Smart Technologies and Innovations in E-Business

Elena G. Popkova
Armenian State University of Economics, Yerevan, Armenia

A volume in the Advances in E-Business Research (AEBR) Book Series

IGI Global
PUBLISHER of TIMELY KNOWLEDGE

Published in the United States of America by
IGI Global
Business Science Reference (an imprint of IGI Global)
701 E. Chocolate Avenue
Hershey PA, USA 17033
Tel: 717-533-8845
Fax: 717-533-8661
E-mail: cust@igi-global.com
Web site: http://www.igi-global.com

Library of Congress Cataloging-in-Publication Data

CIP Pending
ISBN: 978-1-6684-7840-0
EISBN: 978-1-6684-7841-7

British Cataloguing in Publication Data
A Cataloguing in Publication record for this book is available from the British Library.

Advances in E-Business Research (AEBR) Book Series

In Lee
Western Illinois University, USA

ISSN:1935-2700
EISSN:1935-2719

Mission

Technology has played a vital role in the emergence of e-business and its applications incorporate strategies. These processes have aided in the use of electronic transactions via telecommunications networks for collaborating with business partners, buying and selling of goods and services, and customer service. Research in this field continues to develop into a wide range of topics, including marketing, psychology, information systems, accounting, economics, and computer science.

The **Advances in E-Business Research (AEBR) Book Series** provides multidisciplinary references for researchers and practitioners in this area. Instructors, researchers, and professionals interested in the most up-to-date research on the concepts, issues, applications, and trends in the e-business field will find this collection, or individual books, extremely useful. This collection contains the highest quality academic books that advance understanding of e-business and addresses the challenges faced by researchers and practitioners.

Coverage

- E-procurement methods
- E-business systems integration
- Online Consumer Behavior
- E-business technology investment strategies
- Electronic Communications
- E-Business Management
- E-business strategies
- Evaluation methodologies for e-business systems
- Trust, Security, and Privacy
- Telework and Telecommuting

IGI Global is currently accepting manuscripts for publication within this series. To submit a proposal for a volume in this series, please contact our Acquisition Editors at Acquisitions@igi-global.com or visit: http://www.igi-global.com/publish/.

The Advances in E-Business Research (AEBR) Book Series (ISSN 1935-2700) is published by IGI Global, 701 E. Chocolate Avenue, Hershey, PA 17033-1240, USA, www.igi-global.com. This series is composed of titles available for purchase individually; each title is edited to be contextually exclusive from any other title within the series. For pricing and ordering information please visit http://www.igi-global.com/book-series/advances-business-research/37144. Postmaster: Send all address changes to above address.

Titles in this Series

For a list of additional titles in this series, please visit: www.igi-global.com/book-series

New Business Frontiers in the Metaverse
Shivani Inder (Chitkara Business School, Chitkara University, India) Shuchi Dawra (Chitkara Business School, Chitkara University, India) Kyla Latrice Tennin (College of Doctoral Studies, University of Phoenix, USA) and Sandhir Sharma (Chitkara Business School, Chitkara University, India)
Business Science Reference • copyright 2024 • 295pp • H/C (ISBN: 9798369324226) • US $290.00 (our price)

Revolutionizing Customer-Centric Banking Through ICT
Dharmendra Singh (Modern College of Business and Science, Oman) Garima Malik (Birla Institute of Technology Management, India) and Swati Bhatnagar (New Delhi Institute of Management, India)
Business Science Reference • copyright 2024 • 304pp • H/C (ISBN: 9798369320617) • US $315.00 (our price)

Cases on Social Media and Entrepreneurship
Syed Far Abid Hossain (BRAC Business School, BRAC University, Dhaka, Bangladesh)
Information Science Reference • copyright 2024 • 323pp • H/C (ISBN: 9798369317815) • US $255.00 (our price)

Digital Business and Optimizing Operating Strategies
Gökhan Akel (Antalya Belek University, Turkey) and Mustafa Atahan Yılmaz (Pamukkale University, Turkey)
Business Science Reference • copyright 2024 • 313pp • H/C (ISBN: 9798369304280) • US $250.00 (our price)

Building Smart and Sustainable Businesses With Transformative Technologies
Hamed Nozari (Department of Management, Azad University of the Emirates, Dubai, UAE)
Business Science Reference • copyright 2024 • 306pp • H/C (ISBN: 9798369302101) • US $250.00 (our price)

Metaverse Applications for New Business Models and Disruptive Innovation
Muhammad Anshari (Universiti Brunei Darussalam, Brunei) Muhammad Syafrudin (Sejong University, South Korea) and Ganjar Alfian (Universitas Gadjah Mada, Indonesia)
Business Science Reference • copyright 2023 • 265pp • H/C (ISBN: 9781668460979) • US $250.00 (our price)

IGI Global
PUBLISHER of TIMELY KNOWLEDGE

701 East Chocolate Avenue, Hershey, PA 17033, USA
Tel: 717-533-8845 x100 • Fax: 717-533-8661
E-Mail: cust@igi-global.com • www.igi-global.com

Table of Contents

Detailed Table of Contents

In the rapidly evolving digital landscape, E-Business 5.0 represents the latest stage of technology-driven commerce, emphasizing the integration of smart technologies to enhance business processes, customer experiences, and operational efficiencies. This chapter explores the key elements and strategies that define E-Business 5.0, focusing on how artificial intelligence, the internet of things (IoT), blockchain, and advanced data analytics are transforming traditional e-business paradigms. The chapter examine the implications of these technologies on business models, highlighting the shift toward more personalized, automated, and data-driven interactions between businesses and customers. Additionally, it addresses the challenges and opportunities presented by E-Business 5.0, including ethical considerations, cyber security risks, and the need for continuous innovation and adaptation.

The evolution of e-business has traversed various stages, each marked by distinct technological advancements. The current epoch, commonly referred to as E-Business 5.0, signifies a paradigm shift characterized by intelligent systems and interconnected ecosystems. Scholars in the field emphasize the pivotal role of smart technologies and innovations in shaping this new era. A substantial body of research underscores the transformative impact of intelligent automation and robotics in E-Business 5.0. The integration of artificial intelligence (AI) and machine learning (ML) technologies has been demonstrated to significantly enhance operational efficiency. Robotic process automation (RPA), a crucial component of intelligent automation, not only streamlines routine tasks but also contributes to coordinated and responsive business processes. The literature reveals that blockchain technology is foundational to E-Business 5.0. Its decentralized and secure nature provides a tamper-resistant platform for transactions, mitigating the risks associated with data breaches and fraudulent activities

The evolution of e-business into its advanced form, E-Business 5.0, has witnessed a paradigm shift, primarily catalyzed by the integration of smart technologies and innovations. This research embarks on a comprehensive exploration of the leading smart technologies and innovations within the domain of E-Business 5.0, leveraging a robust foundation built upon an extensive literature review. The primary objectives of this study encompass an analysis of the current landscape of E-Business 5.0 technologies, an assessment of organizations' practical experiences in their implementation, a forward-looking evaluation of potential applications, and the provision of recommendations and management frameworks for seamless integration. The research delves into the core questions concerning the pivotal technologies that characterize E-Business 5.0. This study, grounded in a comprehensive literature review, sheds light on the transformative potential of smart technologies and innovations within the dynamic landscape of E-Business 5.0.

The successful use of smart technologies in an enterprise is critical in the ever-changing E-Business 5.0 scenario. In order to improve operations, boost client experiences, and obtain a competitive edge, this chapter examines the necessity of coordinating cutting-edge technologies with corporate goals. It talks about how different smart technologies and their ability to transform conventional corporate processes are important aspects of strategic integration. It also talks about problems like technological complexity and gives advice on how to solve them with strong leadership and changing company culture. Based on actual cases, the chapter offers helpful suggestions for E-Business executives traveling through the process of strategic integration, stressing the critical role that technology plays in fostering competitive advantage and long-term growth.

This chapter was written based on bibliographical research, qualitative, and exploratory studies. The objective of writing the chapter was to highlight the main disruptive technologies and innovations for business 5.0 with application perspectives and recommendations; and, when reading the academic materials, it was noticed that few areas are covered in academic investigations into business 5.0. There are solutions and recommendations, as well as directions for future research. The final considerations, among the conclusions, are that well-being for future generations are the revolutions to be documented for a fairer society, whether in reality or in augmented, virtual, mixed, or extended realities.

The chapter explores entrepreneurial dynamics and development area. An exploration of entrepreneurial forms: social, scalable, large-scale, and small-business enterprises, accompanied by an up-to-date analysis of country-level startup activities as of 2023. The coexistence of technology and entrepreneurship education is examined, with a specific focus on the symbiotic relationship between digital technology and AI collaboration. The study investigates the dynamics of the entrepreneurial ecosystem and elucidates the evolving characteristics of small businesses. The chapter also addresses various dimensions of franchising model, encompassing perspectives of both franchisors and franchisees and as the multi-unit aspects of this entrepreneurial paradigm. An exhaustive exploration is conducted into pivotal interplay between digital leadership of an entrepreneur and digital success of an entrepreneurial teams, focusing on the role that technological innovation and absorptive capacity play.

In today's fast-paced digital landscape, chatbots and artificial intelligence (AI) stand as a revolutionary advancement in the digital marketplace by not only offering more streamlined purchasing experiences and enhanced user engagement for customers but also strengthening the relationships between businesses. This report aims to explore a commonly used self-service tool employed by businesses to support customers at every stage of their purchasing journey, mainly known as chatbots. This 24/7 customer service tool revolutionizes user experiences and drives innovation in the business environment by virtually assisting customers every step of the way in their purchasing journey. The findings and discussion acquired through this study, especially in terms of future research areas, are extremely helpful for comprehending the functions to understand and enhance chatbot technology further enriching user interaction in the evolving business environment.

New technologies have changed the way products are offered today: Nowadays the internet and social

Preface

THE SCIENTIFIC MESSAGE OF THE BOOK

This book is focused on e-business, which changed in the course of the Fifth Industrial Revolution as a scientific category and as an economic subject in the practice of the digital economy. The main novel idea of the book is that the new subject of the digital economy in the conditions of the Fifth Industrial Revolution is e-business 5.0.

Its formation took place under the influence of the Law of dialectics on the "transition from quantitative to qualitative". Thus, initially, technological progress facilitated the growth of the number of subjects of e-business and the expansion of the range of breakthrough technologies of Industry 5.0, used by these subjects, and the spheres of application of these technologies. Then, sustainable practices of using technologies of Industry 5.0 in e-business were formed, organisational models were established, and the business culture was transformed.

As of now, there are clear outlines of e-business 5.0, which is treated in this book as e-business that participates actively in the Fifth Industrial Revolution as its driver; specialises in high-tech products; treats Industry 5.0 not only as a source of technological resources but also as a targeted market.

The scientific message of this book is that e-business 5.0 requires constant implementation of the leading innovations and smart technologies, to remain competitive, preserve market positions, and implement its export potential. The book is devoted to the development of not only innovations and smart technologies (such as artificial intelligence, and virtual and augmented reality) for e-business 5.0 but also fundamental and applied organizational & economic and managerial decisions for flexible and highly effective application of these innovations and technologies in the activities of e-business 5.0.

Overview of the Book's Contents

The book contains twelve chapters, which consecutively disclose the scientific and economic foundations of implementing innovations and smart technologies in e-business. In the first chapter, "Managing Smart Technologies in the Digital Age: E-Business 5.0", the essence of the evolution of e-business during its transition to form 5.0 is disclosed and the character of the influence of the Fifth Industrial Revolution on business models is explained. The authors systematize smart technologies of e-business 5.0, which include robots, the Internet of Things, blockchain, virtual and augmented reality, Big Data, artificial intelligence, and related machine visions.

The second chapter "Leading Smart Technologies and Innovations for E-Business 5.0: Applications and Management Frameworks" explains the influence of smart technologies and innovations on the development of e-business 5.0. This influence is manifested in the transformation of approaches to managerial decision-making, modernization of the management of supply and sales chains, and the change in the character of interaction of e-business 5.0 and consumers. The advantages of applying smart technologies and innovations in the activities of e-business 5.0 in this chapter are an increase in operational effectiveness, openness, and flexibility, and the risks are new cyber threats.

In the third chapter, "E-Business 5.0: Pioneering Smart Technologies and Innovations for Digital Transformation", the authors specify the resource support for e-business 5.0 and the sources of its competitive advantages. Empirical experience of the subjects of e-business 5.0 in the sphere of practical application of smart technologies is disclosed. The authors determine trends and opportunities for the application of smart technologies in e-business 5.0 and offer managerial recommendations for this.

The fourth chapter, "Strategic Integration of Smart Technologies in E-Business", explains the uniqueness of the technological landscape of the Fifth Industrial Revolution. The chapter provides scientific substantiation of the necessity for strategic integration of e-business 5.0 for the accelerated implementation of innovations and maximisation of advantages and distribution of risks of implementing smart technologies. Leading experience from international practice is given and discussed, and case examples are given. Socio-environmental advantages of the application of innovations and smart technologies in e-business 5.0 are explained.

The contents of the fifth chapter "Disruptive Technologies and Innovations in Business 5.0: Trends and Application Perspectives in Phygital Transformation" includes an overview of disruptive technologies of Industry 5.0 and an explanation of the essence of changes that take place in economic systems during the implementation of these technologies. The chapter discloses the scientific essence of the formation of cyber-social systems. Technologies considered in the chapter determine the functioning and development of e-business 5.0 and 3-D printing.

The sixth chapter, "Entrepreneurial Development and Dynamics A Comprehensive Review", substantiates the uniqueness of the nature of entrepreneurship in e-business 5.0, which consists in a flexible combination of automatization and social communications, which take various forms of man-machine interaction. Special attention in this chapter is paid to entrepreneurial teaching and education as a source of highly qualified managerial personnel for e-business 5.0.

The seventh chapter, "Application of Chatbot and Artificial Intelligence in Business", is devoted to justification of the central role of AI in the system of socio-economic interactions and business processes of e-business 5.0. This chapter studies machine learning as a technology of the development of AI, which includes the expansion of its functional capabilities and an increase in the activities' effectiveness.

The chapter "E-Commerce is an Innovative and Efficient Strategy for the Presentation of Products through Quick Response Codes" presents an explanation of the global geography of e-commerce, its typologization, and a comparison of alternative approaches to e-commerce. The chapter proves the preferences for applying QR codes in e-commerce. E-commerce is presented in this chapter as one of the main spheres of production specialization of e-business 5.0.

The ninth chapter, "The Transaction War between Google Pay and Phonepe", describes the digital landscape of modern payment systems. It is focused on the financial infrastructure of e-business 5.0. The authors enumerate technological innovations of modern payment systems and their advantages for e-business 5.0. Strategic partnership with payment systems and services is offered as a promising mechanism, for raising the effectiveness of financial activities of e-business 5.0.

The tenth chapter, "Personalized Healthcare in the Era of E-Business 5.0: Harnessing the Power of Big Data", characterises the current landscape of healthcare and substantiates the necessity for personalization of medical services to raise their quality as a response to modern challenges that are connected with global epidemics and pandemics. Examples from the practice of electronic healthcare are given, and a case study, which discloses the leading experience of patient-centred e-business 5.0 in healthcare, is provided.

The eleventh chapter, "Embracing the Fourth Industrial Revolution in Petrochemical Industry", explains the continuity of industrial revolutions and demonstrates the connection between e-business 4.0 and e-business 5.0. This chapter discloses the character of the influence of the Fourth Industrial Revolution on the petrochemical sphere of the digital economy. The risks and advantages of the high-tech development of e-business in the petrochemical sector in the conditions of industrial revolutions are explained.

In the twelfth chapter, "Omnichannel Supply Chain in India: A Study Using SAP-LAP Approach", describes the leading experience of India in the development of e-business 5.0. The authors' attention is focused on the development of omnichannel supply chains, which are studied with the use of the progressive method of SAP-LAP modelling. A vivid result of this paper, which constitutes the basis for its scientific novelty, is the presented structure of SAP-LAP for the development of the omnichannel supply chain.

The Book's Contribution to the Development of Scientific Literature on E-Business

The book supports the ongoing scientific discussion on the issues of the development of e-business 5.0, explaining the specifics and offering recommendations for the highly effective application of the leading technologies of Industry 5.0 in modern business practice. The main conclusion of this book is that e-business 5.0 requires smart technologies and innovations, which provide advantages and risks of various nature – social, economic, and environmental.

The develop a systemic approach to the management of technological development of e-business 5.0 will allow assuaging the risks of its digital modernization and maximizing advantages, which are expressed in the strengthening of global competitive advantages and acceleration of the rate of economic growth and an increase in the quality of life in the information society. The practical significance of scientific solutions, which are presented in this book, is that they will allow improving the practice of state regulation and corporate management of e-business 5.0.

Elena G. Popkova
Armenian State University of Economics, Yerevan, Armenia

Chapter 1
Managing Smart Technologies in the Digital Age:
E-Business 5.0

S. C. Vetrivel
https://orcid.org/0000-0003-3050-8211
Kongu Engineering College, India

V. Sabareeshwari
Amrita School of Agricultural Sciences, India

V. P. Arun
JKKN College of Engineering and Technology, India

K. C. Sowmiya
Sri Vasavi College, India

ABSTRACT

In the rapidly evolving digital landscape, E-Business 5.0 represents the latest stage of technology-driven commerce, emphasizing the integration of smart technologies to enhance business processes, customer experiences, and operational efficiencies. This chapter explores the key elements and strategies that define E-Business 5.0, focusing on how artificial intelligence, the internet of things (IoT), blockchain, and advanced data analytics are transforming traditional e-business paradigms. The chapter examine the implications of these technologies on business models, highlighting the shift toward more personalized, automated, and data-driven interactions between businesses and customers. Additionally, it addresses the challenges and opportunities presented by E-Business 5.0, including ethical considerations, cyber security risks, and the need for continuous innovation and adaptation.

DOI: 10.4018/978-1-6684-7840-0.ch001

1. INTRODUCTION

1.1. Evolution from E-Business 5.0

The concept of e-business has evolved significantly over the past few decades, reflecting changes in technology, consumer behavior, and business processes. This evolution can be categorized into distinct stages, each with unique characteristics and contributions to the development of the digital economy. Here's a detailed look at the evolution from E-Business 1.0 to E-Business 5.0.

E-Business 1.0: The Beginnings

E-Business 1.0 represents the initial phase of online business, characterized by basic websites and limited interaction with users. In the mid-to-late 1990s, the internet became accessible to a broader audience, and businesses began to explore its potential (Abid & Javaid, 2019). This period focused on establishing an online presence, typically through static websites that offered company information and basic contact details. Companies saw the internet as a new marketing channel but had limited capabilities for e-commerce and customer engagement. The focus was primarily on broadcasting information, with minimal interaction or personalization.

E-Business 2.0: Interactive and Social

With the emergence of Web 2.0 technologies in the early 2000s, E-Business 2.0 introduced interactive elements and user-generated content. This phase saw the rise of social media platforms, blogs, and online communities (Adadi & Berrada, 2018). Companies began to engage with customers through interactive websites, enabling user feedback, reviews, and social sharing. E-commerce platforms like eBay and Amazon gained traction, allowing businesses to sell products online. The focus shifted from simple information delivery to fostering interaction and engagement with customers.

E-Business 3.0: Personalization and Mobility

E-Business 3.0 marked a significant shift toward personalization and mobility. With the proliferation of smartphones and mobile devices in the late 2000s, businesses recognized the importance of mobile-friendly websites and applications. This era introduced advanced data analytics and customer segmentation, allowing companies to tailor their offerings to individual preferences (Angelopoulos et al., 2020). Personalization became a key strategy, with companies using data to understand customer behavior and deliver targeted content. E-commerce platforms evolved to include mobile shopping and seamless payment options, creating a more flexible and customer-centric experience.

E-Business 4.0: Data-Driven Automation

The fourth phase, E-Business 4.0, emerged in the mid-2010s, characterized by the integration of automation and artificial intelligence (AI) into business processes. This era saw the rise of machine learning, chatbots, and predictive analytics. Businesses used data-driven insights to optimize operations and enhance customer experiences (Akter et al., 2016). Automation played a significant role in streamlining tasks, reducing costs, and improving efficiency. Companies began to use AI to personalize customer interactions, automate customer support, and predict market trends. The focus shifted toward data-driven decision-making and enhancing operational agility.

E-Business 5.0: Smart Technologies and Connectivity

E-Business 5.0 represents the latest evolution, driven by the convergence of advanced technologies like AI, the Internet of Things (IoT), blockchain, and edge computing. This phase emphasizes smart technologies that enable real-time connectivity and automation across the entire business ecosystem. E-Business 5.0 introduces the concept of hyper-connectivity, where devices, systems, and people are interconnected, creating a seamless and intelligent business environment. In this phase, companies leverage AI and machine learning for advanced analytics, enabling more precise and efficient decision-making. IoT devices connect physical assets to the digital world, providing real-time data for monitoring and control (Aslam et al., 2020). Blockchain technology enhances security and transparency in business transactions. E-Business 5.0 also emphasizes sustainability and ethical considerations, as businesses seek to use technology to create a positive impact on society and the environment.

1.2. The Impact of the Digital Age on Business Models

The digital age has revolutionized the way businesses operate, fundamentally altering traditional business models and creating new paradigms for value creation and customer engagement. At its core, the digital age is characterized by the proliferation of digital technologies, high-speed internet connectivity, mobile devices, and a rapidly growing digital economy (Arora et al., 2008). These elements have collectively reshaped the business landscape, leading to profound changes in how companies deliver products and services, engage with customers, and structure their internal operations.

a. **Transformation of Business Structures**: The digital age has allowed companies to transition from brick-and-mortar models to more flexible and scalable digital frameworks. Businesses can now operate entirely online, reducing overhead costs associated with physical locations while expanding their reach to global markets (Babamiri et al., 2019). This shift has facilitated the rise of e-commerce platforms, where companies can conduct transactions, provide customer support, and deliver services without traditional geographic constraints. Furthermore, digital platforms enable businesses to create and sustain ecosystems that bring together multiple stakeholders, including customers, suppliers, and partners, fostering a networked approach to business.

b. **Enhanced Customer Engagement and Personalization**: Digital technologies have transformed customer engagement, enabling businesses to interact with their clients in real-time and through multiple channels. Social media platforms, mobile applications, and websites allow companies to reach customers instantly, gather feedback, and adjust their offerings based on customer preferences. This increased interaction has led to personalized customer experiences, where businesses can tailor products and services to meet individual needs. The use of big data analytics and artificial intelligence has further enhanced this personalization, allowing companies to predict customer behavior, segment markets, and create targeted marketing campaigns.

c. **Disruption of Traditional Industries:** The digital age has also disrupted traditional industries, forcing them to adapt or risk becoming obsolete. For example, the rise of streaming services like Netflix and Spotify has disrupted traditional media and entertainment industries, while ride-sharing platforms like Uber and Lyft have transformed the transportation sector. This disruption often leads to a more customer-centric approach, where companies must focus on delivering greater value and convenience to remain competitive. The rapid pace of technological change also requires businesses to be agile and innovative, continually evolving their business models to stay ahead of the competition.

d. **Data-Driven Decision Making:** In the digital age, data has become a critical asset for businesses. Companies now have access to vast amounts of data generated from various sources, including customer interactions, social media, and IoT devices. This data can be analyzed to gain insights into customer behavior, market trends, and operational efficiencies (Berman, 2012). As a result, businesses are increasingly relying on data-driven decision making to inform their strategies, optimize operations, and identify new opportunities for growth. This shift toward data-driven approaches has given rise to new roles within organizations, such as data scientists and analysts, who specialize in extracting actionable insights from complex datasets.
e. **Emergence of Collaborative Business Models:** The digital age has facilitated the emergence of collaborative business models, where companies work together to create shared value. The concept of "sharing economy" has gained traction, with platforms like Airbnb and WeWork exemplifying how businesses can leverage technology to create peer-to-peer marketplaces (Brown & Wobst, 2021). This collaborative approach allows companies to leverage resources and expertise from a broader network, promoting innovation and reducing costs. Additionally, open-source technologies and collaborative development platforms have enabled businesses to accelerate innovation by tapping into a global community of developers and contributors.

1.3. The Role of Smart Technologies in E-Business

Smart technologies have emerged as a transformative force in e-business, revolutionizing how companies operate, interact with customers, and create value. At the heart of this transformation is the convergence of several advanced technologies, including artificial intelligence (AI), machine learning, the Internet of Things (IoT), blockchain, and robotics. These technologies enable businesses to collect, process, and analyze vast amounts of data in real-time, allowing for enhanced decision-making and customer insights. For instance, AI and machine learning algorithms can analyze customer behavior, predict trends, and automate repetitive tasks, leading to more efficient operations and personalized customer experiences. IoT extends connectivity to physical devices, enabling businesses to monitor supply chains, track inventory, and offer smart products and services. Blockchain technology, with its decentralized and secure nature, is redefining trust in transactions, providing new avenues for secure payments and data sharing (Carayannis et al., 2021). Robotics and automation, on the other hand, are streamlining production processes and enhancing productivity. The role of smart technologies in e-business is multifaceted. They are driving the evolution of business models, leading to the creation of data-driven, customer-centric strategies that emphasize agility and flexibility. These technologies are also fostering innovation by providing businesses with the tools to explore new revenue streams and business opportunities. Moreover, they are enabling businesses to respond more effectively to market demands, improving customer satisfaction and loyalty. However, the integration of smart technologies in e-business is not without challenges. Companies must address cybersecurity risks, data privacy issues, and the need for a workforce equipped with the right skills. Despite these hurdles, the potential benefits of smart technologies in e-business are immense, offering a pathway to increased competitiveness, efficiency, and sustainable growth in the digital age.

2. DEFINING SMART TECHNOLOGIES IN E-BUSINESS

2.1. Overview of Smart Technologies (AI, IoT, Blockchain, etc.)

Smart technologies represent a class of advanced technologies that are driving the digital transformation of businesses across industries. This overview delves into the key types of smart technologies and their roles in shaping modern business practices:

- **Artificial Intelligence (AI)**

Artificial Intelligence refers to the simulation of human intelligence in machines designed to think, learn, and perform tasks traditionally requiring human intervention. AI encompasses various subsets like machine learning, deep learning, and natural language processing. In e-business, AI is crucial for automating tasks, enhancing customer service through chatbots, personalizing marketing strategies, and optimizing business operations. Its ability to analyze large datasets quickly makes it an invaluable tool for gaining insights and making informed business decisions.

- **Internet of Things (IoT)**

The Internet of Things involves connecting everyday objects and devices to the internet, allowing them to collect and exchange data. IoT has a significant impact on e-business, enabling businesses to monitor equipment, track inventory in real time, and optimize logistics (Cioffi et al., 2020). In retail, IoT devices are used to enhance customer experiences by offering personalized product recommendations based on user behavior. In manufacturing, IoT sensors can predict equipment failures, leading to proactive maintenance and reduced downtime.

- **Blockchain**

Blockchain is a decentralized, distributed ledger technology that allows for secure, transparent, and tamper-resistant record-keeping. In e-business, blockchain is revolutionizing financial transactions, supply chain management, and data security. Its primary advantage is the creation of trust without intermediaries, reducing costs and increasing efficiency (Deepa et al., 2022). For example, blockchain-based smart contracts can automate contract execution, while blockchain-based cryptocurrencies offer alternative payment methods that reduce reliance on traditional banking systems.

- **Robotics and Automation**

Robotics and automation are key components of smart technologies, focusing on automating physical tasks and processes. In e-business, robotics is used in manufacturing, warehousing, and logistics to improve efficiency and reduce human error. Automation, facilitated by AI, streamlines back-office operations, customer service, and even marketing campaigns, allowing businesses to operate with greater precision and speed.

- **Augmented Reality (AR) and Virtual Reality (VR)**

AR and VR technologies are reshaping customer experiences in e-business. Augmented Reality superimposes digital information onto the real world, while Virtual Reality creates immersive virtual environments. These technologies are used in e-business to enhance product visualization, create virtual showrooms, and offer immersive customer experiences. In the real estate industry, for example,

VR allows potential buyers to take virtual property tours, while AR can enhance online shopping by enabling customers to visualize products in their real-world environment. Smart technologies are at the forefront of innovation in e-business, driving efficiency, customer engagement, and new business models (Danneels, 2003). As these technologies continue to evolve, their integration into various aspects of business operations will likely become even more profound, offering new opportunities for growth and competitiveness in the digital age.

2.2. The Convergence of Technologies and its Impact

The convergence of technologies refers to the blending and interconnection of different smart technologies—such as artificial intelligence (AI), the Internet of Things (IoT), blockchain, robotics, and augmented/virtual reality (AR/VR)—into a unified ecosystem. This convergence is having a profound impact on how businesses operate, innovate, and interact with customers. The seamless integration of these technologies creates a synergy that amplifies their individual benefits and enables new possibilities for e-business in the digital age. One of the most significant impacts of technology convergence is the ability to collect, process, and analyze data from various sources in real time. By integrating AI with IoT, businesses can gain deeper insights into customer behavior, product usage, and operational efficiency. For example, a manufacturing company can use IoT sensors to monitor equipment and feed the data into AI algorithms to predict maintenance needs, reducing downtime and increasing productivity (Föckler et al., 2005). The convergence of technologies allows businesses to create more personalized and immersive customer experiences. By combining AI with AR/VR, companies can offer virtual product demonstrations, virtual tours, and customized recommendations based on individual preferences. This convergence enhances customer engagement, leading to higher satisfaction and loyalty. In retail, for instance, AR-enabled mobile apps can let customers virtually “try on” clothing, while AI-driven chatbots provide instant customer support.

Technology convergence facilitates automation across various business processes. Robotics and AI together enable automated production lines that operate with minimal human intervention, reducing costs and increasing efficiency. In e-business, AI-powered automation can handle routine tasks like order processing, inventory management, and customer service, allowing human employees to focus on more complex and creative tasks. This streamlining of operations can lead to significant cost savings and improved operational agility. Blockchain technology, when combined with other smart technologies, enhances security and transparency in e-business. Blockchain's decentralized nature ensures that data and transactions are tamper-resistant, reducing the risk of fraud and unauthorized access. In supply chain management, the convergence of blockchain with IoT provides end-to-end traceability, allowing businesses and customers to track products from origin to delivery. This increased transparency fosters trust among stakeholders and supports compliance with regulatory requirements (Fraga-Lamas et al., 2021). The convergence of technologies opens the door to innovative business models and revenue streams. For example, the combination of blockchain and IoT enables “smart contracts” that automatically execute agreements when certain conditions are met. This automation can transform traditional business contracts and agreements, reducing administrative overhead and increasing efficiency. Additionally, the convergence of AI and data analytics allows businesses to offer data-driven insights as a service, creating new revenue opportunities.

2.3. Key Characteristics of Smart Technologies

Smart technologies, which encompass a range of advanced tools and systems like artificial intelligence (AI), the Internet of Things (IoT), blockchain, robotics, and augmented/virtual reality (AR/VR), share several key characteristics that define their role and impact in modern business. Here's a detailed look at these characteristics:

2.3.1 Intelligence and Automation

Smart technologies are designed to exhibit a degree of intelligence, often through AI and machine learning. This intelligence allows them to learn from data, make autonomous decisions, and automate tasks. Automation is a key characteristic, leading to greater efficiency and reducing the need for human intervention in repetitive or mundane tasks.

2.3.2 Connectivity and Interoperability

Smart technologies are inherently connected and interoperable, allowing them to communicate with each other and with external systems. The Internet of Things (IoT) exemplifies this characteristic, with devices and sensors connected to networks, enabling seamless data exchange. This connectivity creates a rich ecosystem where different technologies can work together to create comprehensive solutions.

2.3.3 Data-Driven Insights

A significant feature of smart technologies is their ability to collect, analyze, and derive insights from vast amounts of data. AI and machine learning excel at this, processing large datasets to identify patterns, trends, and anomalies. This data-driven approach underpins predictive analytics, personalized experiences, and informed decision-making in business.

2.3.4 Adaptability and Flexibility

Smart technologies are designed to adapt to changing environments and evolving business needs. They can be reconfigured, updated, and scaled to meet new requirements without extensive re-engineering. This adaptability ensures that businesses can stay agile in the face of technological advancements and market shifts.

2.3.5 Real-Time Processing

Many smart technologies operate in real time, allowing for immediate data processing and decision-making. This characteristic is crucial for applications like real-time analytics, IoT sensor monitoring, and automated responses in customer service. Real-time processing enables businesses to react quickly to changing conditions and make timely decisions.

2.3.6 Security and Trust

Security is a fundamental characteristic of smart technologies, particularly in the context of blockchain and AI. These technologies incorporate advanced encryption, decentralized architectures, and secure communication protocols to ensure data integrity and protect against cyber threats (Feedstuffs.com, 2019). Blockchain, with its distributed ledger system, provides a high level of trust and transparency, reducing the risk of fraud and unauthorized tampering.

2.3.7 Customization and Personalization

Smart technologies enable businesses to create highly personalized experiences for customers. Through AI-driven algorithms, companies can tailor products, services, and marketing campaigns to individual preferences and behaviors. This customization extends to business operations, allowing for targeted automation and bespoke solutions.

2.3.8 Efficiency and Productivity

The integration of smart technologies leads to significant gains in efficiency and productivity. Robotics and automation reduce manual labor and increase throughput in manufacturing and logistics. AI-driven automation streamlines back-office processes, while IoT-based monitoring enhances operational efficiency. These improvements contribute to cost savings and competitive advantage.

2.3.9 Collaboration and Interaction

Smart technologies facilitate enhanced collaboration and interaction among users and systems. AR/VR technologies enable immersive experiences that can transform remote collaboration, virtual meetings, and customer engagement. Connectivity features allow different systems to interact seamlessly, fostering collaboration across business functions and with external partners.

2.3.10 Scalability

Smart technologies are inherently scalable, allowing businesses to grow and expand without significant infrastructure changes. This scalability is essential for companies looking to capitalize on new opportunities and adapt to evolving business environments.

Together, these key characteristics define smart technologies and their transformative impact on business operations, customer engagement, and strategic decision-making. As these technologies continue to evolve, their role in shaping the future of business becomes increasingly significant.

3. APPLICATIONS OF SMART TECHNOLOGIES IN E-BUSINESS

3.1. AI and Machine Learning in Business Processes

Artificial Intelligence (AI) and Machine Learning (ML) have become integral components in business processes, offering companies the ability to streamline operations, enhance decision-making, and deliver personalized customer experiences. AI encompasses a range of technologies designed to simulate human intelligence, while ML, a subset of AI, focuses on algorithms that allow systems to learn from data and improve over time. In business processes, AI and ML contribute to automation, predictive analytics, and improved efficiency. For example, in customer service, AI-powered chatbots can handle routine inquiries, providing instant responses and freeing up human agents to focus on more complex issues. In marketing, ML algorithms analyze customer data to deliver targeted campaigns, leading to higher conversion rates and better ROI. In operations, AI can optimize supply chain logistics, forecast demand, and manage inventory, reducing waste and improving productivity. AI and ML are also instrumental in enhancing business intelligence. By analyzing vast amounts of data, they can identify trends, detect anomalies, and provide actionable insights to business leaders. This data-driven approach supports informed decision-making and strategic planning (Garratt, 2018). Additionally, AI-based systems can assist in risk management by predicting potential threats and suggesting mitigation strategies. The adoption of AI and ML in business processes represents a significant shift toward automation and data-driven operations. Companies that effectively harness these technologies can gain a competitive edge, improve customer satisfaction, and achieve greater operational efficiency, ultimately driving business growth and success in a rapidly evolving digital landscape.

3.2. Internet of Things (IoT) for Enhanced Connectivity

The Internet of Things (IoT) has revolutionized the concept of connectivity by embedding everyday objects with sensors, software, and other technologies that enable them to collect, process, and exchange data over the internet. This network of interconnected devices has far-reaching implications for businesses, providing enhanced connectivity that drives efficiency, innovation, and new business models. In business, IoT facilitates real-time data collection and monitoring, allowing companies to track assets, monitor equipment, and optimize operations. For example, in manufacturing, IoT sensors can be deployed on production equipment to monitor performance and detect potential faults before they cause downtime. This proactive approach to maintenance not only reduces costs but also improves productivity and operational efficiency. In supply chain management, IoT plays a crucial role in enhancing visibility and traceability. Companies can track products from the manufacturing stage to final delivery, allowing them to streamline logistics, reduce delays, and improve customer satisfaction. IoT-enabled tracking also helps businesses maintain compliance with regulatory requirements, particularly in industries like food and pharmaceuticals, where traceability is essential for safety and quality control. The IoT's enhanced connectivity extends to customer engagement and personalization (Ghobakhloo et al., 2021). In retail, IoT devices can collect data on customer behavior and preferences, enabling businesses to tailor product offerings and marketing campaigns to individual needs. Smart homes, powered by IoT, offer a new level of convenience and customization, allowing customers to control lighting, temperature, and security systems remotely. IoT also has applications in healthcare, where connected devices can monitor patient health, track medication adherence, and alert healthcare providers to potential issues. This level of connectivity can lead to more personalized healthcare and improved patient outcomes. Despite its many benefits, the widespread adoption of IoT comes with challenges, primarily related to security and data privacy. The interconnected nature of IoT devices creates potential vulnerabilities that can be exploited by cybercriminals. Businesses must implement robust security measures to protect sensitive data and ensure the integrity of their IoT networks.

3.3. Blockchain and Distributed Ledger Technologies for Security

Blockchain and distributed ledger technologies (DLT) represent a significant evolution in data security and transparency, providing robust solutions for secure transactions, data integrity, and decentralized control. These technologies are transforming various business sectors by offering an immutable and tamper-resistant system for recording and verifying data, thus enhancing security and trust.At its core, blockchain is a decentralized and distributed ledger that allows participants to record transactions securely. Once a transaction is added to the blockchain, it becomes part of a permanent record that is virtually impossible to alter or delete. This immutability is achieved through cryptographic hashing and a consensus mechanism, such as proof of work or proof of stake, which ensures that all participants agree on the validity of transactions (Guidotti et al., 2018). This characteristic of blockchain provides enhanced security for businesses, as it significantly reduces the risk of data tampering and fraud. Each transaction on the blockchain is timestamped and linked to the previous transaction, creating a transparent and auditable chain of records. This transparency fosters trust among stakeholders, enabling secure collaboration and reducing the need for intermediaries. One of the key features of blockchain and DLT is decentralization. Unlike traditional databases that rely on a central authority, blockchain operates across a distributed network of nodes, with no single point of control. This decentralization enhances security by eliminating centralized vulnerabilities that could be targeted by malicious actors. The distributed nature of blockchain also promotes trust among participants. In business scenarios where multiple parties interact, such as supply chain management, blockchain provides a trusted environment for recording and verifying transactions. Companies can trace the provenance of goods, ensuring authenticity and compliance with industry standards. This level of trust is especially valuable in industries with complex supply chains, like food and pharmaceuticals. Blockchain's security features are particularly useful for financial transactions. Cryptocurrencies like Bitcoin and Ethereum leverage blockchain technology to enable secure and transparent peer-to-peer transactions without the need for intermediaries like banks. These transactions are protected by advanced cryptography, reducing the risk of fraud and unauthorized access. Another important application of blockchain in business is smart contracts—self-executing contracts with the terms of the agreement directly written into code. Smart contracts automatically execute when certain conditions are met, reducing the need for manual intervention and minimizing the risk of disputes. This automation can streamline business processes and ensure compliance with contractual terms.

While blockchain and distributed ledger technologies offer significant security advantages, they are not without challenges. Scalability and energy consumption are notable concerns, especially in proof-of-work-based blockchains. Additionally, regulatory and legal issues must be addressed to ensure compliance with existing laws and standards. To mitigate these challenges, ongoing developments in blockchain technology aim to improve scalability and efficiency. Proof of stake and other consensus mechanisms are gaining traction as energy-efficient alternatives to proof of work. Interoperability between different blockchains is also a focus, allowing for seamless data exchange across diverse platforms.

3.4. Robotics and Automation in Business Operations

Robotics and automation are transforming business operations by introducing efficiency, precision, and scalability into a wide range of industries. Through advanced robotics, businesses can automate repetitive tasks, reducing labor costs and minimizing human error. In manufacturing, robotic systems are used for assembly lines, quality control, and packaging, allowing for continuous production with minimal downtime (Govindarajan et al., 2011). Automation, driven by technologies like artificial intelligence and machine learning, extends to business processes, where it optimizes workflows, streamlines supply chain management, and enhances customer service through AI-powered chatbots and automated communication. The adoption of robotics and automation not only boosts productivity but also improves safety in hazardous environments by reducing human exposure to dangerous tasks. These technologies empower businesses to scale rapidly, respond to market demands more effectively, and focus human resources on higher-level, strategic activities, ultimately driving innovation and competitiveness in the digital age.

3.5. Augmented Reality (AR) and Virtual Reality (VR) in Customer Engagement

Augmented Reality (AR) and Virtual Reality (VR) are reshaping customer engagement by offering immersive and interactive experiences that go beyond traditional modes of interaction. AR superimposes digital information onto the real world, while VR creates entirely virtual environments. These technologies allow businesses to engage customers in innovative ways, leading to enhanced satisfaction, deeper brand loyalty, and new opportunities for personalized experiences. In retail, AR is revolutionizing the shopping experience by enabling customers to virtually "try on" products, like clothing, makeup, or accessories, without physical contact. This capability helps customers make more informed purchasing decisions and reduces return rates. Similarly, AR-based mobile applications can provide additional product information by scanning items with a smartphone, offering a more engaging and informative shopping experience. VR takes immersion to the next level by creating virtual environments that customers can explore. In industries like real estate, VR allows prospective buyers to take virtual tours of properties, saving time and resources. In the automotive industry, customers can experience virtual test drives, providing a sense of the vehicle's look and feel before visiting a showroom. VR also finds applications in entertainment, with businesses offering virtual gaming experiences, and in education, where virtual simulations enhance learning and training. Beyond retail and real estate, AR and VR are making inroads into customer service and support (Haleem et al., 2019). Virtual showrooms and product demonstrations enable customers to interact with products in a virtual space, while virtual assistants can guide users through troubleshooting or technical support scenarios. This immersive approach to customer service can lead to higher engagement and a more enjoyable experience.

4. TRANSFORMING BUSINESS MODELS WITH E-BUSINESS 5.0

4.1. Customer-Centric Business Models

o Customer-centric business models are at the heart of E-Business 5.0, a concept that emphasizes integrating advanced digital technologies to create experiences that prioritize customer needs, preferences, and satisfaction. E-Business 5.0 represents a shift toward highly personalized and interactive business practices, leveraging artificial intelligence (AI), the Internet of Things (IoT), big data analytics, and other smart technologies to deliver tailored products and services. Here's how customer-centric business models are evolving in the context of E-Business 5.0:

- **Deep Understanding of Customer Behavior**

E-Business 5.0 leverages big data analytics and AI to gather insights into customer behavior, allowing businesses to understand their target audiences more deeply. This analysis goes beyond basic demographics to include browsing habits, purchase history, social media interactions, and even sentiment analysis. The result is a detailed customer profile that businesses can use to personalize their offerings and marketing strategies.

- **Personalized Products and Services**

With E-Business 5.0, businesses can create products and services that align with individual customer preferences. Through AI and machine learning, companies can offer personalized recommendations, tailored promotions, and even custom-made products. This level of personalization enhances customer satisfaction and fosters brand loyalty, as customers feel valued and understood.

- **Seamless Omnichannel Experience**

Customer-centric business models in E-Business 5.0 focus on providing a seamless experience across multiple channels, including online platforms, mobile apps, social media, and brick-and-mortar stores (Hopkins, 2021). IoT plays a crucial role in this integration, connecting various touchpoints to ensure a consistent and cohesive customer journey. Customers can start a purchase on one channel and complete it on another without friction, enhancing convenience and satisfaction.

- **Proactive Customer Support**

E-Business 5.0 also introduces proactive customer support, where businesses anticipate customer needs and address issues before they arise. AI-powered chatbots and virtual assistants are key components of this approach, offering instant responses and 24/7 support. Additionally, IoT sensors can monitor product performance, allowing businesses to alert customers to potential issues or schedule maintenance proactively, creating a smoother customer experience.

- **Customer Engagement and Co-Creation**

A customer-centric business model encourages active customer engagement and co-creation. E-Business 5.0 harnesses AR and VR technologies to create immersive experiences, allowing customers to interact with products in new ways. Businesses can also involve customers in the product development process, using crowdsourcing and feedback mechanisms to gather input and create products that resonate with their target audience.

- **Building Trust and Transparency**

Customer-centric business models emphasize trust and transparency, crucial elements of E-Business 5.0. Blockchain technology helps businesses ensure data security and create transparent supply chains, allowing customers to trace the origin of products and verify their authenticity. This transparency builds trust and reinforces the customer-centric ethos.

o **Continuous Improvement and Innovation**

Finally, customer-centric business models in E-Business 5.0 are designed for continuous improvement and innovation. Companies use data-driven insights to refine their products, services, and customer interactions, ensuring they stay ahead of market trends and evolving customer expectations. This iterative approach enables businesses to remain agile and responsive in the dynamic landscape of E-Business 5.0.

4.2. Data-Driven Decision Making

Data-driven decision making is a process in which organizations leverage data analysis, analytics, and evidence-based insights to guide business strategies, operations, and goals. This approach transforms the traditional reliance on intuition or guesswork, allowing companies to make informed decisions backed by objective data. With the proliferation of big data, businesses can collect vast amounts of information from various sources, such as customer interactions, market trends, and internal processes (Imoize et al., 2021). By applying advanced analytics, artificial intelligence, and machine learning, organizations can identify patterns, uncover trends, and predict future outcomes. This enables them to optimize operations, improve customer experiences, and gain a competitive edge. Data-driven decision making leads to more efficient resource allocation, reduced risk, and enhanced agility, as businesses can quickly adapt to changing conditions and make strategic decisions with greater confidence. Ultimately, this approach is essential for businesses aiming to thrive in the data-rich environment of the digital age.

4.3. Agile and Flexible Operations

Agile and flexible operations are central to the concept of E-Business 5.0, where businesses leverage smart technologies to respond swiftly to changing market dynamics and customer demands. This approach emphasizes adaptability, allowing companies to pivot their strategies, scale resources, and innovate quickly. With tools like artificial intelligence (AI), cloud computing, and the Internet of Things (IoT), businesses can analyze real-time data, automate processes, and collaborate across distributed teams. This flexibility fosters a culture of continuous improvement, where feedback loops drive iterative development and rapid deployment of new products and services. By embracing agile methodologies, such as Scrum or Kanban, organizations can break down silos, improve communication, and deliver value to customers faster. The ability to reconfigure operations and experiment with new business models positions E-Business 5.0 enterprises to thrive in a digital age marked by constant change and heightened competition.

4.4. Integration of Smart Technologies Into Traditional Business Practices

Integrating smart technologies into traditional business practices represents a transformative shift, enabling companies to leverage advanced tools like artificial intelligence (AI), the Internet of Things (IoT), blockchain, and robotics to enhance efficiency, productivity, and customer engagement. This integration allows businesses to automate routine tasks, make data-driven decisions, and create personalized customer experiences (Ietto et al., 2022). For example, AI and machine learning can be used to optimize supply chain operations, reducing costs and improving accuracy. IoT devices can monitor equipment in real-time, predicting maintenance needs and reducing downtime. Blockchain technology, with its secure and transparent ledger system, facilitates trust in financial transactions and supply chain traceability. Robotics and automation streamline manufacturing processes, increasing speed and reducing errors. By incorporating these smart technologies, traditional businesses can evolve into more agile, flexible, and customer-centric organizations, ready to compete in the rapidly changing digital landscape. However, this integration also requires addressing challenges such as cybersecurity risks, data privacy, and workforce adaptation to ensure a smooth transition to a technologically advanced business environment.

5. CHALLENGES AND RISKS IN IMPLEMENTING E-BUSINESS 5.0

5.1. Cybersecurity Risks and Mitigation Strategies

In the context of E-Business 5.0, cybersecurity risks pose significant challenges due to the increasing integration of smart technologies and the reliance on digital networks. The expanded use of artificial intelligence (AI), the Internet of Things (IoT), and blockchain exposes businesses to a broader attack surface, with risks including data breaches, ransomware attacks, phishing scams, and denial-of-service (DoS) incidents. Mitigating these risks requires a multi-faceted approach: implementing robust encryption and authentication mechanisms, regularly updating software to patch vulnerabilities, and adopting a zero-trust security model. Employee training is crucial to prevent social engineering attacks, while comprehensive monitoring and incident response plans help businesses quickly detect and respond to threats. Additionally, businesses must ensure compliance with data protection regulations, such as GDPR and CCPA, to safeguard customer information and maintain trust. By combining technology, processes, and people-focused strategies, companies can effectively address cybersecurity risks and ensure the secure implementation of E-Business 5.0.

5.2. Data Privacy and Ethical Considerations

Implementing E-Business 5.0 with smart technologies like artificial intelligence (AI), Internet of Things (IoT), and big data analytics raises significant data privacy challenges. These technologies inherently involve collecting, processing, and analyzing vast amounts of personal and sensitive data. As businesses gain deeper insights into customer behavior and business processes, the risk of data breaches and unauthorized access increases (Longo et al., 2020). This heightened risk demands stringent data protection measures and compliance with global data privacy regulations, such as the General Data Protection Regulation (GDPR) in Europe and the California Consumer Privacy Act (CCPA) in the United States. One challenge businesses face is ensuring data protection throughout the data lifecycle, from collection to disposal. E-Business 5.0 systems often require data sharing across various platforms and third-party vendors, creating additional risks. Businesses must implement robust encryption, secure data storage, and stringent access controls to safeguard personal information. Moreover, the rapid pace of technological change complicates efforts to keep privacy measures up to date, requiring continuous monitoring and adaptation to evolving threats.

Beyond data privacy, E-Business 5.0 also presents ethical considerations that businesses must address. The use of AI and machine learning algorithms in decision-making can lead to biased outcomes if not properly managed. For example, AI models trained on biased datasets might inadvertently discriminate against certain groups, impacting hiring practices, credit scoring, and customer targeting. Businesses must take proactive steps to ensure their AI systems are transparent, fair, and accountable, which often involves implementing bias detection and correction mechanisms. Another ethical concern arises from the extensive use of personal data for targeted advertising and personalized customer experiences. While these practices can enhance customer engagement, they may also encroach on individual privacy and lead to a sense of surveillance (Mahmood et al., 2020). Businesses must strike a balance between personalization and respecting user autonomy, providing clear information about data collection practices and obtaining informed consent from customers. E-Business 5.0's impact on the workforce also raises ethical issues.

5.3. Workforce Transformation and Skills Gap

E-Business 5.0, driven by smart technologies such as artificial intelligence (AI), machine learning, the Internet of Things (IoT), and robotics, requires businesses to rethink how they structure their workforce. As automation and AI take on more tasks previously handled by humans, organizations must navigate the transition in a way that balances efficiency with human resources. Workforce transformation in this context involves redefining job roles, restructuring departments, and developing new workflows that integrate technology with human labor.

For employees, this transformation can be both challenging and unsettling. Automation might lead to job displacement, especially for roles that are routine or easily automated. This creates a need for retraining and upskilling to prepare workers for new responsibilities and opportunities that arise from the implementation of E-Business 5.0. Companies must also address potential resistance to change, ensuring that employees understand the benefits of the new technologies and feel valued during the transition. Additionally, fostering a culture of continuous learning and adaptation is crucial to help employees thrive in an evolving business landscape.

The rapid advancement of smart technologies has resulted in a significant skills gap, where the demand for skilled labor in emerging technologies far outstrips the supply. This gap poses a considerable risk for companies implementing E-Business 5.0, as they may struggle to find talent with the necessary expertise in AI, data analytics, IoT, blockchain, and other related fields (Masood & Sonntag, 2020). The skills gap can slow down implementation, increase operational costs, and limit the potential benefits of e-business initiatives. To address the skills gap, companies must invest in comprehensive training programs and partnerships with educational institutions. These initiatives can help equip their existing workforce with the skills needed to manage and operate smart technologies.

5.4. Regulatory Compliance and Legal Issues

Implementing E-Business 5.0, with its reliance on smart technologies such as artificial intelligence (AI), the Internet of Things (IoT), blockchain, and advanced analytics, brings a host of regulatory compliance and legal issues. As businesses embrace these technologies, they must navigate a complex landscape of laws, regulations, and standards to avoid legal risks and penalties.

- Compliance with Data Protection Laws

One of the primary challenges in E-Business 5.0 is compliance with data protection laws. With the increasing use of AI and IoT, businesses collect and process vast amounts of personal data, raising concerns about privacy and data security. Regulations like the General Data Protection Regulation (GDPR) in Europe and the California Consumer Privacy Act (CCPA) in the United States impose strict requirements on how businesses handle personal data (Priadythama et al., 2020). Companies must ensure they have appropriate consent from users, implement robust data protection measures, and provide mechanisms for individuals to exercise their rights, such as accessing or deleting their data. Non-compliance with these regulations can result in significant fines, legal action, and reputational damage.

- **Legal Issues in Smart Contracts and Blockchain**

The adoption of blockchain and smart contracts in E-Business 5.0 introduces unique legal challenges. Smart contracts, which are self-executing agreements coded onto a blockchain, can automate complex business processes, but they also raise questions about enforceability and legal interpretation. Since smart contracts operate without human intervention, errors or ambiguities in the code can lead to unintended outcomes or disputes. Additionally, the decentralized nature of blockchain complicates issues like jurisdiction and accountability. Businesses must ensure that their smart contracts comply with applicable laws and that they have mechanisms for dispute resolution if things go wrong.

- **Intellectual Property and AI**

E-Business 5.0's heavy reliance on AI and machine learning brings intellectual property (IP) concerns. As AI systems generate new content, designs, or inventions, questions arise about ownership and IP rights. For example, who owns the copyright to a piece of art or music created by an AI algorithm? Similarly, businesses using AI-driven analytics to develop proprietary insights may need to protect these assets from competitors. Navigating these IP issues requires a clear understanding of intellectual property laws and, in some cases, new legal frameworks to address AI-generated content.

- **Cybersecurity and Liability**

With the proliferation of IoT devices and increased connectivity in E-Business 5.0, cybersecurity is a major concern. Businesses must ensure their systems are secure against cyber threats, including data breaches, hacking, and denial-of-service attacks. Regulatory compliance in this area involves adhering to industry standards, conducting regular security audits, and implementing robust security protocols (Onik et al., 2018). Failure to secure sensitive data can lead to legal liability, lawsuits, and significant financial losses. Furthermore, businesses may need to comply with industry-specific regulations, such as the Health Insurance Portability and Accountability Act (HIPAA) in healthcare or the Payment Card Industry Data Security Standard (PCI DSS) for payment processing.

- **Cross-Border Regulations and International Trade**

E-Business 5.0 often involves cross-border transactions and global supply chains, which bring additional regulatory and legal challenges. Businesses must comply with international trade laws, export controls, and customs regulations. Additionally, they need to consider the legal implications of data transfer across borders, especially in light of varying data protection laws in different countries. Compliance with these regulations requires a comprehensive understanding of international law and effective coordination with legal experts and regulatory authorities.

6. CASE STUDIES AND BEST PRACTICES

6.1. Successful Implementation of Smart Technologies in E-Business

Implementing smart technologies in e-business can significantly transform business operations, customer experiences, and revenue streams. Here are two case studies that demonstrate successful implementations of smart technologies in e-business, showcasing best practices and key lessons learned.

Case One: E-Commerce Giant Using AI and Machine Learning for Personalization

A leading e-commerce company decided to integrate artificial intelligence (AI) and machine learning (ML) into its platform to enhance personalization and customer experience. The goal was to provide personalized product recommendations, improve search accuracy, and optimize marketing campaigns. To achieve this, the company implemented a recommendation engine powered by ML algorithms that analyzed customer data, including purchase history, browsing behavior, and product reviews. The AI-driven recommendation engine allowed the company to offer tailored product suggestions to individual customers, increasing customer engagement and conversion rates (Riedl et al., 2020). The company also used AI to optimize its email marketing campaigns by analyzing customer preferences and behaviors, leading to higher open rates and click-through rates. Additionally, AI-powered chatbots were deployed to handle customer inquiries, providing instant responses and reducing the workload on customer service teams. The successful implementation of AI and ML resulted in a significant increase in sales and customer satisfaction. The personalized approach led to longer customer sessions and higher average order values. The company also reduced its marketing costs by targeting campaigns more effectively. This case study demonstrates the importance of data-driven insights and the value of AI in creating personalized customer experiences in e-business.

Case Two: Manufacturing Firm Implementing IoT for Operational Efficiency

A manufacturing firm specializing in automotive parts sought to improve its operational efficiency and reduce downtime. To achieve this, the company implemented the Internet of Things (IoT) across its production facilities. IoT sensors were installed on key equipment and machinery to monitor performance, track usage, and detect potential faults.The IoT system provided real-time data on equipment health, allowing the company's maintenance team to predict when maintenance or repairs were needed. This predictive approach reduced unplanned downtime and extended the lifespan of critical machinery. The firm also used IoT data to optimize energy consumption, leading to cost savings and a smaller environmental footprint. The successful implementation of IoT resulted in a significant reduction in downtime, improved operational efficiency, and lower maintenance costs. The firm could quickly identify bottlenecks in production and address them proactively, leading to smoother operations and increased productivity. Additionally, the real-time data enabled the company to track inventory more accurately, reducing excess stock and minimizing waste. This case highlights the benefits of IoT in manufacturing and underscores the importance of predictive maintenance and real-time monitoring. It demonstrates how IoT can drive operational efficiency and cost savings while improving overall business performance in the context of e-business.

6.2. Lessons Learned from E-Business 5.0 Implementations

Implementing E-Business 5.0 has provided valuable lessons for businesses navigating the complex landscape of digital transformation. These implementations, driven by smart technologies like AI, IoT, and blockchain, have revealed the importance of adaptability, customer-centricity, and a robust technological foundation. A key lesson is the need for flexibility in business models, allowing organizations to quickly respond to technological advancements and changing customer expectations. Successful E-Business 5.0 implementations often involve iterative processes, where companies embrace continuous improvement and adjust strategies based on real-time feedback and data-driven insights. Another lesson is the critical role of a skilled workforce. As smart technologies become more prevalent, companies that invest in training and upskilling their employees are better positioned to leverage these technologies effectively. This includes not only technical skills but also an understanding of digital ethics and data privacy, which are paramount in the digital age. E-Business 5.0 implementations have also underscored the significance of cybersecurity (Siriwardhana et al., 2021). As businesses adopt more connected technologies, they must proactively address security risks, implement robust encryption, and ensure compliance with regulations. Companies that neglect cybersecurity often face setbacks, including data breaches and reputational damage. Moreover, successful implementations highlight the importance of a customer-centric approach. Businesses that prioritize personalized experiences and seamless digital interactions tend to achieve higher customer satisfaction and loyalty. This involves leveraging AI and data analytics to understand customer behavior and tailor products and services accordingly.

6.3. Industry-Specific Examples

Retail: The retail industry has undergone a significant transformation with the advent of E-Business 5.0, characterized by the integration of smart technologies like artificial intelligence (AI), the Internet of Things (IoT), and augmented reality (AR). Retailers are leveraging AI algorithms to analyze consumer data, enabling personalized recommendations, targeted marketing campaigns, and optimized inventory management. For example, major e-commerce platforms use AI to suggest products based on a customer's past purchases and browsing history, leading to increased sales and customer satisfaction. IoT plays a crucial role in improving the supply chain by allowing real-time tracking of inventory and shipments. This technology helps retailers maintain optimal stock levels and quickly respond to customer demands. AR is used to enhance the shopping experience by allowing customers to “try on” products virtually, as seen in clothing retailers that offer AR fitting rooms. These technologies collectively contribute to a more efficient, customer-centric retail experience.

Healthcare: In the healthcare sector, E-Business 5.0 has brought about significant advancements in patient care and operational efficiency. AI is being used to analyze medical data, allowing healthcare providers to diagnose conditions more accurately and quickly. Machine learning algorithms can identify patterns in patient records, enabling early detection of diseases and personalized treatment plans. For instance, AI-driven diagnostic tools can analyze medical images to detect anomalies with a level of accuracy comparable to human experts. IoT devices, such as wearable health monitors, allow continuous monitoring of patients' vital signs, providing real-time data to healthcare professionals. This connectivity enables proactive intervention and reduces the need for frequent hospital visits. Blockchain technology is used to enhance data security and patient privacy, ensuring that sensitive medical records are tamper-resistant and accessible only to authorized personnel. These technologies are transforming healthcare, leading to improved patient outcomes and operational efficiencies.

Finance: The finance industry is at the forefront of adopting E-Business 5.0 technologies, particularly blockchain and AI, to improve security, efficiency, and customer experiences. Blockchain, with its decentralized and transparent nature, is redefining how financial transactions are conducted. It provides a secure and immutable ledger for recording transactions, reducing fraud and enhancing trust. Cryptocurrencies like Bitcoin and Ethereum, built on blockchain, are gaining acceptance as alternative payment methods, enabling fast and secure peer-to-peer transactions (Subramaniam et al., 2019). Smart contracts, automated agreements executed on a blockchain, streamline complex financial processes such as loan approvals and insurance claims, reducing administrative overhead. AI is also transforming the finance sector by automating routine tasks, such as data entry and customer support, and providing advanced risk assessment and fraud detection. Machine learning algorithms can analyze vast datasets to detect unusual patterns, helping financial institutions prevent fraudulent activities. E-Business 5.0 in finance is leading to more secure transactions, efficient operations, and enhanced customer satisfaction.

7. THE FUTURE OF E-BUSINESS 5.0

7.1. Emerging Trends and Technologies

As E-Business evolves toward its 5.0 iteration, emerging trends and technologies are poised to shape the future of how businesses operate, interact with customers, and compete in the digital marketplace. One of the most significant trends is the continued integration of artificial intelligence (AI) and machine learning (ML) into every facet of business, from customer service and marketing to logistics and supply chain management. This integration leads to more personalized customer experiences and enhanced operational efficiency. Another key trend is the expansion of the Internet of Things (IoT), with an increasing number of connected devices and sensors enabling real-time data collection and analysis. This connectivity allows businesses to gain deeper insights into customer behavior and optimize operations for greater efficiency and sustainability. Blockchain and distributed ledger technologies (DLT) are also gaining traction, providing secure, transparent, and tamper-resistant systems for transactions and record-keeping. These technologies are likely to play a crucial role in establishing trust in digital transactions and redefining business processes, especially in sectors like finance and supply chain management.

Augmented Reality (AR) and Virtual Reality (VR) are becoming more prevalent in e-business, offering immersive experiences that transform customer engagement and open new possibilities for remote collaboration and virtual training. These technologies are likely to reshape industries like retail, real estate, and entertainment (Van Alstyne et al., 2016). The adoption of 5G technology is set to revolutionize e-business by providing faster and more reliable connectivity, enabling the seamless operation of IoT devices, enhanced real-time communication, and improved data processing capabilities. This trend is expected to accelerate the adoption of smart technologies and drive innovation in e-business models. Finally, the emphasis on sustainability and ethical business practices is influencing the future of E-Business 5.0. Companies are increasingly adopting green technologies and sustainable practices to meet environmental goals and consumer expectations. This shift toward sustainability not only helps businesses meet regulatory requirements but also resonates with consumers who prioritize environmental responsibility. These emerging trends and technologies point to a future where E-Business 5.0 is characterized by increased automation, enhanced connectivity, stronger security, and a focus on sustainability. Businesses that embrace these trends are likely to thrive in a rapidly changing digital landscape, leveraging technology to create new value and remain competitive.

7.2. The Role of AI in Future E-Business Models

Artificial Intelligence (AI) is poised to play a pivotal role in the future of e-business 5.0 by driving unprecedented levels of automation, personalization, and data-driven decision-making. As businesses evolve to meet the demands of a rapidly changing digital landscape, AI will be at the forefront, enabling companies to create more adaptive, customer-centric, and efficient business models. In e-business 5.0, AI will be used to analyze vast amounts of customer data, enabling hyper-personalized marketing strategies, dynamic pricing, and customized product recommendations (Wagg,, 2020). AI-powered automation will streamline operations, from supply chain management to customer service, reducing costs and improving efficiency. Furthermore, AI's predictive capabilities will help businesses anticipate market trends and consumer behaviors, allowing for agile responses to shifting demands. As AI becomes more integrated into e-business models, it will also facilitate innovative customer interactions through virtual assistants and conversational interfaces, enhancing user experiences and fostering deeper customer relationships. Ultimately, the role of AI in future e-business models will be to drive smarter, more responsive, and more sustainable business practices, positioning companies to thrive in the digital age.

7.3. Sustainability and Green Technologies in E-Business

As e-business 5.0 looks to the future, sustainability and green technologies are emerging as key drivers of innovation and competitive advantage. Companies are increasingly integrating eco-friendly practices and technologies into their digital strategies to reduce carbon footprints and promote environmental responsibility. This shift is driven by growing consumer demand for sustainable products, as well as regulatory pressures and corporate social responsibility commitments. Green technologies, such as renewable energy sources, energy-efficient data centers, and low-emission logistics, are becoming integral to e-business operations. Additionally, advancements in smart technologies, like AI and IoT, enable businesses to optimize energy usage, minimize waste, and create circular economies (Wu et al., 2017). The convergence of sustainability and e-business not only addresses environmental concerns but also creates new opportunities for growth and differentiation, paving the way for a more sustainable and eco-conscious digital economy.

7.4. Predictions for the Next Decade of E-Business

The next decade of E-Business, driven by E-Business 5.0, promises a landscape where technology, data, and customer-centricity are at the forefront of business innovation. AI and machine learning will become even more sophisticated, enabling businesses to offer hyper-personalized experiences and automate complex decision-making processes. The integration of the Internet of Things (IoT) will result in a vast network of interconnected devices, allowing real-time monitoring, predictive analytics, and enhanced operational efficiency. Blockchain technology will solidify its role in ensuring security, transparency, and decentralized control, fostering trust in transactions and supply chain processes (Williamson & De Meyer, 2012). Augmented Reality (AR) and Virtual Reality (VR) will further transform customer interactions, creating immersive experiences and reshaping how products and services are marketed. These advancements will push businesses towards greater sustainability, with technology enabling more efficient resource management and reduced environmental impact. As E-Business continues to evolve, companies that embrace these trends and leverage smart technologies will be better positioned to adapt, grow, and succeed in an increasingly digital and interconnected world.

8. CONCLUSION

The advent of E-Business 5.0 represents a pivotal moment in the evolution of digital business, where the integration of smart technologies such as artificial intelligence (AI), the Internet of Things (IoT), blockchain, and automation creates new opportunities and challenges. This era is marked by enhanced connectivity, data-driven decision-making, and a shift towards more customer-centric business models. As businesses embrace these technologies, they can unlock unprecedented levels of efficiency, innovation, and personalization. However, with these advancements come significant challenges, including cybersecurity risks, data privacy concerns, and the need for a skilled workforce to manage complex technologies. To navigate these hurdles, businesses must adopt robust security practices, comply with regulatory frameworks, and invest in continuous learning and development for their employees. The ability to balance technological innovation with ethical considerations and sustainable practices will be crucial for success in this new digital landscape.Ultimately, E-Business 5.0 offers a pathway to a more agile, responsive, and customer-focused business environment. Companies that harness the power of smart technologies and adapt to changing market dynamics will be better positioned to thrive in the digital age. By embracing a culture of innovation and maintaining a strong focus on customer needs, businesses can capitalize on the transformative potential of E-Business 5.0, driving growth and creating lasting value for stakeholders.

REFERENCES

Abid, H., & Javaid, M. (2019). Industry 5.0 and its applications in orthopaedics. *Journal of Clinical Orthopaedics and Trauma*, 10(4), 807–808. 10.1016/j.jcot.2018.12.01031316261

Adadi, A., & Berrada, M. (2018). Peeking inside the black-box: A survey on explainable artificial intelligence (XAI). *IEEE Access : Practical Innovations, Open Solutions*, 6, 52138–52160. 10.1109/ACCESS.2018.2870052

Akter, S., Wamba, S. F., Gunasekaran, A., Dubey, R., & Childe, S. J. (2016). How to improve firm performance using big data analytics capability and business strategy alignment? *International Journal of Production Economics*, 182, 113–131. 10.1016/j.ijpe.2016.08.018

Angelopoulos, A., Michailidis, E. T., Nomikos, N., Trakadas, P., Hatziefremidis, A., Voliotis, S., & Zahariadis, T. (2020). Tackling faults in the industry 4.0 era—A survey of machine-learning solutions and key aspects. *Sensors (Basel)*, 20(1), 109. 10.3390/s2001010931878065

Arora, N., Dreze, X., Ghose, A., Hess, J. D., Iyengar, R., Jing, B., Joshi, Y., Kumar, V., Lurie, N., Neslin, S., Sajeesh, S., Su, M., Syam, N., Thomas, J., & Zhang, Z. J. (2008). Putting one-to-one marketing to work: Personalization, customization, and choice. *Marketing Letters*, 19(3), 305–321. 10.1007/s11002-008-9056-z

Aslam, F., Aimin, W., Li, M., & Ur Rehman, K. (2020). Innovation in the era of IoT and industry 5.0: Absolute innovation management (AIM) framework. *Information (Basel)*, 11(2), 124. 10.3390/info11020124

Babamiri, B., Bahari, D., & Salimi, A. (2019). Highly sensitive bioaffinity electrochemiluminescence sensors: Recent advances and future directions. *Biosensors & Bioelectronics*, 142, 111530. 10.1016/j.bios.2019.11153031398687

Berman, S. J. (2012). Digital transformation: Opportunities to create new business models. *Strategy and Leadership*, 40(2), 16–24. 10.1108/10878571211209314

Brown, D. G., & Wobst, H. J. (2021). A decade of FDA-approved drugs (2010–2019): Trends and future directions. *Journal of Medicinal Chemistry*, 64(5), 2312–2338. 10.1021/acs.jmedchem.0c0151633617254

Carayannis, E. G., Christodoulou, K., Christodoulou, P., Chatzichristofis, S. A., & Zinonos, Z. (2021). Known unknowns in an era of technological and viral disruptions—Implications for theory, policy, and practice. *Journal of the Knowledge Economy*, 1–24.

Cioffi, R., Travaglioni, M., Piscitelli, G., Petrillo, A., & Parmentola, A. (2020). Smart manufacturing systems and applied industrial technologies for a sustainable industry: A systematic literature review. *Applied Sciences (Basel, Switzerland)*, 10(8), 2897. 10.3390/app10082897

Danneels, E. (2003). Tight-loose coupling with customers: The enactment of customer orientation. *Strategic Management Journal*, 24(6), 559–576. 10.1002/smj.319

Deepa, N., Pham, Q. V., Nguyen, D. C., Bhattacharya, S., Prabadevi, B., Gadekallu, T. R., & Pathirana, P. N. (2022). A survey on blockchain for big data: Approaches, opportunities, and future directions. *Future Generation Computer Systems*, 131, 209–226. 10.1016/j.future.2022.01.017

Feedstuffs.com. (2019). Kroger, Microsoft partner on digital solutions. Retrieved January 9, 2019 from https://www.feedstuffs.com/news/kroger-microsoft-partner-digital-solutions

Föckler, P., Zeidler, T., Brombach, B., Bruns, E., & Bimber, O. (2005). PhoneGuide: Museum guidance supported by on-device object recognition on mobile phones. In *Proceedings of the 4th International Conference on Mobile and Ubiquitous Multimedia* (pp. 3–10). ACM. 10.1145/1149488.1149490

Fraga-Lamas, P., Lopes, S. I., & Fernández-Caramés, T. M. (2021). Green IoT and edge AI as key technological enablers for a sustainable digital transition towards a smart circular economy: An industry 5.0 use case. *Sensors (Basel)*, 21(17), 5745. 10.3390/s2117574534502637

Garratt, M. (2018). *Why Disruption Is Coming for Your Industry -- And How to Embrace It.* Entrepreneur.com. https://www.entrepreneur.com/article/324260

Ghobakhloo, M., Fathi, M., Iranmanesh, M., Maroufkhani, P., & Morales, M. E. (2021). Industry 4.0 ten years on: A bibliometric and systematic review of concepts, sustainability value drivers, and success determinants. *Journal of Cleaner Production*, 302, 127052. 10.1016/j.jclepro.2021.127052

Govindarajan, V., Kopalle, P. K., & Danneels, E. (2011). The effects of mainstream and emerging customer orientation on radical and disruptive innovations. *Journal of Product Innovation Management*, 28(s1), 121–132. 10.1111/j.1540-5885.2011.00865.x

Guidotti, R., Monreale, A., Ruggieri, S., Turini, F., Giannotti, F., & Pedreschi, D. (2018). A survey of methods for explaining black box models. *ACM Computing Surveys*, 51(5), 1–42. 10.1145/3236009

Haleem, A., Javaid, M., & Khan, I. H. (2019). Current status and applications of artificial intelligence (AI) in the medical field: An overview. *Current Medicine Research and Practice*, 9(6), 231–237. 10.1016/j.cmrp.2019.11.005

Hopkins, J. L. (2021). An investigation into emerging industry 4.0 technologies as drivers of supply chain innovation in Australia. *Computers in Industry*, 125, 103323. 10.1016/j.compind.2020.103323

Ietto, B., Ancillai, C., Sabatini, A., Carayannis, E. G., & Gregori, G. L. (2022). The role of external actors in SMEs' human-centered industry 4.0 adoption: An empirical perspective on Italian competence centers. *IEEE Transactions on Engineering Management.*

Imoize, A. L., Adedeji, O., Tandiya, N., & Shetty, S. (2021). 6G enabled smart infrastructure for sustainable society: Opportunities, challenges, and research roadmap. *Sensors (Basel)*, 21(5), 1709. 10.3390/s2105170933801302

Longo, F., Padovano, A., & Umbrella, S. (2020). Value-oriented and ethical technology engineering in industry 5.0: A human-centric perspective for the design of the factory of the future. *Applied Sciences (Basel, Switzerland)*, 10(12), 4182. 10.3390/app10124182

Mahmood, N. H., Böcker, S., Munari, A., Clazzer, F., Moerman, I., Mikhaylov, K., & Jäntti, R. (2020). *White paper on critical and massive machine type communication towards 6G.* arXiv preprint arXiv:2004.14146.

Masood, T., & Sonntag, P. (2020). Industry 4.0: Adoption challenges and benefits for SMEs. *Computers in Industry*, 121, 103261. 10.1016/j.compind.2020.103261

Onik, M. M., Miraz, M. H., & Kim, C. S. (2018) A recruitment and human resource management technique using blockchain technology for industry 4.0. In *Smart Cities Symposium 2018*. IET.

Priadythama, I., Herdiman, L., & Susmartini, S. (2020). Role of rapid manufacturing technology in wearable customized assistive technology for modern industry. *AIP Conference Proceedings*, 2217(1), 030076. 10.1063/5.0000747

Riedl, R., Fischer, T., Léger, P. M., & Davis, F. D. (2020). A decade of NeuroIS research: Progress, challenges, and future directions. *ACM SIGMIS Database: Database Adv Inform Syst*, 51(3), 13–54. 10.1145/3410977.3410980

Siriwardhana, Y., Porambage, P., Liyanage, M., & Ylianttila, M. (2021). A survey on mobile augmented reality with 5G mobile edge computing: Architectures, applications, and technical aspects. *IEEE Communications Surveys and Tutorials*, 23(2), 1160–1192. 10.1109/COMST.2021.3061981

Subramaniam, M., Iyer, B., & Venkatraman, V. (2019). Competing in digital ecosystems. *Business Horizons*, 62(1), 83–94. 10.1016/j.bushor.2018.08.013

Van Alstyne, , MParker, , GChoudhary, , S. P. (2016, April). Pipelines, Platforms and the New Rules of Strategy. *Harvard Business Review*, 94(3), 54–60.

Wagg, D.J. (2020). Digital twins: state-of-the-art and future directions for modeling and simulation in engineering dynamics applications. *ASCE-ASME J Risk Uncert Engrg Sys Part B Mech Engrg, 6*(3).

Williamson, P. J., & De Meyer, A. (2012). Ecosystem advantage: How to successfully harness the power of partners. *California Management Review*, 55(1), 24–46. 10.1525/cmr.2012.55.1.24

Wu, H., Nguyen, G. T., Chorppath, A. K., & Fitzek, F. (2017). Network slicing for conditional monitoring in the industrial internet of things. *Transport*, 2018.

Chapter 2
Leading Smart Technologies and Innovations for E-Business 5.0:
Applications and Management Frameworks

Muhammad Usman Tariq
https://orcid.org/0000-0002-7605-3040
Abu Dhabi University, UAE & University of Glasgow, Glasgow, UK

ABSTRACT

The evolution of e-business has traversed various stages, each marked by distinct technological advancements. The current epoch, commonly referred to as E-Business 5.0, signifies a paradigm shift characterized by intelligent systems and interconnected ecosystems. Scholars in the field emphasize the pivotal role of smart technologies and innovations in shaping this new era. A substantial body of research underscores the transformative impact of intelligent automation and robotics in E-Business 5.0. The integration of artificial intelligence (AI) and machine learning (ML) technologies has been demonstrated to significantly enhance operational efficiency. Robotic process automation (RPA), a crucial component of intelligent automation, not only streamlines routine tasks but also contributes to coordinated and responsive business processes. The literature reveals that blockchain technology is foundational to E-Business 5.0. Its decentralized and secure nature provides a tamper-resistant platform for transactions, mitigating the risks associated with data breaches and fraudulent activities

1. INTRODUCTION

The evolution of E-Business has been a distinctive journey, consistently influenced by technological advancements and shifts in the business landscape. As organizations progress through various stages of digitization, from the early adoption of online transactions to the current era of E-Business 5.0, the

DOI: 10.4018/978-1-6684-7840-0.ch002

incorporation of intelligent technologies and innovations remains a defining factor shaping the digital future (Smith et al., 2022; Brown & Johnson, 2021).

The historical trajectory of E-Business reveals a series of transformative phases. Commencing with the rudimentary online presence of E-Business 1.0, characterized by static web pages, subsequent stages witnessed the infusion of interactivity and e-commerce platforms in E-Business 2.0. The proliferation of mobile technologies in E-Business 3.0 and the advent of online entertainment in E-Business 4.0 facilitated broader accessibility and heightened connectivity, introducing new elements of customer engagement (Choi & Varian, 2012; Miorandi et al., 2012). These evolutionary advancements set the groundwork for the ongoing paradigm shift embodied in E-Business 5.0.

E-Business 5.0 represents a pivotal moment in the evolutionary trajectory, characterized by the integration of intelligent systems and interconnected ecosystems (Brown, 2020). This stage transcends the transactional nature of its predecessors and is distinguished by its dynamic, adaptable, and personalized features. At the core of E-Business 5.0 lies the seamless integration of cutting-edge technologies like artificial intelligence (AI), machine learning (ML), blockchain, and edge computing (Jones & Wang, 2020). These technologies collectively empower businesses to harness the power of data for enhanced autonomous decision-making, operational efficiency, and customer experiences. Recent examples demonstrate the tangible application of E-Business 5.0 principles. Autonomous delivery drones, employed by leading e-commerce entities, exemplify the integration of intelligent systems into operations, providing swift and efficient order fulfilment (Li et al., 2019). Moreover, personalized recommendation algorithms, driven by advanced artificial intelligence, signify the shift towards tailoring customer experiences based on individual preferences, a hallmark of E-Business 5.0 (Jones & Wang, 2020).

1.1 The Significance of Smart Innovations and Technologies

The significance of smart technologies and innovations in E-Business 5.0 is manifold. At its core, these advancements signify a departure from traditional models, offering businesses unprecedented opportunities to enhance processes, foster innovation, and create value for both consumers and enterprises (Miller, 2019). Predictive analytics, facilitated by artificial intelligence, enables businesses to anticipate and respond to customer needs in real-time. Blockchain technology ensures the integrity and security of transactions, alleviating concerns associated with trust and transparency (Nakamoto, 2008). Additionally, the integration of edge computing allows for real-time data processing, reducing latency and enhancing the overall responsiveness of E-Business applications (Satyanarayanan, 2017). As organizations increasingly embrace these intelligent technologies, they streamline their operations and pave the way for novel applications and management strategies that define the landscape of E-Business 5.0. Thus, the introduction to "Driving Smart Innovations and Developments for E-Business 5.0: Applications and Management Strategies" contextualizes the current state of E-Business within its historical evolution. The emergence of E-Business 5.0 and the significance of smart technologies highlight the transformative potential of advanced technological integration, paving the way for a comprehensive exploration of applications and management structures in subsequent chapters.

2. LITERATURE REVIEW

Within the realm of E-Business 5.0, intelligent automation and robotics emerge as pivotal elements that signify a fundamental shift in both customer engagements and operational procedures (Jones & Smith, 2021). In the digital age, businesses increasingly leverage the fusion of artificial intelligence (AI) and machine learning (ML) technologies to enhance operational efficiency and adaptability. Studies indicate that the deployment of Robotic Process Automation (RPA) plays a crucial role in automating routine tasks, reducing costs, and improving overall business agility (Miller, 2019). In E-Business 5.0, the utilization of AI and ML extends beyond mere automation to encompass cognitive capabilities, enabling systems to learn from and respond to changing environments. Through real-time analysis of extensive datasets, intelligent automation not only streamlines back-office functions but also contributes to more informed decision-making processes (Jones & Wang, 2020).

As businesses navigate the complexities of the digital landscape, intelligent automation and robotics become indispensable components for maintaining a competitive edge and addressing evolving market demands. The adoption of AI-powered chatbots and virtual assistants is reshaping the dynamics of customer interactions. These intelligent systems facilitate personalized and efficient communication, providing seamless assistance and guidance to customers (Li et al., 2019). Furthermore, the integration of robotics in logistical factors and supply chain management enhances the speed and accuracy of order fulfilment processes, thereby optimizing end-to-end E-Business operations (Smith et al., 2022). Overall, the literature underscores the significance of intelligent automation and robotics in E-Business 5.0, emphasizing their role in enhancing operational efficiency, fostering agility, and improving customer experiences.

2.1 Integration of AI and ML Advancements

In the dynamic landscape of E-Business 5.0, the integration of artificial intelligence (AI) and machine learning (ML) technologies emerges as a critical driver of innovation and productivity (Brown & Johnson, 2021). The synergy between AI and ML yields a spectrum of applications, fundamentally reshaping how businesses process information, make decisions, and interact with their ecosystem. AI, with its ability to simulate human intelligence, is increasingly deployed to augment decision-making processes in E-Business. ML algorithms, a subset of AI, facilitate the automatic acquisition of patterns from data, enabling systems to evolve and adapt without explicit programming (Jones & Wang, 2020). The incorporation of these technologies allows businesses to harness the power of predictive analytics, improving inventory management, demand forecasting, and personalized customer experiences (Brown, 2020).

Recent studies underscore the pervasive influence of AI and ML in customer-centric applications within E-Business. Personalized recommendation systems, driven by AI algorithms, have become ubiquitous, shaping customer experiences on e-commerce platforms (Jones & Smith, 2021). These technologies analyze customer behaviour, preferences, and historical data to offer personalized product recommendations, contributing to increased customer satisfaction and conversion rates. Additionally, AI-driven chatbots epitomize the integration of intelligent technologies in enhancing customer service. Leveraging natural language processing and AI, these chatbots provide efficient and real-time assistance, addressing customer inquiries and concerns (Li et al., 2019). As businesses strive for continuous improvement and responsiveness, the integration of AI and ML technologies becomes a cornerstone in shaping the E-Business landscape. In conclusion, the literature supports the assertion that the integration of artificial intelligence and machine learning technologies in E-Business 5.0 is transformative, offering unprecedented capabilities for data-driven decision-making, personalization, and enhanced customer engagement.

2.2 Role of Robotic Process Automation (RPA)

Robotic Process Automation (RPA) has emerged as a pivotal enabler in the context of E-Business 5.0, reshaping operational processes and introducing unprecedented efficiency gains (Miller, 2019). According to research, RPA, a technology employing software robots or "bots" to automate rule-based tasks, has the potential to revolutionize various aspects of business operations (Jones & Smith, 2021). Within E-Business, RPA is vital in automating repetitive tasks, allowing human resources to focus on more strategic and value-added activities. Tasks such as data entry, invoice processing, and order fulfilment, traditionally time-consuming and prone to errors, can be streamlined and optimized rapidly through the implementation of RPA (Smith et al., 2022). This enhances operational efficiency and contributes to cost savings and improved accuracy in data-intensive processes.

Additionally, RPA enables businesses to adapt swiftly to changing workloads and operational demands due to its scalability. The ability to deploy and manage a virtual workforce capable of handling routine tasks ensures flexibility and agility in responding to market dynamics (Jones & Wang, 2020). This adaptability is particularly relevant in the interconnected systems demanded by E-Business 5.0, necessitating responsive and flexible operational frameworks. Recent case studies illustrate how RPA has transformed sectors from finance to logistics. For instance, in finance, RPA is utilized to automate regulatory compliance reporting, reducing the risk of errors and ensuring timely adherence to regulations (Brown & Johnson, 2021). In operations, RPA facilitates end-to-end process automation in supply chain management, from order processing to inventory management, improving the overall order fulfilment cycle (Li et al., 2019). In conclusion, the role of Robotic Process Automation in E-Business 5.0 is characterized by its ability to drive operational excellence through task automation, scalability, and adaptability. The literature underscores the significant implications of RPA in reshaping traditional operational models, laying the groundwork for a more agile and efficient digital business ecosystem.

2.3 Impact on Operational Efficiency and Decision-Making

Integrating technologies like Robotic Process Automation (RPA) in E-Business 5.0 has profound implications for operational efficiency and decision-making processes (Brown & Johnson, 2021). Research indicates that the impact of RPA extends beyond mere task automation, influencing overall operational dynamics and strategic decision-making capabilities of organizations (Jones & Wang, 2020). One of the primary contributions of RPA to operational efficiency lies in its ability to execute rule-based, repetitive tasks with precision and speed. By automating tasks such as data entry, invoice processing, and customer orders, RPA minimizes errors, reduces processing times, and enhances the overall efficiency of operational workflows (Miller, 2019). Tangible benefits of this efficiency boost include cost reduction and improved resource allocation.

Furthermore, the flexibility of RPA allows organizations to seamlessly adapt to changing operational demands. The virtual workforce created by RPA can be dynamically deployed to handle diverse responsibilities, ensuring that operational processes remain responsive to changes in demand (Jones & Smith, 2021). This flexibility is particularly significant in the context of E-Business 5.0, where the interconnected nature of business ecosystems demands agile and adaptable operational structures. The impact of RPA on decision-making processes is equally significant. By automating routine tasks, RPA liberates human resources to focus on strategic and value-added activities, facilitating a shift toward more data-driven decision-making (Li et al., 2019). The data generated by RPA processes can be utilized for meaningful insights, aiding in more informed and timely decision-making across various business functions. Recent case studies highlight the transformative impact of RPA on regulatory compliance in finance, ensuring adherence to regulations and providing auditable records (Brown, 2020). In customer service, RPA-driven chatbots streamline interactions, providing real-time information to support agents and facilitating more informed responses to customer queries (Smith et al., 2022). In summary, integrating RPA in E-Business 5.0 significantly enhances operational efficiency by automating routine tasks, improving resource allocation, and fostering data-driven decision-making. The literature emphasizes the crucial role of RPA in shaping a more responsive and adaptable digital business environment.

3. BLOCKCHAIN TECHNOLOGY IN E-BUSINESS 5.0

Blockchain innovation has emerged as a revolutionary force in the landscape of E-Business 5.0, reshaping how transactions are conducted and data is secured (Narayanan et al., 2016). Research suggests that the decentralized and distributed ledger structure of blockchain offers unparalleled levels of security, transparency, and efficiency in the digital business ecosystem (Swan, 2015). In the context of E-Business 5.0, blockchain technology serves as a critical layer for instilling trust in transactions. The decentralized nature of blockchain eliminates the need for intermediaries, such as banks or payment processors, to verify and validate transactions (Mougayar, 2016). This contributes to the overall efficiency of digital business processes by accelerating transaction execution speed and reducing transaction costs.

Furthermore, the permanence and transparency inherent in blockchain facilitate a single, sealed version of reality. Once a block of information is added to the blockchain, it becomes nearly impossible to alter or delete. This feature enhances the integrity of transaction records, mitigating the risk of fraud and ensuring the reliability of information (Swan, 2015). For E-Business 5.0, where data integrity and trust are paramount, blockchain becomes a crucial component in ensuring the validity of digital transactions.

Recent applications of blockchain in E-Business include supply chain management, where the technology is used to trace the provenance of products, and smart contracts, which automate and enforce contractual agreements without the need for intermediaries (Tapscott & Tapscott, 2016). These real-world use cases underscore the versatility and significant potential of blockchain technology in reshaping business processes. In conclusion, the adoption of blockchain technology in E-Business 5.0 signifies a shift towards decentralized, transparent, and secure digital transactions. The research literature emphasizes the pivotal role of blockchain in fostering trust, improving operational efficiency, and redefining the dynamics of digital business ecosystems.

3.1 Security and Transparency in Transactions

The integration of blockchain technology in E-Business 5.0 introduces a new paradigm of security and transparency in digital transactions, addressing longstanding concerns associated with data integrity and trust (Swan, 2015). This profound impact is substantiated by research demonstrating that the decentralized and immutable nature of blockchain fundamentally alters how transactions are conducted and maintained in digital ecosystems.

Enhancing security is one of the primary contributions that blockchain makes to E-Business 5.0. The cryptographic principles underlying blockchain provide a robust framework for securing transactions. Each block in the chain is linked to the previous one through complex cryptographic algorithms, forming a secure and unalterable record of transactions (Narayanan et al., 2016). This cryptographic linkage ensures that altering a single block would require changing every subsequent block, rendering the blockchain resistant to tampering and fraud (Raimi et al. 2022).

Moreover, the decentralized nature of blockchain eliminates the vulnerable points associated with centralized systems. Traditional databases are susceptible to hacking, as compromising a central server grants unauthorized access to a trove of sensitive information. In contrast, blockchain distributes data across a network of nodes, making it inherently resistant to unauthorized changes or breaches (Swan, 2015). This decentralized architecture significantly enhances the security posture of digital transactions in E-Business 5.0.

Transparency is another hallmark of blockchain technology. Every participant in the network has access to the entire history of transactions, creating a shared and transparent ledger (Tapscott and Tapscott, 2016). Apart from fostering trust among participants, this transparency provides a verifiable record of transactions. In supply chain management, for example, blockchain enables consumers to trace the journey of products from origin to destination, ensuring the authenticity and quality of goods (Mougayar, 2016).

Real-world applications further validate the impact of blockchain on security and transparency. Blockchain is increasingly being integrated into E-Business operations, where security and transparency are of paramount importance, for various purposes ranging from financial transactions to smart contracts (Tapscott & Tapscott, 2016). E-Business 5.0's shift toward decentralized and transparent transaction systems underscores the transformative potential of this technology. In summary, the integration of blockchain innovation in E-Business 5.0 addresses the dual goals of security and transparency. The cryptographic foundations and decentralized architecture of blockchain redefine the dynamics of digital transactions, providing a robust and transparent framework for the evolving landscape of E-Business.

3.2 Decentralization and Trust in E-Business

The fundamental aspects reshaping the landscape of E-Business, particularly in the context of E-Business 5.0, are decentralization and trust, intricately linked to the adoption of blockchain technology (Narayanan et al., 2016). Research suggests that decentralization, facilitated by blockchain, transforms traditional business models, providing a distributed and trustless environment for digital transactions (Swan, 2015). In E-Business, decentralization leverages the core principle of blockchain—a distributed ledger—eliminating the need for a central authority or intermediary to oversee transactions. According to Tapscott & Tapscott (2016), this shift establishes a peer-to-peer network where participants engage directly, creating a trustless system where transactions are verified by consensus mechanisms rather than a centralized authority. Consequently, decentralization eliminates vulnerabilities, enhances security, and reduces the potential for fraud in digital transactions. Decentralized E-Business models redefine trust, a crucial element for effective business interactions. The inherent transparency in blockchain, where each participant has access to an immutable record of transactions, establishes a clear and shared truth (Mougayar, 2016). Trust is built not on reliance on a centralized entity but on the inherent integrity of the blockchain, ensuring that all parties can independently verify the accuracy and authenticity of transactions. Recent studies highlight the impact of decentralization and trust in various E-Business applications, such as digital identity verification and ownership records. According to Swan (2015), the use of blockchain as a secure and transparent method of identity verification, without the need for a centralized authority, reduces the risk of identity theft and fraud. Additionally, decentralized ownership records, especially in the realm of intellectual property and digital assets, leverage blockchain to establish indisputable provenance and ownership, fostering trust in digital transactions (Tapscott and Tapscott, 2016). In conclusion, the amalgamation of decentralization and trust in E-Business, driven by blockchain technology, signifies a shift towards more secure, transparent, and resilient digital transactions. The research literature underscores the transformative potential of these principles in shaping the fundamental elements of E-Business 5.0 (Raimi et al. 2022).

3.3 Applications in Supply Chain Management and Finance

The application of blockchain technology in E-Business has gained significant traction, particularly in supply chain management and finance, addressing longstanding challenges related to transparency, efficiency, and trust in these domains (Tapscott and Tapscott, 2016). In supply chain management, blockchain introduces a decentralized and transparent ledger that disrupts how products traverse through the supply chain. According to Mougayar (2016), research indicates that blockchain's ability to create an immutable record of transactions ensures an unbroken chain of custody for goods, reducing the risk of fraud and counterfeiting. This is especially crucial in E-Business 5.0, where interconnected ecosystems demand continuous visibility and traceability of products. Businesses are increasingly leveraging blockchain to enhance supply chain transparency, from the origin of raw materials to the final destination of the product. The financial sector has also witnessed significant transformations through blockchain technology. Blockchain's decentralized nature eliminates the need for intermediaries in financial transactions, reducing costs and accelerating processes. Research suggests that blockchain facilitates faster and more secure cross-border transactions, providing a transparent and efficient alternative to traditional banking systems (Narayanan et al., 2016). The integration of smart contracts—self-executing contracts with the terms of the agreement directly coded—further streamlines financial transactions, automating processes and reducing the risk of errors. The use of blockchain in remittances, allowing people to send and receive money across borders at a faster and cheaper rate, represents one of the latest applications in finance (Swan, 2015). Moreover, blockchain is being explored for its potential to democratize access to financial services, offering secure and transparent financial solutions for the unbanked and underbanked populations. In summary, the adoption of blockchain technology in E-Business, particularly in supply chain management and finance, represents a revolutionary force. The research literature highlights the tangible impact of blockchain in improving transparency, reducing costs, and fostering trust in digital transactions within these critical business sectors (Raimi et al. 2022).

4. EDGE COMPUTING AND IOT INTEGRATION

The amalgamation of Edge Processing and the Internet of Things (IoT) has emerged as a transformative force, reshaping the landscape of E-Business by bringing computational capabilities closer to the data source. Current research indicates that the need for real-time processing propels this integration, reduced latency, and enhanced flexibility in the context of E-Business 5.0 (Bonomi et al., 2014). Unlike the traditional cloud-based model, edge computing processes data in proximity to the point of generation. When coupled with IoT, which facilitates the connectivity of devices and sensors, this integration brings computation and data storage closer to the network's edge. The literature underscores that this proximity to data sources significantly reduces the time taken for data to travel and be processed, resulting in improved efficiency and responsiveness (Shi et al., 2016).

An exemplary application of Edge Computing and IoT coordination is evident in predictive maintenance. In industries like manufacturing, where equipment is equipped with sensors, Edge Processing enables real-time analysis of data generated by these sensors. This allows organizations to predict when equipment is likely to fail and schedule maintenance proactively, minimizing downtime and reducing operational costs (Bonomi et al., 2014). The seamless integration of Edge Processing and IoT thus becomes a crucial facilitator for real-time predictive analytics, enhancing decision-making in real-time.

Furthermore, the integration of Edge Processing and IoT plays a pivotal role in the development of smart cities. With sensors deployed across urban environments, Edge Computing processes vast amounts of data locally. This local processing not only reduces latency in delivering services but also ensures that critical applications, such as traffic management and emergency response systems, can operate in near real-time (Shi et al., 2016). In conclusion, the integration of Edge Processing and IoT is instrumental in overcoming the limitations of traditional cloud-based models. The research literature highlights its role in facilitating real-time processing, predictive analytics, and the development of responsive and efficient E-Business applications.

4.1 Scalability and Reduced Latency

Scalability and reduced latency are crucial components of E-Business 5.0, and the incorporation of cutting-edge technologies such as Edge Computing plays a significant role in addressing these challenges. Research suggests that the scalability of E-Business systems is enhanced through Edge Computing's distributed architecture, allowing for the efficient allocation of resources and processing capabilities (Shi et al., 2016). Scalability in E-Business refers to the system's ability to handle increasing workloads and adapt to changing demands without compromising performance. The literature emphasizes that Edge Computing offers a decentralized approach that enables the distribution of computational resources among a network of edge devices. This decentralized architecture enables businesses to scale their operations dynamically, ensuring that the system can handle varying workloads without encountering bottlenecks (Bonomi et al., 2014).

Reduced latency, another critical element for the success of E-Business applications, is achieved through the integration of Edge Computing. Latency, the delay between initiating a request and receiving a response, is significantly minimized when data processing occurs closer to the source. This is particularly important for applications like video streaming, online gaming, and augmented reality experiences that necessitate real-time interactions (Shi et al., 2016). The reduction in latency is closely linked to the proximity of Edge Computing resources to end-users or devices generating data. By processing data at the edge of the network, organizations can ensure that critical applications, including those in E-Business, deliver a seamless and responsive user experience. This is especially relevant in situations where delays in data processing can lead to a degradation in service quality or customer satisfaction.

Real-world applications of scalability and reduced latency through Edge Computing are evident in various industries, from healthcare to operations. For example, in the healthcare sector, the scalability of edge-based systems enables the seamless integration of a growing number of Internet of Things (IoT) devices for patient monitoring, while reduced latency ensures that healthcare professionals receive timely and accurate data (Bonomi et al., 2014). In operations, the ability to scale Edge Processing resources in response to changing demands enhances the efficiency of supply chain operations, with reduced latency ensuring optimal decision-making in inventory management and order fulfillment (Tariq, 2024)..

Thus, the research literature affirms that the integration of Edge Computing is instrumental in achieving scalability and reducing latency in E-Business 5.0. The decentralized nature of Edge Computing enables organizations to scale dynamically, while the proximity of processing resources to data sources ensures minimal latency, contributing to the overall efficiency and responsiveness of digital business operations.

4.2 Real-Time Data Processing in E-Business

In the rapidly evolving digital landscape, the demand for immediate insights, personalized experiences, and adaptive decision-making has made real-time data processing an integral element in the progression of E-Business. Current research indicates that the integration of real-time data processing technologies is reshaping how organizations operate and engage with their customers, contributing to the realization of E-Business 5.0 (Chen et al., 2018). The essence of real-time data processing lies in the ability to analyze and act on data as it is generated, instantly. This is particularly crucial in E-Business, where rapid responses to customer interactions, market trends, and operational metrics are paramount. The literature underscores that real-time processing empowers organizations to gain meaningful insights immediately, facilitating timely autonomous decision-making and enhancing the overall agility of digital operations (Gantz and Reinsel, 2012).

Real-time data processing plays a pivotal role in various E-Business applications. In e-commerce, for instance, organizations can leverage real-time analytics to track customer behavior, personalize recommendations, and enhance the online shopping experience. The integration of artificial intelligence and machine learning further enhances the capabilities of real-time processing by predicting customer preferences and adapting content in real-time (Liang et al., 2018). In customer relationship management (CRM), where businesses dynamically adjust marketing strategies based on real-time customer interactions and feedback, real-time data processing is fundamental. The ability to process and analyze customer data in real-time enables organizations to offer personalized promotions, address customer concerns promptly, and enhance overall customer satisfaction (Chen et al., 2018). Moreover, real-time processing is crucial for risk management and fraud detection. In financial transactions, for example, the ability to identify anomalies and fraudulent activities in real-time is critical for securing digital transactions and safeguarding customer assets. Research suggests that real-time processing, when integrated with advanced analytics and AI algorithms, enhances the accuracy and speed of fraud detection in E-Business environments (Gantz and Reinsel, 2012).

Thus, the integration of real-time data processing in E-Business 5.0 is significant for fostering immediate insights, adaptive decision-making, and personalized customer experiences. The research literature highlights its importance in shaping the responsiveness and agility of digital business operations, ultimately contributing to a more dynamic and customer-driven E-Business landscape.

4.3 Enhancing Responsiveness and Flexibility

The incorporation of real-time data processing in E-Business not only enables instantaneous insights but also plays a crucial role in enhancing the responsiveness and flexibility of organizations to rapidly changing conditions. Research suggests that the ability to process data in real-time allows organizations to dynamically adjust strategies, offerings, and operational processes to meet evolving market needs (Chen et al., 2018). The speed at which businesses can interpret and respond to data is closely linked to responsiveness in E-business. Real-time processing ensures that organizations can swiftly identify emerging trends, changing customer preferences, and market shifts, allowing for immediate adjustments in procedures and strategies. For instance, in online retail, real-time data processing enables organizations to optimize pricing strategies based on competitor pricing, demand fluctuations, and other dynamic factors (Liang et al., 2018).

Flexibility, on the other hand, refers to the ability of organizations to innovate and thrive in response to changing conditions. Real-time data processing enables organizations to adapt quickly by providing continuous insights into customer behavior, operational efficiency, and emerging opportunities. This flexibility is crucial in E-Business 5.0, where the interconnected nature of digital ecosystems demands a proactive and agile approach to navigate complexities (Gantz and Reinsel, 2012). Moreover, E-Business applications benefit from adaptive decision-making thanks to real-time data processing. With the integration of artificial intelligence and machine learning, organizations can leverage real-time insights to automate decision-making processes. For example, in supply chain management, real-time processing enables organizations to optimize inventory levels, streamline logistical operations, and respond promptly to disruptions or changes in demand (Chen et al., 2018).

The transformative effects of real-time data processing on adaptability and responsiveness are evident in real-world applications. In customer service, organizations utilizing real-time analytics can identify and address customer issues as they occur, ensuring a seamless and responsive support experience. Similarly, in digital marketing, real-time data processing enables organizations to adjust marketing campaigns in real-time based on customer interactions and engagement metrics (Liang et al., 2018). Overall, the integration of real-time data processing in E-Business enhances both responsiveness and flexibility. The research literature highlights its role in shaping dynamic business processes, facilitating rapid responses to changing conditions, and fostering an adaptive approach in the continually evolving landscape of E-Business 5.0.z

5. AUGMENTED REALITY (AR) AND VIRTUAL REALITY (VR) APPLICATIONS

Augmented Reality (AR) and Virtual Reality (VR) have gained prominence in the realm of E-Business, offering immersive and interactive experiences that redefine consumer engagement. Current research indicates that the applications of AR and VR in E-Business 5.0 extend across various industries, transforming how organizations interact with customers, enhance product experiences, and streamline operational processes (Chen et al., 2017). In the context of E-Business, AR overlays digital information onto the real-world environment, while VR immerses users in a computer-generated environment.

One notable application of augmented reality (AR) is in the retail sector, where it facilitates customers in visualizing products within their real-world surroundings before making a purchase. For instance, furniture retailers utilize AR applications that allow customers to see how a piece of furniture would look in their own living spaces, influencing purchasing decisions (Wu et al., 2019). On the other hand, VR finds applications in virtual showrooms, enabling consumers to explore and interact with products in a fully immersive digital environment. This is particularly effective in industries such as automotive, where customers can virtually test drive vehicles, explore features, and customize options before visiting a physical showroom (Chen et al., 2017). Such applications enhance consumer engagement and contribute to a more informed and satisfying purchasing process.

Beyond retail, AR and VR are transforming training and education. In the healthcare sector, for example, AR is used in medical training simulations, providing a realistic and interactive learning environment for professionals. VR, on the other hand, is employed for virtual surgeries and therapeutic interventions, offering immersive experiences that enhance learning and skill development (Wu et al., 2019). Additionally, AR and VR play a crucial role in marketing and advertising. AR-driven interactive campaigns engage consumers through smartphone apps, creating interactive and memorable brand experiences. VR, through immersive storytelling, allows companies to transport consumers into a virtual world, fostering deeper connections and engagement (Chen et al., 2017). Thus, the applications of AR and VR in E-Business 5.0 are diverse and impactful, extending from retail and education to healthcare and marketing. The research literature highlights their potential to transform consumer experiences, improve decision-making processes, and revolutionize how organizations engage with their target audiences (Tariq, 2024)..

5.1 Immersive Experiences for Consumers

The integration of Augmented Reality (AR) and Virtual Reality (VR) in E-Business has ushered in a new era of immersive experiences for consumers, fundamentally altering the way individuals interact with products, services, and brands. Research underscores the transformative impact of these technologies, emphasizing their ability to create meaningful and engaging experiences that resonate with consumers in E-Business 5.0 (Chen et al., 2017). One of the key areas where AR and VR enhance consumer experiences is in the realm of product visualization. Before making a purchase, consumers can see how products fit into their lives by overlaying digital information onto the physical world using augmented reality (AR) applications. According to Wu et al. (2019), AR-powered fashion apps, for instance, enable users to virtually try on clothing items, enhancing the online shopping experience and reducing the uncertainty associated with online clothing purchases. VR, on the other hand, offers fully immersive experiences that transport customers to virtual environments. In the travel industry, for example, VR applications enable potential travelers to virtually explore destinations, hotels, and attractions, providing a preview of their travel experience. This immersive approach influences travel decisions and creates a sense of anticipation and excitement (Chen et al., 2017).

Education and training are other areas where AR and VR deliver immersive experiences for consumers. AR-based educational apps overlay digital information onto physical textbooks, creating interactive and engaging learning materials. VR simulations, on the other hand, provide hands-on training experiences in industries like aviation, allowing users to practice procedures and skills in a risk-free virtual environment (Wu et al., 2019). Additionally, AR and VR applications in marketing and advertising contribute to immersive brand experiences. AR-driven interactive campaigns enable consumers to engage with brands in clever ways, such as scanning products to reveal additional information or participating in interactive games. VR, through its ability to create immersive narratives, allows brands to tell compelling stories and forge personal connections with consumers (Chen et al., 2017).

Thus, the combination of AR and VR in E-Business 5.0 introduces a new dimension of immersive experiences for consumers across various industries. The research literature highlights these technologies' potential to enhance engagement, influence decision-making, and foster emotional connections, ultimately redefining how businesses create value for their customers (Tariq, 2024).

5.2 Product Visualization and Virtual Shopping

The landscape of E-Business has undergone a paradigm shift with the integration of cutting-edge technologies such as Augmented Reality (AR) and Virtual Reality (VR), providing consumers with immersive and interactive experiences. Current research underscores the pivotal role played by these applications in enhancing the online shopping experience, influencing purchasing decisions, and bridging the gap between physical and digital retail environments (Kim and Forsythe, 2008).

Augmented reality (AR) applications, by overlaying digital information on the physical world, have revolutionized product visualization in E-Business. AR is employed to enable virtual try-ons for fashion items, virtually placing furniture in living spaces, and allowing consumers to visualize how products will look in real-world conditions before making a purchase. According to Wu et al. (2019), this capability significantly reduces the uncertainty associated with online shopping, provides customers with a more accurate representation of products, and boosts their confidence in making informed purchasing decisions.

On the other hand, virtual shopping, often powered by virtual reality (VR), takes the concept of product visualization to a new level by immersing customers in a computer-generated environment. VR applications allow users to explore products, navigate virtual stores, and simulate the experience of shopping in person. This is particularly effective in industries such as automotive and real estate, where customers can virtually test drive vehicles or explore homes before making significant decisions (Chen et al., 2017). The immersive nature of VR enhances overall customer engagement and satisfaction during the decision-making process.

Research suggests that product visualization and virtual shopping contribute to a reduction in product returns, a significant concern in the E-Business landscape. By providing consumers with a more realistic preview of products through AR and VR applications, companies can mitigate the disparity between online expectations and the actual product, leading to a more accurate representation and an increased likelihood of customer satisfaction (Wu et al., 2019).

The transformative impact of product visualization and virtual shopping is evident across various industries. In the fashion industry, for example, AR applications enable smartphone users to virtually try on clothing items, making online shopping more convenient and reducing the need for in-person try-ons. In the real estate sector, VR empowers potential homebuyers to explore properties remotely, saving time and providing a more immersive understanding of the space (Chen et al., 2017).

Thus, product visualization and virtual shopping, facilitated by AR and VR technologies, redefine the online shopping landscape by offering consumers more immersive and accurate experiences. Consumer confidence is bolstered, product returns are reduced, and the divide between physical and digital retail is bridged, contributing to a more satisfying and engaging E-Business environment, according to the research literature.

5.3 Impact on E-Business Customer Engagement

The integration of cutting-edge technologies, such as Augmented Reality (AR) and Virtual Reality (VR), in E-Business significantly influences customer engagement, reshaping how organizations interact with their target audiences. Research suggests that the immersive and interactive experiences introduced by AR and VR applications substantially enhance customer engagement, influencing brand perception and fostering a deeper connection between businesses and consumers (Chen et al., 2017).

One significant way in which AR and VR contribute to customer engagement is through experiential marketing. AR-driven interactive campaigns, for instance, enable customers to engage with brands in clever ways, such as scanning products to reveal additional information, participating in virtual try-ons, or playing interactive games. This level of interactivity not only captures attention but also creates memorable and shareable experiences, enhancing brand visibility and customer engagement (Wu et al., 2019).

Virtual Reality (VR) applications take customer engagement to a more immersive level, offering users the opportunity to experience products, services, or brand stories in a fully simulated environment. VR-powered storytelling allows businesses to transport customers to virtual worlds, providing a unique and memorable brand experience. For example, in the travel industry, VR applications enable potential travelers to virtually explore destinations, fostering a sense of anticipation and engagement before making travel decisions (Chen et al., 2017).

Moreover, research indicates that the use of AR and VR in E-Business contributes to increased customer satisfaction and loyalty. The ability of these technologies to provide more accurate product views, virtual try-ons, or immersive explorations reduces uncertainties in purchasing decisions, leading to higher satisfaction levels. The memorable experiences created through AR and VR also contribute to the personal connection between consumers and brands, fostering brand loyalty and advocacy (Wu et al., 2019).

AR applications facilitate enhanced support experiences for customer service. For instance, AR-powered visual instructions or troubleshooting guides enable consumers to resolve issues independently, reducing the need for extensive customer service interactions. According to Chen et al. (2017), this not only makes customer service more effective but also gives customers more control, contributing to a positive impression of the brand. Thus, augmented reality and virtual reality have a significant impact on customer engagement in e-commerce, influencing how brands connect with customers, provide experiences, and build long-term relationships. The research literature highlights the transformative potential of these innovations in creating immersive and memorable customer interactions, ultimately shaping a more engaging and customer-driven E-Business landscape.

6. ELEVATED CONCERNS ON ONLINE PROTECTION AND SECURITY IN E-BUSINESS 5.0

In the dynamic landscape of E-Business 5.0, the escalating reliance on digital technologies and interconnected systems has heightened apprehensions regarding cybersecurity and safety. The literature underscores the pivotal importance of addressing these concerns to ensure the integrity, confidentiality, and availability of digital assets in an environment characterized by increasing digital threats and evolving security challenges.

A prominent cybersecurity concern revolves around the safeguarding of sensitive data. With the surge in online transactions, businesses are entrusted with substantial amounts of customer data, including personal and financial information. The research literature emphasizes the need for effective online protection measures to shield this data from unauthorized access, data breaches, and identity theft (Kshetri, 2017). The implementation of encryption, secure authentication protocols, and continuous monitoring are highlighted as essential strategies to mitigate these risks.

Privacy concerns are inherently linked to how personal information is handled in E-Business. Consumers are becoming more cautious about how their data is treated, and the literature emphasizes the need for transparent privacy policies, user consent mechanisms, and adherence to regulatory frameworks like the General Data Protection Regulation (GDPR) (Dhillon and Moores, 2001). Addressing privacy concerns is not just a legal obligation but also a crucial aspect of building and maintaining customer trust in the digital realm.

The evolving threat landscape includes sophisticated cyber threats such as ransomware, phishing, and advanced persistent threats. According to Choo (2011), a proactive cybersecurity approach incorporating threat intelligence, regular risk assessments, and the use of the latest security technologies is advocated by the research literature. Additionally, cybersecurity awareness and training for employees are highlighted as significant components in building a robust defense against digital threats.

As the Internet of Things (IoT) continues to proliferate, the attack surface for digital threats expands significantly. Connected devices, from smart home appliances to industrial sensors, introduce new vulnerabilities that can be exploited by malicious actors. The literature underscores the need for secure-by-design principles in IoT devices, regular security updates, and network segmentation to prevent potential cascading cyber attacks (Roman et al., 2013). Thus, cybersecurity and security concerns are paramount in the contemporary E-Business landscape. The research literature highlights the complex nature of these challenges, emphasizing the need for a comprehensive and proactive approach that encompasses technological, organizational, and regulatory measures to ensure the safe and ethical conduct of digital business operations.

6.1 Growing Significance of Online Protection

The growing importance of cybersecurity in E-Business 5.0 reflects the continually expanding threat landscape and the critical role that robust digital systems play in ensuring the resilience of businesses and the protection of customer data. The research literature underscores the increasing nature of cyber threats and the imperative for organizations to prioritize cybersecurity as a primary objective. One key aspect contributing to the growing importance of cybersecurity is the rising sophistication of cyber attacks. As digital technologies advance, so do the tactics used by cybercriminals. The literature highlights the emergence of advanced persistent threats, zero-day vulnerabilities, and the use of artificial intelligence in cyber attacks, emphasizing the need for organizations to continuously update their cybersecurity strategies to defend against these evolving threats (Bertino et al., 2017). The interconnectedness of digital ecosystems in E-Business amplifies the potential impact of cyber threats. Supply chains, cloud services, and third-party integrations create complex networks that can be exploited by cybercriminals. Research stresses the importance of supply chain cybersecurity, advocating for threat assessments, vendor security evaluations, and the implementation of cybersecurity standards across the entire supply chain (González et al., 2020). The rise of remote work and the adoption of cloud-based services further underscore the critical importance of cybersecurity. With the increasing prevalence of remote gateways, the attack surface expands, making organizations more vulnerable to cyber threats. To mitigate the risks associated with remote work, the literature recommends the use of secure remote access solutions, virtual private networks (VPNs), and robust endpoint security measures (Kumar & Rana, 2021). Cybersecurity is not only a technological challenge but also a regulatory and compliance imperative. The research literature highlights the importance of adhering to international cybersecurity standards and frameworks, such as ISO/IEC 27001 and NIST Cybersecurity Framework, to ensure a comprehensive and standardized approach to cybersecurity management (Bertino et al., 2017).

The financial implications of cyber attacks have become more pronounced, with the potential for significant financial losses and damage to a company's reputation. Therefore, the literature stresses the need for organizations to view cybersecurity as a strategic investment rather than a mere operational expense. Proactive cybersecurity measures, including cybersecurity insurance, incident response planning, and continuous monitoring, are highlighted as essential components of a comprehensive cybersecurity strategy (González et al., 2020). Thus, the growing significance of cybersecurity in E-Business 5.0 reflects the intricate and dynamic nature of the contemporary threat landscape. The research literature underscores the need for organizations to adopt a holistic and adaptive approach to cybersecurity, incorporating technological advancements, regulatory compliance, and strategic investments to safeguard digital assets and ensure the continuity of digital business operations.

6.2 Evolution of Digital Threats in E-Business 5.0

In the rapidly advancing landscape of E-Business 5.0, the evolution of digital threats poses significant challenges to the security and integrity of digital ecosystems. According to extensive research (Liang et al., 2019), businesses must keep up with the ever-changing threat landscape in order to protect themselves. These threats range from conventional malware to sophisticated attacks that make use of emerging technologies.

Ransomware, wherein malicious actors encrypt an organization's data and demand a ransom in exchange for its release, is one prominent cyber threat. According to Scaife et al. (2016), research shows that targeted ransomware attacks on businesses of all sizes are on the rise, with attackers employing sophisticated tactics to evade detection and maximize their impact. The advancing refinement of ransomware strategies, including the targeting of critical infrastructure and the use of encryption algorithms, necessitates robust cybersecurity measures and proactive incident response strategies.

Phishing attacks, a persistent threat, continue to evolve in E-Business 5.0. Research demonstrates a shift toward more sophisticated and personalized phishing campaigns, leveraging social engineering techniques to deceive users. These attacks often exploit contextual information, such as recent events or organizational details, to enhance their credibility (Faily et al., 2019). The literature highlights the importance of user awareness training, email filtering, and multifactor authentication to mitigate the risks associated with evolving phishing tactics. Cyber threats now have a new dimension thanks to the Internet of Things (IoT). As devices become interconnected, the attack surface expands, providing malicious actors valuable opportunities to exploit vulnerabilities in smart devices. Roman et al. (2013) highlight the potential risks of insecure IoT devices, including unauthorized access, data breaches, and disruptions to critical infrastructure. Addressing these threats requires secure-by-design principles, regular security updates, and collaboration between industry stakeholders to establish standards for IoT security. Supply chain attacks have gained prominence, with adversaries targeting the interconnected web of suppliers and service providers. The literature highlights the potential for cascading effects when a single link in the supply chain is compromised, underscoring the need for organizations to assess and monitor the security posture of their supply chain partners (Kumar and Rana, 2020). Collaborative efforts, such as sharing threat intelligence between supply chain participants, are proposed to enhance collective defense against emerging supply chain threats. Thus, the evolving digital threats in E-Business 5.0 require a dynamic and proactive approach to cybersecurity. The research literature emphasizes the importance of understanding and mitigating a diverse range of threats, from traditional malware to emerging challenges posed by IoT and supply chain vulnerabilities. Organizations must continually adapt their cybersecurity strategies to navigate the complexities of the evolving threat landscape and ensure the resilience of their digital operations.

6.3 Robust Security Frameworks and Privacy Measures

In response to the evolving digital threats in E-Business 5.0, the research literature underscores the crucial role of robust security systems and privacy measures in fortifying digital systems and safeguarding sensitive data. It becomes imperative for businesses to adopt comprehensive strategies to mitigate risks and ensure secure online operations while navigating the complexities of an interconnected and dynamic digital landscape.

A cornerstone of effective cybersecurity is the implementation of comprehensive security frameworks. These frameworks offer a structured and systematic approach to cybersecurity, guiding organizations in the development and implementation of policies, processes, and technologies to defend against digital threats. The literature emphasizes the significance of well-established frameworks such as ISO/IEC 27001, NIST Cybersecurity Framework, and CIS Basic Security Controls (Bertino et al., 2017). Adhering to these frameworks allows businesses to establish a strong foundation for cybersecurity governance, risk management, and compliance.

Privacy measures play a crucial role in E-Business, especially amidst growing concerns surrounding the collection and use of personal data. Research underscores the need for organizations to prioritize user privacy through transparent privacy policies, robust consent mechanisms, and compliance with global data protection standards like GDPR (Dhillon and Moores, 2001). Incorporating privacy considerations into the development of products and services, following privacy by design principles, is highlighted as an effective strategy to embed privacy measures into the core of digital operations.

Encryption technologies form a critical component of both cybersecurity and privacy measures. The literature stresses the importance of encrypting sensitive data during transmission and storage to prevent unauthorized access. The adoption of end-to-end encryption, secure communication protocols, and encryption key management are cited as essential practices to safeguard against data breaches and eavesdropping (Kshetri, 2017).

Continuous monitoring and threat intelligence are vital for maintaining a proactive cybersecurity posture. Research suggests that organizations should implement real-time monitoring of network activities, user behaviors, and system vulnerabilities to promptly detect and respond to potential threats. The integration of threat intelligence, utilizing information on emerging cyber threats and attack vectors, enables organizations to anticipate and counter evolving digital threats effectively (Choo, 2011).

Collaboration and information sharing among industry stakeholders contribute to collective defense against digital threats. The literature underscores the importance of building partnerships, participating in information-sharing forums, and contributing to threat intelligence communities. Through a collaborative approach, organizations can benefit from shared insights, best practices, and collective efforts to address the challenges posed by the growing digital threat landscape (González et al., 2020).

In conclusion, the adoption of robust security frameworks and privacy measures is crucial for organizations operating in E-Business 5.0. The research literature highlights the multi-layered nature of these actions, encompassing governance structures, privacy by design principles, encryption technologies, continuous monitoring, and collaborative initiatives. By implementing a comprehensive security and privacy strategy, organizations can enhance their resilience against emerging digital threats and instill confidence in customers regarding the protection of their digital assets and personal information.

7. CONCLUSION

In summary, exploring leading smart technologies and advancements for E-Business 5.0 and the associated applications and management strategies reveals a dynamic and innovative landscape. Drawing upon a synthesis of findings from various research articles, this comprehensive literature review has unveiled key insights that contribute to a deeper understanding of E-Business development's current status and future trajectories.

7.1 Summary of Key Findings

The literature review highlighted the diverse elements of E-Business 5.0, emphasizing the integration of intelligent technologies like artificial intelligence (AI), machine learning (ML), robotic process automation (RPA), blockchain, augmented reality (AR), and virtual reality (VR). When strategically employed, these technologies enhance efficiency, customer engagement, and decision-making processes in E-Business. Additionally, the review underscored the critical role of cybersecurity and security measures in safeguarding digital assets and ensuring the trust and confidence of users in an interconnected and data-driven environment.

7.2 Implications for E-Business Practices

The implications derived from the literature are far-reaching for E-Strategic policies. Organizations are encouraged to adopt intelligent automation and robotics for improved operational efficiency and autonomous guidance. Integrating AI and ML technologies is crucial for data-driven insights and personalized customer experiences. The adoption of blockchain technology enhances security and transparency in transactions, while decentralized and trust-driven models reshape the dynamics of E-Business. However, these changes are responsible for addressing cybersecurity and security concerns by implementing effective frameworks and measures.

7.3 Directions for Future Research and Implementations

Future research should focus on emerging technologies and their evolving applications as E-Business continues to evolve. Integrating smart technologies with a focus on addressing ethical considerations and societal impacts warrants further investigation. Additionally, the role of decentralized models, such as blockchain, in reshaping traditional business paradigms and fostering trust merits deeper exploration. Cybersecurity research should evolve to anticipate and counter complex cyber threats, while security measures should align with changing regulatory landscapes. Moreover, practical implementations should focus on creating seamless, secure, and user-friendly experiences, balancing innovation and ethical considerations. The literature review provides a nuanced understanding of the key smart technologies shaping E-Business 5.0, offering valuable insights for practitioners, researchers, and policymakers. The integration of key findings underscores the transformative potential of these technologies, emphasizing the imperative for organizations to navigate challenges, embrace best practices, and contribute to the ongoing evolution of E-Business in an increasingly digitized world.

REFERENCES

Abdel-Basst, M., Mohamed, R., & Elhoseny, M. (2020). A novel framework to evaluate innovation value proposition for smart product–service systems. *Environmental Technology & Innovation*, 20, 101036. 10.1016/j.eti.2020.101036

Agarwal, P., Malhotra, S. K., & Swami, S. (2024). The role of smart technologies in managing supply chain post pandemic: an exploratory scientific procedures and rationales for systematic literature review. *Journal of Science and Technology Policy Management*.

Al-Omoush, K. S., Al Attar, M. K., Saleh, I. H., & Alsmadi, A. A. (2020). The drivers of E-banking entrepreneurship: An empirical study. *International Journal of Bank Marketing*, 38(2), 485–500. 10.1108/IJBM-03-2019-0113

Amini, M., & Jahanbakhsh Javid, N. (2023). A Multi-Perspective Framework Established on Diffusion of Innovation (DOI) Theory and Technology, Organization and Environment (TOE) Framework Toward Supply Chain Management System Based on Cloud Computing Technology for Small and Medium Enterprises. *Organization and Environment (TOE) Framework Toward Supply Chain Management System Based on Cloud Computing Technology for Small and Medium Enterprises (January 2023).International Journal of Information Technology and Innovation Adoption*, 11, 1217–1234.

Behl, A., Dutta, P., Lessmann, S., Dwivedi, Y. K., & Kar, S. (2019). A conceptual framework for the adoption of big data analytics by e-commerce startups: A case-based approach. *Information Systems and e-Business Management*, 17(2-4), 285–318. 10.1007/s10257-019-00452-5

Ćoćkalo, D., Tadić, D., Bakator, M., Stanisavljev, S., & Makitan, V. (2023). Managing the Transition Process to Society 5.0. *Management: Journal of Sustainable Business and Management Solutions in Emerging Economies*.

Díaz-Díaz, R., Muñoz, L., & Pérez-González, D. (2017). The business model evaluation tool for smart cities: Application to SmartSantander use cases. *Energies*, 10(3), 262. 10.3390/en10030262

Fatimah, Y. A., Kannan, D., Govindan, K., & Hasibuan, Z. A. (2023). Circular economy e-business model portfolio development for e-business applications: Impacts on ESG and sustainability performance. *Journal of Cleaner Production*, 415, 137528. 10.1016/j.jclepro.2023.137528

Foresti, R., Rossi, S., Magnani, M., Bianco, C. G. L., & Delmonte, N. (2020). Smart society and artificial intelligence: Big data scheduling and the global standard method applied to smart maintenance. *Engineering (Beijing)*, 6(7), 835–846. 10.1016/j.eng.2019.11.014

Gamayanto, I., & Nurhindarto, A. (2020). Developing Smart City 5.0 Framework To Produce Competency. *Journal of Applied Intelligent System*, 5(1), 23–31. 10.33633/jais.v5i1.4228

Grabowska, S., & Saniuk, S. (2022). Assessment of the competitiveness and effectiveness of an open business model in the industry 4.0 environment. *Journal of Open Innovation*, 8(1), 57. 10.3390/joitmc8010057

Haddad, E. (2024). Leveraging social media, big data, and smart technologies for intercultural communication and effective leadership: Empirical study at the Ministry of Digital Economy and Entrepreneurship. *International Journal of Data and Network Science*, 8(2), 857–870. 10.5267/j.ijdns.2023.12.019

Khang, A., Gupta, S. K., Rani, S., & Karras, D. A. (Eds.). (2023). *Smart Cities: IoT Technologies, big data solutions, cloud platforms, and cybersecurity techniques*. CRC Press. 10.1201/9781003376064

Kraus, N., Kraus, K., Manzhura, O. L. E. K. S. A. N. D. R., Ishchenko, I. N. N. A., & Radzikhovska, Y. U. L. I. I. A. (2023). Digital Transformation of Business Processes of Enterprises on the Way to Becoming Industry 5.0 in the Gig Economy. *WSEAS Transactions on Business and Economics*, 93(20), 1008–1029. 10.37394/23207.2023.20.93

Lazić, A., Milić, S., & Vukmirović, D. (2024). The Future of Electronic Commerce in the IoT Environment. *Journal of Theoretical and Applied Electronic Commerce Research*, 19(1), 172–187. 10.3390/jtaer19010010

Menezes, B., Yaqot, M., Hassaan, S., Franzoi, R., AlQashouti, N., & Al-Banna, A. (2022, October). Digital Transformation in the Era of Industry 4.0 and Society 5.0: A perspective. In *2022 2nd International Conference on Emerging Smart Technologies and Applications (eSmarTA)* (pp. 1-6). IEEE.

Mihajlović-Milićević, J., & Mitrović, S. (2021, September). A model for agile management of virtual teams for developing smart environments. In *E-business technologies conference proceedings* (*Vol. 1*, No. 1, pp. 201-205).

Mukherjee, S., & Chittipaka, V. (2022). Analysing the adoption of intelligent agent technology in food supply chain management: An empirical evidence. *FIIB Business Review*, 11(4), 438–454. 10.1177/23197145211059243

Nozari, H. (Ed.). (2023). *Building Smart and Sustainable Businesses With Transformative Technologies*. IGI Global. 10.4018/979-8-3693-0210-1

Oppong, S. A., Yen, D. C., & Merhout, J. W. (2005). A new strategy for harnessing knowledge management in e-commerce. *Technology in Society*, 27(3), 413–435. 10.1016/j.techsoc.2005.04.009

Paschek, D. (2020). *Business process management using artificial inteligence-an important requirement, success factor and business need for industry 5.0* [Doctoral dissertation, Universitatea „Politehnica" Timişoara, Şcoala Doctorală de Studii Inginereşti, Domeniul de Doctorat Inginerie i Management].

Perera, S., Jin, X., Das, P., Gunasekara, K., & Samaratunga, M. (2023). A strategic framework for digital maturity of design and construction through a systematic review and application. *Journal of Industrial Information Integration*, 31, 100413. 10.1016/j.jii.2022.100413

Raimi, L., Kah, J. M., & Tariq, M. U. (2022). The Discourse of Blue Economy Definitions, Measurements, and Theories: Implications for Strengthening Academic Research and Industry Practice. In Raimi, L., & Kah, J. (Eds.), *Implications for Entrepreneurship and Enterprise Development in the Blue Economy* (pp. 1–17). IGI Global. 10.4018/978-1-6684-3393-5.ch001

Raimi, L., Tariq, M. U., & Kah, J. M. (2022). Diversity, Equity, and Inclusion as the Future Workplace Ethics: Theoretical Review. In Raimi, L., & Kah, J. (Eds.), *Mainstreaming Diversity, Equity, and Inclusion as Future Workplace Ethics* (pp. 1–27). IGI Global. 10.4018/978-1-6684-3657-8.ch001

Rashid, M. A., Riaz, Z., Turan, E., Haskilic, V., Sunje, A., & Khan, N. (2012, July). Smart factory: E-business perspective of enhanced ERP in aircraft manufacturing industry. In *2012 Proceedings of PICMET'12: Technology Management for Emerging Technologies* (pp. 3262-3275). IEEE.

Razak, M., Gunawan, B. I., Fitriany, F., Ashoer, M., Hidayat, M., & Halim, P. K. P. A. (2019). Moving From Traditional to Society 5.0 Case study by Online Transportation Business. *Journal of Distribution Science*, 17(9), 93–102. 10.15722/jds.17.9.201909.93

Roblek, V., Meško, M., Bach, M. P., Thorpe, O., & Šprajc, P. (2020). The interaction between internet, sustainable development, and emergence of society 5.0. *Data*, 5(3), 80. 10.3390/data5030080

Salem, A. B. M., & Parusheva, S. (2018). Developing a web-based ontology for e-business. *International Journal of Electronic Commerce Studies*, 9(2), 119–132. 10.7903/ijecs.1654

Tariq, M. U. (2024). Equity and Inclusion in Learning Ecosystems. In Al Husseiny, F., & Munna, A. (Eds.), *Preparing Students for the Future Educational Paradigm* (pp. 155–176). IGI Global. 10.4018/979-8-3693-1536-1.ch007

Tariq, M. U. (2024). Empowering Educators in the Learning Ecosystem. In Al Husseiny, F., & Munna, A. (Eds.), *Preparing Students for the Future Educational Paradigm* (pp. 232–255). IGI Global. 10.4018/979-8-3693-1536-1.ch010

Tariq, M. U. (2024). Revolutionizing Health Data Management With Blockchain Technology: Enhancing Security and Efficiency in a Digital Era. In Garcia, M., & de Almeida, R. (Eds.), *Emerging Technologies for Health Literacy and Medical Practice* (pp. 153–175). IGI Global. 10.4018/979-8-3693-1214-8.ch008

Tariq, M. U. (2024). Emerging Trends and Innovations in Blockchain-Digital Twin Integration for Green Investments: A Case Study Perspective. In Jafar, S., Rodriguez, R., Kannan, H., Akhtar, S., & Plugmann, P. (Eds.), *Harnessing Blockchain-Digital Twin Fusion for Sustainable Investments* (pp. 148–175). IGI Global. 10.4018/979-8-3693-1878-2.ch007

Tariq, M. U. (2024). Emotional Intelligence in Understanding and Influencing Consumer Behavior. In Musiolik, T., Rodriguez, R., & Kannan, H. (Eds.), *AI Impacts in Digital Consumer Behavior* (pp. 56–81). IGI Global. 10.4018/979-8-3693-1918-5.ch003

Tariq, M. U. (2024). Fintech Startups and Cryptocurrency in Business: Revolutionizing Entrepreneurship. In Kankaew, K., Nakpathom, P., Chnitphattana, A., Pitchayadejanant, K., & Kunnapapdeelert, S. (Eds.), *Applying Business Intelligence and Innovation to Entrepreneurship* (pp. 106–124). IGI Global. 10.4018/979-8-3693-1846-1.ch006

Tariq, M. U. (2024). Multidisciplinary Service Learning in Higher Education: Concepts, Implementation, and Impact. In S. Watson (Ed.), Applications of Service Learning in Higher Education (pp. 1-19). IGI Global. 10.4018/979-8-3693-2133-1.ch001

Tariq, M. U. (2024). Enhancing Cybersecurity Protocols in Modern Healthcare Systems: Strategies and Best Practices. In Garcia, M., & de Almeida, R. (Eds.), *Transformative Approaches to Patient Literacy and Healthcare Innovation* (pp. 223–241). IGI Global. 10.4018/979-8-3693-3661-8.ch011

Tariq, M. U. (2024). Advanced Wearable Medical Devices and Their Role in Transformative Remote Health Monitoring. In Garcia, M., & de Almeida, R. (Eds.), *Transformative Approaches to Patient Literacy and Healthcare Innovation* (pp. 308–326). IGI Global. 10.4018/979-8-3693-3661-8.ch015

Tariq, M. U. (2024). Leveraging Artificial Intelligence for a Sustainable and Climate-Neutral Economy in Asia. In Ordóñez de Pablos, P., Almunawar, M., & Anshari, M. (Eds.), *Strengthening Sustainable Digitalization of Asian Economy and Society* (pp. 1–21). IGI Global. 10.4018/979-8-3693-1942-0.ch001

Tariq, M. U. (2024). Metaverse in Business and Commerce. In Kumar, J., Arora, M., & Erkol Bayram, G. (Eds.), *Exploring the Use of Metaverse in Business and Education* (pp. 47–72). IGI Global. 10.4018/979-8-3693-5868-9.ch004

Tang, J., Zheng, Q. H., Wang, W. Z., Deveci, M., Bacanin, N., & Aws, A. A. Z. (2023). Analyzing Information Security Factors in Adoption of Intelligent Technologies for Medical Waste Management Systems. *IEEE Transactions on Consumer Electronics.*

Tornjanski, V., Knežević, S., Ljubanić, D., Glišić, V., Žižić, D., & Travica, J. (2021, September). Towards secured digital business ecosystems: From threats to opportunities. In *E-business technologies conference proceedings* (*Vol. 1*, No. 1, pp. 1-14).

Tornjanski, V., Knežević, S., & Mirčetić, V. (2023, June). The role of healthy e-business in Society 5.0: The empowerment of the human-centric era. In *E-business technologies conference proceedings* (*Vol. 3,* No. 1, pp. 22-27).

Treiblmaier, H., Rejeb, A., & Strebinger, A. (2020). Blockchain as a driver for smart city development: Application fields and a comprehensive research agenda. *Smart Cities*, 3(3), 853–872. 10.3390/smartcities3030044

Chapter 3
E-Business 5.0:
Pioneering Smart Technologies and Innovations for Digital Transformation

Nitish Kumar Minz
https://orcid.org/0009-0000-4770-0336
K.R. Mangalam University, India

ABSTRACT

The evolution of e-business into its advanced form, E-Business 5.0, has witnessed a paradigm shift, primarily catalyzed by the integration of smart technologies and innovations. This research embarks on a comprehensive exploration of the leading smart technologies and innovations within the domain of E-Business 5.0, leveraging a robust foundation built upon an extensive literature review. The primary objectives of this study encompass an analysis of the current landscape of E-Business 5.0 technologies, an assessment of organizations' practical experiences in their implementation, a forward-looking evaluation of potential applications, and the provision of recommendations and management frameworks for seamless integration. The research delves into the core questions concerning the pivotal technologies that characterize E-Business 5.0. This study, grounded in a comprehensive literature review, sheds light on the transformative potential of smart technologies and innovations within the dynamic landscape of E-Business 5.0.

1. INTRODUCTION

1.1 Background to the Study

In the ever-evolving landscape of business, the concept of E-Business has transcended traditional paradigms, ushering in a new era known as E-Business 5.0. This transformation, driven by the infusion of smart technologies and innovations, has led to a fundamental shift in the operational dynamics of organizations. The advent of Industry 4.0 and the confluence of digitalization, automation, and data-driven decision-making have had profound effects on businesses, particularly on Small and Medium-sized Enterprises (SMEs) (Ballester, Malo, & Paché, 2020). This paradigm shift is underpinned by the idea that

DOI: 10.4018/978-1-6684-7840-0.ch003

organizations must adapt and integrate advanced technologies to remain competitive and agile (Görög, Zabál, & Szűts, 2021).

The theoretical underpinning of this transformation can be traced to the resource-based view (RBV) of firms (Barney, 1991; Barney, 1995; Barney & Arikan, 2001). This view asserts that organizations gain a sustained competitive advantage by leveraging their unique and valuable resources (Wernerfelt, 1984). In the context of E-Business 5.0, it translates to the strategic utilization of innovative technologies and smart solutions, which become the resources for creating and sustaining superior performance (Peteraf, 1993).

Furthermore, the role of digital transformation in organizational performance, particularly in the context of Industry 4.0, has gained prominence (Park, 2020). A study by Islam et al. (2022) reveals the intricate relationships among digital innovation, digital transformation, and organizational performance, underscoring the pivotal role of digital leadership. These insights emphasize that the effective adoption and integration of digital technologies can catalyze performance improvements and innovation within organizations.

In this context, the integration of digital technologies, as exemplified by Industry 4.0 and E-Business 5.0, presents a compelling area of study. The strategic adoption of these technologies offers the potential for enhanced competitiveness and sustainable development, particularly among SMEs (Ghobakhloo, Hong, Sabouri, & Zulkifli, 2017; Gupta, Kumar, & Kumar, 2021). To this end, there is an increasing recognition of the need for strategies that facilitate successful information technology adoption and digital transformation (Kamble, Gunasekaran, Gawankar, & Papadopoulos, 2019).

1.2 Purpose of the Study

The purpose of this research is to investigate the transformative impact of smart technologies and innovations in the context of E-Business 5.0, particularly concerning their integration into Small and Medium-sized Enterprises (SMEs). The study aims to explore how the strategic adoption of digital technologies and smart solutions can lead to competitive advantage and sustainable performance, aligning with the resource-based view (RBV) of firms. It will delve into the relationships between digital innovation, digital transformation, and organizational performance, with a particular focus on the role of digital leadership in facilitating this transformation.

1.3 Importance of the Study

Understanding the dynamics of E-Business 5.0 and the integration of smart technologies in the context of SMEs is of paramount importance. This research holds significance for SMEs seeking to enhance their competitiveness and sustainability in the digital age (Valenzuela, Guenole, & Ferrar, 2021). By elucidating the relationships between digital technologies, innovation, and performance, the study will provide valuable insights for businesses and decision-makers aiming to navigate the complexities of digital transformation (Chae, Koh, & Prybutok, 2014). Furthermore, it has implications for the development of strategic frameworks that can support SMEs in their journey towards digital maturity, aligning with the principles of Industry 4.0 (Kannan, Senthil, & Tiwari, 2015).

This research addresses a critical need to examine how smart technologies and innovations are shaping E-Business 5.0 and the practical implications for SMEs, contributing to the ongoing discourse on digital transformation and its role in driving competitiveness and sustainability. Through empirical investigations and a synthesis of existing knowledge, this study seeks to equip organizations with the knowledge and strategies necessary to thrive in an environment where innovation, technology, and adaptability are the keys to sustained success.

1.4 Research Objectives

i. To analyze the current landscape of smart technologies and innovations within the domain of E-Business 5.0.
ii. To assess the practical experiences of organizations in implementing smart technologies in the context of E-Business 5.0.
iii. To evaluate the potential applications of smart technologies and innovations in E-Business 5.0.
iv. To provide recommendations for organizations seeking to maximize the benefits of smart technologies in E-Business 5.0.
v. To develop management frameworks for the efficient and effective implementation and governance of smart technologies in E-Business 5.0.

1.5 Research Questions

i. What are the key smart technologies and innovations that characterize E-Business 5.0?
ii. How have organizations experienced the integration of these technologies into their E-Business strategies?
iii. What are the anticipated future trends and applications of smart technologies in E-Business?
iv. What recommendations can be made for businesses looking to leverage E-Business 5.0 technologies?
v. How can management frameworks be established to ensure efficient implementation and governance of these technologies?

2. METHODOLOGY

The methodology for this research involves a comprehensive literature review conducted using Scopus to gather relevant data and articles. This literature review will serve as the primary method for answering the research question and fulfilling the research objectives. Through a systematic examination of existing scholarly works, we aim to gain insights into the evolving landscape of E-Business 5.0, the integration of smart technologies and innovations, and their impact on various aspects of business operations, particularly in Small and Medium-sized Enterprises (SMEs). This approach will allow us to synthesize and analyze the existing body of knowledge in the field, providing valuable insights into the transformative potential of smart technologies in the context of E-Business 5.0.

3. LITERATURE REVIEW

In 1984, Wernerfelt laid the groundwork for understanding competitive advantage. His work underscored the pivotal role of resources in gaining a competitive edge. In the context of E-Business 5.0, where organizations increasingly leverage digital resources and smart technologies, the resonance of his resource-based view is more profound than ever.

Moving forward to 1991, Barney et al. introduced the concept of "Firm resources and sustained competitive advantage." This work provided a robust theoretical foundation for comprehending how organizations achieve and maintain a competitive edge through the strategic utilization of their unique and valuable resources. This perspective remains a cornerstone in discussions of technological advancements and their profound impact on organizational performance.

Building upon this foundation, Barney (1995) continued his exploration of competitive advantage in the "Looking inside for competitive advantage" article published in the Academy of Management Executive. In this study, he delved deeper into the internal aspects of organizations, emphasizing the significance of tangible and intangible resources. This approach strongly aligns with the essence of E-Business 5.0, where businesses increasingly rely on smart technologies and innovations as invaluable resources to bolster their competitiveness and overall performance.

In 2003, Dehning et al. conducted a comprehensive study that compared the financial performance of internet and non-internet firms, as published in the Journal of Electronic Commerce Research. This research underscored the pivotal role of internet-based technologies in influencing business performance. Such a comparison remains highly relevant in the context of E-Business 5.0, where digital transformation is at the core of an organization's competitive advantage.

Further advancing in time to 2004, Chen and Paulraj introduced the constructs and measurements that are crucial "Towards a theory of supply chain management." They emphasized the integration of technology and information systems within the supply chain context, a concept that has gained increasing importance within the realm of E-Business 5.0. This new era witnesses the evolution of supply chain management to accommodate smart technologies and digitalization as integral components.

In the year 2009, Teo et al. conducted an empirical study examining "Adopters and non-adopters of e-procurement in Singapore," as published in Omega. This study underscored the importance of e-procurement and the patterns of its adoption. Such findings are highly relevant in the context of E-Business 5.0, where e-procurement plays a pivotal role in the digital transformation process.

Prajogo and Olhager (2012) delved into "Supply chain integration and performance" in the International Journal of Production Economics. Their research shed light on the effects of long-term relationships, information technology, and logistics integration on supply chain performance. These aspects are central to E-Business 5.0, where digital integration and relationships play pivotal roles in shaping the new business landscape.

Chae et al. (2014) contributed valuable insights by investigating "Information Technology Capability and Firm Performance" in the MIS Quarterly. Their study revealed contradictory findings and possible causes, emphasizing the significance of effectively harnessing information technology to improve organizational performance. This discussion aligns closely with the challenges and opportunities presented by E-Business 5.0, where digital capabilities play a central role in reshaping business operations.

In 2015, Kannan et al. provided a comprehensive "Review of lean manufacturing implementation techniques" in Procedia CIRP. Their work underlined the importance of implementing lean manufacturing techniques effectively, a concept that resonates with E-Business 5.0. In this new era, the efficient utilization of resources, including smart technologies, is more pivotal than ever.

Ghobakhloo et al. (2017) explored "Strategies for successful information technology adoption in small and medium-sized enterprises" in their work published in Information Systems. The study emphasized the importance of effective technology adoption strategies, aligning directly with the challenges faced by SMEs in embracing E-Business 5.0 and its associated smart technologies.

In 2018, Makkonen et al. conducted a "Configurational study of competitive advantage and SMEs" in the Journal of Small Business Management. Their research delved into various configurations for gaining a competitive edge. This study offers valuable insights for SMEs adapting to E-Business 5.0, where the configurations of smart technologies and digital solutions are pivotal for success.

Benitez-Amado et al. (2019) explored the relationship between organizational learning, innovation, and performance in the context of high-tech firms in their study published in the Journal of Business Research. They highlighted the moderating role of the human resource management approach in fostering innovation, underscoring the importance of effectively managing human resources in the context of E-Business 5.0, where the integration of smart technologies and innovations significantly impacts organizational performance.

Kamble et al. (2019) proposed an "Industry 4.0 and lean management integration model" in Production Planning and control. This integration model emphasized the relevance of lean principles within the context of Industry 4.0. This model and its associated research agenda are critical in understanding the dynamics of E-Business 5.0, where lean principles and smart technologies merge for enhanced efficiency and competitiveness.

Kim (2020) conducted an "Empirical investigation of digital marketing activity, digital marketing environment, and organizational performance" in the Journal of Organizational and End User Computing. This study emphasized the role of digital marketing in organizational performance. It holds significance in the context of E-Business 5.0, where digital marketing is an essential component of business operations.

Park (2020) investigated "The Influence of Digital Transformation on innovation performance in the Context of Industry 4.0" in the Journal of Open Innovation: Technology, Market, and Complexity. This research highlighted the transformative impact of digital transformation on innovation performance. These insights have direct relevance to the ongoing evolution of E-Business into its advanced form, E-Business 5.0, where digital transformation is central to driving innovation.

Gupta et al. (2021) investigated "The antecedents of digital transformation for sustainable development in Indian manufacturing SMEs" in the Journal of Manufacturing Technology Management. Their research provided insights into the factors driving digital transformation for sustainable development. This aligns with the objectives of E-Business 5.0, where sustainable performance is a central concern.

Valenzuela et al. (2021) conducted a comprehensive literature review exploring "The Future of Work" in the International Journal of Management Reviews. Their review addressed the evolving landscape of work in the digital age. This discussion is central to E-Business 5.0, where the changing nature of work and employment is a critical aspect of digital transformation.

This literature review offers an in-depth exploration of the evolving business landscape, technological advancements, and their profound impact on organizational performance. These studies collectively underscore the pivotal role of smart technologies and innovations in the context of E-Business 5.0, where the effective integration of these resources is essential for sustaining competitiveness and driving sustainable development in the digital age.

4. THEORETICAL FRAMEWORK

4.1 Resource-Based View (RBV) of Firms (Wernerfelt, 1984)

The Resource-Based View (RBV) of firms, as conceptualized by Wernerfelt (1984), serves as a foundational theory underpinning the understanding of how organizations can attain a sustained competitive advantage. This theory posits that organizations gain a competitive edge by leveraging their unique and valuable resources. In the context of E-Business 5.0, this translates to the strategic utilization of innovative technologies and smart solutions as essential resources for creating and sustaining superior performance.

Wernerfelt's RBV theory emphasizes that not all resources are equal; some are rare, inimitable, and non-substitutable, providing organizations with a distinct competitive advantage. E-Business 5.0 embodies this principle as organizations strive to harness the advantages of cutting-edge technologies, creating a competitive edge in the digital landscape.

Smart technologies and innovations are at the forefront of these valuable resources. Their integration into business operations, decision-making processes, and customer interactions signifies the embodiment of the RBV theory in the digital age. As firms increasingly rely on digital assets and intellectual capital to innovate and adapt, the RBV theory becomes more pertinent than ever.

To fully grasp the implications of E-Business 5.0 and its transformational potential, understanding the RBV theory is essential. This theory underlines the critical importance of recognizing, developing, and effectively deploying smart technologies and innovations as key resources in the pursuit of competitive advantage and sustainable success in the digital era.

4.2 Competitive Advantage (Barney, 1991, 1995)

Barney's work on competitive advantage, especially his seminal paper in 1991, introduced the concept of “Firm resources and sustained competitive advantage.” This research provided a robust theoretical foundation for understanding how organizations achieve and maintain a competitive edge by strategically utilizing their unique and valuable resources.

In the context of E-Business 5.0, the central theme revolves around how smart technologies and innovations have evolved into invaluable resources for businesses. The journey from E-Business to E-Business 5.0 represents a paradigm shift, largely driven by the infusion of these technologies.

Barney's perspective echoes through the modern digital landscape. Organizations, particularly Small and Medium-sized Enterprises (SMEs), must adapt and integrate advanced technologies to remain competitive and agile. The adoption of smart technologies and innovations is a strategic move to create and sustain superior performance, aligning with the principles of the RBV theory.

As organizations navigate the complexities of digital transformation, the significance of Barney's research becomes increasingly evident. The strategic utilization of digital resources, encompassing smart technologies and innovations, defines E-Business 5.0. To maximize competitive advantage in this dynamic environment, businesses must embrace these resources as core elements of their strategic repertoire.

In conclusion, Barney's work underscores the enduring importance of recognizing smart technologies and innovations as essential components of competitive advantage in E-Business 5.0. It highlights the need for organizations to strategically leverage these resources to secure their position in the digital ecosystem.

4.3 Digital Transformation and Performance (Park, 2020; Islam et al., 2022)

The theoretical framework of digital transformation and performance, informed by the works of Park (2020) and Islam et al. (2022), highlights the central role of digitalization in shaping organizational performance in the context of Industry 4.0 and E-Business 5.0. Park's study delves into the influence of digital transformation on innovation performance within the landscape of Industry 4.0, emphasizing how digital transformation catalyzes innovation and ultimately enhances organizational performance.

Islam et al. (2022) provide valuable insights into the relationships among digital innovation, digital transformation, and organizational performance. Their research underscores the significance of digital leadership in driving successful digital transformation. These findings emphasize that the effective adoption and integration of digital technologies, particularly smart technologies and innovations, are pivotal in achieving performance improvements and fostering innovation within organizations.

In the context of E-Business 5.0, digital transformation is not merely a buzzword but a fundamental aspect of business operations. The infusion of smart technologies and innovations represents a substantial facet of this transformation. As organizations increasingly rely on digital resources, the concepts of digital innovation, digital transformation, and the leadership that guides these processes become central to understanding how to enhance organizational performance.

These theoretical perspectives provide essential foundations for understanding how digital transformation, augmented by smart technologies and innovations, impacts organizational performance. They underscore that the strategic adoption of digital resources results in improved performance, innovation, and adaptability, which are pivotal in the dynamic landscape of E-Business 5.0.

4.4 Supply Chain Management (Chen & Paulraj, 2004; Prajogo & Olhager, 2012; Lambert & Cooper, 2000; Zhu et al., 2012)

The theoretical framework of supply chain management encompasses insights from multiple sources, including the works of Chen and Paulraj (2004), Prajogo and Olhager (2012), Lambert and Cooper (2000), and Zhu et al. (2012). These theories collectively emphasize the importance of integrating technology and information systems into supply chain operations, shedding light on the significance of technology in enhancing supply chain efficiency and performance.

Chen and Paulraj (2004) introduce the constructs and measurements crucial to "Towards a Theory of supply chain management," highlighting the role of technology in supply chain optimization. Prajogo and Olhager (2012) delve into "Supply chain integration and performance," elucidating the effects of long-term relationships, information technology, and logistics integration on supply chain efficiency and, consequently, performance.

Lambert and Cooper (2000) contribute by discussing key issues in supply chain management, emphasizing the complexities and challenges associated with managing supply chains. These challenges are exacerbated in the digital age, making the integration of smart technologies and innovations essential to address them effectively.

Zhu et al. (2012) focus on "Green supply chain management in China," underlining the importance of integrating technology and sustainable practices into the supply chain. Their research demonstrates that technology plays a pivotal role in greening the supply chain, which aligns with the sustainability goals of E-Business 5.0.

The combination of these theoretical perspectives underscores that smart technologies and innovations are integral to optimizing supply chain efficiency and enhancing overall business performance. In E-Business 5.0, where supply chains are becoming more complex and global, technology is the linchpin for achieving competitiveness and sustainability.

4.5 Lean Management (Kamble et al., 2019; Kannan, Senthil, & Tiwari, 2015)

Lean management, as investigated by Kamble et al. (2019) and Kannan, Senthil, and Tiwari (2015), represents a critical theoretical perspective that emphasizes the importance of minimizing waste and maximizing efficiency in production processes. The application of lean principles is well-established in manufacturing and is becoming increasingly relevant in E-Business 5.0, as organizations seek to optimize digital processes and workflows.

Kamble et al. (2019) propose an "Industry 4.0 and lean management integration model" that highlights the compatibility of lean management principles with the principles of Industry 4.0, which aligns with the goals of E-Business 5.0. This integration model underscores how smart technologies can automate and streamline operations, enabling lean practices in digital contexts.

Kannan, Senthil, and Tiwari (2015) review various techniques for lean manufacturing implementation. They highlight the significance of minimizing operational waste, improving efficiency, and reducing costs in manufacturing processes. In E-Business 5.0, these principles are adapted to digital processes and workflows.

These theories collectively reinforce the importance of integrating smart technologies into lean management practices within E-Business 5.0. They underline that the adoption of digital solutions can help organizations achieve greater efficiency and reduce operational waste, ultimately contributing to improved performance in digital environments.

These theoretical perspectives provide a solid foundation for understanding the impact of smart technologies and innovations in E-Business 5.0. They highlight the critical role of technology in enhancing competitiveness, sustainability, and overall organizational performance in the digital era.

5. DISCUSSION

The discussion synthesizes the key findings from the literature review and provides insights into the transformative impact of smart technologies and innovations in the context of E-Business 5.0, especially in Small and Medium-sized Enterprises (SMEs). The discussion will also address the research questions and objectives outlined in the introduction.

5.1 Key Smart Technologies and Innovations in E-Business 5.0

The analysis of the literature has highlighted several key smart technologies and innovations that characterize E-Business 5.0. These include but are not limited to:

i. **Internet-Based Technologies:** The research conducted by Dehning et al. (2003) emphasized the significant role of internet-based technologies in influencing business performance. The comparison between Internet and non-internet firms underscores the importance of digitalization and the Internet in E-Business 5.0. Internet technologies have become the backbone of E-Business 5.0, enabling organizations to expand their digital reach, connect with global markets, and enhance customer experiences.
ii. **Digital Supply Chain Management:** The study by Chen and Paulraj (2004) introduced the critical constructs and measurements that are essential for supply chain management. E-Business 5.0 witnesses the evolution of supply chain management, with a strong focus on digitalization and technology integration. Smart technologies play a pivotal role in optimizing supply chain processes, enhancing visibility, and ensuring seamless operations.
iii. **E-Procurement:** Teo et al.'s empirical study in 2009 shed light on the patterns of e-procurement adoption. In the context of E-Business 5.0, e-procurement technologies continue to evolve and play a crucial role in procurement efficiency, cost reduction, and supply chain integration.
iv. **Digital Leadership:** The research by Islam et al. (2022) emphasizes the importance of digital leadership in the context of digital innovation and transformation. In E-Business 5.0, effective leadership is essential to drive the strategic adoption of smart technologies and innovations. Leaders guide organizations in navigating the complexities of digital transformation, ensuring that these technologies are effectively integrated into the business strategy.

5.2 Organizations' Experiences in Implementing Smart Technologies

A recurring theme in the literature is the need for organizations, especially SMEs, to adapt and integrate advanced technologies to remain competitive and agile (Görög, Zabál, & Szűts, 2021). This adaptation often involves a process of digital transformation where organizations embark on the journey of adopting and implementing smart technologies. Several key insights emerge:

i. **Digital Transformation Challenges:** Implementing smart technologies can be challenging, and organizations often face hurdles related to change management, cost, and resource constraints. Successful digital transformation requires a strategic and well-managed approach (Gupta, Kumar, & Kumar, 2021).
ii. **Role of Digital Leadership:** As highlighted by Islam et al. (2022), the role of digital leadership is pivotal. Effective leaders are essential in driving the digital transformation journey, fostering a culture of innovation, and ensuring that the organization reaps the full benefits of smart technologies.
iii. **Digital Innovation and Performance:** The study by Islam et al. (2022) underscores the intricate relationships among digital innovation, digital transformation, and organizational performance. The effective adoption and integration of smart technologies can catalyze performance improvements and innovation within organizations.

5.3 Future Trends and Applications of Smart Technologies

E-Business 5.0 is a dynamic landscape, and future trends and applications of smart technologies are expected to shape the business environment further. Some anticipated trends include:

i. **Artificial Intelligence (AI) and Machine Learning:** AI and machine learning are set to play a more prominent role in E-Business 5.0. They enable organizations to make data-driven decisions, automate processes, and enhance customer experiences.
ii. **Internet of Things (IoT):** IoT devices are becoming integral in E-Business 5.0, facilitating real-time data collection and analysis, leading to improved efficiency and product/service innovation.
iii. **Blockchain Technology:** Blockchain is gaining traction as a means to secure transactions and data in E-Business 5.0, particularly in supply chain management and financial transactions.
iv. **Digital Marketing Innovations:** E-Business 5.0 will continue to witness innovations in digital marketing, personalization, and customer engagement, as emphasized by Kim (2020).

5.4 Recommendations and Management Frameworks

Based on the findings and insights from the literature, the following recommendations and management frameworks can be proposed:

i. **Invest in Digital Leadership:** Organizations should invest in digital leadership, ensuring that leaders are equipped to guide digital transformation initiatives effectively.
ii. **Prioritize Change Management:** Recognize the significance of change management in the digital transformation process. Allocate resources and efforts to ensure a smooth transition for employees and stakeholders.
iii. **Embrace a Culture of Innovation:** Foster a culture of innovation within the organization. Encourage employees to explore and implement new technologies that can drive business growth.
iv. **Continuous Learning and Adaptation:** Given the dynamic nature of E-Business 5.0, organizations should commit to continuous learning and adaptation. Stay updated on emerging technologies and industry trends.
v. **Data Security and Privacy:** As organizations leverage smart technologies, a robust data security and privacy framework is imperative. Invest in cybersecurity measures and compliance with data protection regulations.

5. CONCLUSION

The journey of E-Business has undergone a remarkable transformation, giving birth to E-Business 5.0, a new era characterized by the infusion of smart technologies and innovations. This evolution has disrupted traditional paradigms, ushering in a digital landscape where organizations, particularly Small and Medium-sized Enterprises (SMEs), must harness advanced technologies to remain competitive and agile.

At the heart of this paradigm shift is the Resource-Based View (RBV) of firms (Wernerfelt, 1984). The RBV theory posits that organizations gain a sustained competitive advantage by leveraging their unique and valuable resources. In the context of E-Business 5.0, these invaluable resources are the innovative technologies and smart solutions that empower organizations to create and sustain superior performance. In essence, the RBV theory is more pertinent than ever in the digital age, where firms increasingly rely on digital assets and intellectual capital to innovate and adapt.

The competitive advantage theory by Barney (1991, 1995) is central to understanding the impact of smart technologies in E-Business 5.0. Barney's work highlights that organizations achieve and maintain a competitive edge by strategically utilizing their unique and valuable resources. As organizations transition to E-Business 5.0, this transition is predominantly powered by the strategic infusion of smart technologies, making these resources pivotal in the quest for competitive advantage.

The integration of digital technologies and smart solutions in E-Business 5.0 holds vast potential for SMEs. As seen in the work of Ghobakhloo et al. (2017) and Gupta et al. (2021), the strategic adoption of digital technologies offers SMEs the potential for enhanced competitiveness and sustainable development. However, the journey of digital transformation is not without its challenges, necessitating effective strategies for successful technology adoption (Kamble et al., 2019).

Moreover, the significance of digital leadership cannot be understated (Islam et al., 2022). Effective leaders are essential to navigate the complexities of digital transformation, foster a culture of innovation, and ensure the strategic integration of smart technologies. Their guidance is pivotal in realizing the full potential of these technologies.

The future of E-Business 5.0 promises even more profound changes. Anticipated trends include the broader use of Artificial Intelligence (AI) and Machine Learning, the proliferation of Internet of Things (IoT) devices, blockchain technology, and continuous innovations in digital marketing (Kim, 2020). These trends will further shape the competitive landscape and the strategies of organizations.

In conclusion, E-Business 5.0's transformation is anchored in the strategic utilization of smart technologies and innovations. The literature review and discussions underscore the pivotal role of leadership, innovation, and adaptability in navigating the complexities of this digital landscape. As organizations evolve within E-Business 5.0, their ability to optimally harness smart technologies becomes a critical factor for success.

By embracing the insights from the literature, learning from early adopters, and implementing recommended strategies and frameworks, organizations can position themselves to thrive in this era of dynamic digital transformation. Leadership, innovation, and adaptability will be the guiding principles to leverage smart technologies effectively, achieve competitive advantage, and sustain superior performance in the exciting journey of E-Business 5.0.

REFERENCES

Ballester, D., Malo, S., & Paché, G. (2020). The effects of the industry 4.0 on the operational performance of SMEs. *Journal of Manufacturing Technology Management*, 31(4), 950–972. 10.1108/JMTM-06-2019-0187

Barney, J. B. (1991). Firm resources and sustained competitive advantage. *Journal of Management*, 17(1), 99–120. 10.1177/014920639101700108

Barney, J. B. (1995). Looking inside for competitive advantage. *The Academy of Management Perspectives*, 9(4), 49–61. 10.5465/ame.1995.9512032192

Barney, J. B., & Arikan, A. M. (2001). The resource-based view: Origins and implications. In Hitt, M. A., Freeman, R. E., & Harrison, J. S. (Eds.), *The Blackwell Handbook of Strategic Management* (pp. 124–188). Blackwell Publishers.

Benitez-Amado, J., Llorens-Montes, J., & Perez-Arostegui, M. N. (2019). Organizational learning, innovation, and performance in high-tech firms: The moderating role of the human resource management approach. *Journal of Business Research*, 95, 319–326. 10.1016/j.jbusres.2018.10.036

Chae, B. K., Koh, S., & Prybutok, V. R. (2014). Information technology capability and firm performance: Contradictory findings and their possible causes. *Management Information Systems Quarterly*, 38(1), 305–326. 10.25300/MISQ/2014/38.1.14

Chen, I. J., & Paulraj, A. (2004). Towards a theory of supply chain management: The constructs and measurements. *Journal of Operations Management*, 22(2), 119–150. 10.1016/j.jom.2003.12.007

Dehning, B., Stratopoulos, T. C., & Zan, L. (2003). The financial performance of internet versus non-internet firms: A comprehensive study. *Journal of Electronic Commerce Research*, 4(3), 143–157. 10.1108/eb028855

Ghobakhloo, M., Hong, T. S., Sabouri, M. S., & Zulkifli, N. (2017). Strategies for successful information technology adoption in small and medium-sized enterprises. *Information Systems*, 65, 41–53. 10.1016/j.is.2017.01.006

Görög, M., Zabál, P., & Szűts, Z. (2021). Digital transformation and its role in enhancing the competitiveness of SMEs. *Sustainability*, 13(12), 6999. 10.3390/su13126999

Gupta, H., Kumar, A., & Kumar, S. (2021). Investigating the antecedents of digital transformation for sustainable development in Indian manufacturing SMEs. *Journal of Manufacturing Technology Management*, 32(7), 1521–1547. 10.1108/JMTM-04-2020-0181

Islam, J. U., Ahmed, S., Ali, M., Islam, S., & Moe, T. N. (2022). Investigating the relationships among digital innovation, digital transformation, and organizational performance: The role of digital leadership. *Information Systems Frontiers*, 1–20. 10.1007/s10796-022-10440-0

Kamble, S. S., Gunasekaran, A., Gawankar, S. A., & Papadopoulos, T. (2019). Industry 4.0 and lean management: A proposed integration model and research agenda. *Production Planning and Control*, 30(8-9), 698–710. 10.1080/09537287.2019.1601963

Kannan, D., Senthil, S., & Tiwari, M. K. (2015). A review of lean manufacturing implementation techniques. *Procedia CIRP*, 26, 12–17. 10.1016/j.procir.2015.07.005

Kim, S. (2020). Empirical investigation of digital marketing activity, digital marketing environment, and organizational performance. *Journal of Organizational and End User Computing*, 32(2), 52–71. 10.4018/JOEUC.2020040104

Lambert, D. M., & Cooper, M. C. (2000). Issues in supply chain management. *Industrial Marketing Management*, 29(1), 65–83. 10.1016/S0019-8501(99)00113-3

Law, R., Buhalis, D., & Cobanoglu, C. (2014). Progress on information and communication technologies in hospitality and tourism. *International Journal of Contemporary Hospitality Management*, 26(5), 727–750. 10.1108/IJCHM-08-2013-0367

Makkonen, H., Olkkonen, R., & Frank, L. (2018). Competitive advantage and SMEs: A configurational study. *Journal of Small Business Management*, 56(2), 289–306. 10.1111/jsbm.12319

Park, S. (2020). The influence of digital transformation on innovation performance in the context of Industry 4.0. *Journal of Open Innovation*, 6(4), 98. 10.3390/joitmc6040098

Peteraf, M. A. (1993). The cornerstones of competitive advantage: A resource-based view. *Strategic Management Journal*, 14(3), 179–191. 10.1002/smj.4250140303

Porter, M. E. (1985). *Competitive advantage: Creating and sustaining superior performance*. Free Press.

Prajogo, D., & Olhager, J. (2012). Supply chain integration and performance: The effects of long-term relationships, information technology, and sharing, and logistics integration. *International Journal of Production Economics*, 135(1), 514–522. 10.1016/j.ijpe.2011.09.001

Teo, T. S. H., Lin, S., & Lai, K. H. (2009). Adopters and non-adopters of e-procurement in Singapore: An empirical study. *Omega*, 37(5), 972–987. 10.1016/j.omega.2008.11.001

Turker, D., & Altuntas, S. (2014). Sustainable supply chain management in the fast fashion industry: An analysis of corporate reports. *European Management Journal*, 32(5), 837–849. 10.1016/j.emj.2014.02.001

Valenzuela, F., Guenole, N., & Ferrar, J. (2021). The future of work: A literature review. *International Journal of Management Reviews*, 23(3), 453–471. 10.1111/ijmr.12233

Wang, Y. S., & Tang, T. I. (2003). Assessing international Internet marketing performance: The application of the balanced scorecard. *Industrial Management & Data Systems*, 103(4), 253–266. 10.1108/02635570310464625

Wernerfelt, B. (1984). A resource-based view of the firm. *Strategic Management Journal*, 5(2), 171–180. 10.1002/smj.4250050207

Zhu, Q., Sarkis, J., Lai, K. H., & Geng, Y. (2012). Green supply chain management in China: Pressures, practices, and performance. *International Journal of Operations & Production Management*, 32(5), 519–543. 10.1108/01443571211228747

Chapter 4
Strategic Integration of Smart Technologies in E-Business

Anita Chaudhary
https://orcid.org/0009-0002-5815-5331
Eternal University, India

ABSTRACT

The successful use of smart technologies in an enterprise is critical in the ever-changing E-Business 5.0 scenario. In order to improve operations, boost client experiences, and obtain a competitive edge, this chapter examines the necessity of coordinating cutting-edge technologies with corporate goals. It talks about how different smart technologies and their ability to transform conventional corporate processes are important aspects of strategic integration. It also talks about problems like technological complexity and gives advice on how to solve them with strong leadership and changing company culture. Based on actual cases, the chapter offers helpful suggestions for E-Business executives traveling through the process of strategic integration, stressing the critical role that technology plays in fostering competitive advantage and long-term growth.

1. INTRODUCTION

Technology is advancing so quickly that it has completely changed the e-business scene and ushered in a new era where smart technologies are integrated. With the strategic use of cutting-edge technologies like artificial intelligence (AI), the Internet of Things (IoT), block chain, and augmented reality, classic business models are being rethought and reinvented in what is known as "e-business 5.0." With the potential to transform customer engagement, operational efficiency, and value creation in the digital economy, these smart technologies offer enormous potential.

The strategic integration of smart technology into e-business operations has become essential for firms looking to maintain their competitiveness and relevance in this dynamic and always changing ecosystem. A few examples of how smart technologies are changing business operations are the integration of AI-powered Chabot's for customer service, IoT-enabled devices for real-time supply chain monitoring, block chain-based platforms for secure transactions, and augmented reality applications for immersive shopping experiences. However, careful preparation, financial commitment, and alignment with overarching company goals are necessary for the successful integration of these technologies.

DOI: 10.4018/978-1-6684-7840-0.ch004

The context for examining the complex effects of intelligent technology integration in e-business is established by this introduction. This study aims to investigate the possible influence of E-Business 5.0 on organizational performance, consumer experiences, and social welfare. It will also look at best practices and emerging trends in the implementation of smart technology. This research intends to inform and encourage enterprises to embrace innovation and harness the transformative power of technology in the digital age by offering a thorough overview of the strategic integration of smart technologies in e-business.

2. LITERATURE SURVEY

A wide range of research publications that provide insight into the incorporation of smart technologies in e-business are included in the literature review. (Smith et al., 2021) conducted a ground breaking study in which they conducted a systematic review to comprehend the effects of artificial intelligence (AI) in a variety of e-business areas. Their results shed light on how implementing AI might improve operational effectiveness, customize client experiences, and support data-driven decision-making. In a similar way, (Brown & Garcia, 2019) explore the uses and consequences of the Internet of Things (IoT) in electronic commerce. Their analysis reveals how IoT solutions handle issues like data security and interoperability while enabling predictive maintenance, enhancing inventory management, and optimizing supply chains.

The use of block chain technology in e-business is thoroughly examined by (Chen et al., 2020). Their analysis explores how block chain technology might improve supply chain management and digital payments in particular, as well as transaction security, transparency, and efficiency. (Kim & Lee, 2018), on the other hand, offer insights into the uses of augmented reality (AR) in e-business, emphasizing its potential to produce immersive shopping experiences and enable remote help. They also talk about difficulties including user acceptability and technological constraints.

A conceptual framework for comprehending smart technology adoption in e-business is provided by (Garcia & Martinez, 2017). According to their synthesis, the three main elements impacting adoption are perceived usefulness, technological difficulty, and organizational readiness. Last but not least, (Wang & Liu, 2022) look at E-Business 5.0 disruption management techniques, stressing the critical role that cutting-edge technologies like AI, IoT, block chain, and AR play in promoting innovation and preserving competitive advantage. All of these studies add to our understanding of the opportunities, risks, and effects of incorporating smart technologies into e-business processes.

When taken as a whole, these research articles provide a thorough overview of the ever-changing e-business world within the framework of intelligent technology integration. They draw attention to the difficulties and factors that come with adopting technologies like AI, IoT, block chain, and augmented reality in addition to their promise for transformation. The literature review highlights the complexity of incorporating smart technology into e-business operations, from improving customer experiences and operational efficiency to handling security and interoperability concerns. Additionally, by offering conceptual frameworks, empirical insights, and strategic perspectives, these studies help firms navigate the intricacies of E-Business 5.0 with invaluable counsel. E-businesses can use smart technology to promote innovation, support sustainable growth, and add value for stakeholders in the digital age through on-going research and development.

3. PROPOSED SYSTEM

3.1 Introduction and Context Setting:

Give a brief overview of the role that smart technologies play in contemporary e-business settings. Talk about how technology is advancing so quickly and how this is affecting consumer and business behaviour.

Emphasize the necessity of integrating smart technology strategically in order to fulfil changing client demands and maintain competitiveness.

Smart Technologies Landscape: Review all of the major smart technologies that are pertinent to e-business, such as big data analytics, block chain, IoT, AI, and AR.

Describe each technology's capabilities and its uses in the context of e-business, highlighting how it might improve operational effectiveness, customize customer experiences, and support creative business models.

Framework for Strategic Integration: Create a strategic framework that will allow smart technologies to be systematically incorporated into e-business processes. Describe the main elements of the framework, such as:

- Evaluation of the organization's objectives and technological adoption preparedness.
- Determining the pertinent smart technologies based on industry requirements and company objectives.
- Creation of an implementation strategy that takes into account aspects like talent acquisition, data governance, technology infrastructure, and change management.
- Technology performance and business outcomes are continuously monitored and evaluated, and adjustments and optimizations are made as needed.

Best Practices and Case Studies: Give instances of successful smart technology deployments in various e-business fields, together with case studies from the real world.

Examine the tactics used by businesses to successfully integrate smart technologies, taking into account obstacles including cultural differences, interoperability problems, and data protection issues.

Emphasize the best practices and takeaways from these case studies, demonstrating the revolutionary effects of integrating smart technologies on customer happiness, revenue growth, and business efficiency.

Evaluation and Impact Assessment: Talk about how to measure how smart technology integration affects e-business performance indicators. Take into account both qualitative and quantitative metrics, such as employee satisfaction and brand perception, in addition to quantitative measures like ROI, revenue growth, cost savings, and customer engagement.

In order to evaluate the effectiveness of smart technology efforts and promote continued improvements, it is critical to stress the significance of on-going monitoring and feedback channels.

Future Trends and Outlook: Examine new developments and potential paths for intelligent technology integration in the context of e-business. Talk about how developments in fields like edge computing, cyber security, AI-driven personalization, and regulatory frameworks affect e-business tactics. Provide an analysis of the possible advantages and difficulties that may result from these developments, as well as suggestions for how businesses may continue to be creative and flexible in their response to technology.

4. RESULT AND DISCUSSION

Several important themes and insights have come to light during our investigation into the strategic integration of smart technologies in e-business. First, we discover that companies using smart technologies see significant improvements in their ability to make decisions, be agile, and operate more efficiently. By deploying IoT sensors, AI algorithms, and sophisticated analytics, companies may streamline resource distribution, automate repetitive processes, and extract valuable insights from massive data sets. These upgrades help to provide leaner operations, lower expenses, and better market responsiveness.

Our investigation also highlights the revolutionary effect that intelligent technology integration has on the consumer experience. Through the implementation of personalized interactions, customized product recommendations, and seamless Omni channel experiences, companies may cultivate heightened customer engagement, loyalty, and advocacy. Furthermore, smart technologies provide up new avenues for income generation and business model innovation, enabling fresh approaches to value creation and market distinction.

But our conversations also bring to light some of the difficulties in integrating smart technology, such as security, privacy, and ethical issues. Maintaining client trust and adhering to laws like the GDPR become increasingly important as businesses gather and examine ever-larger volumes of customer data. Furthermore, there are implementation issues arising from the intricacy of integrating diverse technologies and legacy systems, necessitating meticulous planning, investment, and organizational alignment.

In conclusion, e-businesses can generate development, innovation, and competitive advantage through the strategic integration of smart technologies, but doing so also necessitates careful assessment of the risks, obstacles, and ethical implications. Organizations must place a high priority on flexibility, adaptation, and prudent innovation going ahead in order to successfully traverse the rapidly changing digital landscape. Through the adoption of a customer-centric and ethically-driven strategy to technology adoption, e-businesses can fully leverage smart technologies to provide value for all stakeholders and society at large.

4.1 Advantages of the Proposed System

The following are some benefits of the suggested approach for the strategic integration of smart technologies in e-business:

1. **Enhanced Operational Efficiency:** Businesses may minimize manual labor, maximize resource usage, and simplify processes by utilizing smart technologies like automation, IoT, and artificial intelligence. By streamlining processes and automating tedious jobs, this boosts output, speeds up decision-making, and reduces expenses.
2. **Better Customer Experience:** As a result of intelligent technology integration, customer happiness and loyalty are increased through personalized interactions, customized recommendations, and seamless Omni channel experiences. Businesses may provide pertinent and timely answers, build lasting relationships, and encourage repeat business by comprehending and predicting client needs through data analytics and AI-driven insights.
3. **Innovation and Competitive Advantage:** By embracing smart technology, businesses may stay ahead of the curve in a market that is changing quickly by innovating their goods, services, and business models. Through the utilization of cutting-edge technologies such as block chain, AR/VR,

and machine learning, companies may forge distinctive value propositions, set themselves apart from rivals, and seize fresh market prospects.

4. **Making Decisions Based on Data:** Large volumes of data can be gathered, analyzed, and used by businesses to gain insights that can be put into action through smart technology integration. Organizations may find chances for growth and optimization, see trends and patterns, and make well-informed decisions by utilizing the power of big data analytics and AI algorithms.
5. **Adaptability and Agility:** The suggested approach places a strong emphasis on the value of these traits in addressing evolving technological trends and shifting market conditions. Organizations can remain flexible and adaptable, taking advantage of opportunities and reducing risks in a world that is becoming more complicated and unpredictable by cultivating a culture of innovation, experimentation, and continuous learning.

All things considered, the suggested framework for the strategic incorporation of smart technologies into e-business enables enterprises to leverage technology's transformative ability to spur development, creativity, and long-term competitive advantage in the digital era.

4.2 Social Welfare of the Proposed System

There are various ways in which the suggested system for the strategic integration of smart technology in e-business could improve social welfare.

Accessibility and Inclusivity: Businesses can make sure that their goods and services are available to a wider audience, including people with disabilities or restricted access to traditional channels, by utilizing smart technologies to improve digital accessibility. This promotes equality of opportunity and inclusivity in the digital economy, so advancing social justice and empowering individuals.

Employment Creation and Economic Growth: The use of smart technologies in e-business promotes employment growth in a number of industries, such as digital marketing, technology development, data analytics, and customer service. Businesses provide job possibilities and boost economic growth as they innovate and increase their digital presence; this eventually raises living standards and lowers unemployment rates.

Education and Skill Development: As smart technologies proliferate, workers must constantly learn new skills and upgrade their existing ones to keep up with changing employment demands and technological breakthroughs. Companies have a significant impact on fostering possibilities for career growth and lifetime learning by funding employee education and skill development programs. This human capital investment promotes social mobility, increases employability, and gives people the tools they need to succeed in the digital economy.

Environmental Sustainability: Through programs like energy-efficient operations, sustainable supply chain management, and eco-friendly product design, smart technologies help organizations maximize resource usage, decrease waste, and lessen their impact on the environment. Organizations may protect the welfare of present and future generations by addressing urgent global issues like resource depletion and climate change, as well as by supporting sustainable business practices.

Cooperation and Community participation: By utilizing digital platforms, social networks, and online communities, the incorporation of smart technology into e-business enables increased community participation and cooperation. Companies can use these platforms to engage with stakeholders, such as clients, vendors, staff members, and local communities, to promote communication, get input, and jointly develop solutions. By encouraging openness, responsibility, and trust, this participatory strategy builds social cohesiveness and group resilience in the face of common difficulties.

In general, the suggested framework for the deliberate incorporation of smart technologies into e-business has promise for yielding substantial social welfare advantages through the advancement of environmental sustainability, job creation, accessibility, inclusivity, education, and community involvement. Businesses can use smart technologies to produce good social impact and improve the general well-being of society by adopting ethical and responsible practices.

4.3 Future Enhancement

The suggested approach for the strategic integration of smart technologies in e-business may be improved in a number of ways in subsequent versions. First off, consumer engagement and feedback analysis could be completely transformed by the application of sophisticated natural language processing (NLP) and sentiment analysis technologies. Businesses can better adjust their products, services, and marketing campaigns by gaining deeper insights into customer preferences, attitudes, and emerging trends through real-time analysis of customer queries, feedback, and social media conversations.

Secondly, there is potential to improve product presentation and engagement through the incorporation of immersive virtual reality (VR) experiences into e-commerce platforms. Businesses may close the gap between online and offline shopping experiences by giving customers the ability to virtually explore things in 3D surroundings, virtually try on apparel or accessories, or virtually picture furniture in their living spaces. This lowers uncertainty and increases confidence in making purchases. Furthermore, unforgettable brand experiences may be produced by VR-powered virtual showrooms and experiential marketing initiatives, which encourage client advocacy and loyalty.

Finally, the use of tokenization and decentralized finance (DeFi) technology has the potential to completely transform financial transactions and payment methods in e-business. Businesses may improve security and transparency in financial transactions, expedite cross-border payments and lower transaction costs by utilizing decentralized platforms and block chain-based smart contracts. Additionally, tokenizing assets like digital collectibles, fractional real estate ownership, or loyalty points might open up new investment avenues and revenue sources while giving consumers more freedom and liquidity over how they manage their digital assets.

5. CONCLUSION

In summary, e-business's strategic integration of smart technologies is a critical first step in promoting innovation, accelerating growth, and boosting competitiveness in the digital age. Businesses can discover new avenues for increasing operational efficiency, consumer engagement, and income production by utilizing technologies like block chain, augmented reality, IoT, and AI. Organizations may surpass conventional limits and develop value propositions that appeal to today's tech-savvy consumers by utilizing tailored experiences, data-driven insights, and seamless interactions.

However, a strategic and all-encompassing approach that takes organizational alignment, technological readiness, and ethical considerations into account is necessary for the successful adoption of smart technology. Prioritizing investments in cyber security, infrastructure modernization, and talent development is essential for firms looking to reduce risks and take advantage of the revolutionary potential of emerging technologies. Furthermore, in the quickly changing digital landscape, cooperation, knowledge exchange, and partnerships across industries and disciplines are crucial for fostering innovation and resolving difficult problems. Businesses may use smart technology to create a more equitable, sustainable and prosperous future for society at large by adopting a culture of constant learning, flexibility, and responsible innovation.

REFERENCES

Chen, M., Mao, S., & Liu, Y. (2014). Big data: A survey. *Mobile Networks and Applications*, 19(2), 171–209. 10.1007/s11036-013-0489-0

Davenport, T. H., & Harris, J. (2007). *Competing on analytics: The new science of winning*. Harvard Business Press.

Gubbi, J., Buyya, R., Marusic, S., & Palaniswami, M. (2013). Internet of Things (IoT): A vision, architectural elements, and future directions. *Future Generation Computer Systems*, 29(7), 1645–1660. 10.1016/j.future.2013.01.010

Hair, J. F., Hult, G. T. M., Ringle, C. M., & Sarstedt, M. (2017). *A primer on partial least squares structural equation modeling (PLS-SEM)*. Sage Publications.

Kshetri, N. (2018). Blockchain's roles in meeting key supply chain management objectives. *International Journal of Information Management*, 39, 80–89. 10.1016/j.ijinfomgt.2017.12.005

Lee, J., Kao, H. A., & Yang, S. (2014). Service innovation and smart analytics for Industry 4.0 and big data environment. *Procedia CIRP*, 16, 3–8. 10.1016/j.procir.2014.02.001

McAfee, A., & Brynjolfsson, E. (2012). Big data: The management revolution. *Harvard Business Review*, 90(10), 60–68.23074865

Porter, M. E., & Heppelmann, J. E. (2014). How smart, connected products are transforming competition. *Harvard Business Review*, 92(11), 64–88.

Schwalbe, K. (2015). *Information technology project management*. Cengage Learning.

Shi, W., Cao, J., Zhang, Q., Li, Y., & Xu, L. (2016). Edge computing: Vision and challenges. *IEEE Internet of Things Journal*, 3(5), 637–646. 10.1109/JIOT.2016.2579198

Thakur, V. K., Gularte, M. S., Raj, R. G., & Kessler, M. R. (2015). *Green composites: Polymer composites and the environment*. Springer.

Turban, E., Sharda, R., Aronson, J. E., & King, D. (2015). *Business intelligence: A managerial approach*. Pearson Education.

Voigt, K. I., Buliga, O., & Michl, K. (2017). Industry 4.0–Empirical evidence on productivity gains and employment challenges. *Journal of International Business Studies*, 48(5), 601–606.

Wang, S., Wan, J., Li, D., & Zhang, C. (2016). Implementing smart factory of Industrie 4.0: An outlook. *International Journal of Distributed Sensor Networks*, 12(1), 3159805. 10.1155/2016/3159805

Wei, L., Zhu, H., Cui, Y., Ren, Y., Li, B., & Liu, J. (2017). Scalable and efficient blockchain-based data sharing scheme for cloud storage. *IEEE Transactions on Cloud Computing*, 6(2), 384–392.

West, D. M. (2018). *Blockchain for government: Benefits and implications of distributed ledger technology for information sharing*. Brookings Institution.

Xu, L. D., He, W., & Li, S. (2014). Internet of Things in industries: A survey. *IEEE Transactions on Industrial Informatics*, 10(4), 2233–2243. 10.1109/TII.2014.2300753

Yang, K., Chen, M., Zhang, Y., & Wang, S. (2017). Big data and cloud computing: Innovation opportunities and challenges. *International Journal of Digital Earth*, 10(1), 13–53. 10.1080/17538947.2016.1239771

Zhang, S., & Wen, J. (2018). Research on construction of smart tourism service system based on big data and cloud computing. In *2018 IEEE International Conference on Big Data (Big Data)* (pp. 5155-5162). IEEE.

Zhu, Q., Huang, L., & Wang, W. (2016). The adoption of blockchain technology in financial services: A comparative study. In *2016 13th International Conference on Service Systems and Service Management (ICSSSM)* (pp. 1-6). IEEE.

Chapter 5
Disruptive Technologies and Innovations in Business 5.0:
Trends and Application Perspectives in Phygital Transformation

Neli Maria Mengalli
https://orcid.org/0000-0002-3782-3807
Faculdade São Bernardo do Campo, Brazil

Antonio Aparecido Carvalho
Faculdade São Bernardo do Campo, Brazil

ABSTRACT

This chapter was written based on bibliographical research, qualitative, and exploratory studies. The objective of writing the chapter was to highlight the main disruptive technologies and innovations for business 5.0 with application perspectives and recommendations; and, when reading the academic materials, it was noticed that few areas are covered in academic investigations into business 5.0. There are solutions and recommendations, as well as directions for future research. The final considerations, among the conclusions, are that well-being for future generations are the revolutions to be documented for a fairer society, whether in reality or in augmented, virtual, mixed, or extended realities.

1. INTRODUCTION

Over the years, developers have sought to make technologies smarter in a strategic sense to mitigate the waste of human time. The world has undergone physical and digital transformations to enable phygital experiences for human beings. Disruptive innovations proved to originate from disruptive strategies, because they were leveraged for the development of a service or a product that enables the use in a differentiated market for business 5.0 with the (de) stabilization of competitors that dominated the market.

In faster transformations, the existing opportunities for a present market tend to evidence conventional strategies and innovations. New opportunities in current markets tend to provide incremental strategies and innovations. In new opportunities in markets where products or services exist, strategies and innovations are architected. When the market and opportunities are new, strategies and innovations

DOI: 10.4018/978-1-6684-7840-0.ch005

are radical. Existing opportunities and new markets make possible the origin of disruptive strategies and innovations, because, in theory, markets are created from the most demanding use of a demand that wants to have a better experience as a consumer.

The advent of disruptive technologies makes new markets possible. Păvăloaia and Necula (2023) wrote about the disruptive impact of technologies and showed that the most prominent examples are artificial intelligence, the Internet of Things (IoT), blockchain, 5G and 3D printers. Pang, Lee, and Murshed (2023) ratify artificial intelligence and the Internet of Things (IoT) and include Machine Learning in the list of examples.

It is added that the disruptive effects, both strategic and innovative, of artificial intelligences are in phygital transformation second by second. Business 5.0 plans must be (re) written in their entirety. Regarding the management of people, careers, and benefits, they need to be reflected, because the professions will have names and profiles different from the current ones and layoffs are not myths. However, as expressed in the article by Păvăloaia and Necula (2023, p. 9), they will not affect all of society and (cyber) society, only those who carry out routine activities and actions with many repetitions. The uses of artificial intelligence in business 5.0 show new career models that can be sustainable careers based on human varnish.

The purpose of this chapter is to highlight the main disruptive technologies and innovations for business 5.0 with application perspectives and recommendations based on an exploratory and bibliographic study that involves literature review and business reports. Although it is known that human beings have values when interacting with machines, as Pang, Lee and Murshed (2023, p. 2) wrote about the concept of industry 5.0, which seeks to highlight a more human-centered approach as a transformer in business and the authors emphasize the importance of collaboration between people and machines, in this chapter, technologies are highlighted. In recommendations, humans must have the power skills expressed.

The target audience of this chapter are researchers who investigate business 5.0, entrepreneurship with innovation, the fifth industrial revolution and the phygital transformation in business and undergraduate and graduate professors and students, business professionals, artificial intelligence analysts, metaverse developers and designers, public policy makers, and scientists in the humanities and social sciences.

Researchers from the economic area, startups, innovation management, computerization processes, people management and economic management are public for this chapter, as well as specialists, entrepreneurs, investors, and people interested in business 5.0. Chapter division is background, chapter focus, methodology, solutions and recommendations, directions for future research, and concluding remarks.

2. BACKGROUND: HIGHLIGHT AND CONTEXT FOR MAIN SCENES

When thinking about innovations and disruptive technologies, episodes of The Jetsons (1962 - 1987) come to mind. How many people of the 50^{+} diversity have not watched episodes of the cartoon created by Joseph Barbera (1911 - 2006) and William Hanna (1910 - 2001) for two decades of the 20th century? It is not known for sure, but the certainty is that countless people, when witnessing a utopian future, wanted to have homes like those of the main characters, to drive (aero) cars, to have robotic employees, to have a reduction in the journey of work and have more leisure time.

The intelligent technology Internet of Things (IoT) is a reality, and the Vertical Take-Off and Landing is a prototype of Embraer in Brazil. Soon, science fiction will be completed in reality. It is expected that dystopias will be mitigated in the development of equipment for daily uses connected according to the needs and demands of users. Machines seem to learn as in prosopopoeia or personifications.

In the same prosopopoeia, digital transformation is fueled by technologies such as cloud services, artificial intelligence, the Internet of Things (IoT), the voices that interact with machines, drones, Big Data, 3D printing, robotics, blockchain and business intelligence [not necessarily in this gradation], among other possibilities for technological food. In the phygital transformation, metaverse ecosystems tend to leverage businesses with experiences that need virtual reality, augmented reality, mixed realities, and extended realities.

Figure 1. Digital transformation and phygital transformation

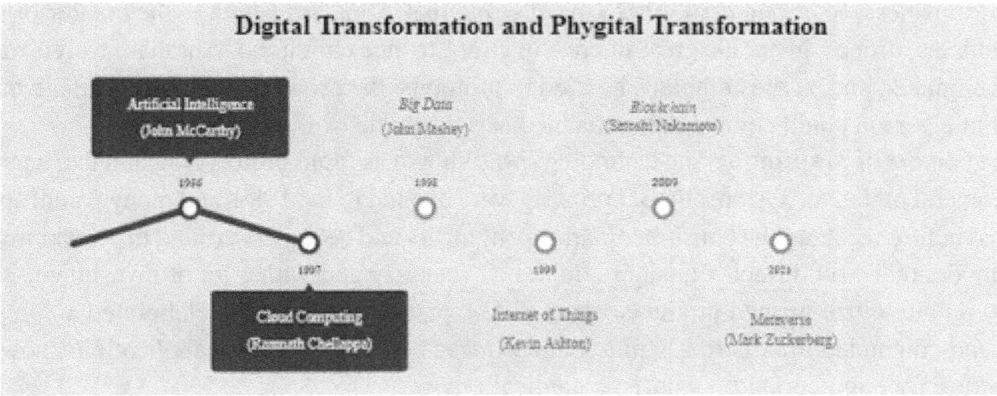

Digital transformation and phygital transformation are changes that have elements with names. In Figure 1, it is possible to see a timeline. The names that people know were devised by researchers, mainly, in the field of computing. Mishra (2014, p 204) wrote that Professor Ramnath Chellappa created the word cloud for computing in the lecture "Intermediaries in Cloud-Computing: A New Computing Paradigm" in 1997.

Artificial intelligence is a definition attributed to John McCarthy, because, in 1956, he was one of the members of the event for "A Proposal for the Dartmouth Summer Research Project on Artificial Intelligence" and because he organized the initial meeting at the higher education institution where he worked. The conference was based on "to proceed on the basis of the conjecture that every aspect of learning or any other feature of intelligence can in principle be so precisely described that a machine can be made to simulate it." (Artificial Intelligence Coined at Dartmouth, 1956) and there was the advent of the birth of the research field with a small group of scientists.

Understanding human intelligence and how to make machines more conscious was a mention made by James H. Moor / Daniel P. Stone, Professor in Intellectual and Moral Philosophy at Dartmouth College for the event that John McCarthy (Dartmouth College), Marvin Lee Minsky (Harvard University), Nathaniel Rochester (I.B.M. Corporation) and Claude Elwood Shannon (Bell Telephone Laboratories) proposed. McCarthy (2007, p. 2) in the 2004 article revised in 2007 wrote that artificial intelligence was known as intelligent computer programs, as it was related to the task of using hardware and software to understand human intelligence, however this chapter does not limit it to methods that are observable in biologically developed organisms.

When it comes to robotics, the term resembles science fiction. Sims (1987, p. 8) wrote that the scientific community was slow to accept the term originating from science fiction and that the term robot is of Czech origin with connotations of forced labor or servitude. The author wrote that the Czech writer Karel Čapek (1890 - 1938) in the first decade of the 20th century assigned the name robot to a series of mechanical objects, electronic humanoids, androids, and mannequins that served people. During the 20th century, based on the book by Karel Čapek (1890 - 1938), several properties of a real mechanical robot were developed. The fictional connected worker was designed with new connotations for new businesses and for teaching and learning in robotics-related classes.

In relation to the drone, the name is reminiscent of the buzzing sound when flying and the revolution did not use the world wide web. The author of the word drone for unmanned aerial vehicle was not found, as it is an informal nickname given. However, since the 70s of the 20th century, models have been made viable for business. Siddiqui, et al. (2023, p. 2) wrote that Abraham Karen is the creator of unmanned aerial vehicles, drones, given his great interest in aircraft since childhood. Abraham Karen was an aeronautical engineer, and, at the company, he tried to prototype the product with more suitable materials so that just one person could control the unmanned aerial vehicle or UAV technology.

In the context of 3D printing, the technology was known as rapid prototyping and had a patent application. Several precursor systems for 3D printing were created in the 1980s and many patent applications were filed before reaching the consumer market. Engineers and designers around the world were looking for the model that would impact business. In the 21st century and with a lot of investment, 3D printers began to revolutionize printed products. Irons (2020, p. 43), in the thesis, elaborated a compilation of models and concluded that there is still a lot of work to be done for future applications, however there is a structure for engineering for futuristic applications.

The technological revolution does not necessarily include the world wide web, but Irmak and Bozdal (2018, p. 20) wrote that there have been two major revolutions for humans, the world wide web and the Internet of Things that have the potential to change the world. The term Internet of Things was mentioned in a 1999 presentation by sensor expert, and innovator Kevin Ashton.

In the revolution created with the world wide web, there was a huge amount of data. Diebold (2012, p. 3) wrote that John Mashey produced a presentation with slides that highlights the existence of a phenomenon called Big Data. The presentation is in the references for additional reading in this chapter. The author reported in the article that the creator of the name Big Data adopted the reference for advertising and as a unifying theme for technical seminars and concluded that the term Big Data covers computer science, statistics and econometrics and that it may have arisen in conversations at the company Silicon Graphics Inc. (SGI), but the highlight is given to John Mashey.

Strategic decision-making in business had technological devices that over the years were perfected by professionals in the field of computer science and data analysis. Chen (2010, p. 2) wrote that the term Business Intelligence was created in 1989 and the information technology sector strengthened the skills, computational resources, applications, and practices for business management. Gartner, Inc. is credited with boosting the term in reports on product projection and analysis for Business Intelligence. The company consulted Chief Executive Officers to validate the insights and reports circulating in organizations and, according to the author, Gartner, Inc. highlighted that Business Intelligence surpassed security and was the main priority in information technology. In 2011, Gartner, Inc. produced the "Magic Quadrant for Business Intelligence" report (Sallam, et al. (2011)) with a global view of the main Business Intelligence platform software providers.

Studies about platforms were focused on the digital sphere and businesses were revolutionized with blockchain technology, because the effects ranged from the financial area to production and included the educational area. In 2009, Satoshi Nakamoto, according to Sakız and Gencer (2019, p. 99) released a whitepaper that provided details of how blockchain technology had a decentralized aspect so that no one could control anything. The evolution of business, Bitcoin and other cryptocurrencies have revolutionized the financial system globally.

The idea of Bitcoin and blockchain goes back to the efforts of Nick Szabo in the late 1990s, however Satoshi Nakamoto implemented the well-known digital currency. The authors wrote that Nakamoto can be a group of developers who used blockchain technology to create Bitcoin, there is little information about Nakamoto and that he or she could be a group of people or just one person. Decentralized inspires people and businesses that have created immersive worlds.

In 2021, Mark Zuckerberg renamed the company to Meta and reported how the business would be developed based on decentralization in the metaverse, a combination of virtual reality and augmented reality in an immersive world that would merge the virtual universe and the physical world. The founder's speech was given at an annual conference with great global repercussions. The future was in the present modified by Zuckerberg. According to Moenandar, *et al.* (2022, p. 130), despite the rhetoric that the company's name was changed, there was an intention to announce a new mode of social interaction that would be made possible by the metaverse through technological resources and would impact the business both internally and externally.

Both digital transformation and phygital transformation have driven changes in business. At the end of the 20th century and into the 21st century, innovations and technologies were better known through the world wide web, and it was perceived that they were engines for social, cultural, and economic development. From the knowledge society with the information economy to the interlocution with machines that learn and are named as artificial intelligences, industry 4.0 gives way to Industry 5.0. Digital transformation transcends physics and has joined the virtual with the physical for humans to transform business phygitally.

Business advances with disruptive technologies and the intangibility of human capital that constantly develops emotional intelligence and a growth mindset in a world economy that fluctuates and changes markets. People are the subjects of new cultures and economic developments, and public policies seek government regulations to advance innovative activities.

Stimulating the development of businesses is a government demand for high technologies in partnerships between companies and universities. Research and development in teaching and extension activities so that the curricula prescribed in higher education institutions are not just the reductionist reproduction of historical contents and exercises that do not contribute to contemporary practice.

Concerns about the decline in jobs and the professions of the future are mitigated by company reports, for example, researchers from the IBM Institute for Business Value suggest, according to research insights, that artificial intelligence will not be the will replace human beings in jobs, but people who do not know how to use and interact with artificial intelligence can be replaced by human beings who know how to work with mastery and fluent interaction with artificial intelligence.

In the aforementioned research insight, there is a belief that the global skills deficit threatens workers, that is, the threat is human and has reference to higher education, reskilling, and upskilling. Over a period of five years (2023 to 2028), according to Augmented Work for an Automated, AI-driven World. (2023, p. 2) based on the World Economic Forum, 44% of workers' skills will be modified. Four out of five executives believe generative artificial intelligence will change employee roles and skills, but only 28% of Chief Executive Officers in the 2023 study assessed the potential impact of generative artificial intelligence on their current workforce.

Mengalli and Carvalho (2024, p. 80) concluded that, in business plans, human skills must be valued and praised in relation to artificial intelligence and the authors highlighted that there may be a conflict between machines and humans, especially in the context of debates regarding generative artificial intelligence, in this chapter, there is an emphasis that it is necessary to pay attention to (co) creation with machines and give due credit to what was written by artificial intelligence programming. Ethical issues deserve research, as do the skills and abilities that converge with morals and ethics in interactions with machines.

Completing the background that began with the classic The Jetsons (1962 - 1987), there is part of the reality in the business world from the McKinsey & Company report, The Economic Potential of Generative AI: The Next Productivity Frontier (2023, p. 3): around 75% of generative artificial intelligence use cases are in the following areas: operations involving consumers, marketing and sales, software engineering and research and development. Sixty-three cases were examined where technologies could address specific business challenges and ways of producing one or more measurable results.

Companies have advanced with the use of generative artificial intelligence with the ability to support interactions with consumers, with the generation of content for marketing and sales [creativity is a human characteristic], with the writing of computer code based on natural language instructions, in addition to research for the development of new products and services. The anatomy of work is changing with the increase in employees' individual capabilities in automating activities.

Business 5.0 allows employees to have time for productivity because disruptive technologies allow work automation to absorb around 70% of employees' time, according to the aforementioned McKinsey & Company report, that is, the forecast was to automate half the time and there has been an overcoming so that the human varnish can be shown in terms of communication, creativity, negotiation, the ability to help the company and colleagues, among other human functions that combine with emotional intelligence.

2.1 Focus of the Chapter: The Lens and Efforts to Emphasize the Business 5.0 Context

Human beings and society are the basic elements for business 5.0. The name 5.0 represents the fifth transformation and the confrontation of countless challenges that include inequality, poverty, unemployment, corruption, conflicts over ideologies, crimes, climate change and human and government debts and doubts. Businesses with the name 5.0 propose the presentation of solutions for the phygital transformation that Mengalli, Carvalho and Galvão (2023, p. 56) reported is supported by objects and applications that involve physical mechanisms with interfaces and virtual contents in overlapping places and physical and virtual spaces which may include scents and perfumes.

Phygital solutions are realistic and encompass knowledge and practice for problem solving and strategic decisions in environmental and social governance. There is a predominance of facing adversities for the well-being of people and their families with the facilitation of processes and organizational routines and with respect for human beings and their time so that knowledge of emotions, control of emotions and feelings, self-motivation, empathy, compassion, and healthy relationships that presuppose help in carrying out shared activities.

Sharing hopes in activities shows that the present changes a more human future and, when the chapter's focus lens sought to centralize business 5.0, industry 6.0 emerged through the prism of Almusaed, Yitmen and Almssad (2023, p. 1) who described the sixth transformative phase of the architecture, engineering and construction sector as a pioneer in advances in quantum computing, nanotechnology, artificial intelligence and cloud-based energy solutions for effectiveness, precision and sustainability.

If transformation 5.0 uses artificial intelligence, the metaverse and robotics to increase productivity, creativity, and supply chain alignment, as the authors wrote, data culture reigns with the use of real-time monitoring for decisions strategies using intelligent sensors and algorithms guided by artificial intelligence so that operational bottlenecks are mitigated, and processes are optimized. Humans enable analytical insights when (co) creation is with other humans and, when (co) creating with computer programming in machine interface, they bring to life ideas with unknown authors that need to be ethically referenced when they [ideas] are used in the organization.

In the intelligent bases for business 5.0 and 6.0, there are ecological and culturally respected processes, products and services, such as, for example, the employee experience and the consumer experience in relation to diversity and social adversities, after all, the interoperability of systems forms ecosystems that connect human skills and abilities with antifragility and the sustainability of the planet so that there are no (ego) systems driven by small and fragile powers that compromise business in branded ways that involve human work, process design, and disruptive technologies created with languages for artificial intelligence.

Leadership is based on data culture, design, environmental and social context and, above all, human ethics that seeks innovative solutions for aesthetic effectiveness that include climate and energy issues. Such effectiveness can be supported by realities: augmented, virtual, mixed, and extended, in addition to olfactory augmented reality so that the tangibility of human notions is simulated to mitigate errors in reality. The information and data from the realities mentioned above show that the physical world and the digital universe coexist in synchronous time.

The new business models favor the coexistence of synchronous time in different experiences in immersive worlds and the Gartner Inc. Press Release (2022) reported that 25% of people will spend at least one hour a day in the metaverse in 2026 and the areas that make use of the metaverse increase and Big Techs create software and mobile devices to improve people's experience in communication, creativity, mitigating errors in simulations and in the reality of telemedicine, and design iterations. Interdisciplinarity and people with diverse backgrounds work towards the reality of the metaverse and artificial intelligence for business.

Ecological and sustainable depend on interdisciplinary prisms and disruptive technologies for prospecting consumption patterns that include renewable energy or not for the option of materials that enhance human comfort which, within the scope of the employee experience, has robots and mechanizations enabled by artificial intelligence for the (co) creation of inventiveness, simulations and improvements to processes, products and services, as well as for the speed of solutions and strategic decisions.

Effectiveness, creativity, and innovation have the interface between human and machine. The intelligent part of business is done by systems that include artificial intelligence in the development and design of the user interface for physical security that requires repairs to technological gaps to mitigate business vulnerability. Digital twins are present in the business and can be developed to emphasize the holistic and human nature of disruptions, including mental configuration in quantum dimensions because thinking transcends atoms and binary bytes.

Acting occurs based on thoughts and can be enhanced with the main technologies presented. In this section, disruptive technologies were highlighted and could be present in this chapter because they provide new sets of characteristics for businesses and, according to Păvăloaia and Necula (2023, p. 1), they add value to new applications and new businesses, after all they stimulate the development of new products and create distinct markets with unique experiences. In recent years, disruptive technologies have promoted unexpected impacts on consumer markets in relation to technologies that existed and did not provide satisfactory experiences for customers and users, as they had low performance, little applicability and, sometimes, gave brands a bad reputation.

Disruptive technologies, in business 5.0, can be initially evaluated in the most different niches or can be verified in small markets until they become competitive in the main market and replace old routines and processes. In some cases, disruptive technologies cause experiences that employees are not always prepared for the use and results and must go through upskilling and reskilling processes to change habits for new appropriations and performances with radical computing power and with technological advances that bring about social transformation with changes in the local and regional economy and consumer behavior.

Edwards, *et al.* (2022, p. 3) wrote that disruptive technologies, over time, overtake and are surpassed by other disruptive technologies and consumers switch to new disruptive technologies. The authors developed a new model and methodology to identify the inflection point of a disruptive technology in market dynamics to define whether the technology will succeed or fail in a disruptive situation. Although technologies can present notable advantages, it is important to investigate whether the investment will have a return compatible with the structured business.

The market seeks interconnectivity and optimization for global business. The use of digital twins has shown favorable results, especially when there are physical structures that combine with digital knowledge in synchronous time. However, the users involved need adaptability and such human competence can provide opportunities for the use of digital twins or not when it comes to appropriation in use, even though there is the creation of opportunities for new possibilities for environmentally conscious actions.

Environmentally conscious and socially coherent actions have been part of governance in companies that have sought disruptive innovation since the 90^{s} of the 20th century. Khan and Arif (2023, p. 1) wrote that disruptive innovation was often called hidden innovation because it incorporated recent technologies or methods into the market. Emerging technology was generally inferior to technology that was in use. According to the authors, the modern technology was more expensive, had fewer functions, was more difficult to operate and was less attractive, but after several rounds, it surpassed the old technology and destroyed the business.

According to Ataman, Myhr and Nistor. (2023, p. 105) disruptions impact network markets and innovators can attract significant attention in an industry that is established for innovative solutions or consumer niches that are underserved. The authors wrote that investigations into disruptive innovations were carried out mainly by companies focused on products with traditional technologies and that most markets operate in a business ecosystem that trusts each other and is integrated into a network of business partners.

Businesses are in the fifth industrial revolution and teaching, research and extension activities must present innovative and successful practices to show that there is quality in the process of teaching and learning in higher education. Starting from business 5.0 in a society with consumption 5.0, the models for undertaking include both human intelligence and phygital experiences as well as artificial intelligence produced and developed by humans so that human beings and machines can have dialogue in user languages, not languages, not from developers.

The closer the interlocution interfaces are friendly, the more consumers will have the best experiences and the collaborators will be able to produce quality for the business. The junctions designed by knowledge and artificial intelligence show the intersections between human learning, the growth mindset and the emotions and feelings systemically in business as a way to deny not producing disruptive and sustainable innovations so that environmental and social governance become a reality in economic systems surrounded by machines with disruptive technologies.

The main disruptive technologies and innovations are presented to enhance business 5.0 with the respective perspectives and recommendations so that there are neither dystopias nor utopias, after all technologies are strategies, as Silva (2001, p. 842) wrote about the machines that are concrete objects and instruments as products of techniques and it is added that the processes are human with intentions and with techniques that are in the conception and use of disruptive technologies.

Recommendations are necessary in business 5.0, because they involve creations, (co) creations, developments, prototyping and systems that need cybersecurity and social monitoring for secrecy. Data culture must have levels of access for the strategic decision to be disruptive for the market. The future of professions is a present that is in daily transformation, because technologies are increasingly intelligent, artificially parameterized by humans who are developing a society in which careers and functions show the human varnish insofar as the repetitive is with the days numbered for human beings and that people seek assertive communication and creativity from employees and service providers to boost business.

Sustainable innovation and disruptive innovation are increasingly complementing each other, because the first has problems that are understood with existing markets, changes are incremental, there is performance promotion, the cost is low, consumers trust brands in a market predictable and business methods are traditional and, second, it has problems that are not understood, markets are new, innovation carries the incremental, the architectural and the radical, consumers do not trust brands in an unpredictable market and the methods for business 5.0 management are far from traditional given phygital experiences.

According to the McKinsey & Company report: Value Creation in the Metaverse: The Real Business of the Virtual World. (2022, p.47), clothing and luxury goods companies use the metaverse for advertising [...], the metaverse presents an opportunity for retailers to (re) imagine and personalize the store environment both to individuals as well as groups of customers [...], and shopping malls are created in the metaverse. In the aforementioned report, virtual reality is mentioned in relation to shopping, however it is necessary to create consistent experiences for consumers to bridge the gap between the physical and digital.

Yazici, Özkan, and Özkan (2024, p. 23) wrote that the value of the metaverse for companies and employees impacts the future of work. The authors wrote that the metaverse offers opportunities for companies to create innovative business models on product or service sales platforms that can interact with customers in new and unique ways and reported that technologies with augmented, virtual, mixed, or extended reality and digital twins or mirror worlds are important technological paths for the metaverse. It is emphasized that, in this chapter, technology will not be emphasized, but digital or phygital businesses, for this reason there will be no emphasis on references to explain the realities mentioned here.

Within the scope of the perspectives of adopting the metaverse for business, Knox (2022, p. 213) wrote the question: "So why is the metaverse being taken so seriously, when the idea itself seems a bit 'old hat'?" in conclusion. The author's response is that there is an attempt to revive the frontiers that characterized the early days of Silicon Valley and because it makes sense from a business perspective. It is a reflection that deserves to be made in business models to verify the feasibility or not of having immersive worlds for brands.

Meepung and Kannikar (2022, p. 277 - 278) wrote that the metaverse reduces physical constraints on business without concern for consumer location or construction period to increase business opportunities as well as enabling new dimensions of the system payment method with the smart contract. Payments can be made through cryptocurrencies and contracts can be made on blockchain. Phygital transformation helps brands design creative experiences that stimulate feelings and happiness among consumers and employees who drive emotional connections in business.

Innovations for business 5.0 are enabled by disruptive technologies so that products or services have more affordable costs and get more people to have access. It is noteworthy that people's data is important for verifying consumer behavior. In innovative businesses, consumers are an important part of the business and Marketing models.

It is necessary to bring in customers who did not consume or include populations that did not have the income to consume. The network, in business 5.0, has consistent value for stakeholders so that technologies improve disruptive innovations for the well-being of society and (cyber) society.

2.2 The Paths to Systematization to Achieve Understanding

The quality of life and well-being of society and (cyber) society are achieved with disruptive innovations that require technologies that are increasingly user and consumer friendly. It is difficult to predict the influence of innovation in relation to disruption. Company leaders have difficulty recognizing whether innovations are valuable to the market. Even though there is evidence about innovation, leaders could help companies identify disruptive changes.

This statement showed that more research could help businesses identify disruptive innovations and technologies. The objective of this chapter, as described in the introduction, was to highlight the main disruptive technologies and innovations for business called 5.0, and concomitantly inform application perspectives, and recommendations. At the beginning of writing this chapter, the term “business 5.0” was searched for in academic mechanisms and it was possible to realize that the business repertoire in the fifth generation of transformation was not yet included in many academic texts.

The bibliographic review was carried out in the years 2024 and 2023 and the year, area and where the academic material was published will be presented. The references will include the completeness of the authors, the year, the title, and subtitle, if any, and where the academic material was published, as well as the Uniform Resource Locator [URL] for later consultation and continuity of the investigation. What was highlighted in this chapter shows the trends and application perspectives in phygital transformation and over the years, new research must be conducted around business 5.0 and 6.0.

continued on following page

Table 1. Continued

Table 1. Research area and publication

Year	Area	Publication
2024	Information Security	Institute of Electrical and Electronics Engineers (IEEE Access)
2023	Software Engineering	International Journal of Intelligent Systems and Applications in Engineering (IJISAE)
2023	Organizational Management	Routledge
2023	Human Resources	Routledge
2023	Business Administration	IGI Global
2023	Financial Sector	Journal of Business and Social Sciences
2023	Supply Chain	Supply Chain Insider
2023	Financial Sector	IGI Global
2023	Financial Sector	IGI Global
2023	Medicine	International Journal of Computer Trends and Technology
2023	Business Administration	Social Science Research Network
2023	Business Administration	IGI Global
2023	Supply Chain	IGI Global
2023	Supply Chain	IGI Global
2023	Economy	IGI Global

Source: Selections made by the authors

The bibliographical research showed that, in academic works, there is mention of the term "business 5.0", however the terms "disruptive technologies" and "disruptive innovations" were not present in all research materials. The term "phygital transformation" was not found in academic materials. Therefore, the proposal of this chapter has become unique, but needs to be renewed every year or decade, as it contemplates the trend and perspectives that change as new disruptive technologies are made available to the market, and disruptive innovations occur. It is always good to clarify that, after business 5.0, business 6.0 will be the reality in the market.

Figure 2. Quantity of publication by area (2024 / 2023)

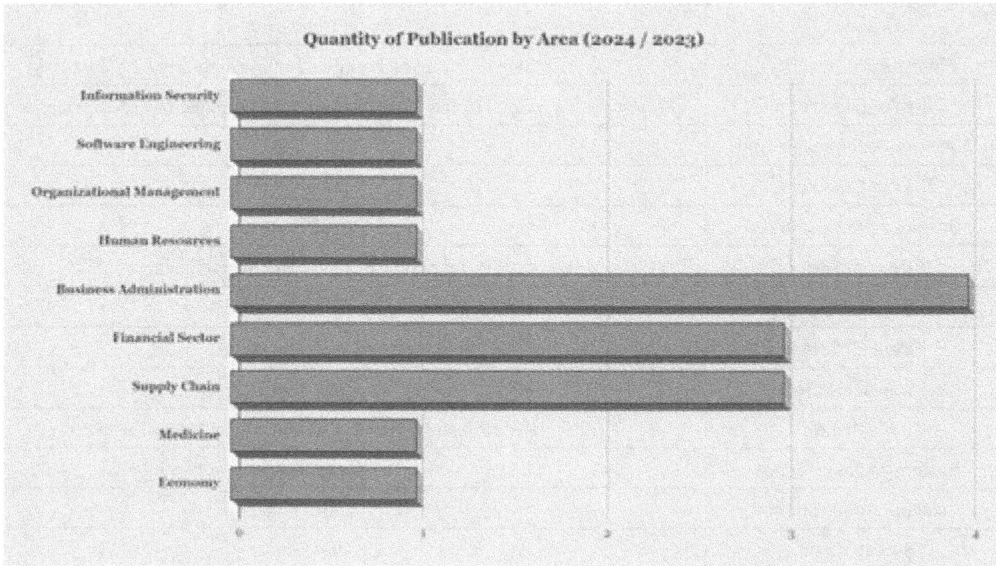

In the search, based on academic mechanisms, figure 2, it was possible to notice that the Business Administration area had four publications, three book chapters and one article. Publications in the areas of concentration Organizational Management (one publication), Human Resources (one publication), Financial Sector (three publications) and Supplies (three publications) can be understood as being part of the Business Administration area. Therefore, the Administration area had a greater concentration of publications found. Software Engineering (one publication), Medicine (one publication) and Economics (one publication) were areas that highlighted the combination of business 5.0 in publications.

Even though the academic search engines had brought forty-five results, after reading each text, two texts were not included in the table because they were in a language other than English and the others because they did not contain topics related to business 5.0 in depth. In the search to learn about academic materials about business 5.0, it was possible to read chapters from the book: "Opportunities and Challenges of Business 5.0 in Emerging Markets" (2023), with the motto emerging markets, and from the book: "Innovation in Digital Economy: New Approaches to Management for Industry 5.0" (2023), with a focus on management and innovation in the digital economy.

The calls per chapter were answered by the authors, so business 5.0 was the theme and the macro area was Business Administration. The concentration in the area was organizational management, human resources, financial sector, and supply chain. The economy permeated across contexts, because both business 5.0 and industry 5.0 changed the lives of people in companies and in local and regional environments. Kunwar and Kumar (2023, p. 6) concluded, in the article that focuses on the financial sector, that specialized creativity and innovation have the potential to help and design value-added solutions, therefore, banking issues interfere with business.

Businesses need money that has been modified in format with blockchain and modifying supply chains and the healthcare sector lacks more competent and quality-oriented products. Dave (2023, p. 7-8) wrote that Industry 5.0 emphasizes the fusion of cyber-physical systems, the Internet of Things

(IoT), systems, artificial intelligence and cloud computing and manufacturers must detect and resolve any problems promptly and precisely so that there is quality control in production.

As the market's need for quality, techniques and technologies increasingly depend on clouds increases, information security and software engineering need development. Shaikh. et al. (2024, p. 7166) concluded that the study brought some potential answers to technological maturity and future advances in the context of information security and Ahmed (2023, p. 135), within the scope of software engineering, wrote that future work will include longitudinal studies to evaluate the effects of long-term sustainability for different solutions, therefore, environmental and social governance must be included in research and business 5.0.

The business 5.0 ecosystem involves research and perspectives on implementation in the most different areas, both those contained in the table presented and in areas that were not contained in the table, because, in the evolution of society from 1.0 to 6.0, technology transforms civilization, according to Almusaed, Yitmen and Almssad (2023, p. 4) in the context of smart and sustainable environments built for the future.

3. SOLUTIONS AND RECOMMENDATIONS: POSSIBILITIES FOR IMPROVEMENT IN RESEARCH

The future is modified in the present and, in recent years, the concepts involving 5.0 and 6.0 have emerged with transformative principles within the scope of disruptive technologies and innovations. Paradigm changes not only focus on product and service processes, but they redefine the relationships between those who are (bio) technologized and those who are not (bio) technologized, that is, at each transition it is necessary to understand that there is an evolution of scenarios, as that more research is needed that includes human interaction with machines and mechanization.

Physical work boosted the economy, however, in contemporary times, communication, creativity, technologies and innovations are necessary for mechanization and robotization, after all, after physical and work in the digital era, the transformation is phygital. Transport can be Vertical Take-Off and Landing, like the Eve Air Mobility that will be produced by Embraer in Brazil, the human being can interact with artificial intelligence and the digital human can remain in the metaverse, just like brands. It is a reality that transcends fiction and that must take care of people's well-being.

No matter how far we go with technologies and innovations, human beings are the basis of business 5.0 and 6.0. The private initiative and the public sector can make use of technologies and disruptive innovations to mitigate inequalities, solve social problems and address the aging of the population with sustainability and improvements in the areas of health and transport. Technologies and innovations that improve society can leverage phygital solutions for the real world with economic balance and growth to solve social and historical challenges.

Food and industrialization are elements that need to be included in research. Sikder, et al. (2023, p. 10) wrote that the solution can be understood as a way to identify the risks that leaders, in industry, face to prevent people from catastrophes, as well as improve the performance of industrial systems. The authors wrote about different research investigations that include lean, agile, green, as well as environmentally conscious supply chain practices to create hybrid supply chain models. Leaders can check results in the palm of their hands.

Disruptive innovation includes many products and services nowadays. The advent of smartphones showed new habits and customs in people and such changes in behavior made it possible for people to stay in homes in a more accessible way via the application. People who travel manage to rent residences with a price comparison that, in many cases, is lower than those charged by conventional hotels.

In the phonographic market, there was a change in habits. People use platforms to listen to music and podcasts, so in addition to consumers having different experiences, artists and producers have had to change to be closer to their audiences. From live music to music on smartphones, people had different behaviors for listening to music on record players or turntables, on radios, on cassette players, on home audio systems, on compact disc and on mp3.

People changed their behavior to watch movies and series. It was no longer necessary to leave home to rent movies, the world wide web and mobile and fixed devices made it possible to subscribe to watch movies and series. Companies grow their business with subscription capabilities. The cost started with low subscription prices and the business model became attractive to consumers. Satisfactory consumer experience changes markets.

The employee's experience begins to be valued and companies earn seals to show that it is a good place to work. Managers are paid to have a strategic vision so that long-term goals can be achieved, so paying attention to people, whether at work or in consumption, is a strategy considered consistent with the markets. The power to mobilize people to work on projects in organizations is considered as the potential of mobilization capacity.

People transform the use of technologies for disruptive innovations and knowing how to manage crises or emergencies with emotional intelligence is strategic. Solving problems involving complex elements requires skills and abilities, including socio-emotional skills. It is challenging to be creative and know how to (co) create solutions in the market. Results orientation differentiates people in demonstrating commitment and achieving established goals. Well-trained people are solutions and investments for disruptions.

3.1 Future Research Directions: The Investigations that Enable Disruptions

In this chapter, in the search in academic bases with a focus on "business 5.0", it was possible to verify that the Business Administration area had more articles or book chapters, twelve publications, including the areas of concentration Organizational Management (one publication), Human Resources (one publication), Financial Sector (three publications) and Supplies (three publications). Information Security (one publication) and Software Engineering (one publication) had academic dissemination with the motto "business 5.0" and were in the area of computer science.

Business 5.0 involves Administration and Economics, which was found in one publication because there are changes in companies and entrepreneurship that impact places locally and regionally. Therefore, more studies must be carried out in these areas and must involve computer sciences so that the disruption highlights the software and hardware that were used for digital or phygital transformation in business.

Research should include business 5.0, and 6.0, disruptive technologies and innovations, and people who lead companies that break paradigms. The (cyber) society must be investigated in higher education institutions so that economic developments are known in the causes and consequences. In contemporary times, there is an increase in automation in people's lives and there is a scalability that dominates business, and it is necessary to place the transformation.

In relation to the area of Medicine, which had one publication found with the motto "Business 5.0", in the conclusion of the article written by Dave (2023, p. 9) it involves the manufacturing sector and the need for paradigms to guide the industry and the area technological because the results of the author's research have ramifications for the manufacture of implants. A look at diversity must consider contemporary conditions and the discovery of diseases and the repair of damages suffered by people so that there is equity in the job market and so that people are economically active in business.

Diversity has been more respected, including in the ways projects are implemented. It is necessary to verify to what extent the disruptive technologies and those considered as artificial intelligences have modified professions and careers to show the human varnish. People are important in business and human capital with emotional intelligence has intangible value and economic research can show the development of business and public policies. The labor market must be understood in relation to artificial intelligences and metaverses. The phygital transformation in industry 5.0 needs a lot of studies.

Business 5.0 management and business plans need research to verify to what extent there are disruptive innovations with which types of technologies and whether the life of society and (cyber) society has improved. Palermo (2023, p. 3) wrote that the premise of conscious capitalism is that companies need to look for ways to make a profit while doing business, however it is necessary to consider the social, environmental, and cultural well-being of employees and society. It is believed to be an effective way to maximize long-term profits.

Business 5.0 and 6.0 still has little research, whether in manufacturing systems, company automation, sustainable production, cyber-physical systems or metaverses that transform the concept of brands. Artificial intelligence is a topic that is focused on business in academic investigations, however it does not facilitate the reconnection with human nature, because working together with mechanizations requires the different computational vision that can be gained from upskilling and reskilling.

If the target is the consumer experience, investigations need to include the experience of employees so that no product or service is offered with human suffering. Developing personalized robots without critical thinking can unbalance the power of technology in relation to human desires. Even though the cyclical nature of business and paradigm shifts within brands are realities, research must move towards quantum advances, neural integration, autonomous and decentralized systems and immersive worlds for sustainable productions and that human beings are at the center of business power.

Pan, et al. (2023, p. 13) wrote that the quantum technology revolution is receiving attention in research as it has new advances and, with such advances, businesses are changing in a technological way. The authors wrote that quantum technologies are becoming the cornerstone and driving force in social development and if they are the cornerstone and driving force, researchers will be able to build studies that transform business in terms of infrastructure and in terms of humanization, after all, from the cornerstone, other stones were defined in the construction and the driving force transmits movement in the machines.

4. CONCLUSION

In conclusion, it is possible to state that the advances were many and that it is necessary to go beyond profit and have the participation of stakeholders for the creation of values in business 5.0 with the interconnection of interests, given that there is an interdependence of all business systems and winning means enabling common well-being for employees and consumers, as well as everyone who participates in the process in the company.

Business 5.0 is done by entrepreneurs and by (intra) entrepreneurs for society and for (cyber) society. An attempt was made to systematize disruptive technologies and innovations with the value of people and management in exploratory and bibliographic study. Although the evidence was of an economic nature, the recommendations are of human value for the management of disruptive technologies in companies in full physical transformation in industry 5.0.

The fifth industrial revolution shows signs, disruptions show changes in behavior with disruptive technologies. Organizations change structures and models, companies and startups are pivoting to transform, otherwise the business cannot thrive. The contribution of this chapter is in the concepts and theory gathered to show the business 5.0 revolution. It is noteworthy that research with public policies must take place to understand how governments are or are not subsidizing and supporting business 5.0 in nations economically.

In the introduction, the speed was in the transformations and existing opportunities for strategies and innovations and, in the directions for future research, quantum technologies were present for further investigations that could enable social advances, even though the demands seek the best experiences as consumers. From the introduction to further research, theories from the most different areas were revealed and, in the bibliographic study, there was an understanding that many areas must be present in academic research for business 5.0.

In relation to the objective of the chapter, the main innovations, and technologies for business 5.0 were highlighted from the perspective of application and recommendations in a bibliographic and exploratory study, given that academic investigations still present little theory regarding the main theme of the book. In business reports, immersive experiences are present and, by 2026, it is predicted that people will spend at least one hour a day in the metaverse. In relation to artificial intelligence, people who do not master the specifics of computational parameters will be replaced by human beings who know the software programmed by developers.

Throughout the research to write this chapter, new problems were discovered and the focus for resolution is on the studies of quantum computing, because the world of atoms and bytes were unveiled in the concepts and principles of the industry from the first revolution to the fifth transformation and the human being is not always included as an active agent of phygital change in academic investigations, nor are physical and mental well-being mentioned in business.

Future research into business 5.0 must enable technological developments and verify the nature of the human workforce, however, they must ensure that socioeconomic inequalities are mitigated with science, just as it is necessary to solve social and environmental problems through governance in metaverse and artificial ecosystems. Well-being for future generations are the revolutions to be documented for a fairer society, whether in reality or in augmented, virtual, mixed, or extended realities.

It was possible to notice that the terms written in the background of the chapter were not created at the same time, nor did they appear in the creation of the names. Both digital transformation and phygital transformation are the result of development over the years and over centuries, that is, businesses to become 5.0 or 6.0 needed legacies from researchers or inventors who created products that were perfected by many people. Users or consumers had to adopt and make adjustments until they appropriated a new way of including business models to improve the customer experience. Many stakeholders were needed to perform the businesses that people know, in contemporary times, as innovative or disruptive. Paradigms have been modified.

The publications found in the search on academic bases are concentrated in the area of Business Administration and need to involve more areas, after all, business and entrepreneurship change with business 5.0 and 6.0 and need to be more interdisciplinary for brands, given that the paradigms of modern business are not the same in the contemporary context. The speed of information is much greater, and technologies change exponentially to meet new experiences for both consumers and employees who, from a youthful age, are exposed to small screens and which include science fiction and immersive games in their personal lives.

The paradigms to be prioritized must have the human being at the center of management and leadership so that ethical dilemmas are resolved and the labor implications can ensure well-being and mental health with disruptive technologies as strategies for creativity and human communication for the human varnish to show that despite the acceleration of automation and the development of artificial intelligence capacity, the time available for humans to delve into data culture for business improvement.

The conclusion, in the report "The CEO's Guide to Generative AI What You Need to Know and Do to Win with Transformative Technology" (2024, p. 133), illustrated what companies should invest in: using decades of experience in creating technologies and the driving business transformation to help consumers navigate the unknown and then inviting stakeholders to create the coming and move forward together to (co) write future chapters.

REFERENCES

Ahmed, E. O. (2023). The Study of Software Engineering for Development and Maintenance of Software Systems. *International Journal of Intelligent Systems and Applications in Engineering*, 12(8s), 128–137. https://ijisae.org/index.php/IJISAE/article/view/4102

Almusaed, A., Yitmen, I., & Almssad, A. (2023). Reviewing and Integrating AEC Practices into Industry 6.0: Strategies for Smart and Sustainable Future-Built Environments. *Sustainability (Basel)*, 15(18), 13464. 10.3390/su151813464

Artificial Intelligence Coined at Dartmouth. (1956). Dartmouth. https://home.dartmouth.edu/about/artificial-intelligence-ai-coined-dartmouth

Ataman, K., Myhr, N., & Nistor, C. (2023). Disruptive Innovation as a Network Dilemma: A Conceptual Model. *Journal of Behavioral and Applied Management*, 23(2), 104–113. https://jbam.scholasticahq.com. 10.21818/001c.84555

Augmented Work for an Automated, AI-driven World. (2023). *IBM Institute for Business Value.* https://www.ibm.com/thought-leadership/institute-business-value/en-us/report/augmented-workforce

Chandel, A., & Sharma, R. (2023). Artificial Intelligence and Value Creation at the Crossroads of Industry 5.0: A Bibliometric and Content Analysis Discourse. In Dadwal, S. (Eds.), *Opportunities and Challenges of Business 5.0 in Emerging Markets* (pp. 58–78). IGI Global., 10.4018/978-1-6684-6403-8.ch004

Chawla, S., & Mehta, K. (2023). Cryptocurrency Adoption in the Era of Industry 5.0: Opportunities, Challenges, and the Intellectual Landscape – SLR and Bibliometric Analysis. In Dadwal, S., (Eds.), *Opportunities and Challenges of Business 5.0 in Emerging Markets* (pp. 240–262). IGI Global. 10.4018/978-1-6684-6403-8.ch013

Chen, H. (2010). Business and Market Intelligence 2.0. *IEEE Computer Society*. IEEE. https://citeseerx.ist.psu.edu/document?repid=rep1&type=pdf&doi=2a143d9d55854e0852a1401054b2fa12839987b2

da Silva, B. D. (2001). A Tecnologia é uma Estratégia. In Dias, P. (Ed.), *Freitas, C. V. de (Org.). Actas da II Conferência Internacional Desafios 2001* (pp. 839–859). Centro de Competência da Universidade do Minho do Projecto Nónio.

Dadwal, S. (Eds.). (2023). *Opportunities and Challenges of Business 5.0 in Emerging Markets.* IGI Global., 10.4018/978-1-6684-6403-8

Dadwal, S. (Eds.). (2023). *Opportunities and Challenges of Business 5.0 in Emerging Markets.* IGI Global., 10.4018/978-1-6684-6403-8

Dave, D. M. (2023). Revolutionizing Medical Device Implants: Unleashing the Power of Industry 5.0. *International Journal of Computer Trends and Technology*, 71(10), 1–11. 10.14445/22312803/IJCTT-V71I10P101

Diebold, F. X. (2012). On the Origin(s) and Development of the Term 'Big Data'. PIER Working Paper n. 12-037. https://ssrn.com/abstract=2152421

Edwards, C. (2022). Evaluating the Tipping Point of a Complex System: The Case of Disruptive Technology. *TechRxiv.*https://www.techrxiv.org/doi/full/10.36227/techrxiv.21126292.v1

Gartner Predicts 25% of People Will Spend at Least One Hour Per Day in the Metaverse by 2026 (2022). *Gartner Inc. Press Release.* Newsroom. https://www. gartner.com/en/newsroom/press-releases/2022-02-07-gartner-predicts-25-percentof-people-will-spend-at-least-one-hour-per-day-in-the-metaverse-by-2026

Gross-Gotacka, E. (2023). Integration of Intellectual Capital, Sustainable Development, and Business 5.0. In: Rzepka, A. *Innovation in Digital Economy: New Approaches to Management for Industry 5.0* [Translated by Jakub Prachowski] (pp.135-148). Routledge. https://www.routledge.com/Innovation-in-the-Digital-Economy-New-Approaches-to-Management-for-Industry/Rzepka/p/book/9781032469935

Gross-Gotacka, E. (2023). The Concept of Inclusion and Diversity as an Accelerator for Building Society 5.0 and Creating a Managed Organization in the 5.0 Era. In: Rzepka, A. *Innovation in Digital Economy: New Approaches to Management for Industry 5.0* [Translated by Jakub Prachowski] (pp. 62-72). Routledge. https://www.routledge.com/Innovation-in-the-Digital-Economy-New-Approaches-to-Management-for-Industry/Rzepka/p/book/9781032469935

Hussain, A. (2023). Developing a Model for the Adoption of Industrial Revolution 5.0 Among Malaysian Manufacturing SMEs for Sustainable Growth. In Dadwal, S., (Eds.), *Opportunities and Challenges of Business 5.0 in Emerging Markets* (pp. 40–57). IGI Global. 10.4018/978-1-6684-6403-8.ch003

Irmak, E., & Bozdal, M. (2018) Internet of Things (IoT): The Most Up-To-Date Challenges, Architectures, Emerging Trends and Potential Opportunities. *International Journal of Computer Applications* (0975 – 8887). https://core.ac.uk/download/pdf/286715999.pdf

Irons, B. T. (2020). Current and Future Applications of 3D Printing Using Custom-Made Material. [Thesis, USD]. https://red.library.usd.edu/honors-thesis/89/

Kankekar, S. S., Dadwal, S. S., & Ali, A. (2023). Investigating the Factors, Challenges, and Role of Stakeholders in Implementing Industry 5.0 and Its Impact on Supply Chain Operations: A Study of the Global Agri-Food Supply Chain. In Dadwal, S. (Ed.), *Opportunities and Challenges of Business 5.0 in Emerging Markets* (pp. 124–150). IGI Global. 10.4018/978-1-6684-6403-8.ch007

Khan, R., & Arif, Z. U. (2023). *Systematic Review of Disruptive Innovation (DI).* Research in Agriculture and Future Direction of Research. 10.1016/j.teler.2023.100079

Knox, J. (2022). The Metaverse, or the Serious Business of Tech Frontiers. *Postdigit Sci Educ*, 4(2), 207–215. 10.1007/s42438-022-00300-9

Kumar, R. (2023). India-ASEAN Economic Engagement: Challenges and New Lessons for Trade Integration. In Dadwal, S., (Eds.), *Opportunities and Challenges of Business 5.0 in Emerging Markets* (pp. 212–226). IGI Global. 10.4018/978-1-6684-6403-8.ch011

McCarthy, J. (2007). *What is Artificial Intelligence?* Stanford. https://www-formal.stanford.edu/jmc/whatisai.pdf

Meepung, T., & and Kannikar, P. (2022). Metaverse; Virtual World Challenges and Opportunities for Digital Business. *Journal of Economics, Business and Management, 10.*

Mengalli, N. M., & Carvalho, A. A. (2024). The Learning Experience and the Behavioural Profile: Artificial Intelligence, Upskilling, and Reskilling for the Professions of the Future. In Hai-Jew, S. (Ed.), *Generative AI in Teaching and Learning* (pp. 66–84). IGI Global. 10.4018/979-8-3693-0074-9.ch004

Mengalli, N. M., de Carvalho, A. A., & Galvão, S. M. (2023). Metaverse Ecosystem and Consumer Society 5.0: Consumer Experience and Influencer Marketing in Phygital Transformation. In Bansal, R., Qalati, S., & Chakir, A. (Eds.), *Influencer Marketing Applications Within the Metaverse* (pp. 33–56). IGI Global. 10.4018/978-1-6684-8898-0.ch003

Moenandar, S.-J., Beerends-Pavlovic, S., van den Berg, B., & Coughlan, G. (2022). A Brave New Internet: Hacking the Narrative of Mark Zuckerberg's 2021 Introduction of the Metaverse. *Narrative Works*, 11, 125–148. 10.7202/1108958ar

Mohammed Jamil, M. I. (2023). An Overview and Synthesis of Entrepreneurial Theories for Start-Ups and MSMEs in the Era of Industry 5.0. In Dadwal, S., (Eds.), *Opportunities and Challenges of Business 5.0 in Emerging Markets* (pp. 1–24). IGI Global. 10.4018/978-1-6684-6403-8.ch001

Pan, D., Ren, X., Zhang, L., Song, Z., Nie, Y., Zhang, L., Ma, M., & Han, D. (2023). A Disruptive Technology Identification Method for New Power Systems Based on Patent Evolution Analysis. *Electronics (Basel)*, 12(9), 2045. 10.3390/electronics12092045

Pang, T. Y., Lee, T.-K., & Murshed, M. (2023). Towards a New Paradigm for Digital Health Training and Education in Australia: Exploring the Implication of the Fifth Industrial Revolution. *Applied Sciences, 13*(11), 6854. MDPI AG. .10.3390/app13116854

Păvăloaia, V.-D., & Necula, S.-C. (2023). Artificial Intelligence as a Disruptive Technology - A Systematic Literature Review. *Electronics, 12*(5), 1102. MDPI AG. .10.3390/electronics12051102

Rzepka, A. (Ed.). (2023). *Innovation in Digital Economy: New Approaches to Management for Industry 5.0* [Translated by Jakub Prachowski]. Routledge. https://www.routledge.com/Innovation-in-the-Digital-Economy-New-Approaches-to-Management-for-Industry/Rzepka/p/book/978103246993510.4324/9781003384311

Sakız, B., & Gencer, A. H. (2019). Blockchain Technology and its Impact on the Global Economy. *International Conference on Eurasian Economies*. https://avekon.org/papers/2258.pdf

Sallam, R. L. (2011). *Magic Quadrant for Business Intelligence*. Gartner, Inc.https://in2015.in1.com.br/sites/default/files/magic_quadrant_for_business__210036.pdf

Sekaran, A., Dadwal, S. S., & Ali, A. (2023). Industry 5.0 and Environmental, Social, and Governance Initiatives in Supply Chain Sustainability: A Study of the European Fast Fashion Industry. In Dadwal, S., (Eds.), *Opportunities and Challenges of Business 5.0 in Emerging Markets* (pp. 151–171). IGI Global. 10.4018/978-1-6684-6403-8.ch008

Shaikh, Z. A., Hajjej, F., Uslu, Y. D., Yüksel, S., Dınçer, H., Alroobaea, R., Baqasah, A. M., & Chinta, U. (2024). A New Trend in Cryptographic Information Security for Industry 5.0: A Systematic Review. *IEEE Access : Practical Innovations, Open Solutions*, 12, 7156–7169. https://ieeexplore.ieee.org/abstract/document/10384336. 10.1109/ACCESS.2024.3351485

Siddiqui, W. A. (2023). Design and Fabrication of FPV Racing Drone. *Journal of Mechanical and Construction Engineering*. .10.54060/a2zjournals.jmce.38

Sikder, M. R. (2023). Integrating Circular Economy and Industry 5.0 for Sustainable Supply Chain Management in the Food Industry. *Supply Chain Insider, 9*(1). https://supplychaininsider.org/ojs/index.php/home/article/view/73

Sims, P. (1987). *Basic Robotics Curriculum: An Introductionary Unit for Junior High School Students.* [Thesis, UNF]. https://digitalcommons.unf.edu/etd/52

Swati, K., & Brijesh, K. (2023) Application of Industry 5.0 in Financial Sector. *Journal of Business and Social Sciences*, (13), 1-7. http://eprints.intimal.edu.my/1822/

The CEO's Guide to Generative AI What You Need to Know and Do to Win with Transformative Technology. (2024). *IBM Institute for Business Value*. IBM. https://www.ibm.com/downloads/cas/BN9Y6QPN

The Economic Potential of Generative AI: The Next Productivity Frontier. (2023). McKinsey & Company. https://www.mckinsey.com/~/media/mckinsey/business%20functions/mckinsey%20digital/our%20insights/the%20economic%20potential%20of%20generative%20ai%20the%20next%20productivity%20frontier/the-economic-potential-of-generative-ai-the-next-productivity-frontier-vf.pdf?shouldIndex=false

Verma, D., Kansra, P., & Kumar, P. (2023). Significance of Blockchain Technology and Industry 5.0 in Indian Banking Sector. In Dadwal, S., (Eds.), *Opportunities and Challenges of Business 5.0 in Emerging Markets* (pp. 263–269). IGI Global., 10.4018/978-1-6684-6403-8.ch014

Yazici, A. M., Özkan, A., & Özkan, H. (2024). Meta: XR-AR-MR and Mirror World Technologies Business Impact of Metaverse. *Journal of Metaverse*, 4(1), 21–32. 10.57019/jmv.1344489

ADDITIONAL READINGS

Abuhantash, A. (2023). The future of HR management: Exploring the potential of e-HRM for improving employee experience and organizational outcomes. *World Journal of Advanced Research and Reviews*, 18(02), 647–651. 10.30574/wjarr.2023.18.2.0883

Asante, . (2023). Optimization of Consumer Engagement with Artificial Intelligence Elements on Electronic Commerce Platforms. *Journal of Electronic Commerce Research*, 24(1). http://www.jecr.org/sites/default/files/2023vol24no1_Paper2.pdf

Ashton, K. (2009). That "Internet of Things" Thing: In the Real World Things Matter More than Ideas. *RFID Journal*. http://www.rfidjournal.com/articles/view?4986

Chellappa, R. (1997). *Cloud Computing: Emerging Paradigm for Computing*. Informs Meeting, Dallas.

FGV - Fundação Getúlio Vargas. (2023). *Perspectivas para o Mercado de Trabalho e Renda*. Webinário. https://www.linkedin.com/events/webinar-perspectivasparaomercad7077615352418906112/comments/

Kim, T., & Kim, S. (2021). Digital Transformation, Business Model and Metaverse. *Journal of Digital Convergence*, 19(11), 215–224. 10.14400/JDC.2021.19.11.215

Mashey, J. R. (1999). *Big Data ... and the Next Wave of InfraStress*. UNENIX. https://www.usenix.org/legacy/publications/library/proceedings/usenix99/invited_talks/mashey.pdf

Palermo, S. (2023). Giving Behavior and Social Decision-Making in the Age of Conscious Capitalism: A Case for Neuroscience. *Frontiers in Psychology*, 14, 1073632. https://www.frontiersin.org/articles/10.3389/fpsyg.2023.1073632/full. 10.3389/fpsyg.2023.107363237057169

Seok, W. H. (2021). Analysis of Metaverse Business Model and Ecosystem. *Electronics and Telecommunications Trends*, 36(4), 81–91. 10.22648/ETRI.2021.J.360408

Zoox Smart Data. (2023). *Além dos Dados: Como Prever Tendências e Oportunidades*. Webinário. https://www.linkedin.com/events/webinar-perspectivasparaomercad7077615352418906112/comments/

KEY TERMS AND DEFINITIONS

Consumer Experience: In times of recommendations made by artificial intelligence in digital environments, time spent is usually mitigated in choosing products or services. Satisfactory experiences provide consumers with feelings of attention and dedication towards platforms that show behaviors related to psychological engagement and trigger observable attitudes through data to improve other consumption experiences. The recommendations, in computational systems, enhance behavioral engagement based on psychological involvement with the e-commerce platform. It is believed that the recommendation system made by artificial intelligence influences behavioral and psychological engagement in consumption. It is noteworthy that emotions do not end with purchases, because brands can, with or without data referring to engagements, modify the ways in which they relate to consumers in the transaction cycle and shopping journeys.

Employee Experience: In a time when mobility, social networks and phygital transformation are reinforced for work, the crossing of data and emotions are elements for analysis and interpretation. Employee experience has strategic value for companies and is part of organizational goal initiatives because they are remissive to the impact of experience on business results. By collaborators, it is understood that they (co) work for the advances of companies in the market, therefore, the experiences they have in activities and organizational actions reflect on productivity and assertiveness. Customer service and improved communication impact the experience of employees. The artificial intelligences will be part of the experiences and the data contained in the interactions are of an emotional nature and feelings.

Human Varnish: Term brought to the business area and linked to professions that need physical work or continuous use of computational resources that can be supported by artificial intelligence bases. Although there is social interaction to perform functions, professions with these characteristics tend, in the future, to have artificial intelligence to support or to perform most of the human function in the job. The professional in the area tends to be necessary regarding decisions involving elements that only exist in human beings.

Sustainable Career: Combines mental health, happiness, time management and productivity. Mental health becomes a public health issue when it is not reflected as a center of sustainability. Work activities can show harm to human life and careers need to be fully sustainable. The happiness element is present in studies that have conclusions about the contribution of happiness in the employee's professional life. Neural connections relate to health, well-being, feelings, emotions, and actions. The productivity represented by performance and deliveries is related to the management of enjoyment and work time. Sustainable employability is contained in the sustainable career, just as the sustainable career is at the intersection of mental health, happiness, and time management. Personal life influences the professional and the professional trajectory interferes in people's way of life.

Chapter 6
Entrepreneurial Development and Dynamics: A Comprehensive Review

Varun Mundhada
https://orcid.org/0009-0004-2952-8682
Symbiosis Institute of Technology, Symbiosis International University (Deemed), India

Gagandeep Kaur
https://orcid.org/0009-0004-2834-9850
Symbiosis Institute of Technology, Symbiosis International University (Deemed), India

Poorva Agrawal
https://orcid.org/0000-0001-6720-9608
Symbiosis Institute of Technology, Symbiosis International University (Deemed), India

Suhashini Awadhesh Chaurasia
https://orcid.org/0000-0002-7443-0105
Rashtrasant Tukadoji Maharaj Nagpur University, India

Satyam Kalihari
Symbiosis Institute of Technology, Symbiosis International University (Deemed), India

Vladlen Jayden Rebello
Symbiosis Institute of Technology, Symbiosis International University (Deemed), India

P. D. Shobhane
Symbiosis Institute of Technology, Symbiosis International University (Deemed), India

Latika Pinjarkar
Symbiosis Institute of Technology, Symbiosis International University (Deemed), India

Shruti Maheshwari
Symbiosis Institute of Technology, Symbiosis International University (Deemed), India

Sumukh Chourasia
Symbiosis Institute of Technology, Symbiosis International University (Deemed), India

ABSTRACT

The chapter explores entrepreneurial dynamics and development area. An exploration of entrepreneurial forms: social, scalable, large-scale, and small-business enterprises, accompanied by an up-to-date analysis of country-level startup activities as of 2023. The coexistence of technology and entrepreneurship education is examined, with a specific focus on the symbiotic relationship between digital technology and AI collaboration. The study investigates the dynamics of the entrepreneurial ecosystem and elucidates the evolving characteristics of small businesses. The chapter also addresses various dimensions of

DOI: 10.4018/978-1-6684-7840-0.ch006

franchising model, encompassing perspectives of both franchisors and franchisees and as the multi-unit aspects of this entrepreneurial paradigm. An exhaustive exploration is conducted into pivotal interplay between digital leadership of an entrepreneur and digital success of an entrepreneurial teams, focusing on the role that technological innovation and absorptive capacity play.

1. INTRODUCTION

An economy's resilience and capacity for good change can both be greatly enhanced by entrepreneurship. The efficacy of an economy is markedly influenced by one's adeptness in initiating and overseeing a personal enterprise. Recent research indicates that engaging in entrepreneurship can substantively contribute to both national prosperity and individual welfare. It revolves around the conception of novel ideas with the overarching objective of ameliorating societal conditions. Entrepreneurship not only holds the capacity to influence economic dimensions but also exerts an impact on cognitive and emotional states. Corporate entrepreneurship, social entrepreneurship, and sustainable entrepreneurship stand as noteworthy manifestations within the spectrum of entrepreneurial activities (S. Avelar, 2024).

The rising prominence of sustainable entrepreneurship and environmentally and socially conscious businesses is evident. Such enterprises prioritize not only financial gains but also aim to contribute positively to societal well-being. In order to adequately address current global challenges, it is necessary to look at this emerging paradigm in business practices from a multidisciplinary perspective, which has the potential to lead to innovative solutions. Nevertheless, divergent perspectives exist within the academic discourse, with varying studies offering distinct viewpoints on the efficacy of these businesses in enhancing societal welfare (A. Bonfanti, 2004).

Entrepreneurship, as a multifaceted domain, encompasses the creation of novel ventures with a pronounced emphasis on specific determinants. The advancement of entrepreneurship development has been instrumental in catalyzing the formulation of business plans and entrepreneurial initiatives, especially among students. Concurrently, it has played a pivotal role in cultivating a more inclusive and participatory environment. This inclusive approach extends to nurturing students' creativity, fostering active citizenship, elevating learning outcomes, engaging stakeholders, demystifying career options, and augmenting overall employability (D. Hyams-Ssekasi, 2022).

Business today faces numerous challenges, which necessitate the effective management of natural resources and the placement of entrepreneurial strategies. The entrepreneurial process assumes a pivotal role in cultivating innovation, discerning diverse market opportunities, and strategically guiding a company toward sustained success. The profound relevance of the entrepreneurial approach is underscored by its capacity to empower entrepreneurs in addressing intricate challenges associated with resource extraction, environmental conservation, and economic advancement. Given the indispensability of natural resources to business operations, meticulous handling of these resources becomes imperative for the viability and continuity of most enterprises (R. Regmi, 2023).

Academic institutions are increasingly investigating innovative methodologies to enhance the entrepreneurial decision-making capabilities of their students. Research indicates that the cultivation of entrepreneurship is paramount for students to develop an entrepreneurial orientation. A comprehensive understanding of the intricate connections between students' characteristics and their awareness of entrepreneurship support programs sponsored by universities necessitates further research (M.J. Mustafa, 2023).

Entrepreneurship, a pivotal driver of income generation, involves the strategic realignment of existing production factors. Entrepreneurs explore innovative solutions, undergoing iterative processes to enhance economic viability. Scholars posit that the effectiveness of entrepreneurship in fostering economic progress is contingent upon well-structured institutional frameworks (N. Ahmad, 2008).

Figure 1 illustrates entrepreneurial activity, showcasing the entrepreneur's dual focus on forward-looking markets and resource utilization. This strategic synthesis, termed inventing, underscores the entrepreneur's capacity for insightful strategies. Operating within the dynamic business environment— encompassing industry, competition, and national economic structures—the entrepreneur is influenced by broader environmental factors, including political and economic perspectives. At the core of entrepreneurial pursuits is the objective of value creation, emphasizing the entrepreneur's role as a creator and innovator in the nexus of markets, resources, and environmental influences(E. Stan, 2011).

Figure 1. Entrepreneurial Activity in the Commercial Environment

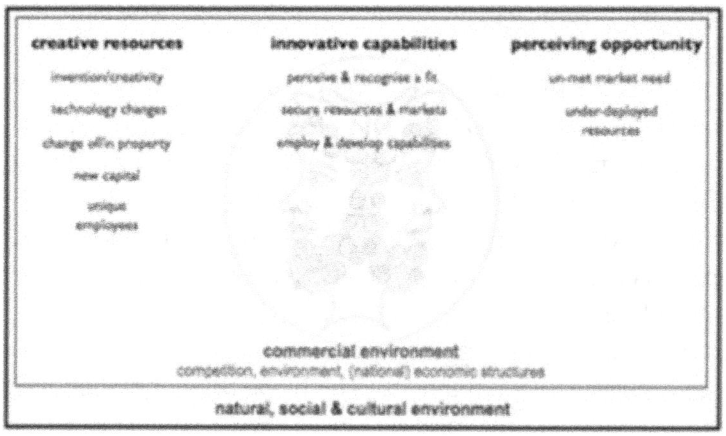

2. TYPES OF ENTREPRENEURSHIP

2.1 Traditional Entrepreneurship

Everybody has a different idea of the kind of business they want to start and a different set of objectives. Some people find that success comes from hard work, while others find success comes from having enough money. Some business owners prioritize social good over other considerations.

Finding the kind of entrepreneurship, a company practices is pivotal in assessing its compatibility with prospective employees. The type of entrepreneurship not only shapes the organizational working environment but also delineates the attributes of the entrepreneur. Consequently, aligning one's career aspirations with the nature of entrepreneurship is crucial. For instance, pursuing a role in social entrepreneurship or imitation may not align with working for an organization that champions innovation and creativity. Companies that embrace cutting-edge technology or embody creative entrepreneurship may prove to be the ideal workplace for individuals seeking a dynamic and innovative professional milieu.

In contemporary times, a predominant proportion of businesses are classified as small enterprises. Constituting 99.7% of all companies in the United States, these small businesses play a pivotal role in employing 50% of the non-governmental workforce. Typically operating on modest profit margins sufficient for sustaining owners and their families, small businesses often encounter challenges in securing venture capital, relying predominantly on financial support from family, friends, or small business loans. Small businesses span a variety of professions, including hairdressers, electricians, grocery stores, carpenters, consultants, plumbers, etc.

2.2 Scalable Startup Entrepreneurship

In this form of entrepreneurship, individuals initiate their own companies with a strong belief that their vision has the potential to create a global impact. They secure financial support from venture capitalists and aim to recruit top-notch talent. Their primary objective is to identify a business model that can be expanded and replicated successfully. When they reach this milestone, venture capitalists will be required to provide additional funding for their business growth. Since they require significant risk capital and promise significant returns, scalable startups account for only a small proportion of all companies. Among the most notable scalable startups are Facebook, Instagram, and online electronics retailers.

2.3 Large Company Entrepreneurship

Entrepreneurship within large corporations involves enduring innovation, wherein these companies create new products based on variations of their core offerings. These novel products are designed to align with evolving customer demands and technological advancements. Frequently, these companies achieve this by forming partnerships or acquiring innovative firms. Notable instances of large corporate entrepreneurship can be observed in companies like Google, Microsoft, and Samsung (E. Stam, 2011).

2.4 Social Entrepreneurship

Social entrepreneurship involves developing products and services to address societal challenges and needs. Their primary objective is to positively impact the world rather than focusing on generating profits or accumulating wealth. Social enterprises can be for-profit, non-profit, or a mix of the two. Safepoint Trust, founded by Marc Koska, is an example of social entrepreneurship. This organisation is committed to redesigning medical instruments and introducing low-cost, single-use syringes for healthcare facilities in resource-constrained areas around the world. As a result of Safepoint Trust's innovative Auto-Disable needle technology, 4 billion safe injections have been delivered across 40 countries, contributing significantly to the global healthcare safety agenda (M.A. AI-Awlaqi, 2018)

2.5 Digital Entrepreneurship

It entrepreneurship is building business on the internet, providing services, selling products online, without investing on physical infrastructure. Some of the example of digital business are e-commerce web sites, online courses, social media WhatsApp, Facebook, Instagram, YouTube, blogs. These are good means of earning. Some features to implement digital entrepreneurship are as follows: planning, effective communication, adaptability, require knowledge, seeking new opportunities, technically strong entrepreneur, skills to work, learns from hindsight, requires grit. Apart from some features, there are some tips to become a good entrepreneur. These are: entrepreneur mindset, keep the expenditure under observation, plan and set objectives, develop sales and marketing skills, encourage employees, efforts to talk to other entrepreneurs etc (Vikrant Nangare, 2021).

3. TECHNOLOGY AND ENTREPRENEURSHIP EDUCATION

Emerging technologies such as Internet of Things, artificial intelligence, big data, robotics, and 3D printing have matured and are becoming more widely used. These advanced digital technologies have the potential to have a significant impact on entrepreneurship, businesses, innovation, and society on a large scale. According to our research, more than half of businesses that use Next-Generation Digital Technologies (NGDTs) do so collectively, demonstrating diverse approaches and rapid implementation across various business types and sectors. There is an interesting interaction between technologies like the Internet of Things, big data, cloud computing, and artificial intelligence, all of which generate large amounts of data.

Recently, researchers have explored the potential of digital entrepreneurship to address economic and social challenges in entrepreneurship. Noteworthy is the realization that entrepreneurship, when leveraged digitally, affords increased control, heightened influence, and a more comprehensive understanding of the underlying causes and implications of poverty, surpassing mere assistance (S. Si, 2023).

3.1 Integrating Digital Technology in Entrepreneurship Education and Enterprise

Educational institutions strive to benefit society by imparting knowledge, conducting research, and contributing to economic growth through technology-driven businesses or by fostering students and educators to establish enterprises. Entrepreneurship and enterprise education programs are designed to enhance crucial skills and competencies, yielding significant positive outcomes. Educational technology creates a curriculum that blends theoretical concepts with practical computer hardware and software applications, thus bridging the gap between students studying science and business and equipping them with the skills required for the modern workforce. The incorporation of modern technologies like robotics, artificial intelligence (AI), virtual reality (VR), and augmented reality (AR), presents creative teaching approaches that can be applied in business school and science and technology program curricula (A. AI-Gindy, 2022).

3.2 AI in Collaboration With Entrepreneurship

Within the educational landscape, Artificial Intelligence (AI) emerges as a transformative force, wielding tools such as virtual classrooms, AI tutors, intelligent boards, augmented reality, simulations, and robust data systems. While AI showcases the capacity to perform tasks once exclusive to human expertise, its broader integration into education prompts questions and concerns. This section explores the trends in AI adoption, assessing its potential to reshape curricula, teaching methodologies, and assessment practices, while also delving into its overarching impact on the teaching and learning experience.

Additionally, this subsection scrutinizes the substantial potential of AI in entrepreneurship education. It investigates the prerequisites for effective collaboration between instructors and AI, emphasizing the pivotal components necessary for seamless cooperation. This collaborative partnership is presented to enhance teaching strategies, inspire students, and foster increased participation, thereby contributing to the attainment of desired learning outcomes. The section concludes by asserting that, despite the initial investment, the incorporation of AI into entrepreneurship education holds intrinsic value. This value lies in providing personalized support without imposing constraints on individual choices and fostering overall student progress (A. AI-Gindy, 2022).

3.3 Entrepreneurial Mindset and Psychological Aspects

The success or failure of entrepreneurs is significantly influenced by the presence of an entrepreneurial mindset, a critical factor in entrepreneurship studies that corresponds to profound cognitive processes associated with entrepreneurial activities. Notably, in certain developing countries, insufficient business success can be attributed to a deficient entrepreneurial mindset. The cultivation of a business-oriented mindset involves a complex interplay of factors such as entrepreneurial education, attitudes toward entrepreneurship, and self-efficacy.

Entrepreneurship education emerges as a pivotal component in enhancing self-efficacy, encompassing tasks that include the analysis of business feasibility, the formulation of business plans, and the reception of peer feedback. These educational initiatives contribute to the development and reinforcement of skills and competencies necessary for fostering a robust entrepreneurial mindset among individuals engaged in entrepreneurial pursuits. Recognizing and addressing the multifaceted dimensions of this mindset is essential in promoting entrepreneurial success and sustainability.

Scholars emphasize the significance of cultivating an entrepreneurial attitude, considering it a determinant variable within the domain of entrepreneurship studies. This attitude pertains to an individual's response to information, events, and feedback concerning opportunities and encompasses an intricate interplay of feelings, thoughts, beliefs, and actions.. Recognizing the cognitive aspect of entrepreneurship is critical because it has a significant impact on the formation, management, and evolution of businesses. According to researchers, perceived self-efficacy is an explanatory factor that links cognitive processes with entrepreneurial attitudes.

Furthermore, the entrepreneurial mindset and attitudes are shaped by personal backgrounds and environmental factors. Researchers identify a bidirectional relationship between attitudes and entrepreneurial mindsets, conceptualized as an entrepreneurial image formed by interpreting these variables. The cultivation of a positive entrepreneurial image involves the recognition and pursuit of suitable opportunities. Successful entrepreneurship requires specific mindset attributes, including a proclivity for risk-taking, opportunity-seeking, action orientation, continuous learning, and a broad vision.

This study makes significant contributions in three key areas. Firstly, it explores the underexplored relationship between entrepreneurial attitudes and mindsets within the existing body of research. It is imperative to devote more attention to studying entrepreneurial mindsets, despite the growing interest in entrepreneurship. Secondly, it examines self-efficacy, entrepreneurship education, and entrepreneurial attitudes across diverse regions, including Malaysia, Africa, India, and Indonesia, shedding light on less-explored contexts. Lastly, the study delves into the mediating role of entrepreneurial attitudes and self-efficacy in elucidating students' entrepreneurial mindsets, ultimately impacting their capacity to initiate new ventures (L.W. Wardana, 2020).

Figure 2 featured in this context brings attention to business categories based on size, maturity, or growth stage dimensions. Nonetheless, it is imperative to acknowledge that these frameworks exhibit limitations when applied to small businesses, and the text, unfortunately, does not explicitly specify these constraints.

Figure 2. Growth Phases of organization

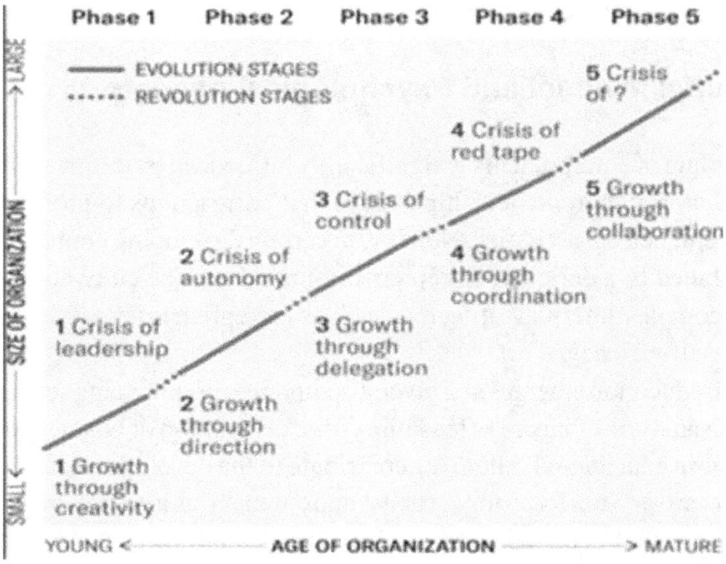

Figures 2 and 3 systematically evaluate previous business growth models, elucidating three principal shortcomings inherent in their design. Firstly, these models presume that a company must navigate through all developmental stages for success. Secondly, they tend to overlook the pivotal early stages of a company's formation and growth. Thirdly, these models predominantly rely on the assessment of company size solely based on annual sales, neglecting salient factors such as value-added, geographical presence, product complexity, and technological advancements. In response to these identified limitations, the authors have formulated a novel framework tailored for SM and burgeoning businesses. Drawing upon their experiential insights, extensive literature research, and empirical studies, this framework is manifested as a five-stage development model, visually represented in the below graph.

Figure 3. Growth Stages of organization

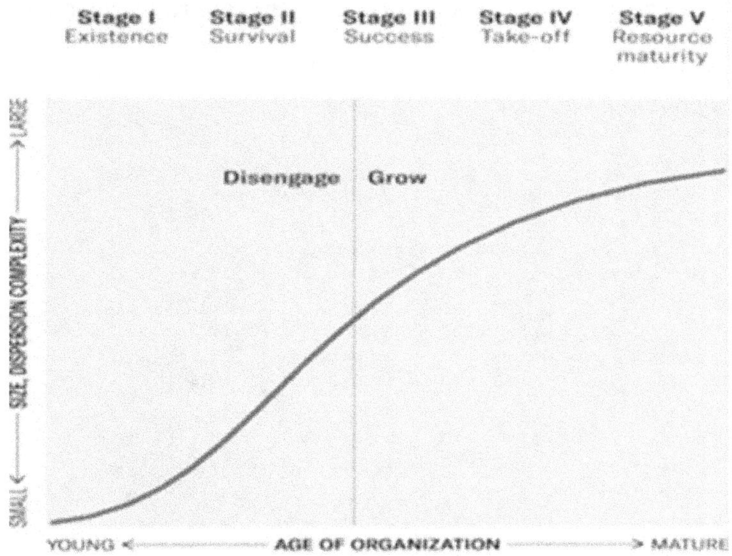

Figure 4 shows the characteristics of small businesses at each stage of development. Those steps are Existence, Survival, Success-Disengagement, Success-Growth, and Take-Off. The table includes information about the company's size, diversity, complexity, and the owner's involvement in the business. For example, in the Existence Stage, the company is small and straightforward, and the owner is involved in all aspects of the business. The company is large and complex in the Take-Off Stage, and the owner is less involved in the business's day-to-day operations.

Figure 4. Characteristics of small business at each stage of development

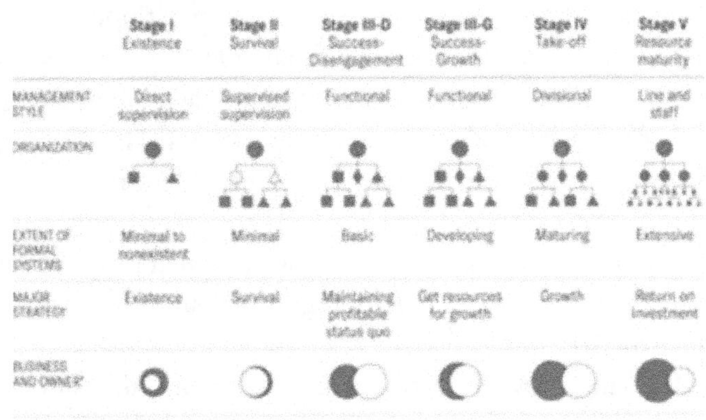

Figure 5 shows the possible paths of small businesses as they evolve. The exhibit has four stages: I. Existence, II. Survival, III. Success, and IV. Take-off. Each step is divided into two substages: -D (Disengagement) and - G (Growth). The arrows show the possible transitions between stages. For example, a company in Stage I can move to Stage II or leave the business. A company in Stage II can move to Stage III or return to Stage I. A company in Stage III can move to Stage IV or stay in Stage III. A company in Stage IV can continue to grow or experience a downturn and return to Stage III.

Figure 5. Evolution of Small Companies

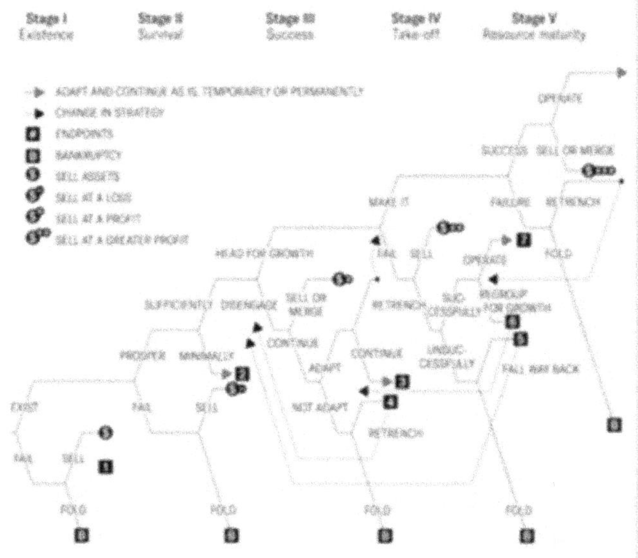

4. SMART TECHNOLOGIES AND TOOLS IN E-BUSINESS

Internet of things (IoT) is one of the new digital technologies used for the enhancement of any business. It has wide applications in various companies and one of the most important area is entrepreneurship. By integrating IoT based smart technologies, there will be dramatic changes in the company. It also provides many entrepreneurial opportunities for entrepreneurs to develop new business ideas. Opportunity searching is the most important aspect of entrepreneurial process. This how any entrepreneurs identify innovative goods or services to enter in market by evaluating, identifying and exploiting opportunities (Mona Jami, 2024).

D2K (Data to Knowledge) is a visual programming tools which provides various layouts along with content mining. It also provides transformative strategies for building various essential hereditary calculations (Kanupriya Verma, 2019).

As per (Micheael J., 2001) the knowledge from marketing for any decision support system is provided by basically three main sources. The first one is customer knowledge from retailer, second consumer knowledge from the research of market and the last one is data provider for third party. Figure 6 shows the complete picture of various e-business strategies. Shared marketing knowledge from customer knowledge, supply chain partners from supplier to knowledge management and then to retailer. And end marketing decision support application which includes various parameters category analysis, shelf space management, product development, product promotion and customer relations management.

Figure 6. E-Business Strategies

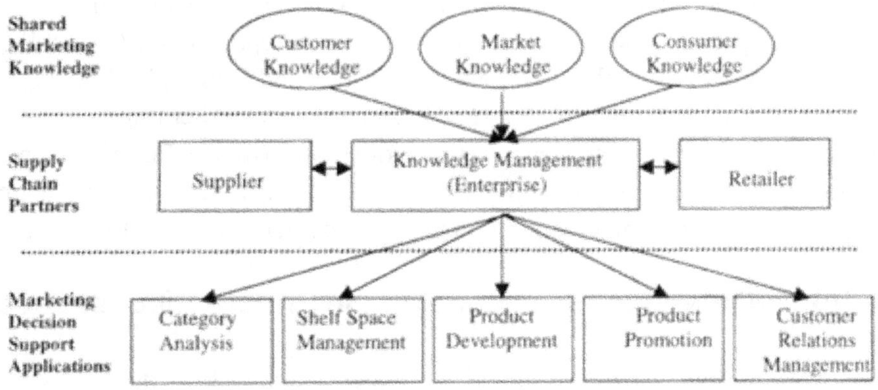

Artificial Intelligence(AI) in e-Business(Richard Fedorko, 2022): AI plays a vital role in increasing the e-Business for the entrepreneur. It creates new opportunities for various fields, exploring work efficiency, reducing costs, better decision making, improving product quality and optimizing human resource structure. AI assistance Chatbots provides 24 by 7 services to the customer. It is a virtual platform for providing free assistance facility to user. AI anchor for renewed news reader has been launched by various news channels In house studio news reading is done by these AI anchors.

Gig economy is one the good way to get the work done. It is a temporary positions of an organization which are filled by skilled employees for a period of time. It is the position which is meant for a small period of time. These are any person who are prominent in companies who handles short projects on hourly or contract basis. By using these type of gig employees companies get different skill based people to work for them(G.R. Preena, 2020).

5. ENTREPRENEURIAL RESILIENCE

Researchers have studied how entrepreneurs bounce back from challenges and noticed some of the problems. First, it only partially aligns with recent psychology research on resilience as an all-encompassing concept, focusing more on specific factors like optimism and hardiness. Secondly, one needs to fully understand entrepreneurial strength changes over time, which means the ability to stay emotionally and psychologically stable. Most research only looks at power at one point in time and needs to explore how it develops. For example, psychologists have identified two common patterns after a traumatic event or loss: one where people recover after a few months and another where they continue to struggle for years. There are also patterns in between these extremes.

Thirdly, the existing research on resilience focuses on successful and aspiring entrepreneurs, leaving little knowledge about whether stability is possible when business ventures fail. Given that, about half of new businesses fail within the first five years (P.D. Crner, 2017).

Entrepreneurial resilience has become a popular term in psychology and is being used in a variety of studies. The entrepreneur needs to be capable of handling many personal and market situations and disruptive events. The Resilient In addition to finding solutions for an unpredictable and difficult market, businesses see the bright side of bad circumstances. Entrepreneurs are remarkably resilient and may apply this to their enterprises because of how well they perform in challenging circumstances, how they overcome obstacles, and the informal organizational environments in which they operate. Because the information provided needs to be more accurate, entrepreneurs occasionally have to make better decisions or poorer decisions. Whereas Quadruple Helix and Quintuple Helix (Q/Q) models can offer multidimensionality and are relevant as a flag or a guide, many other things, such as institutional collaboration, training, and direction, are necessary to avoid these errors by fostering a knowledge-based entrepreneurial environment. As a result, entrepreneurs need to stay abreast of changing circumstances by modifying their priorities and implementing numerous other tactics (M.I. Hossain, 2023).

5.1 The Quadruple/Quintuple Helix Model in the Entrepreneurial Ecosystem

The research and development process described by Etzkowitz and Leydesdorff's is a macro-level model of innovation, known as the triple helix model of the knowledge production system, which encompasses government, industry, and universities. These domains include official and informal establishments particular to their respective fields. The government provides contractual relations that ensure stable interactions and exchanges; universities provide new knowledge and technology; and the generative principle of knowledge-based economies works in a triple helix as the center of production. This model has been expanded to include civil society (the Quadruple Helix model) and the natural environment (the Quintuple Helix model). These additional spheres represent external actors and factors that can influence the knowledge production system.

The Q/Q Helix model is more suitable for studying entrepreneurial ecosystems (EEs) because it considers the broader institutional context of EEs. Formal and informal institutions play a crucial role in shaping the entrepreneurial dynamics of EEs.

When civil society and the environment are included in the Q/Q Helix model, a Mode 3 knowledge generation system that is multi-layered, multi-nodal, and multi-lateral in nature is produced. In the dynamic and complicated EE, this model permits Modes 1 and 2 to coexist and coevolve.

By adopting the Q/Q Helix model, researchers can better understand the entrepreneurial dynamics of EEs and how institutions influence these dynamics (A. Cloitre, 2023).

5.2 Entrepreneurial Ecosystem

KISE (Knowledge-Intensive Social Entrepreneurship) events and entrepreneurial ecosystems have garnered significant attention from researchers, professionals, and policymakers. However, the connections between these two concepts have not been thoroughly explored. This section aims to bridge this gap and establish a conceptual framework for understanding how entrepreneurial ecosystems can prepare for and support KISE activities.

The ecosystem concept underscores the importance of identifying the critical elements of local entrepreneurial structures, their connections, and their impact on the emergence and growth of entrepreneurial ventures.

Nonetheless, KISE ventures exhibit unique characteristics that differ from the traditional framework of entrepreneurial ecosystems. These businesses involve a broader range of stakeholders dedicated to enhancing social and environmental performance and promoting sustainable transitions. Consequently, they face more challenges than conventional organizational forms that align well with existing institutions.

Recent research indicates that ecosystem configurations supporting KISE activities encounter distinct challenges compared to general entrepreneurial endeavors. This is primarily due to the lack of readiness within entrepreneurial ecosystems to address entrepreneurial activity's social and environmental aspects. Consequently, the conditions within entrepreneurial ecosystems have a more limited impact on fostering KISE events than nurturing innovative startups.

In summary:

A positive relationship exists between the Framework Conditions of entrepreneurial ecosystems and the emergence of KISE events.

The correlation between Framework Conditions and KISE events is weaker than the association between Framework Conditions and 'traditional' Knowledge-Intensive Entrepreneurship (KIE) activities (E.H. Siqueira, 2023).

6. FRANCHISING IN ENTREPRENEURSHIP

6.1 Context of Entrepreneurship

Historically, the discourse around entrepreneurship has primarily revolved around a manufacturing framework. Within this framework, the focus has been on examining the resourcefulness and innovation of individual leaders often referred to as “captains of industry.” These early manufacturing pioneers showed their capacity to develop novel products and inventive production techniques (e.g., computers and vehicles), serving as excellent role models for entrepreneurship. Research on manufacturer-entrepreneurs has also demonstrated their difficulties in running their businesses and the organizational changes they must make as they grow.

However, confining the conversation to the industrial sector limits the investigation of entrepreneurship to companies with highly centralized and productive output. The issues of regional distribution faced by the retail industry are very different from the fixed production process characteristics of manufacturing. This differentiation provides a unique context for exploring entrepreneurship in the retail and, more precisely, franchise industries.

6.2 Franchisor as a Retail Entrepreneur

The first sector to adopt franchising was the retail sector. Although the U.S. Department of Commerce (1988) indicated that the largest segment of franchising was for products like automobiles and petrol, business format franchising—represented by brands like McDonald's and Holiday Inn—distinguishes this organizational structure from other distribution methods. The heart of franchising entrepreneurship also beats in business format franchising.

Retail industry entrepreneurs have been creating new niche concepts at a rapid pace over the last 25 years. While some of these ideas—like video rental stores— are original, others might come across as copycats and require more significant ingenuity. However, even seemingly identical photos of already-existing non-franchise retail establishments, like photo-finishing shops, frequently acquire a competitive advantage by creating unique and effective operational frameworks that "industrialize" their service offerings. (as described by Levitt in 1983). Moreover, the entrepreneur-franchisors responsible for making these systems must invest resources in developing the concept and operational framework to allow for a seamless transfer to operating franchisees.

6.3 The Entrepreneurial Partnership of Franchising

Retail franchising goes beyond the basic idea of a single entrepreneur running a business. It's a collaborative effort involving the franchisor (the company offering the franchise) and the franchisee (the individual running the franchise). This partnership requires a more complex entrepreneurial role from both parties.

Traditional retail businesses rely on physical customer presence. Customers consider the cost and distance they need to travel to a store, so the location is crucial for attracting shoppers. To grow, retailers must open new stores because each site can only serve a limited customer base.

6.4 The Franchisee as an Entrepreneur

In economics, two distinct viewpoints have emerged to explain why franchising exists, and both have relevance when discussing entrepreneurship. The first perspective is the capital acquisition model, which contends that retail businesses seeking to grow can effectively obtain financial capital from franchisees. This concept has been debated in the literature, but it aligns with the idea of an entrepreneurial partnership. In this partnership, while the franchisor invests in developing the brand, the franchisee invests in developing local markets. Often, franchisees have a better understanding of their local markets, making them more suitable to take on the risks associated with introducing the franchisor's concept to new and untested territories. Additionally, since franchisors often rely on franchisees' local expertise and contacts, they must create unique marketing strategies that adapt to their specific environment.

6.5 Multi-Unit Franchisee

One of the fascinating aspects of franchising is the common occurrence of multiunit franchisees. This means franchisees can own multiple outlets by gradually acquiring more units after starting with just one or by securing area development rights to build a network of stores in an exclusive territory. Considering how these two forms of multi-unit ownership differ and are similar raises interesting entrepreneurship research questions.

Conversely, as a franchisee, you bear a lot more risk when you sign an area development contract, which can be pretty demanding, than when you buy the franchise rights for one unit. Another area of research that ought to pique the interest of mainstream entrepreneurship scholars is figuring out who these area developers are and how they determine the profitability of different franchise offerings (P.J. Kaufmann, 1999).

7. ENTREPRENEURIAL LEADERSHIP

The success of an entrepreneurial team's digital endeavours is closely linked to the lead entrepreneur's digital leadership, and this relationship is critical to the team's overall performance. Here are some key points that illustrate this relationship:

Digital Vision and Strategy: A lead entrepreneur with digital leadership skills is better equipped to set a clear digital vision for the entrepreneurial team. They can define strategic approaches in the digitalization field and align business plans accordingly. This ensures that the team's efforts are directed towards relevant and effective digital strategies.

Technology Integration: Digital leadership encourages the lead entrepreneur to stay updated on the latest digital technological developments. This knowledge is shared with the team, enabling them to effectively adopt and leverage digital technologies. This technical integration can lead to more efficient and innovative business processes.

Resource Allocation: Digitally savvy lead entrepreneurs effectively allocate team resources. This involves giving funds to digital projects and technologies with the best chance of success. The team's digital initiatives are supported, and this sensible resource allocation avoids waste.

Digital Culture and Learning: The lead entrepreneur cultivates a digital culture within the entrepreneurial team by Modeling digital leadership behaviours'. This culture encourages lifelong learning and flexibility in response to digital changes. Members of the group are inspired to investigate digital solutions, which improve innovation and problem-solving skills.

Error Reduction: Making educated decisions and minimizing errors are two benefits of digital leadership. Because of the lead entrepreneur's familiarity with digital technologies and trends, the team is more likely to make wise decisions and focus their efforts on more promising digital entrepreneurial opportunities.

Flexibility and adaptability are encouraged in digital leadership. Thanks to their expertise in that area, the lead entrepreneur can lead the team in adapting to changes in the digital landscape. The ability to change with the times is essential for long-term success as a digital entrepreneur.

Team Performance and Motivation: A lead entrepreneur with expertise in digital leadership can inspire team members by highlighting the advantages and possibilities of digital technologies. This motivation can improve team performance because members are encouraged to take advantage of new opportunities and support the team's online success.

7.1 The Connection Between the Team's Effectiveness on the Digital Front and the Lead Entrepreneur's Digital Leadership

In today's highly competitive market, organizations must adapt and embrace new technological concepts to transform their operations in the traditional way and different managerial practices. This shift in business operations has elevated the importance of digital capabilities alongside conventional leadership skills. This approach is called digital leadership, which combines leadership expertise with digital knowledge. Digital leadership also entails leaders formulating precise plans for significant digitalization procedures and putting plans into action to reach objectives.

Digital leadership is essential for organizations to stay up with the rapidly changing digital landscape when the digital mindset of the modern era is prioritized. Other studies have demonstrated the additional advantages of digital leadership for businesses, including improved innovation management, staff motivation, and the development of dynamic organizational capabilities.

In addition to changes in leadership, technological advancements have spurred entrepreneurship developments that give rise to digital entrepreneurial teams. These teams are made up of professionals with backgrounds in software development, marketing, sales, industry knowledge, and digital technologies. By consistently providing digital goods and services for entrepreneurship success, they collaborate to put strategies and operations for digital firms into practice.

Within these entrepreneurial teams, a lead entrepreneur typically assumes higher authority positions and significantly shares the team's operations, structure, processes, and outcomes. Due to their founder status, the lead entrepreneur has considerable autonomy in steering the team's direction.

Based on this study, lead entrepreneurs with skills in digital leadership are more likely to support their employees' achievement in digital entrepreneurship. The social learning idea states that people learn by observing other people. In an entrepreneurial team, the entrepreneurs mentor the other team members. They demonstrate digital leadership skills and approaches, motivating the group to utilize new tools and stay knowledgeable of technological developments.

Lead entrepreneurs with digital leadership also excel in developing business plans aligned with digitalization strategies, enabling them to guide the team effectively and allocate resources efficiently. These skills lead to well-planned digital entrepreneurship projects and creating a digital culture within the group.

7.2 The Ability of the Entrepreneurial Team to Innovate and Absorb New Technologies as a Mediating Factor

In today's digital age, organizations must bolster their technological capabilities to remain competitive in a constantly changing and uncertain environment shaped by technological advancements. To do so, entrepreneurial teams must cultivate their technical abilities, particularly in two key aspects: technology absorptive capacity and technological innovation capability. Technology absorptive capacity involves recognizing, integrating, and effectively applying new technology for business purposes. With the use of this capacity, businesses may introduce, integrate, and apply new technology while fusing it with their current knowledge base to produce useful results.

The ability to absorb technology takes precedence over other absorbent skills, such as understanding marketing, sourcing, or distribution, according to Becker, Peters, Nelson, and Wolff. With a high degree of technology absorption, new ventures are empowered to create new products, expand operations, and boost productivity. A technological innovation capability, on the other hand, refers to the abilities and skills necessary to understand, master, and improve existing technologies as well as to innovate new ones. To develop a technological innovation strategy, organizations must possess this capability across a range of critical domains, including knowledge, technology, adaptability, production, and experience.

Secondly, because of the digital era's interconnectedness and complexity, digital leadership is defined by the capacity for successful collaboration and communication, which is essential for working together with clients and staff to accomplish digital organizational objectives. In entrepreneurial teams, this collaborative culture is fostered by leaders modelling and teaching followers how to do the same. This learning process fosters ongoing cooperation and develops flexible tech-knowledge network structures at work, eventually improving technology-related capacities within the digital entrepreneurial team, including absorptive and innovation capacity (Y. Xia, 2023).

8. CHALLENGES, ISSUES, AND PROBLEMS

Some of the few challenges faced by many entrepreneurs are listed here (T. Vignesh, 2020).

- Developing business and Vision
- Business investment of start up
- Business team to work with
- Location to work
- Skill based employees

9. CONCLUSION AND FUTURE RESEARCH DIRECTIONS

The study addresses the varied terrain of entrepreneurship, covering both large and small businesses as well as startups. The report emphasizes several crucial points.

It might be hard to get accurate and up-to-date data for international comparisons. Because it is so specific to the situation, entrepreneurship requires careful consideration of many regions, sectors, and cultural contexts. While the combination of digital technology and AI collaboration is discussed, more research into cutting-edge technologies such as quantum computing and blockchain is advised.

The possible routes for further research are listed below:

Longitudinal studies: To learn more about how small firms have changed over time.

Cross-cultural analysis: To find out how culture affects the actions of entrepreneurs.

Quantitative analysis: To evaluate how success is impacted by technology's ability to absorb new information.

Researching franchisors' and franchisees' ability to adjust to shifting market conditions is an innovative approach to franchising.

Government policies effects to examine how they affect various forms of entrepreneurship.

Psychological resilience to investigate how entrepreneurs grow and preserve resilience under trying circumstances.

Impact of industry disruption: To comprehend how different types of entrepreneurships are impacted by disruptive industries and technology. To summarize the necessity of ongoing learning and adaptability in the dynamic business ecosystem is emphasized by this review. Promoting an innovative, cooperative, and resilient culture is essential to advancing entrepreneurial success in the future.

REFERENCES

Al-Gindy, A., Yasin, N., Aerabe, M., & Omar, A. A. C. (2022). *"Integrating Digital Technology in Enterprise and Entrepreneurship Education," in Technology and Entrepreneurship Education: Adopting Creative Digital Approaches to Learning and Teaching*. Springer International Publishing.

Avelar, S., Borges-Tiago, T., Almeida, A., & Tiago, F. (2024). Confluence of sustainable entrepreneurship, innovation, and digitalization in SMEs. *Journal of Business Research*, 170, 114346. 10.1016/j.jbusres.2023.114346

Bonfanti, A., De Crescenzo, V., Simeoni, F., & Adaui, C. R. L. (2024). Convergences and divergences in sustainable and social entrepreneurship research: A systematic review and research agenda. *Journal of Business Research*, 170, 114336. 10.1016/j.jbusres.2023.114336

Cloitre, A., Dos Santos Paulino, V., & Theodoraki, C. (2023). The quadruple/quintuple helix model in entrepreneurial ecosystems: An institutional perspective on the space case study. *R & D Management*, 53(4), 675–694. 10.1111/radm.12547

Corner, P. D., Singh, S., & Pavlovich, K. (2017). Entrepreneurial resilience and venture failure. *International Small Business Journal*, 35(6), 687–708. 10.1177/0266242616685604

Fedorko, R., Krail, S., & Bacik, R. (2022). Artificial Intelligence in E-Commerce: A Literature Review. Springer.

Hossain, M. I., Tabash, M. I., Siow, M. L., Ong, T. S., & Anagreh, S. (2023). Entrepreneurial intentions of Gen Z university students and entrepreneurial constraints in Bangladesh. *Journal of Innovation and Entrepreneurship*, 12(1), 1–34. 10.1186/s13731-023-00279-y36919091

Hyams-Ssekasi, D., & Yasin, N. (2022). *Technology and Entrepreneurship Education*. Springer International Publishing. 10.1007/978-3-030-84292-5

Janadari, N., & Preena, G. R. (2020). *"The Gig Economy and Workforce", Contemporary Developments in Human Resource Management book, I*. SSN.

Kaufmann, P. J., & Dant, R. P. (1999). Franchising and the domain of entrepreneurship research. *Journal of Business Venturing*, 14(1), 5–16. 10.1016/S0883-9026(97)00095-5

Michael J. (2001). *Knowledge Management and Data Mining for marketing*. Elsevier.

Mustafa, M. J., Chin, J. W., Nungsari, M., & Morris, K. J. (2023). Do proactive students benefit more from university support for entrepreneurship when choosing entrepreneurship as a career choice? An examination of Ghanaian and Malaysian students. *International Journal of Management Education*, 21(3), 100868. 10.1016/j.ijme.2023.100868

Por, M. J., Hosseinzadeh, M., & Moradi, M. (2023). IoT based entrepreneurial opportunities in smart transportation: a multidimensional framework. *International Journal of Entrepreneur behavior and Research*, 1355-2554

Regmi, R., Zhang, Z., & Zhang, H. (2023). Entrepreneurship strategy, natural resources management, and sustainable performance: A study of an emerging market. *Resources Policy*, 86, 104202. 10.1016/j.resourpol.2023.104202

Si, S., Hall, J., Suddaby, R., Ahlstrom, D., & Wei, J. (2023). Technology, entrepreneurship, innovation and social change in digital economics. *Technovation*, 119, 102484. 10.1016/j.technovation.2022.102484

Siqueira, E. H., Fischer, B. B., Bin, A., & Kickul, J. (2023). Entrepreneurial ecosystems' readiness towards knowledge-intensive sustainable entrepreneurship: Evidence from Brazil. *Technovation*, 126, 102820. 10.1016/j.technovation.2023.102820

Verma, K., Bhardwaj, S., & Arya, R. (2019). Latest Tools for Data Mining and Machine Learning. *International Journal of Innovative Technology and Exploring Engineering (IJITEE).*

Wardana, L. W., Narmaditya, B. S., Wibowo, A., Mahendra, A. M., Wibowo, N. A., Harwida, G., & Rohman, A. N. (2020). The impact of entrepreneurship education and students' entrepreneurial mindset: The mediating role of attitude and self-efficacy. *Heliyon*, 6(9), e04922. 10.1016/j.heliyon.2020.e0492232995616

Xia, Y., Liu, X., Wang, X., Deng, H., Han, C., Liu, Z., & Tsai, S. B. (2023). The power of role models in a team: The impact of lead entrepreneur's digital leadership on digital entrepreneurial success. *Information Processing & Management, 60*(6).

Chapter 7
Application of Chatbot and Artificial Intelligence in Business

Wan Syiffawiaam Alya'a Farhah Zulkiflee
https://orcid.org/0009-0007-9241-2027
Universiti Brunei Darussalam, Brunei

Mohammad Nabil Almunawar
https://orcid.org/0000-0001-5296-2576
Universiti Brunei Darussalam, Brunei

ABSTRACT

In today's fast-paced digital landscape, chatbots and artificial intelligence (AI) stand as a revolutionary advancement in the digital marketplace by not only offering more streamlined purchasing experiences and enhanced user engagement for customers but also strengthening the relationships between businesses. This report aims to explore a commonly used self-service tool employed by businesses to support customers at every stage of their purchasing journey, mainly known as chatbots. This 24/7 customer service tool revolutionizes user experiences and drives innovation in the business environment by virtually assisting customers every step of the way in their purchasing journey. The findings and discussion acquired through this study, especially in terms of future research areas, are extremely helpful for comprehending the functions to understand and enhance chatbot technology further enriching user interaction in the evolving business environment.

INTRODUCTION

With the rise of technologies and the Internet, it is inevitable for consumers to move online and join the herd of using their digital devices for their basic daily needs. Almost everything can be done online now, from ordering groceries to buying a whole KitchenAid tool and getting it shipped to your doorstep the very next day, even hiring a personal chef to cook the recently bought groceries using the new KitchenAid tool that was recently purchased. In short, consumers can find almost anything and everything on the Web with just the tip of their fingers but the question begs, "How often are their needs and expectations met during this purchasing stage?". While it's true that the Internet offers an endless option for products and services, the ease of finding these offerings and the level of customer information

DOI: 10.4018/978-1-6684-7840-0.ch007

vary widely. Customers may not always be well informed about all available options for a certain product or service, and they may not receive proper guidance during their online journey to make informed purchase decisions. This raises the question of how businesses address these challenges and assist their consumers effectively to ensure a smooth purchasing journey throughout.

The popular use of the Internet has become an essential component in everyone's daily lives and it has consequently resulted in a significant shift in the way people make their purchases today (Misischia et al., 2022). This chapter aims to explore a commonly used self-service tool employed by businesses to support customers at every stage of their purchasing journey, mainly known as Chatbots. With the advancements in technologies such as Artificial Intelligence (AI), the growing consumer preference for self-service is driving companies to adopt chatbots into their businesses. This is primarily due to the round-the-clock availability of customer support via chatbots, leading to reduced operational expenses in comparison to using real human assistants for addressing customer inquiries (Lee, 2020). Businesses are constantly refining their strategies to remain competitive amidst rivals offering similar products/services and the utilization of chatbots has emerged as a popular approach to maintaining relevance and effectiveness in this competitive landscape.

Recent industry reports indicate that over 80% of businesses are considering integrating chatbots within the next five years. However, numerous service providers are already incorporating chatbots into their operations to emphasize cost-saving measures and automation, partially replacing human service encounters (Hildebrand & Bergner, 2019). This trend may be attributed to the exceptional possibilities offered by chatbots, driven by artificial intelligence and machine learning. Furthermore, the increasing adoption of chatbots across various sectors is depicted in Figure 1 below, highlighting their growing integration in education, tourism, and e-commerce. This trend is projected to continue growing in the coming years. They can be utilized in various domains, including facilitating engagement with students in educational environments, interacting with visitors in tourism destinations, and assisting customers in online commerce (Selamat & Windasari, 2021).

Figure 1. Search results in Scopus

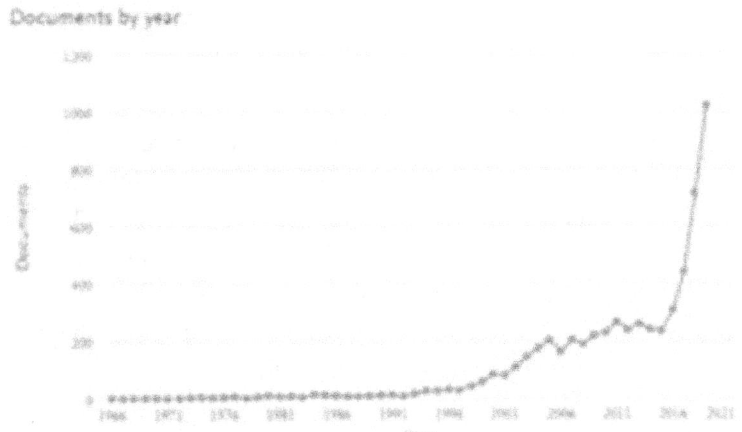

(Scopus preview—Scopus—Welcome to Scopus, 2020), from 1966 to 2019 for the keywords "chatbot" or "conversation agent" or "conversational interface", Source: Adamopoulou and Moussiades, 2020)

A chatbot is defined as an AI-powered service agent that engages in "natural" interactions with users to deliver personalized information. The term "bot" derives from "robot," suggesting that chatbots are programmed to engage in automated communication with users. On the other hand, "chat" implies conversing with users, either in place of a human or as part of a system that incorporates such a program (Selamat & Windasari, 2021). Modern chatbots are designed to mimic human-like conversations to such an extent that customers may not realize they are talking to a chatbot rather than a human service assistant (Selamat & Windasari, 2021)

According to the market forecasting agency Markets and Markets (2023), the chatbot market is expected to grow from USD 13.2 billion in 2024 to USD 49.9 billion by 2030, at a CAGR (compounded annual growth rate) of 24.9% during the forecast period. Figure 2 indicates the trajectory growth of the global chatbot market. This increasing demand is signified because trading products or services via the Internet is synonymous with speed, efficiency and a vast range of offers which inevitably translates into the convenience of consumers' daily lives. As people increasingly engage with digital platforms, businesses are compelled to adjust their strategies accordingly (Misischia et al., 2022). This adaptation involves expanding their service offerings to meet the needs of customers in the digital realm by integrating chatbots, powered by AI, to deliver a more comprehensive and seamless service that caters to the demands of the modern market.

Figure 2. Chatbot market global forecast to 2030 (USD BN)[1]

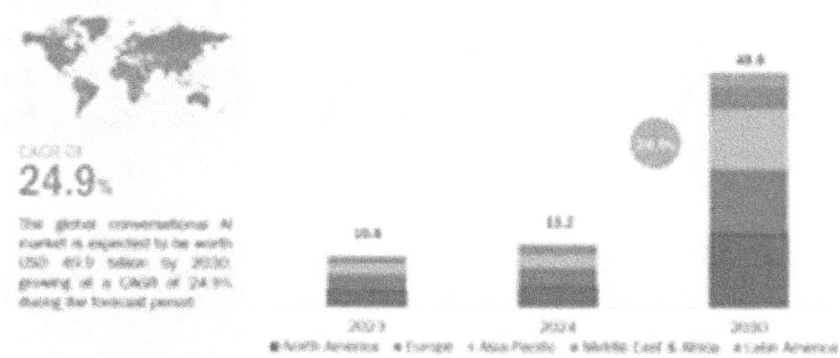

The rest of the chapter is structured as follows: The next section presents a comprehensive literature review, followed by an in-depth exploration of chatbots and AI. Subsequently, the following section will discuss key features of chatbots and the impact it has on user engagement. This is then followed by a detailed examination of their applications in business with a deep dive into real-life applications, providing practical examples of how chatbots are utilized across different industries, while also discussing the benefits of chatbots as well as the challenges they present. Finally, the chapter concludes with an analysis of future trends and developments in chatbot technology.

LITERATURE REVIEW

Chatbots have evolved significantly since their inception, initially serving the purpose of automating basic inquiries that are typically handled by customer service centers. In their early stages, chatbots operated on predetermined rules and simple keyword searches. However, with the advancement of technology in this day of age, modern chatbots have surpassed their initial intended use and now execute a diverse range of tasks that do not require face-to-face interaction. These tasks include facilitating processes such as delivery, returns, and cancellations, making reservations, processing job interviews, providing personalized product recommendations based on purchase history, and even handling complaints related to public services. This transformation highlights the versatility and adaptability of chatbots, which have become indispensable tools for businesses across various industries in streamlining operations and enhancing customer experiences (Lee, 2020).

Businesses are witnessing a significant shift towards online engagement as customers increasingly prefer digital platforms for their shopping and service needs. This transition has prompted fierce competition among businesses to deliver exceptional online customer experiences. Consequently, companies are now investing in advanced technologies such as chatbots and AI to address these changing consumer demands, with the objective to enhance their online presence and refine their customer interactions. Figure 3 below showcases chatbot usage among companies of various sizes ranging from micro-businesses to big businesses.

Figure 3. Chatbot technology adoption by businesses based on size (2022)[2]

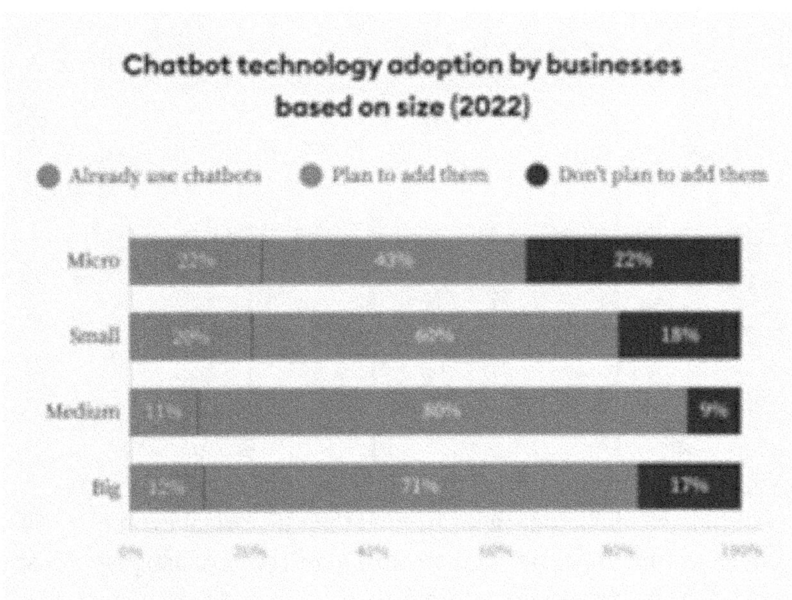

The capabilities of chatbots have evolved dramatically in recent years, enabling them to assist customers across various aspects of their online journey. Chatbots are also now equipped to read reviews, browse and research products, compare options, access discounts and coupons, facilitate purchases, track orders, and even reward customers with loyalty points (Selamat & Windasari, 2021). These advancements demonstrate the increasing sophistication and versatility of chatbots in enhancing the customer experience and streamlining business operations. Moreover, as consumers increasingly transition to the digital realm, businesses of all sizes are endeavoring to meet evolving consumer demands by implementing personalized recommendation systems, seamless online shopping experiences, virtual shopping assistants, and e-service agents integrated into their chatbot service (Selamat & Windasari, 2021).

These newly integrated AI tools were not widely popular in the early 2000s but have now experienced a significant surge in adoption over the past two decades, becoming almost indispensable on various business platforms. The inception of chatbots predates the 2000s by several decades. Dating back to 1966, the pioneering chatbot ELIZA, developed by Weizenbaum, laid the groundwork by employing basic pattern recognition to generate responses. However, the first chatbot was developed by Alan Turing in 1950 when he proposed a test to see if a machine could communicate so well that people couldn't tell it apart from a human, an idea that has led to the creation of modern chatbots that can have lifelike conversations with users. Since then, the chatbot industry has undergone a remarkable evolution, leveraging advancements in Natural Language Processing and Deep Learning, as seen in Figure 4 below. These technological advancements have culminated in the integration of sophisticated chatbot applications into modern business environments. For instance, ALICE, introduced in 2009, showcased the potential of Artificial Intelligence Markup Language (AIML) and surpassed its predecessors (ELIZA) in terms of speed and interoperability (Jwala et al., 2019).

Figure 4. A brief history of chatbots[3]

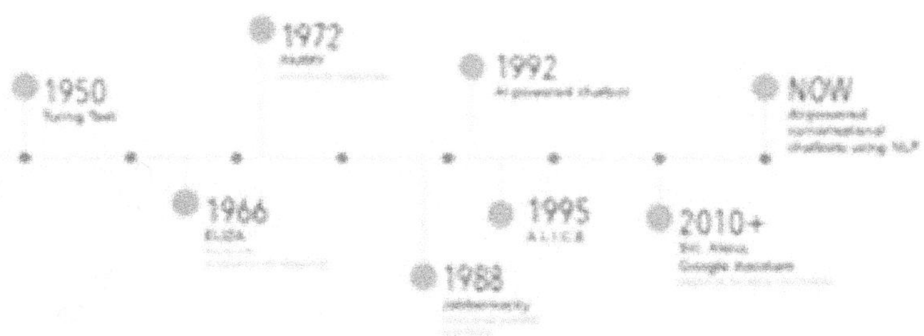

However, the significance of chatbots goes beyond their historical evolution. Modern research helps to understand the diverse functionalities and the different types of language processing mechanisms employed by these AI-driven chatbots. Recent studies have shown that the type of chatbot deployed can significantly influence consumer behavior and how they operate. For instance, research by Hildebrand & Bergner (2019) revealed that customers are more inclined to upgrade to a higher-priced car rental option when interacting with personalized chatbots compared to neutral chatbots or traditional website interfaces. Figure 5 below illustrates the significant impact different types of chatbots can have on consumer behavior and business success.

Figure 5. Willingness to trade up to a more costly car rental option depending on bot-type

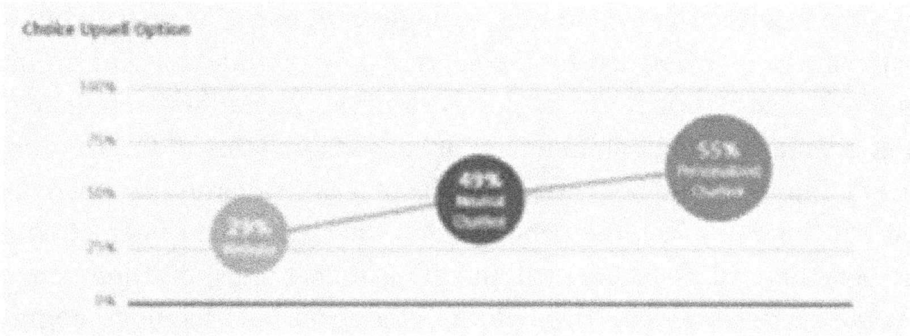

(Source: Hildebrand and Bergner, 2019)

Chatbots can be classified into different types based on various parameters such as knowledge domain, service provided, goals, and input processing/response generation method. Figure 6 showcases the different classifications of chatbot categories, providing a clear overview of how chatbots are designed and utilized according to their specific functionalities and applications. This classification helps in understanding the diverse capabilities and appropriate use cases for each type of chatbot.

Figure 6. Classification of chatbots

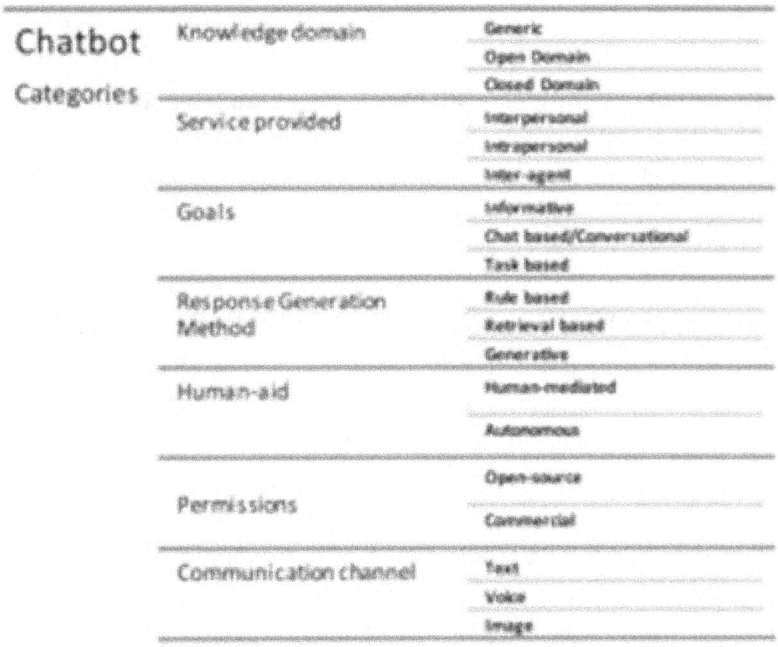

(Source: Adamopoulou and Moussiades, 2020)

Firstly, based on the knowledge domain, chatbots are categorized into open-domain, which are only capable of discussing general topics, and closed-domain, which focuses on specific knowledge domains (Nimavat & Champaneria, 2017). Open-domain chatbots offer the advantage of being versatile and able to engage in a wide range of conversations, but they may struggle with providing accurate or relevant information on specialized topics. Closed-domain chatbots, on the other hand, excel in providing precise information within their defined scope but may struggle with handling queries outside their domain.

Secondly, chatbots can be classified by the service they provide, ranging from interpersonal bots facilitating tasks like restaurant or flight bookings to intrapersonal bots integrated into personal chat apps to inter-agent bots facilitating communication between systems in IoT environments (Nimavat & Champaneria, 2017). Interpersonal bots offer the advantage of streamlining tasks and interactions with external services, but they may lack the personalized touch of human interaction. Intrapersonal bots, however, provide personalized assistance within personal chat apps, offering convenience but limited functionality beyond the app's scope. Meanwhile, Inter-agent bots facilitate communication between systems by enhancing automation and efficiency but they require robust integration capabilities.

Additionally, chatbots are categorized by their goals, such as informative bots providing pre-stored or fixed-source information, conversational bots engaging users in human-like conversations, and task-based bots performing specific tasks like booking flights or assisting with browsing (Nimavat & Champaneria, 2017). Informative bots offer the advantage of quick access to relevant information but may lack engagement. Conversational bots mimic human-like interactions, enhancing user experience but requiring sophisticated natural language processing capabilities. Task-based bots efficiently perform specific tasks but may struggle with handling complex or ambiguous requests.

Lastly, chatbots can be classified by their input processing and response generation method, with truly intelligent systems employing natural language understanding, rule-based systems using pattern matching, and hybrid systems combining rules and machine learning techniques (Nimavat & Champaneria, 2017). Truly intelligent systems offer the advantage of understanding nuanced language and context, providing more accurate and relevant responses but requiring extensive training data. Rule-based systems offer simplicity and reliability but may struggle with handling ambiguity or complex queries. Hybrid systems combine the strengths of both approaches, offering flexibility and accuracy but requiring careful design and maintenance. These classifications help manage user expectations and facilitate understanding of chatbot functionalities, enabling businesses to leverage chatbots effectively in various contexts.

UNDERSTANDING CHATBOTS AND ARTIFICIAL INTELLIGENCE

This section delves into the intricate mechanisms behind chatbots and artificial intelligence (AI), unraveling their profound significance in modern technology and applications. By exploring the nuanced functionalities and capabilities of chatbots and AI, this section aims to provide a comprehensive understanding of their roles in various domains, including customer service, e-commerce platforms, and beyond.

A chatbot is defined as a conversational agent that is powered by Artificial Intelligence (AI), designed to mimic human-like conversations. It utilizes natural language processing (NLP) algorithms to interpret conversations with users and generate organic responses (Casheekar et al., 2024). Figure 7 illustrates the chatbot workflow, providing a visual representation of the step-by-step process involved in how the chatbot interacts with users. From the initial user input to the generation of responses, the figure demonstrates the intricate flow of information and decision-making within the chatbot system. For optimal performance, users are encouraged to input accurate information and queries, enabling the chatbot to discern their intentions effectively and deliver the desired responses with precision and clarity.

This synergy between AI-driven technology and user input underscores the chatbot's ability to provide a seamless and user-centric conversational experience.

Figure 7. Workflow of natural language processing algorithm for chatbots[4]

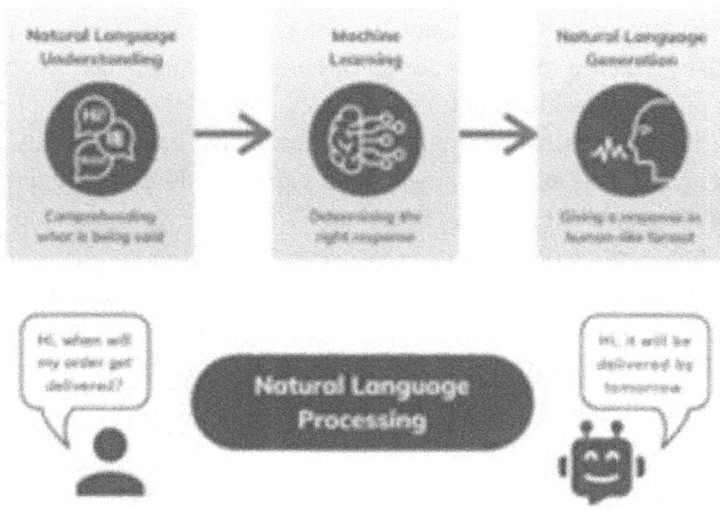

Chatbots are now also often integrated with Artificial Intelligence to amp up the functionalities and features. Before the rise of AI, the chatbot was merely a conversational program that generated responses based on predetermined rules involving keywords. Nowadays, the popular chatbot often utilizes AI technologies such as Machine Learning (ML) and Deep Learning (DL) to interpret users' requests and give out personalized human-like conversational experiences. These technologies enable machines to accomplish activities that have traditionally required human intelligence. It also utilizes AI to gather insights into preferences, behaviors, and trends. This wealth of information empowers businesses to tailor product recommendations, marketing strategies, and customer interactions to individual preferences, ultimately enhancing the overall customer experience. Table 1 below explains the various types of AI integrated into chatbots:

Table 1. AI technology used in a chatbot (Source: Choi & Nam, 2019)

Technology	Explanation
Natural language processing	Pattern recognition technology that can recognize and identify voices, texts, and figures.
Semantic web	Natural language processing technology that recognizes natural language and uses it for information search, automatic translation, and answering questions.
Text mining	Semantic web technology enables information to be searched from among data composed of characters.
Context-aware computing	Context-aware computing technology that can grasp the context of conversation.

Earlier versions of chatbots, exemplified by ELIZA, were limited to only text-based interactions. However, with advancements in technologies like Machine Learning, modern chatbots have significantly improved their conversational abilities. They are now equipped with features such as Recurrent Neural Networks (RNNs) and Long Short-Term Memory (LSTM) networks, enabling them to retain information from previous interactions. Overall, chatbots continue to evolve and become increasingly sophisticated, enhancing their utility and appeal to users. (Jwala, 2019).

However, the development and implementation of chatbots and AI in customer service are not without challenges. The absence of human forms of communication, such as voice and gestures, can heighten interaction problems, while emotional nuances pose additional complexities. Chatbots must be equipped with attributes like trustworthy personalities, active listening skills, and socially oriented interaction styles to engage users authentically and this can all be done by integrating AI. Moreover, the ability to convey empathy and foster rapport is crucial for building lasting relationships with customers and ensuring satisfactory service performance (Misischia et al., 2022)

In conclusion, understanding the intricacies of chatbots and AI is essential for businesses seeking to enhance customer service and drive success in the digital age. By leveraging these technologies effectively, businesses can streamline operations, personalize interactions, and ultimately deliver superior customer experiences that foster loyalty and drive growth.

KEY FEATURES AND IMPACT ON USER ENGAGEMENT

Figure 8. Chatbot capabilities and features[5]

Chatbots offer a multitude of features that enhance customer interactions and streamline service delivery in businesses. Firstly, they excel in providing fast and accessible information 24/7 round the clock, drawing from diverse databases to address customer inquiries promptly and comprehensively (Følstad et al., 2018; Quah & Chua, 2018; Chen et al., 2019). By providing immediate responses 24/7, chatbots meet customer demands for prompt assistance, thereby enhancing user satisfaction. Moreover, their ability to draw from diverse databases ensures comprehensive and accurate information delivery, fostering trust and reliability among users. This accessibility not only resolves queries quickly but also improves the overall customer experience, leading to higher engagement and loyalty. Chatbots facilitate interactions with users, enhancing their overall experience with technology by providing efficient and effective responses to queries and requests (Svenningsson & Faraon, 2019).

Secondly, chatbots offer convenience by simplifying complex information and interactions by utilizing efficient wording and providing options to assist customers in identifying their needs swiftly (Brandtzaeg, 2018; Følstad et al., 2018; Kasilingam, 2020). Chatbots simplify complex information and interactions, making it easier for users to find relevant information and solutions to their queries. This convenience enhances user satisfaction and encourages continued engagement with the chatbot. Additionally, by offering options and guiding users through the interaction process, chatbots reduce friction and frustration, leading to smoother user experiences and increased engagement levels. Chatbots help meet user expectations by avoiding trivial chatter, maintaining formality in language, and providing accurate and useful information, leading to a positive perception of technology and encouraging continued interaction (Svenningsson & Faraon, 2019).

Moreover, modern chatbots engage in natural dialogue by employing sophisticated natural language processing (NLP) techniques to understand nuanced conversations and respond with depth, sensitivity, and even humor, fostering a sense of interaction akin to human-to-human communication (Luo et al., 2017; Murtarelli, 2020; Schanke et al., 2019; Youn & Jin, 2018). The ability of modern chatbots to engage in natural dialogue while employing sophisticated NLP techniques enhances user engagement by creating a more personalized and human-like interaction experience. Users feel understood and valued, leading to higher levels of satisfaction and a stronger emotional connection with the brand or service. Moreover, the inclusion of humor and sensitivity in responses adds an element of comfort, further enhancing user engagement and loyalty. Chatbots recognize user tone and preferences, generating responses that mimic human agents' empathy and passion, thereby enhancing user engagement and satisfaction (Hu, et al., 2018).

Additionally, chatbots excel in providing personalized recommendations tailored to individual customer profiles by leveraging data analytics to offer tailored assistance and suggestions (Rese et al., 2017; Pantano & Pizzi, 2019). This personalized assistance enhances user engagement by providing relevant and valuable recommendations that meet the specific needs and preferences of each user (Selamat & Windasari, 2021). By delivering personalized experiences, chatbots foster a sense of loyalty and connection with users, driving repeat interactions and increased engagement over time.

Furthermore, they are adept at handling large volumes of data and automating tasks, further assisting in data management and communication processes (Luo et al., 2017; Ko & Lin, 2020) as well as reducing manual effort and streamlining processes. This capability enhances user engagement by ensuring efficient and timely responses to queries, leading to a more seamless and satisfying user experience. Additionally, automation reduces wait times and improves service delivery, further enhancing user satisfaction and engagement with the chatbot. Not only that, but chatbots empower users by providing access to information and services in a user-friendly manner, contributing to user satisfaction and engagement (Huang & Chueh, 2021).

Lastly, chatbots promote customer actions by facilitating various tasks during interactions, such as showcasing product catalogs, placing orders, and offering personalized recommendations, thereby enhancing customer engagement and their decision-making processes (Rese et al., 2017; Pantano & Pizzi, 2019). Users are more likely to engage with the chatbot and take desired actions when these features are seamlessly integrated into the interaction process. This promotes user engagement and drives conversions, ultimately contributing to the success of the business. Chatbots streamline processes such as ordering, consultations, and information retrieval, saving users time and effort compared to traditional methods (Leung & Wen, 2020).

In addition to the aforementioned features, recent exploratory studies have identified four key chatbot features deemed important for not only users but specifically small and medium-sized enterprises (SMEs). These features include responsive chatbots, simple action steps to trigger customer actions, humanized conversations, and personalized recommendations (Selamat & Windasari, 2021) and they are incorporated into chatbot prototypes and empirically tested on larger SMEs' customers. The results revealed that the featured chatbot prototypes had a significant impact on higher anthropomorphism, perceived enjoyment, and perceived usefulness compared to standard chatbots. Additionally, anthropomorphic cues in SMEs' chatbots were found to influence customer shopping intentions. The study done by Selamat & Windasari, 2021 highlights the importance of creating enjoyable and useful chatbot features tailored to SMEs' needs, as merely having user-friendly chatbots may not significantly impact customer usage and shopping intentions.

APPLICATIONS IN BUSINESSES

The integration of chatbots in small and medium-sized enterprises (SMEs) holds significant potential for enhancing customer interactions and service delivery. The study mentioned before, done by Selamat and Windasari (2021) emphasizes the importance of chatbots in facilitating customer encounters and relationships during the purchasing process within SMEs. They suggest that SMEs' customers place a high value on natural and casual conversations, indicating the need for anthropomorphic features to be carefully implemented in SME chatbots. Additionally, these chatbots should prioritize usefulness and enjoyment over ease of use, aligning with the preferences of SME customers.

Furthermore, Misischia et al. (2022) highlight several essential functions of chatbots that contribute to improving service performance and fulfilling customer expectations (seen in Table 2 below). Firstly, chatbots enhance service performance through functions such as interaction, entertainment, and problem-solving. They emulate trustworthy personalities, exhibit empathy, and engage in socially oriented interactions, resulting in higher-quality interactions and positive user experiences. Additionally, chatbots' ability to provide entertainment positively influences consumer attitudes and enhances service performance. Their problem-solving capabilities are particularly valuable in handling various customer inquiries and complaints efficiently, thereby improving overall service quality.

continued on following page

Table 2. Continued

Table 2. Determination of the chatbots' objective categories on scientific literature (source: Misischia et al., 2022)

Objective category	Customer-related function	Quality
Improvement of service performance	Interaction	Show language expertise, emotionality, openness, empathy, trustworthiness, listening capacity, reactivity, social orientation, and engagement.
	Entertainment	Improve customer's attitude through funny content.
	Problem-Solving	Support by information requests, search queries, complaints, returns, exchanges, refunds, etc. Store data for future requests.
Fulfillment of customer's expectations	Trendiness	Updates the user's current news about new products or emerging trends Capture user-related information such as interests and preferences
	Customization	Save and store data from conversations, purchase history and other activities. Prepares customize content

Moreover, chatbots meet customer expectations by offering trendiness and customization. Trendiness involves providing customers with up-to-date information about the latest trends and products, ensuring that SMEs stay relevant in today's dynamic market. Customization enables chatbots to deliver personalized products and services tailored to individual customer preferences, thereby enhancing overall customer satisfaction and brand loyalty. (Misischia et al., 2022)

In summary, the application of chatbots in SMEs enables efficient handling of customer interactions, fosters closer relationships with customers, and enhances overall service performance. By incorporating anthropomorphic features, prioritizing usefulness and enjoyment, and fulfilling customer expectations through trendiness and customization, SMEs can leverage chatbots to deliver exceptional customer experiences and stay competitive in the digital marketplace.

REAL-LIFE EXAMPLES

By 2025, it is anticipated that chatbots will power 95% of consumer online service interactions (Clark, 2020), playing a substantial role in generating $112 billion in retail sales (Williams, 2019). This prediction is supported by the current capability of AI-driven chatbots to address a minimum of 80% of standard customer inquiries (Suthar, 2020). Considering this trajectory, industry giants such as Alibaba and Sephora have already been utilizing this AI-driven tool to facilitate their sales. The two case examples below illustrate the success it has driven them to.

Alibaba

Alibaba, as the world's largest e-commerce platform, faces a monumental challenge in meeting the soaring demand for customer service while maintaining efficiency and scalability. With millions of active consumers and sellers engaging in transactions daily, traditional customer service methods are no longer sustainable. To address this challenge, Alibaba has turned to intelligent customer service solutions, with its flagship AI chatbot, AliMe, leading the charge (Wang et al., 2023). Subsequently, Alibaba experiences both pros and cons in terms of customer engagement, as outlined in the table below.

Table 3. Pros and cons of using AI or human agents in customer engagement in Alibaba (source: Yitong Wang, Offer Mintz, Depin Chen, Kehan Chen, 2024)

	Artificial Intelligence	Human	Examples
Pros	Faster and more accurate responses for cases with clearly defined questions and answers. Easily scalable, low marginal cost. High supply elasticity.	More accurate responses for complex and non-standardized cases. Useful when customers need to detail evidence of problems. Better understanding of long-tail problems not well defined by algorithmic rules.	Lead Time: For Taobao's Double 11 shopping festival, human services typically need three months for hiring, preparations, and training in comparison to ASI services that require only a one-day lead time focusing primarily on increasing cloud computing capacity. Costs: AI-based customer service costs less than 1 percent of human customer service.
Cons	Unable to handle complex scenarios with many rounds of conversation. Strong dependence on algorithms and training data. Weak emotional connection with customers.	Slower responses. Quality is highly dependent on personnel. Low supply elasticity. High cost.	Interpretability: AI-based bots need to be provided with at least hundreds of training samples; humans can read the question and (mostly) understand the problem. Number of interactions per customer: the current AI-based bot service is limited to two rounds of customer dialogue; humans can continue for longer customer dialogues.

AliMe, launched in 2015, serves as an intelligent human-computer interaction (IHCI) platform for both sellers and customers on Alibaba's e-commerce platforms. Powered by advanced AI technologies such as speech recognition, semantic understanding, and deep learning, AliMe can proactively analyze customer needs and provide personalized assistance. During the Singles' Day shopping festival in 2019, AliMe handled a staggering 300 million queries, equivalent to the capacity of 85,000 human service staff (Amanda Dong, 2020).

AliMe's capabilities extend beyond basic inquiries, offering a range of services throughout the customer journey. It provides pre-sales promotion by recommending products and facilitating transactions, automates tasks such as generating invoices and reminding sellers of inventory needs during sales, and offers post-sales support, including address changes and delivery reminders. Additionally, AliMe can understand customer emotions and alert human agents when intervention is needed, enhancing the quality of service provided (Amanda Dong, 2020).

In the short term, Alibaba aims to establish the AliMe bot platform, offering solutions tailored to different domains and infrastructure types. This includes AliMe Assistant for Alibaba's business, TiMi for Taobao merchants, and Bee Bot for external enterprises. These platforms provide comprehensive chatbot solutions, ranging from the user interface to AI capabilities for developers (Amanda Dong, 2020). Figure 9 explains the three domain solutions – AliMe, TiMi, and Bee Bot, supporting either one of the two types of infrastructures: SaaS, providing a complete end-to-end solution including the chat user interface, and PaaS, supplying AI interface capabilities for developers to build their systems.

Figure 9. Alibaba's domain solutions

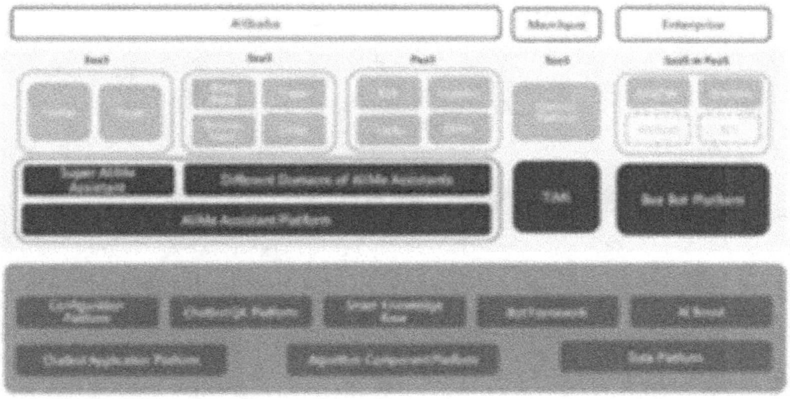

(source: Amanda Dong, 2020)

Beyond e-commerce, Alibaba envisions expanding the reach of intelligent customer service robots to other platforms it has invested in, such as social media, video streaming, and offline retail. This interconnected ecosystem allows Alibaba to seamlessly connect touchpoints along the entire customer journey, providing a cohesive and personalized experience.

However, Alibaba faces important questions regarding data privacy and the commercialization of individual data. As an internet giant with access to vast amounts of user data, Alibaba must balance its desire for monetization with corporate responsibility and respect for user privacy. Navigating these challenges will be crucial as Alibaba continues to leverage AI and chatbot technologies to enhance customer service and drive business growth.

Sephora

Sephora, a leading global beauty retailer, has embraced chatbot technology to provide personalized recommendations and enhance the customer shopping experience. With over 2,300 stores worldwide, Sephora leverages chatbots to connect with customers through platforms like Kik Messenger and Facebook Messenger.

One of Sephora's chatbots, operating on Kik Messenger (as seen in Figure 10 below), offers customers personalized beauty advice and product recommendations. Through a conversational interface, customers can take a quiz to provide key details about their preferences, allowing the chatbot to recommend the perfect products tailored to their needs. This chatbot not only suggests products but also provides beauty tips and reviews, mimicking the experience of interacting with a knowledgeable salesperson in-store. Customers can seamlessly make purchases without leaving the messenger platform, streamlining the shopping process. (Lee, 2020)

Figure 10. Sephora Kik bot[6]

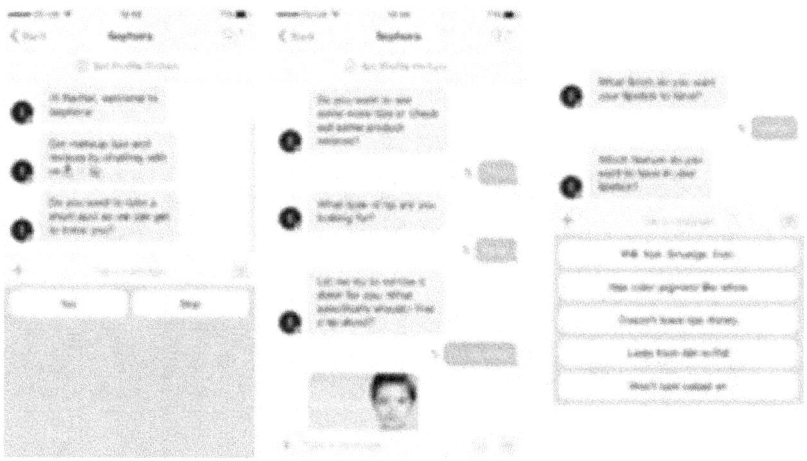

Additionally, Sephora has introduced innovative chatbots on Facebook Messenger to further engage customers. The Sephora Reservation Assistant allows users to book makeover appointments at Sephora stores using natural language processing. This convenient feature has seen an impressive 11% higher conversion rate compared to other booking channels, demonstrating the effectiveness of chatbots in driving customer engagement and conversions (Lee, 2020). Another notable chatbot developed by Sephora is the Color Match for Sephora Virtual Artist. This bot utilizes image recognition technology to match lipstick shades based on photos of celebrities, objects, or even the user's face. By scanning an image, customers can instantly access a list of matching lipsticks, facilitating informed purchase decisions (Lee, 2020). Both of these virtual assistant bots can be seen in action in the example conversation below.

Figure 11. Sephora reservation assistant and Sephora virtual artist[7]

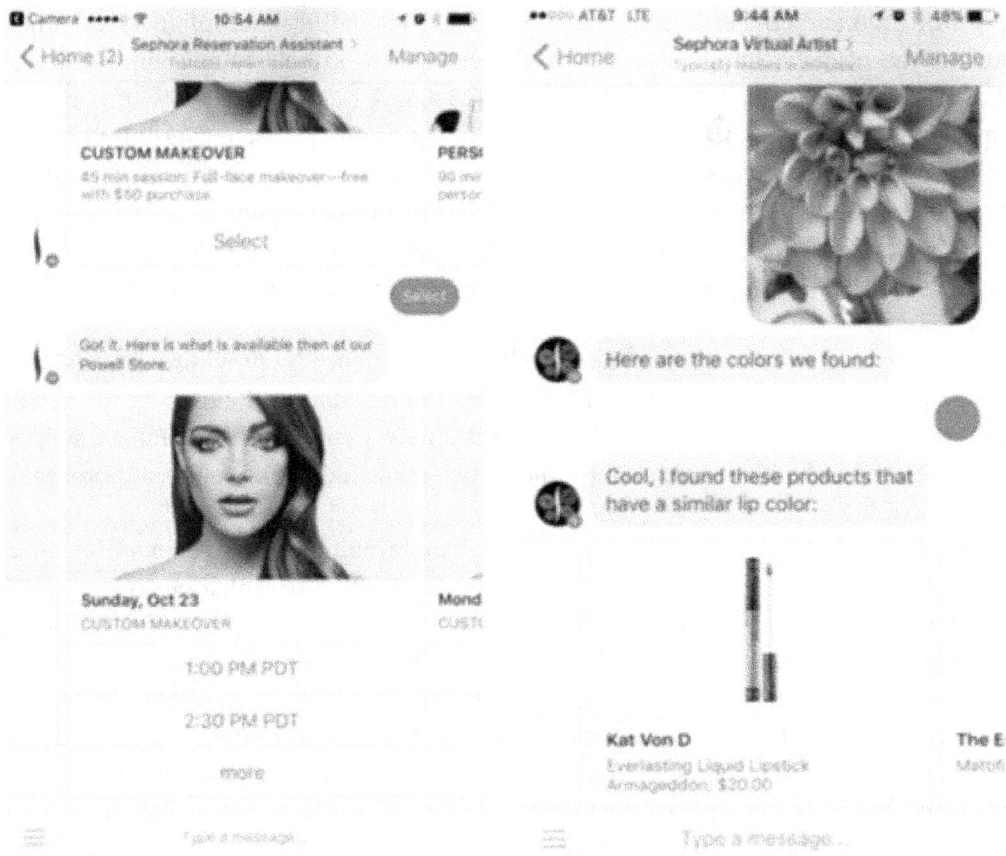

Overall, Sephora's chatbots exemplify how machine-learning-based chatbots can be leveraged to deliver personalized recommendations, streamline booking processes, and enhance the overall shopping experience for customers. By harnessing the power of natural language processing, Sephora continues to innovate in the beauty retail industry, catering to the evolving needs and preferences of modern consumers.

BENEFITS OF CHATBOTS AND ARTIFICIAL INTELLIGENCE

Chatbots and AI offer many benefits for businesses across industries, transforming customer service, sales, and overall efficiency. One of the key benefits of chatbots and AI is their ability to increase upsell potential. Studies have shown that chatbots with human interfaces can dramatically increase consumers' willingness to upsell premium products and add-on services. Since they reveal basic consumer characteristics, chatbots can better motivate consumers to buy more affordable products, ultimately increasing revenue for businesses. (Hildebrand & Bergner, 2019)

In terms of time and cost efficiency, chatbots excel by handling multiple queries simultaneously, thus reducing the need for human agents. They operate 24/7 without human intervention, providing round-the-clock support to customers. According to McGrath (2018), up to 80% of common customer service questions can be addressed by chatbots, leading to potential cost savings of up to 30%.

Additionally, chatbots increase customer confidence by providing instant feedback and personalized recommendations. Even when chatbots make objectively incorrect recommendations, consumers accept them, leading to higher levels of brand trust and acceptance of product recommendations. This increased trust positively impacts and supports brand perception, building long-term customer relationships. (Hildebrand & Bergner, 2019)

Moreover, chatbots and AI improve the overall user experience by providing fast and efficient support. A large proportion of common customer queries can be addressed, reducing the need for human intervention and saving both customers and businesses time. By providing personalized support based on customer preferences, chatbots increase customer satisfaction and facilitate repeat purchases. (Selamat & Windasari, 2021)

Furthermore, this technology enables businesses to handle multiple customer inquiries simultaneously without significantly increasing labor costs. This advancement ensures that businesses can efficiently manage higher volumes of customer interactions, especially during peak periods such as sales promotions or events. (Wibowo et al., 2020)

Chatbots and AI engage consumers by providing engaging and interactive ways for consumers to interact with brands. Chatbots provide a more immersive brand experience which leads to increased customer engagement and loyalty, particularly appealing to millennials. (Lee, 2020)

Additionally, chatbots use big customer data to derive information and provide more informed recommendations by analyzing customer interactions. Moreover, chatbots can identify trends, preferences, and pain points, enabling companies to make data-driven decisions to improve products and services and increase overall customer satisfaction. (Wibowo et al., 2020)

In summary, chatbots and AI offer many benefits for businesses, from increased revenue and customer loyalty to improved operational efficiency and data-driven decision-making. As these technologies evolve, they will play a more significant role in shaping the future of business services and customer interactions.

CHALLENGES AND CONSIDERATIONS

Designing and implementing chatbots present a range of challenges and considerations that stem from their anthropomorphic role, appearance, and interactivity. Firstly, determining the appropriate anthropomorphic role for a chatbot involves understanding how users perceive and interact with these digital agents. Whether acting as assistants, coaches, or co-workers, chatbots must navigate users' expectations and preferences to fulfill their intended roles effectively. However, users may have varying perceptions of chatbots compared to human agents, necessitating careful consideration of how different roles impact user experience and acceptance. (Chong et al., 2021)

Secondly, the appearance of chatbots plays a crucial role in shaping users' perceptions of their capabilities and trustworthiness. Striking a balance between humanlike traits and the risk of raising user expectations too high is paramount. Designing chatbots with a humanlike appearance may enhance social presence and credibility but could also lead to uncanny valley effects if not executed properly. (Chong et al., 2021)

Furthermore, interactivity is essential for fostering user engagement and satisfaction. Chatbots must be equipped with appropriate verbal and nonverbal cues to facilitate seamless communication with users. Achieving accurate understanding and appropriate responses, especially in natural language conversations, poses a significant technical challenge. Additionally, providing a user-friendly experience, particularly in complex tasks, requires careful attention to interaction design and interface usability. (Chong et al., 2021)

User characteristics and preferences also play a crucial role in chatbot design and interaction. Users vary in their tendency to anthropomorphize chatbots, some users may perceive chatbots as more human-like and attribute human qualities to them, while others may not and their desire for control over interactions, Some users may prefer more autonomy and control, while others may be comfortable relinquishing control to the chatbot. Addressing these individual differences is essential for tailoring chatbot design and interaction styles to different user segments. (Chong et al., 2021)

Moreover, the nature of the service provided by the chatbot and users' perceived risks can impact user perceptions and behaviors. These risks stem from privacy concerns, including the exposure of sensitive information, financial data, and other vulnerable data susceptible to online threats. Balancing transactional efficiency with relational rapport-building and addressing users' concerns about functional, financial, and data privacy risks are essential for fostering trust and acceptance. (Chong et al., 2021)

In conclusion, designing effective chatbots requires a holistic approach that considers the interplay between anthropomorphic role, appearance, interactivity, user characteristics, service nature, and perceived risks. Successfully navigating these challenges and considerations is essential for creating chatbots that meet users' needs and expectations while addressing potential pitfalls in implementation.

FUTURE TRENDS AND DEVELOPMENTS

The future of chatbots is poised for significant evolution and refinement across various dimensions, driven by emerging research trends and societal needs. As chatbot technology continues to advance, researchers and developers are increasingly focusing on enhancing the emotional intelligence of AI chatbots. Understanding the intricate relationship between emotion and agency beliefs in AI-chatbot interactions is becoming paramount. Designing chatbots to elicit positive emotions and foster a sense of trust and social bonding can profoundly impact user experience and perception of agency (Chong et al., 2021). Figure 12 illustrates the emerging trends and key developments that will shape the future of chatbots in the coming years.

Figure 12. Overall trends shaping the future of chatbots[8]

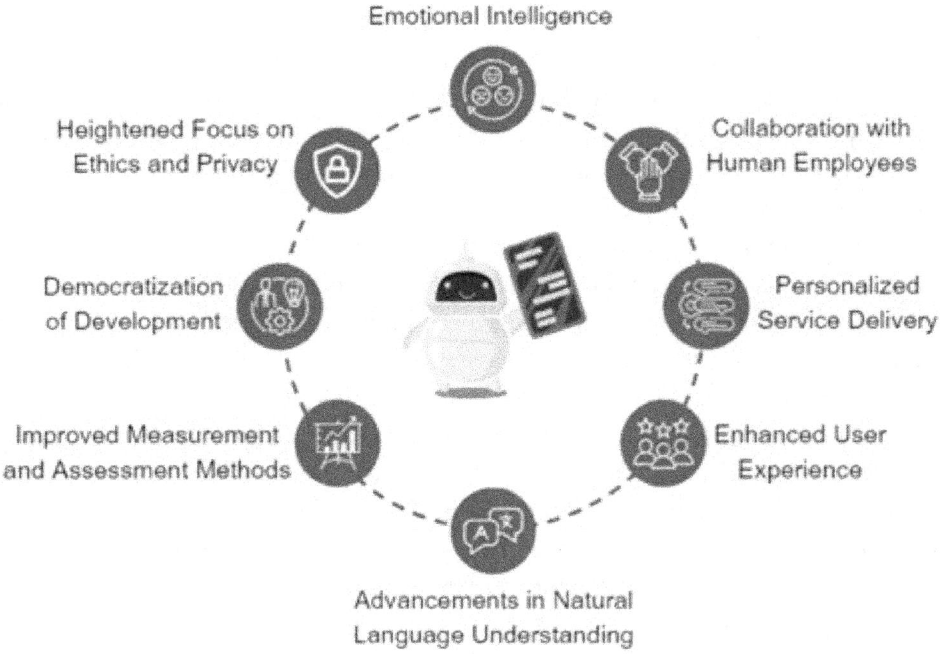

Moreover, there is a pressing need to address the proxy agency dilemma. As users become increasingly reliant on AI chatbots for critical tasks and services, there is a risk of overdependency. Research is essential to understand the consequences of this dependency and develop strategies to mitigate associated risks, especially in situations where chatbots may not be accessible (Chong et al., 2021).

Furthermore, the collaboration between AI chatbots and human employees presents both opportunities and challenges. Optimizing collective agency through effective communication and coordination can enhance operational efficiency in service delivery. However, potential negative consequences, such as increased work pace and decreased creativity due to reliance on AI-driven solutions, need to be addressed (Chong et al., 2021).

Personalization in service delivery through AI chatbots is also on the rise, but it raises concerns about privacy and transparency. Balancing the benefits of personalization with the need for privacy and transparency is crucial for building and maintaining trust among users. Future research will focus on developing solutions that strike this delicate balance effectively (Chong et al., 2021).

However, improving chatbot user experience remains a key area of focus as researchers need to address issues related to both pragmatic and hedonic experiences. This includes understanding user intent, engaging users over time, and translating theoretical insights into practical design improvements to consistently delight and engage users. (Følstad et al., 2021)

Additionally, measuring and assessing chatbot user experience will also be a significant area of research. Developing common definitions, metrics, and validated scales for evaluating key aspects of chatbot performance will enable researchers and developers to gain deeper insights into user satisfaction and process support. (Følstad et al., 2021)

Meanwhile, advancements in natural language understanding will continue to drive progress in chatbot development as more quality training data and techniques involving domain experts will be essential for improving dialogue management and context understanding. (Følstad et al., 2021)

Finally, research on ethics and privacy in chatbots will become increasingly important, particularly in sensitive contexts such as finance, health and education. Identifying and addressing ethical and privacy issues specific to chatbots, as well as integrating ethical principles into chatbot design will be crucial for building trust and ensuring the responsible deployment of chatbot technology. (Følstad et al., 2021)

In summary, the future of chatbots will be characterized by advancements in emotional intelligence, collaboration with human employees, personalized service delivery, enhanced user experience, improved measurement and assessment methods, advancements in natural language understanding, democratization of development, and a heightened focus on ethics and privacy. These trends will shape the next generation of chatbots and their impact on society.

CONCLUSION

The utilization of Chatbots and Artificial Intelligence (AI) stands as a revolutionary advancement in the digital marketplace that not only offers streamlined purchasing experiences but also enriched user engagement and fortified bonds between businesses and their clientele. This report has emphasized the crucial importance of chatbots in reshaping consumer relationships by providing ongoing virtual assistance and personalized engagements, while also improving operational efficiency by automating tasks that traditionally call for human attention. Moreover, the discussion on real-world cases from industry giants like Alibaba and Sephora vividly illustrates the tangible benefits of integrating chatbots and AI, spanning heightened productivity, efficiency, and convenience for both enterprises and consumers.

Nevertheless, as businesses embark on the journey of integrating chatbots and AI, strategic adoption becomes paramount to prioritize empathetic interactions with customers, ensure data privacy is maintained, and align chatbot features with the changing preferences of customers. Emphasizing these aspects ensures the need for businesses to consider the human aspect of technology implementation, ensuring that chatbots are designed to provide meaningful and personalized interactions that truly benefit users rather than mere tools of automation. Looking ahead, the trajectory of chatbots in e-commerce holds immense promise. The findings acquired through this study, especially in terms of future research areas, are extremely helpful for further enhancing chatbot technology and enriching user interaction. In essence, embracing these technologies is essential for businesses to remain relevant and thrive amidst the rapid evolution of the digital landscape.

REFERENCES

Adamopoulou, E., & Moussiades, L. (2020). Chatbots: History, technology, and applications. *Machine Learning with Applications*, 2, 100006. 10.1016/j.mlwa.2020.100006

Capacity. (2023). *Evolution of Chatbots*. Capacity. https://capacity.com/chatbots/evolution-of-chatbots/

AI Business. (n.d.). Case Study: How Alibaba Uses AI Chatbots to Serve a Billion Customers. *AI Business*. https://aibusiness.com/ml/the-alibaba-challenge-how-to-effectively-engage-with-a-billion-customers-

Casheekar, A., Lahiri, A., Rath, K., Prabhakar, K. S., & Srinivasan, K. (2024). A contemporary review on chatbots, AI-powered virtual conversational agents, ChatGPT: Applications, open challenges and future research directions. *Computer Science Review*, 52, 100632. 10.1016/j.cosrev.2024.100632

Chen, Y. W. O. M. D. C. K. (2024, February 14). Case Study: How Alibaba Uses AI Chatbots to Serve a Billion Customers. *AI Business*. https://aibusiness.com/ml/the-alibaba-challenge-how-to-effectively-engage-with-a-billion-customers-#close-modal

Choi, S. W., & Nam, J. H. (2019). The use of AI chatbot as an assistant tool for SW education. *Journal of the Korea Institute of Information and Communication Engineering*, 23(12), 1693–1699.

Chong, T., Yu, T., Keeling, D. I., & de Ruyter, K. (2021). AI-chatbots on the services frontline addressing the challenges and opportunities of agency. *Journal of Retailing and Consumer Services*, 63, 102735. 10.1016/j.jretconser.2021.102735

Cornell, J., & Cornell, J. (2024, January 12). 12 Essential Chatbot Features to Consider in 2024. Chat Blog. https://www.proprofschat.com/blog/chatbot-features/

Dong, A. (2020). AI chatbot behind Alibaba's $38 billion Single's Day sales miracle. *Digital Innovation and Transformation*. Harvard Press. https://d3.harvard.edu/platform-digit/submission/ai-chatbot-behind-alibabas-38-billion-singles-day-sales-miracle/

Get ahead start into the world of conversational messaging. (2023, July 22). Sinch Engage. https://engage.sinch.com/blog/ai-chatbots-in-e-commerce/#:~:text=AI%20chatbots%20can%20be%20great,leave%20with%20the%20best%20product

Hildebrand, C., & Bergner, A. (2019). AI-Driven Sales Automation: Using Chatbots to Boost Sales. *NIM Marketing Intelligence Review*, 11(2), 36–41. 10.2478/nimmir-2019-0014

Jwala, K. (2019). Developing a Chatbot using. *Machine Learning*, 8(1). https://www.ijrte.org/wp-content/uploads/papers/v8i1S3/A10170681S319.pdf

Lee, S. (2020). Chatbots and Communication: The Growing Role of Artificial Intelligence in Addressing and Shaping Customer Needs. *Business Communication Research and Practice*, 3(2), 103–111. 10.22682/bcrp.2020.3.2.103

MarketsandMarkets. (2024). *Conversational AI Market Size, Statistics, Growth Analysis & Trends*. MarketsandMarkets.https://www.marketsandmarkets.com/Market-Reports/conversational-ai-market-49043506.html

Misischia, C. V., Poecze, F., & Strauss, C. (2022). Chatbots in customer service: Their relevance and impact on service quality. *Procedia Computer Science*, 201, 421–428. 10.1016/j.procs.2022.03.055

Nimavat, K., & Champaneria, T. (2017). *Chatbots: An overview. Types, Architecture, Tools and Future Possibilities*. Research Gate. https://www.researchgate.net/publication/320307269_Chatbots_An_overview_Types_Architecture_Tools_and_Future_Possibilities

Sciendo. (2020). *Chatbot Technologies in Customer Service*. Sciendo. https://www.sciencedirect.com/science/article/pii/S2666827020300062

Sephora Bot. (n.d.). ChatbotGuide.org. https://www.chatbotguide.org/sephora-bot

Singh, P., & P. (2023, September 1). *10 Must-have Chatbot Features That Make Your Bot a Success*. REVE Chat. https://www.revechat.com/blog/chatbot-features/

Skuridin, A., & Wynn, M. (2024). Chatbot Design and Implementation: Towards an Operational Model for Chatbots. *Information (Basel)*, 15(4), 226. 10.3390/info15040226

Tidio. (2024). *Chatbot Statistics: Trends and Predictions for 2024*. Tidio. https://www.tidio.com/blog/chatbot-statistics/

Tyrväinen, O., Karjaluoto, H., & Saarijärvi, H. (2020). Personalization and hedonic motivation in creating customer experiences and loyalty in omnichannel retail. *Journal of Retailing and Consumer Services*, 57, 102233. 10.1016/j.jretconser.2020.102233

Vergaray, A. D., Peralta Robles, W. F., & Salazar Jiménez, J. A. (2023). The Impact of Chatbots on Customer Satisfaction: A Systematic Literature Review. TEM Journal, 1407–1417. https://doi.org/10.18421/TEM123-21

Wang, Y., Mintz, O., Chen, D., & Chen, K. (2023). How to Effectively Engage with a Billion Customers. *MBR Journal*. https://mbrjournal.com/wp-content/uploads/2023/07/019_Paper-26_AI-3-by-Mintz-Wang-Typeready.pdf

What Is a Chatbot? (n.d.). IBM. https://www.ibm.com/topics/chatbots

Wibowo, B., Clarissa, H., & Suhartono, D. (2020). The Application of Chatbot for Customer Service in E-Commerce. Engineering, MAthematics and Computer Science (EMACS). *Journal*, 2(3), 91–95. 10.21512/emacsjournal.v2i3.6531

Zemčík, T. (2019). *A Brief History of Chatbots. DEStech Transactions on Computer Science and Engineering*.

ENDNOTES

1 Corversational AI Market, accessed 23 May, 2024, https://www.marketsandmarkets.com/Market-Reports/conversational-ai-market-49043506.html

2 Maria Fikonia, *The Future of Chatbots: 80+ Statistics, Industry Trends & Benchmarks (2024)*, accessed 23 May, 2024, https://www.tidio.com/blog/chatbot-statistics/

3 Team Capacity, *Evolution of Chatbots*, 2020, accessed 23 May, 2024, https://capacity.com/chatbots/evolution-of-chatbots/

4 TheDataScientist, *The Rise of Artificial Intelligence in Customer Service: Transforming Customer Interactions*, accessed 23 May, 2024, https://thedatascientist.com/the-rise-of-artificial-intelligence-in-customer-service-transforming-customer-interactions/

5 This figure was created using Canva based on a paragraph.

6 Sephora, accessed 23 May, 2024, https://www.chatbotguide.org/sephora-bot

7 Sephora, accessed 23 May, 2024, https://www.chatbotguide.org/sephora-bot

8 This figure was created using Canva based on a paragraph.

Chapter 8
E-Commerce is an Innovative and Efficient Strategy for the Presentation of Products Through Quick Response Codes

Gerardo Reyes Ruiz
https://orcid.org/0000-0003-0212-2952
Centro de Estudios Superiores Navales, Mexico

ABSTRACT

New technologies have changed the way products are offered today: Nowadays the internet and social networks play a preponderant role in spreading, in a more efficient and dynamic sense, any kind of product. In this context, e-commerce is a modality for the sale of products and services, that admits the addition of these new technologies through the internet, which transforms it into a tool that allows the discovery of new uses, forms, and consumption habits. E-commerce allows to provide customers products and services with the highest quality, for this it is necessary to implement QR codes that can create a differentiating user experience where the products are displayed in the best possible way and accompany them with content that is valuable to consumers. In this way, it is intended to promote the efficient and rationalized use of all the resources that companies have and, at the same time, motivate the use of new technologies, as a strategic enabler and competitive differentiator, to overcome all their business objectives.

1. INTRODUCTION

In recent decades, there have been significant changes in people's consumption and so-called new technologies (Singh et al., 2021). On the one hand, we have witnessed that some brands have gradually positioned their products in markets that are becoming more competitive every day and, on the other hand, new technologies have shown dizzying advances, which have allowed the creation, precisely, of new consumer markets (Grubor and Milovanov, 2017). With the emergence of the internet, our lives underwent more than evident changes, however, it has been the new technologies, which making use of the internet, which currently allow us to have a more comfortable, pleasant, and safe life. In other words,

DOI: 10.4018/978-1-6684-7840-0.ch008

our daily lives have also been transformed by the proliferation of new technologies, particularly after having lived through the COVID-19 pandemic (Sharma and Bashir, 2020; He, Zhang and Li, 2021). For example, there are currently countless establishments around the world that allow purchases of all kinds of products or services to be made from the comfort and security of the home, simply by using a telephone connected to the Internet or with access to a data plan (Shammar and Zahary, 2020; Forecast GMDT, 2019; Mahr and Huh, 2022; Andersson, 2018). There are also, nowadays, countless establishments that focus on or have the service of bringing purchases, which are generally carried out through a mobile device with internet access, to the door of the home (Massa and Ladhari, 2023; Chemnad, 2022). In the same way, and also with a smartphone connected to the internet, multiple payments for services, bank cards, money transfers, etc. can be made from the comfort and security of the home: of course, banking institutions have been enablers and promoters of these changes with the aim, among other things, of creating a more comfortable and secure life for us (Sharma, 2024; Mefoute Badiang and Nkwei, 2024). These examples establish that contemporary human beings have become co-dependent on new technologies, regardless of whether any technological innovation satisfies their specific needs. In other words, life in the 21st century is far more bearable than life just 100 years ago. This is due to the leaps and bounds with which science and technology have advanced (Lee and Daiute, 2019). Therefore, the benefits of technological advances for the contemporary human being are also more than evident.

Undoubtedly, we are immersed in a world of information (Palvia et al., 2021; Chinese Academy of Cyberspace Studies, 2023). Surely, this is largely because the approach and knowledge of new technologies are becoming easier and more accessible to all people. However, these technological changes are increasingly rapid and it is clear that the interaction between technology and human beings has changed drastically over time (Asongu, 2021). That is, so much information is handled today that contemporary humans must quickly assimilate many technological developments rather than having them adapt to their needs. As a consequence of this interaction, it can be said that the current dynamics of product or service markets have led us, among other things, to be immersed in a global society with cutting-edge technologies (Ameen, Hosany and Tarhini, 2021). Similarly, current marketing trends have also had to adapt to the imminent technological changes, since nowadays it is not enough to implement marketing strategies that only focus on showing a product in a store window or through any other conventional media such as television, radio, some magazines and/or printed catalogs (Sharma, 2023; Clark, Azab and Key, 2024). In other words, how products or services are presented and sold to the end consumer has gradually changed over time (Peña-García, et al., 2020; Ghosh, 2024). However, an important factor to consider is that current marketing strategies, which have survived a globalized world and were able to adapt to technological advances, depend to a large extent on the buying habits of the people who inhabit a country (Peña-García et al., 2020; Munro, Kapitan and Wooliscroft, 2023).

The great impact of using the Internet and its adoption through new technologies has also transformed how people interact: communications are now more impersonal but faster, more efficient, and more secure. The response to new technologies was evident at the onset and throughout the global COVID-19 pandemic (Toussaert, 2021); Lee and Trimi, 2021). In this context, the efficiency of mobile devices, and in particular smartphones (García-Salirrosas, 2022), has reached a level of dependency for people that they are now a necessary and indispensable product with which people can either communicate or shop online and no longer so much in a convenient way but rather in a secure way (Katsumata et al., 2022). Moreover, mobile devices, particularly through social networks, have become an extremely important and sensitive means to introduce and/or disseminate, more efficiently and dynamically, a product or service (Stocchi et al., 2022; Dolega, Rowe and Branagan, 2020). The multiple uses of these innovative applications have not been ignored by companies seeking new and novel ways to sell their products or services (Biswas and Li, 2022).

Of course, large and even medium-sized companies have not been and cannot be indifferent to technological advances, marketing trends, and, obviously, new sales strategies, particularly those carried out over the Internet (Verma and Dixit, 2023; Mohdhar and Shaalan, 2021; Hendricks and Mwapwele, 2024). Companies that invest in new technologies to publicize their products, expand their market, and even position some of their products must be very clear about the sales strategies they will use to achieve their goal (Jing, Lin, Zhang and Qian, 2022; Hoffman, Moreau, Stremersch and Wedel, 2022). Otherwise, it is very likely that they will incur unnecessary expenses or that their products will not be well received by consumers. Undoubtedly, a primary objective in the sales process for a product or service is precisely to arouse the consumer's desire to buy (Lin, Chen and Zhang, 2022). In this context, new sales strategies must consider the entire consumer process, because they need to identify how many and which goods are demanded by their consumers so that the finished product or service manages to please them and they intend to buy it (Lin, 2023; Agmeka, Wathoni and Santoso, 2019). It is also important for these sales strategies to identify the main needs of their consumers; from how to reach them, to the profitability of the product, and to know if the final product or service can be paid for by the consumer or if it is of their total interest (Schwarz and Tan, 2021).

Recent generations of consumers and entrepreneurs have witnessed dizzying changes both in the so-called new technologies and in the consumption habits and forms of payment for some products (Nouri-Harzvili, Hosseini-Motlagh and Zirakpourdehkordi, 2024; Lamine, Fayolle and Audretsch, 2023). Scientific and technological development, as well as technology transfer, have contributed multiple advances, which have supported new sales strategies (Hoyer et al., 2020; Bohórquez, Pérez, Alvarez and Villón, 2024). These new sales strategies have been developed to present to consumers, in a much more accessible and attractive way, a finished product or service that is already on the market, that is about to enter a new market segment, or that its innovation will allow it to create, precisely, a new consumer market (Purnomo, 2023). However, new technologies, seen as a process of innovation, can in no way be considered a synonym of business growth and progress, i.e., as time went by, the companies that managed to survive these rapid technological developments had to face these imminent changes and, consequently, adapt their products or services (Krishen, Dwivedi, Bindu and Kumar, 2021), with new sales strategies, to markets that are becoming more competitive every day (Ali et al., 2023). On the other hand, companies that were not able to adapt or did not understand these multiple technological changes and, unfortunately, could not adopt the new sales strategies were forced to withdraw some of their products or services from the market, and some companies with a long tradition in the market even had to close their operations temporarily or permanently (Bai and Tian, 2020).

As mentioned above, new technologies, particularly those adapted to the Internet, played a preponderant role worldwide during the COVID-19 pandemic (Wang and Wang, 2021; Valamede, de Oliveira, Munhoz and Akkari, 2022; Chemnad et al., 2022). In this stage of crisis, multiple applications emerged that allowed people to communicate through videoconferencing (Zoom, Google Meet, Cisco Webex Meetings, Skype, among others), make all kinds of purchases (both products and services) from the comfort of their homes (Amazon, Chedraui, Costco, The Green Cornen, Superama, Petco, OfficeMax, Postmates, Delivery. com, etc.) and some of these applications became very popular because they bring these purchases to the door of the home (Uber Eats, Rappi, Didi Food, DoorDash, GrubHub, etc.), make all kinds of banking transactions with a smartphone (Paypal, Venmo, Google Wallet, Payoneer, etc.), hire a streaming service (Netflix, Amazon Prime, Disney +, HBO, Tubi, Discovery, etc.). In this context, the sale and purchase of products and services through the Internet (e-commerce) had and continues to grow considerably worldwide. Undoubtedly, this consumer behavior was favored because they avoided, as far as possible, becoming infected and/or suffering from COVID-19 symptoms by having direct contact with another person (Wajid and Alam, 2024; Kalgotra, Gupta and Sharda, 2021). In other words, the Internet became the best ally; it became the default shopping channel. What has become clear is that new technologies are an extremely important factor for people not to risk the most valuable thing they have, their lives. In this global scenario, consumers had to learn to use numerous applications, usually through a mobile device, to satisfy their basic needs through online shopping (Mofokeng and Tan, 2021; Chodak, 2024).

On the other hand, e-commerce or Internet commerce is known as commerce that is carried out electronically, where the purchase and sale of products or services are done through the Internet (Verma and Dixit, 2023; Qin et al., 2022; Chodak, 2024). However, e-commerce is not limited only to the internet, since it can also be done through intranets (Wihardja and Widianto, 2023; Ogunmola and Kumar, 2023) and e-commerce is not limited to the purchase or sale of products or services since it can also be used to transport, trade data, goods, information, communication, among others (Saw and Inthiran, 2022; Munoz, Holsapple and Sasidharan, 2023). Thus, e-commerce became a very popular sales channel that offers products or services to customers (Kremez, Frazer, Weaven and Quach, 2021. This channel, which is now a large global market, originated with the sale of electronic devices and small products, which could have been easily transferred between the seller and the buyer. This is how Amazon, the most popular e-commerce provider, started its online business with the sale of books (Soto Setzke et al., 2023). Consequently, offering goods that exist only in electronic form, such as software, was an even more natural process. Therefore, the rapid growth of this online sales channel resulted in a greater diversity of products to be sold over the Internet. In modern times there are an infinite number of products or services, even large items such as furniture or automobiles, that can be sold or purchased in electronic stores. In this dynamic, most likely the only thing that changes is the shipping method to deliver the product to the customer. Undoubtedly, some important factors that influenced this rapid expansion of e-commerce have been: 1) a low entry barrier of financing for distributors; 2) an explosive growth of mobile devices; 3) a clear expansion of social networks; 4) a disproportionate growth of users on the world wide web and; 5) easy access to the internet (Fouskas, Pachni-Tsitiridou and Chatziharistou, 2020).

Now let's look at some data related to e-commerce worldwide: The increase of internet users has been an important factor in the growth of e-commerce worldwide, since based on figures reported by Internet World Stats (2021) internet users went from 3,696 million (with a global penetration rate of 49.5%) in December 2015 to 5,053 million (with a global penetration rate of 64.2%) in December 2020. This growth in global internet connectivity is positive for the e-commerce industry because all new users are potential customers for online shopping. The number of e-commerce shoppers in the world increased from 1.52 billion in 2016 to 2.05 billion in 2020 (Statista, 2021), which represented a 34.9% variation for this period. Undoubtedly, e-commerce is a representation of how digital transactions continue to shape the behavior and purchasing practices of people around the world. In this context, online retail sales in the world went from 1,845 billion USD in 2016 to 4,206 billion USD in 2020 (Statista, 2021) which represented a 128% variation during the period 2016-2020. In other words, in five years the monetary figures associated with this type of e-commerce increased by five-eighths globally. This implies that the growth in e-commerce sales is also associated with an increase in the number of Internet users, who appreciate the benefits of online shopping compared to traditional means.

E-commerce has changed the way people shop. This type of commerce has changed the way companies conduct their processes from how they design, produce, and deliver their products or services to the way consumers trust suppliers (Laudon and Laudon, 2021). Undoubtedly, e-commerce is here to stay, especially in pandemic times like COVID-19 (Chen and Bashir, 2022; Campisi et al., 2023). According to Digital 2021: Global Digital Overview (Hootsuite, 2021), consumers worldwide made, through e-commerce 2020, approximately 347 billion purchases, which equates to 44.5% of worldwide purchases. Moreover, during the COVID-19 pandemic, in 2020, the total value of the global B2C (Business-to-Consumer) e-commerce market was approximately US$2.44 trillion (Hootsuite, 2021). Due to this dynamic in B2C e-commerce worldwide, there was also an increase in the use of road transport for product distribution (Tae-Woo Lee, Chhetri, Liu and Lin, 2024; Raimbekov et al., 2022). Thus, Figure 1 presents the evolution of electronic commerce until 2021.

Figure 1. E-Commerce Evolution Globally, 2021

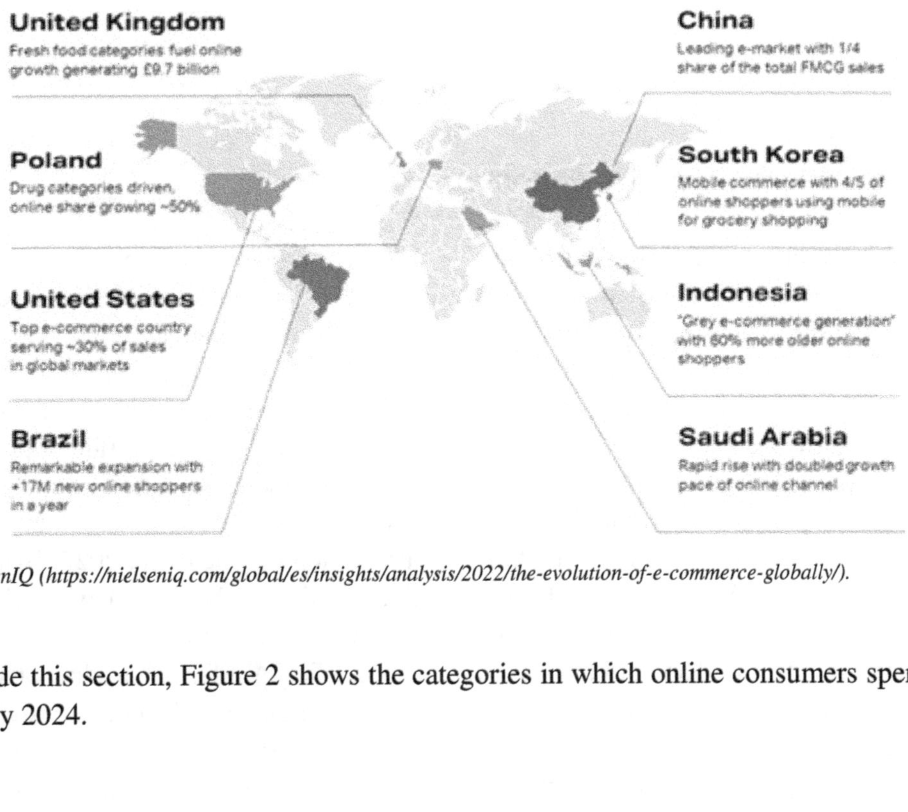

Source: NielsenIQ (https://nielseniq.com/global/es/insights/analysis/2022/the-evolution-of-e-commerce-globally/).

To conclude this section, Figure 2 shows the categories in which online consumers spent the most during January 2024.

Figure 2. Categories in which online consumers spent the most during January 2024

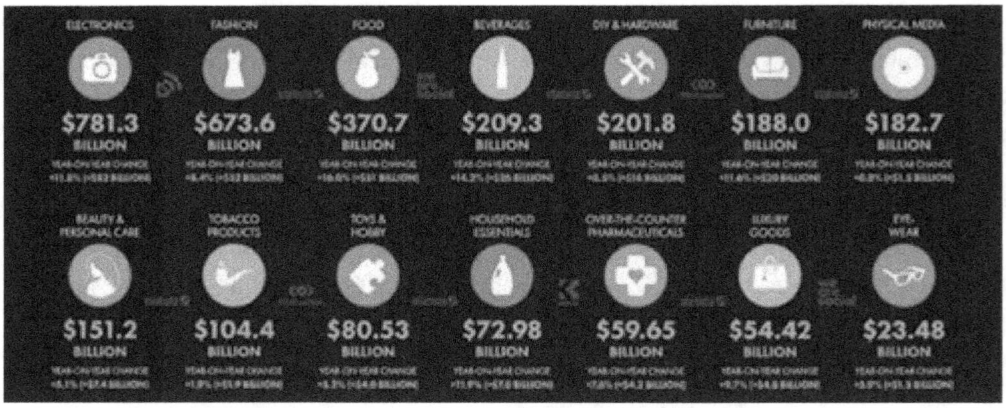

Source: DATAREPORTAL (https://datareportal.com/reports/digital-2024-global-overview-report).

2. BACKGROUND

2.1 Background and Types of E-Commerce

Every company must be very clear that to survive in an environment where there are multiple products or services similar to its own, it is of utmost importance to be different. Porter (1985), one of the pioneers in strategy, commented that there are only two sources of competitive advantage: a) offering a similar product (service) at a lower cost or b) offering a different product (service) at a higher price. This author also states that the first competitive advantage entails a low-cost strategy while the second competitive advantage necessarily leads to a differentiation strategy. However, creating a different product is not as simple as it seems. This is because a different product implies, among other things, quality in the product itself, which requires relatively high levels of investment (usually for research and development), innovation, operating costs, labor remuneration, and promotion (Byrne et al., 2022; Brito, Correia de Souza and Moita, 2024). These high levels of promotion are allowed because they provide high-profit generation (Farmer and Schelnast, 2021). In turn, it is important to mention that in a market segment, multiple brands are identified and offered by different companies. A different product or service indeed entails, among other things, important aspects of innovation, high advertising costs, and considerable investment in research and development (Wisnicki, 2020). However, it is precisely at this point where the advantage of showing a product (service) through a new sales strategy, which aims to show any product (service) in a more interesting and novel way, regardless of the product quality or intrinsic properties of the product, takes on great importance (Xia, Xie, Zhu and Liang, 2021).

Consumers currently have many options for the same type of product (without loss of generality, from this point on we will refer only to the concept of "product", although the term "service" will be implicit), which can even create brand preferences in the customer's mind (Valette-Florence and Valette-Florence, 2020). This behavior has, in the first instance, the purpose of increasing company revenues and, subsequently, increasing consumer trust and loyalty (Zha et al., 2024). In this context, it is important to ask why a consumer chooses a certain product. There are multiple factors for a consumer to buy a product (Permarupan, Xuan and Ling, 2021). Still, it is also true that a factor to consider, to justify the success and preference of a product, is its image or the way it is presented (Kim, Baek and Yoon, 2020; Cassani et al., 2020). This abstract concept can lead the consumer to generate certain perceptions of the product and its presentation (Wang, Chen and Zhang, 2023; Agost, Vergara and Bayarri, 2021). These perceptions should by no means be taken lightly, because the rejection of a product, or even a brand, is because: 1) the consumer has had a negative experience with that product or; 2) the consumer has some negative attitudes, even generated by comments from other consumers, towards a product (Chatzoglou et al., 2022; Camilleri, Cricelli, Mauriello and Strazzullo, 2023). However, we believe that for the image of a product, it is very important how it is presented to the consumer, i.e., in how the product and its characteristics are presented to the consumer. Therefore, we are convinced that the strategy of presenting a product, regardless of all its qualities and characteristics, through a new and novel, economical, and attractive strategy, can serve to position and increase its sales in a market segment.

On the other hand, and as mentioned above, the use of the Internet has changed the way we interact in modern societies, and has even changed the use we currently make of our knowledge. At the same time, mobile devices have gradually become an indispensable product for a person to communicate or carry out multiple online transactions. Nowadays, and in any part of the world, having a smartphone and a wireless network is no longer a luxury or a temporary fad; on the contrary, it has become a necessity, particularly for the new generations. The way much of the world's transactions are now conducted, including the purchase of a product by retail consumers, is undoubtedly online (Hootsuite, 2021). The classification of e-commerce helps to understand this diversified field. In general, electronic sales and purchases can be business-to-consumer (B2C) or business-to-business (B2B). However, it is important to know the different ways in which this e-commerce, or types of e-commerce, is conducted. Below is shown, according to Munoz, Holsapple, and Sasidharan 2023, the main classification of e-commerce based on the nature of the transactions and the relationships between the participants.

Table 1. Types of e-commerce are based on the nature of the transactions and the relationships between the participants

Concept	Description
Business to business (B2B)	Refers to transactions between organizations. Currently, approximately 85% of e-commerce volume is B2B.
Business to consumer (B2C)	This electronic commerce includes retail transactions of products or services from companies to individual buyers. Since sellers are usually retailers, they are also known as e-tailing.
Consumer to business (C2B)	People use the Internet to sell products or services to companies. Alternatively, people use C2B to request offers for products or services.
Intrabusiness EC	It refers to e-commerce transactions between various organizational departments and people in a company.
Business to employees (B2E)	It refers to the delivery of services, information, or products from organizations to their employees. An important category of employees is mobile employees, such as field representatives or repair employees who go to customers. The EC's support for such employees is also called business-to-mobile (B2ME) employees.
Direct delivery	In this model, a seller advertises and sells a product to a buyer and collects payment. The seller then transfers the orders to a supplier and pays the wholesale price. The supplier packages and delivers the product to the buyer.
Consumer to consumer (C2C)	In this category, individual consumers sell or buy from other consumers. Examples of C2C include people who sell computers, musical instruments, or personal services online.

continued on following page

Table 1. Continued

Concept	Description
Collaborative commerce	It refers to online activities and communications carried out by parties working to achieve the same goal.
Electronic government	In this category, a government agency purchases or provides goods, services, or information for businesses (G2B) or for individual citizens (G2C). Governments can also negotiate with other governments (G2G).
Social commerce	The expansion of social media and networks, as well as Web 2.0 tools (wikis, blogs, etc.), allowed new ways of carrying out electronic commerce, making it, precisely, social. That is, multiple new and modified e-commerce models were created, which rejuvenated the field of online transactions worldwide.

Source: Munoz, Holsapple, and Sasidharan (2023).

3. MAIN FOCUS OF THE CHAPTER

3.1 Traditional Approach to E-Commerce

Mobile internet traffic is a huge and inescapable phenomenon, almost every transaction worldwide could be done over a mobile network (social networking services, e-commerce, banking, etc.), i.e. almost every aspect of our daily lives can easily be done just by using a mobile device. In this universe of online transactions, and given that consumers differ considerably, it is difficult to know which elements of a product work best and which should be abandoned or improved. However, quality information associated with a product is necessary and important for consumers to value it and learn more about the products they wish to purchase (Nor Asshidin, Abidin and Borhan, 2016). Therefore, this information is a preponderant factor for consumers to decide whether to prefer products online (Lin et al., 2018). Of course, the decisions that consumers make online are very important for the success of e-commerce (Sharma, Mahajan and Rana, 2019). In this regard, generally, consumers see pictures of the products they are looking for online in a static and boring way (see Figure 3). Moreover, if they need to know more information about the product of their interest then they have to click on multiple links to know more details about the product they are analyzing. Figure 3 shows the traditional way of presenting a product, which can be through a web page or through interactive catalogs with static designs that do not use objects focused on a better perception of the product by the consumer. With the use of an App, a hologram of the finished product can be presented in specific places where the product would not normally be placed. For example, augmented reality is intended to surprise the customer and get his full attention and interest: one of the main objectives, and perhaps the most important, of the sale of products with the use of these new technologies, is to amaze and impact the customer and then motivate him to purchase the final product, which he has already visualized previously through an App (usually with a cell phone).

Figure 3. An example of traditional e-commerce

Source: Blacksip (2021).

Modern e-commerce strategies and increasing technological advances have not been ignored by large and even medium-sized product brands. This behavior, in turn, has allowed some companies or manufacturers to decide to introduce their brands in the market. In this context, Quick Response codes, known as QR (Hill and Whitty, 2021; Denso Wave Incorporated, 2024), are a reliable and fully adaptable tool that allows adding any type of information associated with the product displayed through a web page, which makes it a novel technology to discover new uses, forms and consumption habits but, above all, allows showing a product in an interesting, novel and simple way (Guenther, Eisenbart and Dong, 2020). The information displayed using a QR code, which is easily identifiable if it is presented next to the product, is intended to surprise the customer and get his full attention and interest (Fan et al., 2022; du Plessis, 2022). Of course, the main objective of the sale when making use of this type of new technology is to awaken the consumer's desire and then motivate him to purchase the product that he has already visualized through an App, usually through a cell phone (Yamin and Abdalatif, 2024; Kjeldsen, Nodeland, Fagerstrøm and Pawar, 2023). This approach undoubtedly originates a novel sales strategy and one that is currently used by very few companies (Türker, Altay and Okumuş, 2022). Perhaps the latter is because companies assume that its cost is high, however, this type of technology is highly affordable and has a lot of potential to show a product more attractively and interestingly to the consumer (Pratas and Oliveira, 2023). In other words, the aim is to present only that information that is important and of complete interest to the consumer so that he/she does not feel bombarded with advertising: Currently, a type of marketing is being developed, known as Inbound Marketing, which aims to discard all information that is not important to the consumer (Flynn Meyer, 2021; Chouaib Dakouan and Redouane Benabdelouahed, 2019). However, this type of marketing focuses on the type of information, but not on the form in which it is presented to the consumer.

It is precisely at this juncture that QR codes make sense as a new sales strategy to make more attractive and interesting the way a product is presented to the consumer in an online store (Pratas and Oliveira, 2023). This is because QR codes make it easy to add all kinds of technologies that allow adding, through an image, audio, or video, more interesting and novel product information, such as Augmented Reality, Virtual Reality, images in 360^0, music, etc. (Yao, Wang and Shen, 2022; LaVoila et al., 2017; Korkut and Surer, 2023; Du, Liu and Wang, 2022). This proposal, as a new sales strategy, will use a relatively new technology called QR codes, through which it will be possible to visualize, using a mobile device, virtually and with 3D objects a more detailed panorama of the finished product that a company has available in some of its department stores (Yao, Wang and Shen, 2022; Pingxuan, 2020; Lv, Lloret and Song, 2021). Companies that have a website where they present their products can adapt both their website and the way they display their products so that, through QR codes, the consumer can interact with them from anywhere in the world.

On the other hand, companies that do not have a website to present their products can opt for a catalog that is expressly designed with colors and images attractive to the user's eye: this catalog can be available in any section where their products are offered. The catalog can be conformed by the pictures of the final products and at the side of each image will be the QR code, which will allow the product to be presented, with the application of a smartphone, through 3D images or display any type of information in a multimedia file (Hanan S., Elhadad and Ghareeb, 2021). This procedure can also be carried out using a computer camera: the webcam identifies the marker and immediately displays on the computer screen the superimposed image and all the information that is of total interest to the consumer, which can be downloaded from a website previously designed for this purpose. The superimposed image (in 2D or 3D) is a key element because it is intended to capture the consumer's attention. This image must be attractive to the eye, as it will represent the content and use of the finished product, show its existence in inventories, track the location of the sale, request the consumer's email if they want more information, request a product valuation (via an online survey or email) and even providing a purchase button (commonly known as a shopping cart). In other words, regardless of whether the product is presented on a website or in a catalog, the objective of our proposal is that, in addition to the product, a QR code is presented that is detonated by an image or marker. This QR code will allow, when scanned by a webcam or a mobile device, to view 2D or 3D images, multimedia files, etc. the product and display all types of information associated with it so that it can be consulted by an indeterminate number of consumers (Fridhi and Frihida, 2019).

4. SOLUTIONS AND RECOMMENDATIONS

QR codes can be adapted to any type of e-commerce. However, this work can be considered for that type of e-commerce where the first objective is to present a product for purchase and sale. In this context, B2C, B2B, B2E, C2C, and Social Commerce can be mentioned as a first instance. As a methodology, it can be mentioned that this work aims to model a Service Oriented Architecture (SOA) type system. This system aims to manage other modules or secondary systems, which will be linked to each other to interact, through QR codes, with the buyer of a product. In this sense, the QR codes will be "the module" that will be seen by the buyer, which when "detonated/activated" by the potential buyer will initiate the interaction (showing the modules that are related to each other) with the potential buyer of the previously viewed product, generally through a mobile device. This SOA system is integrated through the OASIS program (Outil Auteur de Simulations Interactives avec Scénarios), which allows the creation and use of standard interfaces, which allow the services of different technologies, and even dissimilar data formats. Furthermore, these interfaces can exchange information without having to resort to bounded interfaces (OASIS, 2024). HTML and Java were used to program the modules. On the other hand, the free program Visualead was used to create the QR codes, while the App known as QR Droid Zapper was used to read these QR codes.

Within the online sales process, different needs can be observed, for example: that the furniture to be purchased is by the decoration, that the product meets their needs, and motivates the consumer's desire to purchase or enhance the purchase. It is necessary to visualize the consumer's process since the main objective is for him to demand some goods that he likes. The perception of a product, through its image, can in no way be taken lightly, since the preference of a product, or even a brand, can occur because the customer has had a pleasant experience with said product or because the customer has some positive attitudes, even generated by comments from other consumers, towards a certain product. At this point, we are convinced that to establish a better sales strategy, even for each market segment established by a group of consumers with heterogeneous consumption habits, a faster, more direct, and efficient interaction is necessary, and even indispensable, which can be carried out by implementing QR codes on the side of the product that is being shown using a device with Internet access (Salina et al., 2023): fast because it only depends on the speed with which the transmission of information is carried out. the data; direct because it allows and facilitates interaction with the consumer through a mobile device and efficient because it shows, dynamically and attractively, the characteristics and all the specific information of the product that is for sale, you can even see all this in real-time (Wara and Dugga, 2019). On the other hand, contemporary consumers are increasingly responsible with what they buy, for example, they are currently interested in viewing the product in more detail, and they are interested in being informed about its composition or how it affects the ecology. Due to this, companies have to migrate towards new technologies to address the new ways of choosing and selecting a product, that is, how to sell their products. Likewise, it is essential to change the culture of offering products because technologies have already proposed and improved new markets (such as online sales or automated points of sale). The sales strategy using QR codes will be able to personalize products, thereby offering quality and convenience in purchases. In this sense, knowledge and comparison of brands with others, of which there may already be knowledge, can make certain brands better known and selected, precisely, for the innovative way in which they are being presented.

4.1 Advantages and Disadvantages of QR Codes, Based on a SOA System, in E-Commerce

It was in 2010 when QR codes were applied as a payment system for the first time. The Korean franchise Tesco, in South Korea, detected that its population spent many hours of the day at train stations, so it created an ingenious payment format to meet their shopping needs. This company offered its consumers an innovative system, which consisted of making their purchases while waiting at the train stations. Koreans made their purchases using QR codes. They did this by scanning a screen on which the products were displayed, each associated with a QR code, as if they were in the supermarket, and a matter of minutes they had them in their hands. houses. This dynamic is a great advantage for both the buyer and the business. For the buyer because it provides a new payment tool based on a mobile device with internet access (such as a smartphone) and for the merchant because it allows them to generate a new and easy payment method, since QR codes can be generated. quickly and efficiently, associated with the amounts, in real-time.

This simplicity of payment allows, in turn, to generate the following benefits: 1) Reduction in risks: This means that you do not have to expose your wallet or carry credit or debit cards in said wallet; 2) Call to Action: This concept refers to sending the consumer the ideal means, generally through a mobile device, to inform them of purchase incentives via discounts or promotions due to their proximity to the business and; 3) Loyalty: This action allows the transaction to be closed, through various marketing and sales strategies and techniques, such as a points program. That is, customer loyalty is a marketing concept that aims to ensure that the consumer, who has previously purchased a product or service, continues buying and becomes a regular customer. Without a doubt, transactions made using QR codes currently represent a challenge for both cash and credit cards, since mobile payments are revolutionizing the lives of people around the world. On the other hand, by associating a credit/debit card with an App to make purchases through QR codes, it even allows you to personalize the payment method. That is, each user can obtain a unique QR Code associated with a payment application, such as Google Pay, which, in turn, is linked to a credit/debit card. In this context, the biggest and perhaps the main disadvantage of using QR codes as a means of payment is the loss or theft of the mobile device, since if you do not have security codes to access this modality then the cost increases. risk of losing the money associated with the credit/debit card.

When using a QR code, the consumer generally expects to find additional useful information about the product they want to buy. In itself, a QR code is a call to action. However, the paucity of additional useful information found when reading them is scarce or uninteresting and this may be one of the main reasons why the use of QR codes is novel. Among the main marketing actions when using a QR Code are: an advertisement, a promotion, a product, or a brand. However, the flexibility and adaptability in the use of these codes allow them to be extended to the following: all types of multimedia files can be associated (sound, 2D and 3D images), one or more Internet pages can be associated, useful information about the product/service, GPS information, link a social network, associate with multiple Apps (even in real-time) in addition to multiple banking transactions. Therefore, we consider that among the main benefits of QR codes are: a) they are easy to generate; b) they are easy to "read"; c) offer additional useful and important information; d) the information associated with the code can be retrieved at any time; e) they are easy to diffuse; f) can generate exclusivity for a product; g) its creation and/or generation is economical and; h) in e-commerce, direct traffic to the company can be generated through the URL address. Similarly, we consider that the main disadvantages that influence not using QR codes are the following: a) at first glance they are aesthetically ugly; b) you need to previously download an App to use them; c) the Internet is needed to use them; d) they are not "social", that is, you cannot interact with them; d) by themselves they do not contain useful information, because they are the "trigger" of other "environments".

5. RESULTS AND DISCUSSION

5.1 Hardware Requirements

The design of the system that we propose must provide for the type of hardware and software that is required for the execution of the system. In this system, the following is proposed:

- Camera, usually contained in mobile devices connected to the Internet. With this, both the QR code and the marker are detected.
- Screen of the device (usually a mobile device), with which you interact with the system. Through this screen, the third-dimensional image of the product, the information, and the characteristics that are intended to be shown to the consumer are displayed.
- Audio, is also provided on mobile devices, since in many cases the images come with sound, generally in a podcast.

The recent evolution of mobile hardware has allowed QR codes to be the "triggers" to reproduce multiple applications and tools on physically small units such as smartphones or tablets. These devices contain all the necessary components to present the consumer with all types of information about a product, such as high-resolution cameras and screens, accelerometers, GPS, wireless connectivity via WLAN, and radio links (Dargan et al., 2023). To execute this product sales system, using QR codes, a camera is used, which produces a point of view to show all the information linked to the product and which will be superimposed on a marker (see Figure 4). In addition, events can be "triggered" to display information such as its price, its existence and its composition, etc. which will be useful for the consumer, because they will be able to compare the products of interest with other well-known brands even displayed on the same shelf. By making the comparison and obtaining the advantages of the products, the consumer is then expected to be inclined to purchase the products that quickly and efficiently show them better information. Additionally, in this interaction, you can be directed to the official site of the product, social networks such as Facebook or Twitter, and even purchase through these means. The interaction can be carried out through buttons with superimposed icons, which when pressed show the objects or links associated with the product.

Figure 4. Reading the QR code

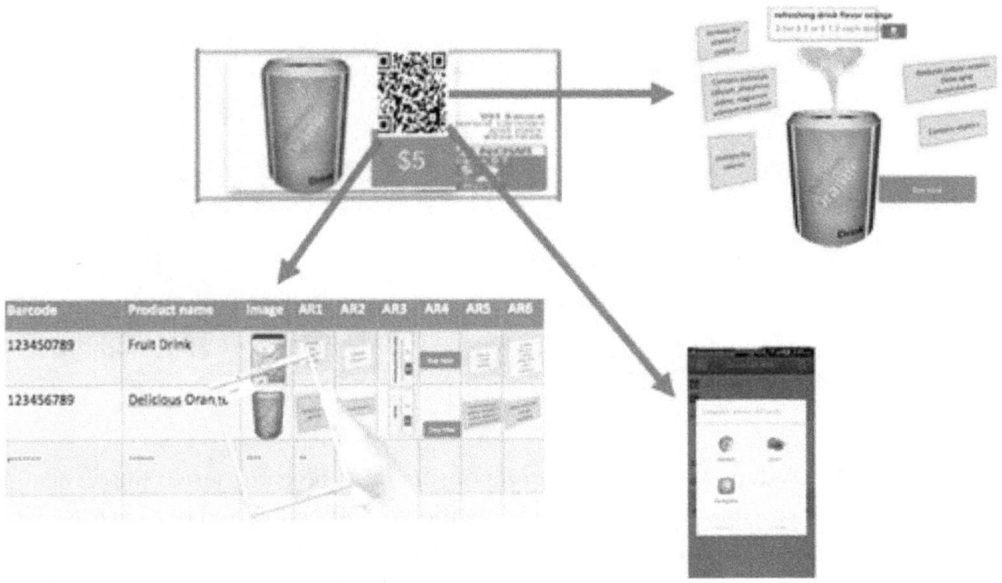

Source: Author's elaboration

5.2 System Architecture

The first action that begins with the design of the system is the determination of the system architecture, which is the hierarchical structure of the program modules, the way its components interact, and the data structure used by its modules. (Kendall and Kendall, 2021). There are several architectural styles of software, however, due to the nature of the system that is proposed to be built, the one that should be modeled is the Service Oriented Architecture (SOA) type, which is an architectural paradigm for designing and developing distributed systems and has been created to provide ease and flexibility of integration with linked systems, as well as establish direct alignment with business processes, thus reducing implementation costs (Haorongbam, Nagpal and Sehgal, 2022). Other advantages of this system are: 1) it implements innovation in services to consumers and, 2) it has agile adaptation to changes, including early reaction to competitiveness (Niknejad et al., 2020). The main characteristic of SOA is that a company's information systems are built on a set of computer standards with the objective that all of them, even those made with different technologies, can operate in an integrated manner and without dependencies between them. SOA represents a model where a logical unit is decomposed into several smaller units; In this architecture, services can be used by other services or other programs (Mishra and Sarkar, 2022). The architecture of the product sales system, using QR codes, is shown in Figure 5.

Figure 5. SOA of the product sales system through QR codes

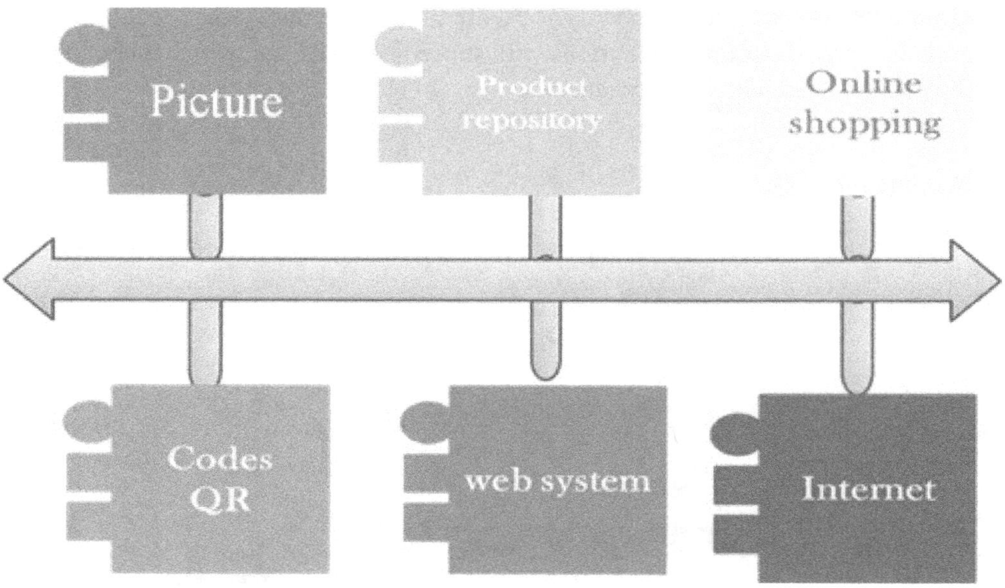

Source: Author's elaboration.

In this product sales system, the following components must be considered: image design, product repository, online purchases, internet, web system, creation of QR codes, and bookmarks. The programming paradigms for this type of architecture require a structure that integrates different modules to be interconnected and, simultaneously, can operate individually; This characteristic is called "low level of service coupling". To graphically show the architecture of this system, it is necessary to construct a diagram to show its operation from the precise moment in which the consumer views a product until he finishes using the system: a technique that can be used is known as "activity diagram" (see Figure 6).

Figure 6. Activity diagram of the catalog sales system for own-brand products

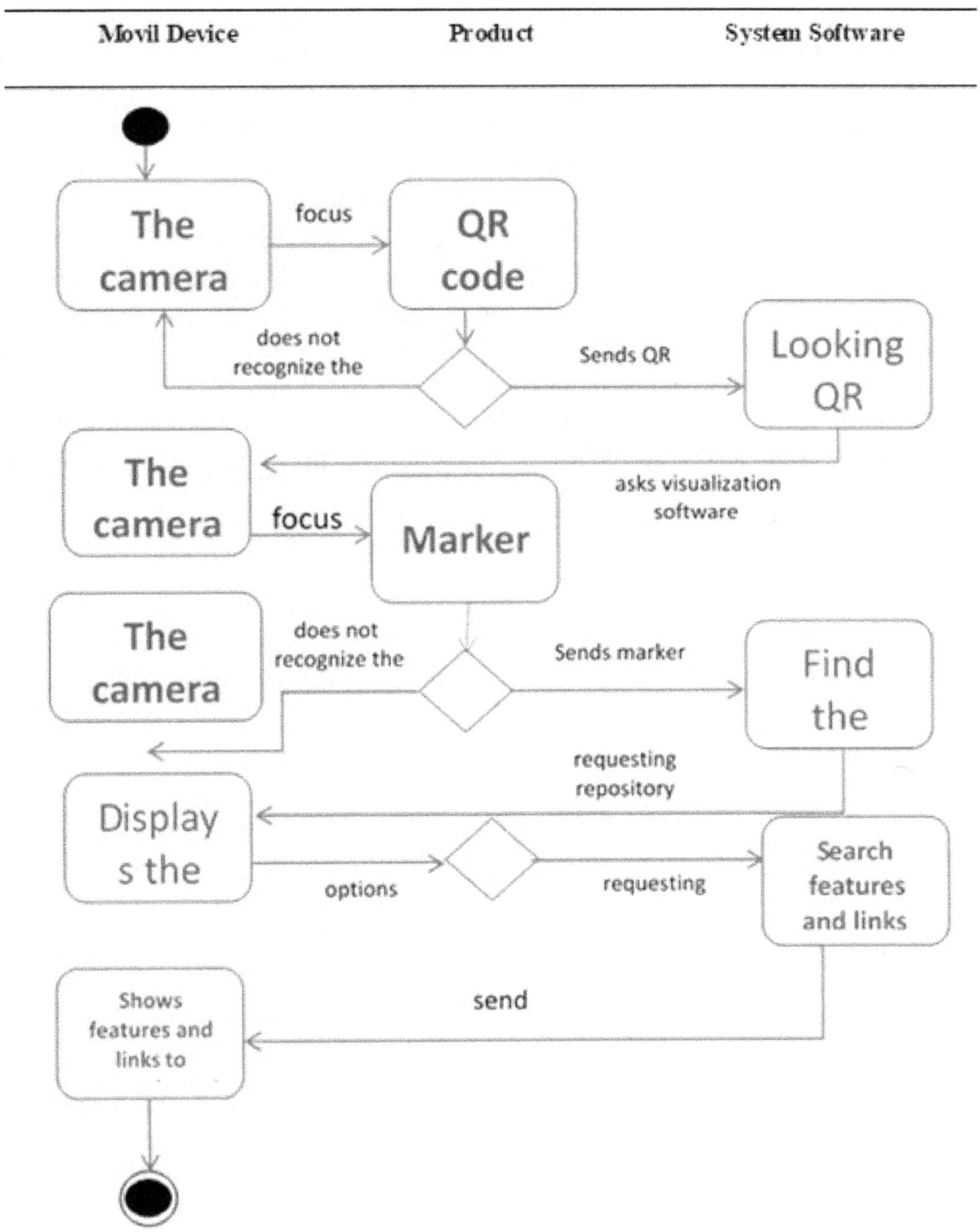

Source: Author's elaboration.

The interfaces to be used must be standard, which will allow services with different technologies, and even dissimilar data formats, to exchange information without having to resort to delimited interfaces (OASIS, 2024).

5.3 Design and Construction of QR Codes

Martins et al (2019) point out that the greater the perception regarding the ease of use, the greater the intention of people to use the telephone and make purchases. Based on this, it can be indicated that when the consumer uses their mobile device to view a product, through a web page, in 2D, 3D, or through AR, they find it attractive and novel. The plus of these websites when adding an online sales system is that it encourages people to perceive being able to make purchases of hedonic and utilitarian products as a pleasure. This interaction with the user allows more and more companies to be interested in promoting their products through this modality, which includes the case of products offered through e-commerce. In this way, the creation of QR codes is as follows:

a. **QR code**. The QR code (see Figure 7) is a two-dimensional image that stores information in a dot matrix or a two-dimensional barcode that was created in 1994 by the Japanese company Denso Wave, a subsidiary of Toyota (Denso Wave Incorporated, 2024). There are different QR code readers (see Table 2), among them some are free to use and ready to be downloaded via the Internet; Even new smartphones already come equipped with this type of software: In these QR codes, you can store text, a website address, a phone number or even a social network domain such as Facebook or Twitter. This type of two-dimensional code is used in these sales systems so that the consumer can locate, using the camera directed towards the QR code, the corresponding application quickly and accurately.

Figure 7. QR code reader

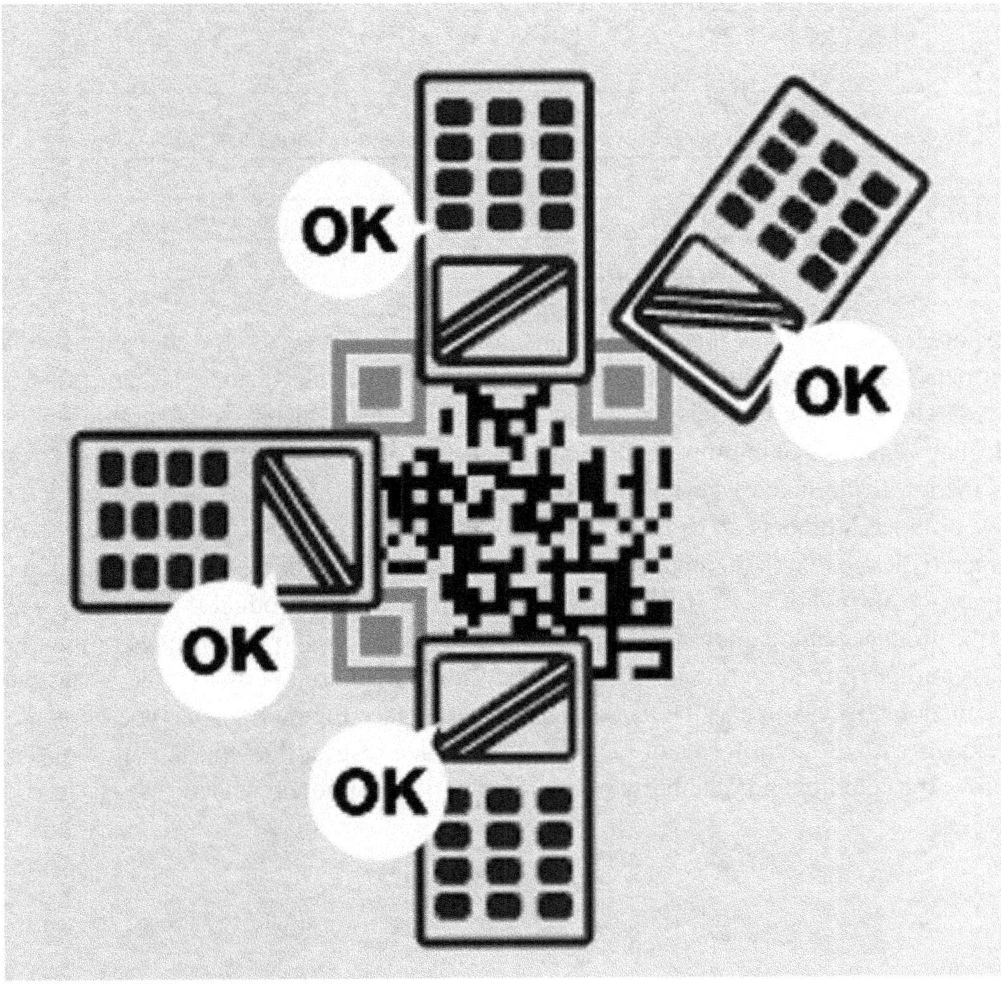

Source: Denso Wave Incorporated (2024).

Table 2. Applications for QR code readers

QR code reader	System for its operation
ScanLife/BIDI	iOS, Android, BlackBerry, Symbian, java.
QR Droid zapper	Android/iOS.
QRafter	iOS.
RedLaser	iOS, Android, Windows Phone.
Tingiz	Android.
Scan	iOS, Android, Windows Phone.
Barcode Scanner	Android.

continued on following page

Table 2. Continued

QR code reader	System for its operation
i-nigma	iOS, Android, BlackBerry, Windows Phone.
1QR	Android.
Beetag Reader	Windows Phone 7, Android iPhone, Bada BlackBerry, BlackBerry Touch, J2me, PalmOS 5. x, Symbian S60 2nd–Symbian S60 3rd, Symbian S60 5th, Symbian UIQ2, Symbian UIQ3, Windows Mobile 5, 6, 6.5.
UpCode Reader	Nokia con Symbian.
QuickMark Reader	sistema iOS, Android, Windows Phone / Mobile and Symbian.
Kaywa Reader	Java como Motorola, Samsung o Sony Ericson.

Source: Author's elaboration.

b. **Marker**. It is a 2D image that, thanks to its predefined color and shape characteristics, allows the information associated with it to be easily extracted. (Ghasemi et al, 2022) In this sense, the marker is used as an activator, which is "triggered" the moment it is detected by the mobile device's camera, to display virtual 3D or multimedia objects as well as to display links with the product characteristics, information from linked websites and, on some occasions, facilitates and motivates the purchase of the product. Markers can be built with a drawing program; These markers require some specific characteristics so that they can be recognized efficiently. Once the marker is designed, it is exported as an image, in any format, to be able to be displayed next to the product shown on the website (print it in the product catalog or even on the packaging of the product to be consulted). A marker contains a black outline (frame) for the camera to detect. Within this outline (frame), a black-and-white pattern is defined that is encoded as the marker identification (see Figure 8). This type of marker has been developed with different forms of identification, which restrict the representation of the marker to improve the stability and scalability of recognition using a mobile device.

Figure 8. Trust marker

Source: Author's elaboration.

After creating the marker, all the information that will be added to the product is generated when the marker is focused by the mobile device's camera. This information, which can be a virtual 3D object, is designed with a wide variety of specialized software, which serves to create innovative content and awaken, in turn, the consumer's interest and desire to purchase. For the scope of this work, the construction of the 3D object is not detailed because each design software has different characteristics; however, Figure 9 shows the result of a product when it is associated, using QR codes, with a or several Apps.

Figure 9. Apps associated with a product using QR codes

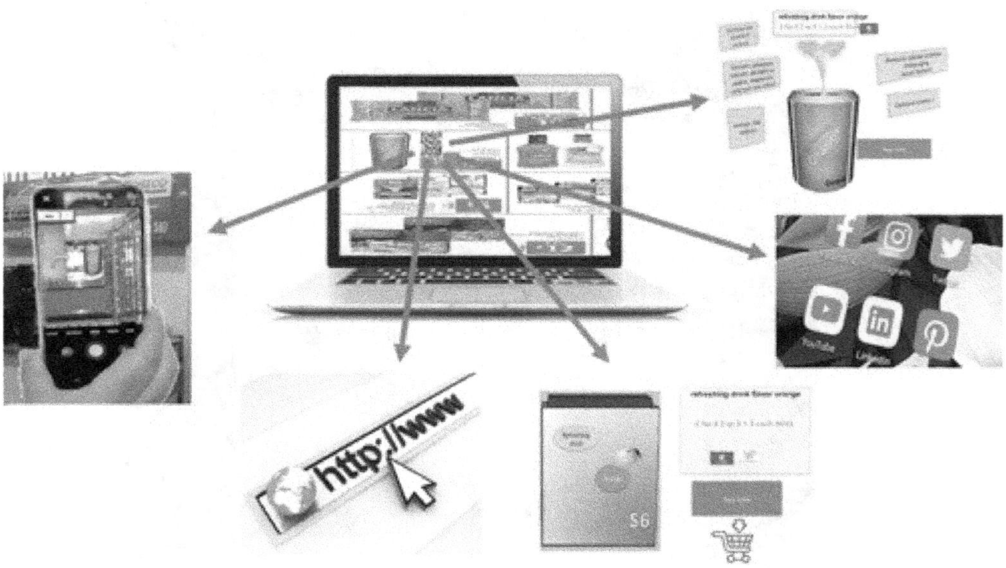

Source: Author's elaboration.

6. FUTURE RESEARCH DIRECTIONS

New technologies, more than being fashionable, are increasingly closer to people, who by using them obtain various benefits; An example is the sale of products online, which makes use of other technologies to make its products better known and, in this way, increase sales. Furthermore, these technologies look for ways to make the product more attractive, through multimedia files, to generate in people the desire to have it in their hands. How many times have people dreamed of observing the details (such as colors, dimensions, music, their operation, their movements, etc.) of their favorite toys before buying them, or the items in operation before opening them, they even wanted to see the clothes. in different colors and try on decorations without removing them from the packaging. This was generally done after purchasing the product, that is until the person appreciated the product when they tried it on in front of a mirror and observed whether that product was to their complete liking. Since flat images do not stimulate emotion or the desire to own the product, companies increasingly use new sales strategies to make people's wishes come true and, consequently, increase people's preference for their products, which will be reflected in an increase in their sales.

Currently, the world is invaded by mobile devices, according to data from Hootsuite (2021), in January 2021 there were 5.22 billion people with a mobile phone, which represented a penetration level of 66.6% worldwide. Likewise, the penetration level of social networks was 53.6% (4.2 billion people in the world). This is a great reason to add new technological elements to the products offered on the web pages; elements that encourage the consumer to enter a world of cutting-edge buying and selling, for this reason, technological resources must be generated that are new and innovative so that users can use them quickly. Furthermore, these technological resources must be designed, built, and sold with software that is used daily. Furthermore, these technological resources must be essential in those programs that are used with devices that are very frequently used by the user, in this case, such as the so-called mobile devices.

Taking into account that computer systems have evolved since the addition of factors such as the mobile platform, the growing use of big data for business, and the increased use of cloud computing (Laundon and Laudon, 2021), it is necessary to look for technologies that make more effective use of the internet and mobile devices that meet consumer requirements. To be at the forefront of these sales issues, our ability to choose must be improved by using information resources that are, to a large extent, the invention and improvement of information and communication technologies, that is, of those systems that involve new technologies with characteristics and capabilities in information management.

Although technological resources and tools that use QR codes have already been developed, it is necessary to introduce more of these resources in the area of e-commerce, for this new systems are proposed that help consumers and sellers to show what they want. You want to express yourself with the display of a product. In other words, the abstract must be extracted from a product to know how to show it to the consumer, which, without a doubt, can be achieved with fairly accessible elements, such as multimedia elements. In this context, and to continue to use QR code technology, it is proposed to use multilevel QR codes (see Figure 10). These multi-level codes contain multiple layers of information, which, independently, can function like a simple QR code. Among the many advantages of using multilevel QR codes, the following stand out: increase the use of information with a single code, encrypt multiple channels of information, use multiple apps simultaneously, can be used as multiple security codes, intertwine information, reduce the use of simple QR codes, motivate the creation, adaptation, and use of new technologies, among others. Furthermore, with the use of these multilevel codes, new sales strategies would be generated.

Figure 10. Multilevel QR codes

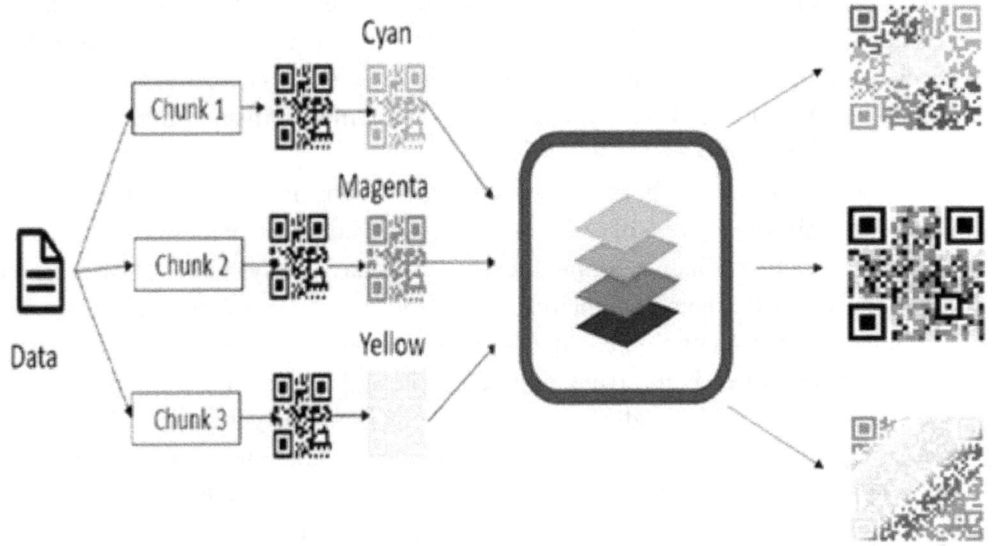

Source: Own elaboration based on Badawi et al (2019).

The information that is added to the product image, using a multi-level QR code, can be information that is downloaded from a website (text, images, sound, video or multimedia files, augmented or virtual reality, etc.) and/or contain from a 3D presentation of the product its correct use, its construction through a manual or video, the sales location, stock in the store, the contact email, a purchase button, set aside the product, track the purchase or shipment, among others. On the other hand, this type of new technology allows the connection with others that, together, can achieve a new shopping experience for the consumer. For example, the shopping experience through mobile commerce (M-commerce)(Oleárová, Bačík and Fedorko, 2021), which includes information services (Google, Yellow Pages, the Cloud, etc.), multiple transactions, location-based services (such as reception discounts, coupons at a local store, taxis, etc.), support services, emergency services, entertainment, etc. All these aspects can be carried out in real time, which will depend, logically, only on the speed at which the data is transmitted. In this context, products that associate a multi-level QR code can be an important component for this type of commerce, since by using these codes the camera of the mobile device would be used as an interaction device. Therefore, through this simple mechanism, the user could view with a mobile device all the information found on the Internet that is associated with the displayed product.

7. CONCLUSION

Multiple scientific and technological advances have supported new online sales strategies, commonly known as e-commerce. To present potential customers with a finished product, which is already for sale in the market or which is about to be introduced into a new market segment, some of these new e-commerce strategies are developed in a way more accessible and attractive. In this context, new e-commerce strategies, based on an SOA-type system, have shown that, over time, how products are presented, but, above all, sold to the consumer, has also changed. Consequently, currently, it is no longer enough to adopt a sales strategy that presents a certain product on display or through any other conventional means to sell it. The use of the Internet has revolutionized the way people interact: communications are now faster and more efficient. In the same way, the development of mobile devices has reached a level of dependency for human beings that are currently a necessary, and almost indispensable, product for a person to communicate or make purchases online.

In the great scenario of online shopping, awakening the consumer's desire to purchase is, without a doubt, one of the main objectives that is immersed in the complex process of selling any product. Therefore, the main objective of using e-commerce, based on an SOA system, is to surprise the customer and, as a consequence, obtain their total interest and attention towards the product that the customer is observing through these new technologies. In this sense, new technologies are an ideal means to awaken consumer desire and subsequently motivate them to purchase the product displayed, generally, through an App with a mobile device. Although this new approach allows the generation of an innovative sales strategy, many companies, despite knowing about it, very few use it, and even fewer dare to develop a system or App specifically for one or some of their products. Without a doubt, this is because companies assume a high cost when implementing a new technology of this nature, which is not necessarily the case.

SOA-type information systems are codes built to help people make decisions in an easy, accessible, and fast way. These decisions would be oriented to different areas ranging from the acquisition of new knowledge, medicine, tourism, education, etc. to other areas that include the sale-purchase of products and the offering of products to consumers in a newer and more innovative way. Currently, there are multiple examples of these information systems that provide this type of facility to consumers and that are distinguished by the way of offering products and services, such as the selection of places in a cinema, theater, or auditorium, to name a few examples, and where its options also contain the date and time. Other types of online information systems can be flight or bus travel reservations where sales also change and adapt to the daily actions and needs of consumers. This could be seen during the COVID-19 pandemic, that is, e-commerce sales were the first response to offer the consumer, in a more innovative, safe, and efficient way, products and services through the internet that were daily offered through catalogs, magazines, or simply on a shelf.

The sales strategy, through QR codes and a SOA system, proposed in this book chapter offers a very accessible format to interact with the consumer through a previously designed website. This e-commerce strategy, based on a SOA-type system, can be acquired by all those companies interested in selling their products online at a fairly affordable price. Without a doubt, among the advantages of this SOA system is adaptability, since it can be quickly adapted to all types of products: this new e-commerce strategy, based on an SOA system, can be offered with the inclusion of a software update and an extra service aimed at technical support. Of course, QR codes allow us to relate this e-commerce strategy, based on an SOA-type system, with other new technologies, social networks, and multiple apps for mobile devices that serve, in turn, to generate more innovative environments (such as augmented reality, virtual reality or mixed reality). This novel e-commerce approach, based on a SOA system, allows all types of products to be displayed originally and innovatively. Furthermore, this e-commerce strategy, based on an SOA system, will favor and position all the products that a company selects to show them from a differentiated perspective. Without a doubt, there is a lot to do with QR codes - in all their modalities - and SOA systems, however, the main priority is to bring these systems closer to companies that are committed to cutting-edge e-commerce, since currently very Few companies use and/or know this technological tool because they consider it expensive.

This work has as its horizon the mass market of consumers due, mainly, to the fact that a large number of products are still sold through the traditional way (radio, television, print media) but they are not presented in a specific segment of the market in a way that arouse consumer interest and "trigger" the need to buy them. Currently, there are still a large number of products that are sold, simultaneously, to large numbers of consumers, who make up an entire target population and who are also waiting to acquire a product in a new way that attracts their attention. Around the world, companies stand out that, regardless of their sales strategy, have the responsibility of providing consumers with quality products. Furthermore, if these companies commit to promoting the use of this type of system, as a strategic precursor and competitive differentiator, then they will be prepared to face the challenge that modernity has prepared for them to position their products in the market: exceed their objectives. of business through new e-commerce strategies.

Undoubtedly, new technologies will be an extremely important factor for companies interested in selling their products or services through e-commerce to position themselves in a better market, even in an international context. In this sense, the system proposed in this work speeds up the sale of any product, since the consumer can have useful information about the product in a truly short time, even in real-time. Another advantage of this system is that, by providing 2D, and 3D images, videos, or multimedia files, the buyer does not need to travel to the store to make their purchases. That is, this system allows the consumer to make all types of purchases from the comfort of their home or even when they are doing other activities, as long as these activities allow them to use a mobile device. For a company, this system allows it to operate multiple online activities, for example, knowing its inventories in real-time, the existence of a product in stores, the sale of a product preferred by consumers, and the information that a consumer reviews the most. a product, manage the price of a product, manage your website to update the information on your products, interact with your consumers through a chat, manage your social networks with the information collected from all your products, and create and disseminate new marketing strategies. sales through your social networks, send promotions to your frequent customers, manage your claims line, view payments, manage your bank accounts, etc. As can be seen, a system of this nature saves considerable time when purchasing/selling a product, mainly because it offers multiple modules that contain, in turn, a large amount of useful information for the consumer of the product of interest. This information can be consulted at any time and, as mentioned above, allows the consumer to purchase any product of interest from a mobile device with internet access. Consequently, a system with these characteristics allows a company to optimize a large part of its processes, which continue to be, for many companies that do not use new technologies, carried out manually by someone responsible for each of those processes.

For all of the above, it can be assured that any company interested in offering its products through this innovative e-commerce strategy, based on a SOA system, will benefit from a sustained increase in its sales. This innovative e-commerce strategy, based on a SOA-type system, is aimed at companies that have products and that have a certain interest in positioning, distributing, or making them known in markets that demand a higher level of innovation and creativity. Without a doubt, companies interested in implementing new e-commerce strategies, based on a SOA system, to their products will be more likely to achieve higher levels of sales, since by creating and implementing new technologies, in addition to supporting the progress of their environment, allow us to glimpse new technological horizons. These new systems aimed at e-commerce are made available to consumers, which will generate, in the not-too-distant future, new needs for the correct application of the products they purchase, but, above all, infinite opportunities will open for technological innovation. That is the innovative ways of presenting a product, providing a special visual and creative interaction generated through QR codes, will facilitate and allow a considerable increase in e-commerce worldwide. Therefore, these systems oriented towards e-commerce make it possible to enhance the advantages in terms of consumer attention, since when interacting with them through the visualization offered by the multiple Apps, triggered by QR codes and With access from any mobile device, the aim is to provoke a different twist to the advertising that is currently known in e-commerce and, as mentioned above, generate new forms of consumer habits.

REFERENCES

Agmeka, F., Wathoni, R. N., & Santoso, A. S. (2019). The Influence of Discount Framing towards Brand Reputation and Brand Image on Purchase Intention and Actual Behaviour in E-commerce. *Procedia Computer Science*, 161, 851–858. 10.1016/j.procs.2019.11.192

Agost, M. J., Vergara, M., & Bayarri, V. (2021). The Use of New Presentation Technologies in Electronic Sales Environments and Their Influence on Product Perception. In Yamamoto, S., & Mori, H. (Eds.), Lecture Notes in Computer Science: Vol. 12765. *Human Interface and the Management of Information. Information Presentation and Visualization. HCII 2021*. Springer. 10.1007/978-3-030-78321-1_1

Ali, O., Osmanaj, V., Kwiatek, P., Alryalat, M., Chimhundu, R., & Dwivedi, Y. K. (2023). The impact of technological innovation on marketing: individuals, organizations and environment: a systematic review. *Ekonomska Istrazivanja*, 36(3), 2210661. 10.1080/1331677X.2023.2210661

Ameen, N., Hosany, S., & Tarhini, A. (2021). Consumer interaction with cutting-edge technologies: Implications for future research. *Computers in Human Behavior*, 120, 106761. 10.1016/j.chb.2021.106761

Andersson, G. (2018). Internet interventions: Past, present, and future. *Internet Interventions : the Application of Information Technology in Mental and Behavioural Health*, 12, 181–188. 10.1016/j.invent.2018.03.00830135782

Asongu, S. A. (2021). The Effects of Mobile Phone Technology, Knowledge Creation and Diffusion on Inclusive Human Development in Sub-Saharan Africa. *Journal of the Knowledge Economy*, 12(3), 1367–1398. 10.1007/s13132-020-00668-8

Badawi, B. (2019). A smart fuzzy auto-suggestion system for a multilayer QR code generator. *Journal of Theoretical and Applied Information Technology*, 19(13), 3585–3603. https://www.jatit.org/volumes/Vol97No13/5Vol97No13.pdf

Bai, Q., & Tian, S. (2020). Innovate or die: Corporate innovation and bankruptcy forecasts. *Journal of Empirical Finance*, 59, 88–108. 10.1016/j.jempfin.2020.09.002

Biswas, P. K., & Li, S. (2022). A hybrid recommender system for recommending smartphones to prospective customers. *Expert Systems with Applications*, 208, 118058. 10.1016/j.eswa.2022.118058

Bohórquez, E., Pérez, M., Alvarez, R., & Villón, S. (2024). Marketing Strategies and Sales: Key Factors for Positioning and Growth in the Market. In Reis, J. L., Del Rio Araujo, M., Reis, L. P., & dos Santos, J. P. M. (Eds.), *Marketing and Smart Technologies. ICMarkTech 2022. Smart Innovation, Systems and Technologies* (Vol. 344). Springer., 10.1007/978-981-99-0333-7_27

Brito, R. D., Correia de Souza, E., & Moita, R. (2024). Separating Vertical from Horizontal Differentiation. *Review of Industrial Organization*, 64(2), 183–218. 10.1007/s11151-023-09924-y

Byrne, D. P., Imai, S., Jain, N., & Sarafidis, V. (2022). Instrument-free identification and estimation of differentiated products models using cost data. *Journal of Econometrics*, 228(2), 278–301. 10.1016/j.jeconom.2021.12.006

Camilleri, M. A., Cricelli, L., Mauriello, R., & Strazzullo, S. (2023). Consumer Perceptions of Sustainable Products: A Systematic Literature Review. *Sustainability (Basel)*, 15(11), 8923. 10.3390/su15118923

Campisi, T., Russo, A., Basbas, S., Bouhouras, E., & Tesoriere, G. (2023). A literature review of the main factors influencing the e-commerce and last-mile delivery projects during COVID-19 pandemic. *Transportation Research Procedia*, 69, 552–559. 10.1016/j.trpro.2023.02.207

Cassani, L., Fiszman, S., Alvarez, M. V., Moreira, M. R., Laguna, L., & Tarrega, A. (2020). Emotional response evoked when looking at and trying a new food product, measured through images and words. A case study with novel fruit and vegetable smoothies. *Food Quality and Preference*, 84, 103955. 10.1016/j.foodqual.2020.103955

Chatzoglou, P., Chatzoudes, D., Savvidou, A., Fotiadis, T., & Delias, P. (2022). Factors affecting repurchase intentions in retail shopping: An empirical study. *Heliyon*, 8(9), e10619. 10.1016/j.heliyon.2022.e1061936158093

Chemnad, K., Alshakhsi, S., Almourad, M. B., Altuwairiqi, M., Phalp, K., & Ali, R. (2022). Smartphone usage before and during COVID-19: A Comparative Study Based on Objective Recording of Usage Data. *Informatics (MDPI)*, 9(4), 98. 10.3390/informatics9040098

Chen, M., & Bashir, R. (2022). Role of e-commerce and resource utilization for sustainable business development: Goal of economic recovery after Covid-19. *Economic Change and Restructuring*, 55(4), 2663–2685. 10.1007/s10644-022-09404-5

Chinese Academy of Cyberspace Studies. (2023). World Information Technology Development. In *World Internet Development Report 2021*. Springer. 10.1007/978-981-19-9323-7_3

Chodak, G. (2024). Measuring the Impact of E-Commerce on the Economy. In *The Future of E-commerce*. Palgrave Macmillan. 10.1007/978-3-031-55225-0_1

Chodak, G. (2024). *The Future of E-commerce. Innovations and Developments*. Springer. 10.1007/978-3-031-55225-0

Chouaib Dakouan, M., & Redouane Benabdelouahed, M. (2019). Digital Inbound Marketing: Particularities of Business-to-Business and Business-to-Customer Strategies. In Kavoura, A., Kefallonitis, E., & Giovanis, A. (Eds.), *Strategic Innovative Marketing and Tourism. Springer Proceedings in Business and Economics*. Springer. 10.1007/978-3-030-12453-3_14

Clark, T., Azab, C., & Key, T. M. (2024). Marketing's next era: The scope and impact of marketing's future, the reach and legacy of Shelby Hunt. *Journal of Business Research*, 170, 114278. 10.1016/j.jbusres.2023.114278

Dargan, S., Bansal, S., Kumar, M., Mittal, A., & Kumar, K. (2023). Augmented Reality: A Comprehensive Review. *Archives of Computational Methods in Engineering*, 30(2), 1057–1080. 10.1007/s11831-022-09831-7

Dolega, L., Rowe, F., & Branagan, E. (2020). Going digital? The impact of social media marketing on retail website traffic, orders and sales. *Journal of Retailing and Consumer Services*, 60, 102501. 10.1016/j.jretconser.2021.102501

Du, Z., Liu, J., & Wang, T. (2022). Augmented Reality Marketing: A Systematic Literature Review and an Agenda for Future Inquiry. *Frontiers in Psychology*, 13, 925963. 10.3389/fpsyg.2022.92596335783783 du Plessis, C. (2022). A Scoping Review of the Effect of Content Marketing on Online Consumer Behavior. *SAGE Open*, 12(2). 10.1177/21582440221093042

Fan, X., Deng, N., Qian, Y., & Dong, X. (2022). Factors Affecting the Effectiveness of Cause-Related Marketing: A Meta-Analysis. *Journal of Business Ethics*, 175(2), 339–360. 10.1007/s10551-020-04639-6

Farmer, K., & Schelnast, M. (2021). Product Differentiation, Decreasing Costs, and Intra-Sectoral Trade. In *Growth and International Trade. Springer Texts in Business and Economics*. Springer. 10.1007/978-3-662-62943-7_13

Flynn Meyer, E. (2021). *Mastering Inbound Marketing: Your Complete Guide to Building a Results-Driven Inbound Strategy* (1st ed.). BookBaby.

Forecast, G. M. D. T. (2019). *Cisco visual Networking index: global mobile data traffic forecast update, 2017-2022*. CISCO. https://www.cisco.com/c/en/us/solutions/service-provider/visualnetworking-index-vni/index.html

Fouskas, K., Pachni-Tsitiridou, O., & Chatziharistou, C. (2020). A Systematic Literature Review on E-Commerce Success Factors. In Kavoura, A., Kefallonitis, E., & Theodoridis, P. (Eds.), *Strategic Innovative Marketing and Tourism. Springer Proceedings in Business and Economics*. Springer. 10.1007/978-3-030-36126-6_76

Fridhi, A., & Frihida, A. (2019). GIS 3D and Science of Augmented Reality: Modeling a 3D Geospatial Environment. *Journal of Soft Computing in Civil Engineering*, 3-4, 78–87. 10.22115/SCCE.2020.212254.1148

García-Salirrosas, E. E., Acevedo-Duque, Á., Marin Chaves, V., Mejía Henao, P. A. M., & Olaya Molano, J. C. (2022). Purchase Intention and Satisfaction of Online Shop Users in Developing Countries during the COVID-19 Pandemic. *Sustainability (Basel)*, 14(10), 6302. 10.3390/su14106302

Ghasemi, Y., Jeong, H., Choi, S. H., Park, K.-B., & Lee, J. Y. (2022). Deep learning-based object detection in augmented reality: A systematic review. *Computers in Industry*, 139, 103661. 10.1016/j.compind.2022.103661

Ghosh, M. (2024). Meta-analytic review of online purchase intention: Conceptualising the study variables. *Cogent Business & Management*, 11(1), 2296686. 10.1080/23311975.2023.2296686

Grubor, A., & Milovanov, O. (2017). Brand strategies in the era of sustainability. *Interdisciplinary Description of Complex Systems*, 15(1), 78–88. 10.7906/indecs.15.1.6

Guenther, A., Eisenbart, B., & Dong, A. (2020). Creativity and successful product concept selection for innovation. *International Journal of Design Creativity and Innovation*, 9(1), 3–19. 10.1080/21650349.2020.1858970

Hanan, S. A. S., Elhadad, A., & Ghareeb, A. (2021). Rapid and Blind Watermarking Approach of the 3D Objects Using QR Code Images for Securing Copyright. *Computational Intelligence and Neuroscience, vol. 2021. Computational Intelligence and Neuroscience*, 2236866, 1–11. 10.1155/2021/2236866

Haorongbam, L., Nagpal, R., & Sehgal, R. (2022). *Service Oriented Architecture (SOA): A Literature Review on the Maintainability, Approaches and Design Process. 12th International Conference on Cloud Computing, Data Science & Engineering (Confluence)*, Noida, India. 10.1109/Confluence52989.2022.9734153

He, W., Zhang, Z. J., & Li, W. (2021). Information technology solutions, challenges, and suggestions for tackling the COVID-19 pandemic. *International Journal of Information Management*, 57, 102287. 10.1016/j.ijinfomgt.2020.10228733318721

Hendricks, S., & Mwapwele, S. D. (2024). A systematic literature review on the factors influencing e-commerce adoption in developing countries. *Data and Information Management*, 8(1), 100045. 10.1016/j.dim.2023.100045

Hill, G. N., & Whitty, M. A. (2021). Embedding metadata in images at time of capture using physical Quick Response (QR) codes. *Information Processing & Management*, 58(3), 102504. 10.1016/j.ipm.2021.102504

Hoffman, D. L., Moreau, C. P., Stremersch, S., & Wedel, M. (2022). The Rise of New Technologies in Marketing: A Framework and Outlook. *Journal of Marketing*, 86(1), 1–6. 10.1177/00222429211061636

Hootsuite. (2021). *Digital 2021: global digital overview*. Hootsuite. https://datareportal.com/reports/digital-2021-global-overview-report

Hoyer, W. D., Kroschke, M., Schmitt, B., Kraume, K., & Shankar, V. (2020). Transforming the Customer Experience Through New Technologies. *Journal of Interactive Marketing*, 51, 57–71. 10.1016/j.intmar.2020.04.001

Jing, F., Lin, J., Zhang, Q., & Qian, Y. (2022). New technology introduction and product rollover strategies. *European Journal of Operational Research*, 302(1), 324–336. 10.1016/j.ejor.2021.12.025

Kalgotra, P., Gupta, A., & Sharda, R. (2021). Pandemic information support lifecycle: Evidence from the evolution of mobile apps during COVID-19. *Journal of Business Research*, 134, 540–559. 10.1016/j.jbusres.2021.06.00234565948

Katsumata, S., Ichikohji, T., Nakano, S., Yamaguchi, S., & Ikuine, F. (2022). Changes in the use of mobile devices during the crisis: Immediate response to the COVID-19 pandemic. *Computers in Human Behavior Reports*, 5, 100168. 10.1016/j.chbr.2022.10016835079660

Kendall, K., & Kendall, J. (2021). *Systems Analysis and Design* (10th ed.). Pearson.

Kim, S., Baek, T. H., & Yoon, S. (2020). The effect of 360-degree rotatable product images on purchase intention. *Journal of Retailing and Consumer Services*, 55, 102062. 10.1016/j.jretconser.2020.102062

Kjeldsen, K., Nodeland, M., Fagerstrøm, A., & Pawar, S. (2023). The relative impact of QR codes on omnichannel customer experience and purchase intention. *Procedia Computer Science*, 219, 1049–1056. 10.1016/j.procs.2023.01.383

Korkut, E. H., & Surer, E. (2023). Visualization in virtual reality: A systematic review. *Virtual Reality (Waltham Cross)*, 27(2), 1447–1480. 10.1007/s10055-023-00753-8

Kremez, Z., Frazer, L., Weaven, S., & Quach, S. (2021). Ecommerce structures for retail and service franchises: Ecommerce implementation in mature franchise systems. *Asia Pacific Journal of Marketing and Logistics*, 33(6), 1292–1308. 10.1108/APJML-11-2018-0461

Krishen, A. S., Dwivedi, Y. K., Bindu, N., & Kumar, K. S. (2021). A broad overview of interactive digital marketing: A bibliometric network analysis. *Journal of Business Research*, 131, 183–195. 10.1016/j.jbusres.2021.03.061

Lamine, W., Fayolle, A., Jack, S., & Audretsch, D. (2023). Impact of digital technologies on entrepreneurship: Taking stock and looking forward. *Technovation*, 126, 102823. 10.1016/j.technovation.2023.102823

Laudon, K. C., & Laudon, J. P. (2021). *Management Information Systems: Managing the Digital Firm* (Global Edition). Pearson Higher Education.

LaVoila, J. J. (2017). *3D User Interfaces: Theory and Practice*. Addison-Wesley Professional.

Lee, C. D., & Daiute, C. (2019). Introduction to Developmental Digital Technologies in Human History, Culture, and Well-Being. *Human Development*, 62(1-2), 5–13. 10.1159/000496072

Lee, S. M., & Trimi, S. (2021). Convergence Innovation in the Digital Age and in the COVID-19 Pandemic Crisis. *Journal of Business Research*, 123, 14–22. 10.1016/j.jbusres.2020.09.04133012897

Lin, B., Chen, Y., & Zhang, L. (2022). Research on the factors influencing the re-purchase intention on short video platforms: A case of China. *PLoS One*, 17(3), e0265090. 10.1371/journal.pone.026509035290393

Lin, S. (2023). The Influential Factors on Consumer Purchase Intention: A Case Study on MINISO. In: Li, X., Yuan, C., Kent, J. (Eds.) *Proceedings of the 6th International Conference on Economic Management and Green Development. Applied Economics and Policy Studies*. Springer, Singapore. 10.1007/978-981-19-7826-5_121

Lin, X., Featherman, M., Brooks, S. L., & Hajli, N. (2018). Exploring gender differences in online consumer purchase decision making: An online product presentation perspective. *Information Systems Frontiers*, 21(5), 1187–1201. 10.1007/s10796-018-9831-1

Lv, Z., Lloret, J., & Song, H. (2021). Real-time image processing for augmented reality on mobile devices. *Journal of Real-Time Image Processing*, 18(2), 245–248. 10.1007/s11554-021-01097-9

Mahr, D., & Huh, J. (2022). Technologies in service communication: Looking forward. *Journal of Service Management*, 33(4/5), 648–656. 10.1108/JOSM-03-2022-0075

Martins, J., Costa, C., Oliveira, T., Gonçalves, R., & Branco, F. (2019). How smartphone advertising influences consumers' purchase intention. *Journal of Business Research*, 94, 378–387. 10.1016/j.jbusres.2017.12.047

Massa, E., & Ladhari, R. (2023). Augmented reality in marketing: Conceptualization and systematic review. *International Journal of Consumer Studies*, 47(6), 2335–2366. 10.1111/ijcs.12930

Mefoute Badiang, A., & Nkwei, E. S. (2024). Mobile banking adoption its antecedents and post-adoption effects: The role of consumers status orientation in an African context. *Cogent Business & Management*, 11(1), 2321787. 10.1080/23311975.2024.2321787

Mishra, S. K., & Sarkar, A. (2022). Service-oriented architecture for Internet of Things: A semantic approach. *Journal of King Saud University. Computer and Information Sciences*, 34(10, 10 Part A), 8765–8776. 10.1016/j.jksuci.2021.09.024

Mofokeng, T. E., & Tan, A. W. K. (2021). The impact of online shopping attributes on customer satisfaction and loyalty: Moderating effects of e-commerce experience. *Cogent Business & Management*, 8(1), 1968206. 10.1080/23311975.2021.1968206

Mohdhar, A., & Shaalan, K. (2021). The Future of E-Commerce Systems: 2030 and Beyond. In Al-Emran, M., & Shaalan, K. (Eds.), *Recent Advances in Technology Acceptance Models and Theories. Studies in Systems, Decision and Control* (Vol. 335). Springer. 10.1007/978-3-030-64987-6_18

Munoz, F., Holsapple, C. W., & Sasidharan, S. (2023). E-commerce. In Nof, S. Y. (Ed.), *Springer Handbook of Automation. Springer Handbooks*. Springer. 10.1007/978-3-030-96729-1_67

Munro, P., Kapitan, S., & Wooliscroft, B. (2023). The sustainable attitude-behavior gap dynamic when shopping at the supermarket: A systematic literature review and framework for future research. *Journal of Cleaner Production*, 426, 138740. 10.1016/j.jclepro.2023.138740

Niknejad, N., Ismail, W., Ghani, I., Nazari, B., Bahari, M., & Hussin, A. R. B. C. (2020). Understanding Service-Oriented Architecture (SOA): A systematic literature review and directions for further investigation. *Information Systems*, 91, 101491. 10.1016/j.is.2020.101491

Nor Asshidin, N. H., Abidin, N., & Borhan, H. B. (2016). Consumer Attitude and Uniqueness towards International Products. *Procedia Economics and Finance*, 35, 632–638. 10.1016/S2212-5671(16)00077-0

Nouri-Harzvili, M., Hosseini-Motlagh, S. M., & Zirakpourdehkordi, R. (2024). Evolutionary Marketing Strategies for New High-Technology Product Sales: Effects of Customers' Innovation Adoption. *IEEE Transactions on Engineering Management*, 71, 3158–3171. 10.1109/TEM.2022.3207685

OASIS. (2024). *Advancing open standards for the information society*. OASIS. https://www.oasis-open .org/news

Ogunmola, G. A., & Kumar, V. (2023). E-commerce research models: A systematic review and identification of the determinants to success. *International Journal of Business Information Systems*, 43(1), 87–106. 10.1504/IJBIS.2023.131093

Oleárová, M., Bačík, R., & Fedorko, R. (2021). Overview of current trends in mobile commerce: Global perspectives. *Marketing Science & Inspirations*, 16(4), 2–9. 10.46286/msi.2021.16.4.1

Palvia, P., Ghosh, J., Jacks, T., & Serenko, A. (2021). Information technology issues and challenges of the globe: The world IT project. *Information & Management*, 58(8), 103545. 10.1016/j.im.2021.103545

Peña-García, N., Gil-Saura, I., Rodríguez-Orejuela, A., & Siqueira-Junior, J. R. (2020). Purchase intention and purchase behavior online: A cross-cultural approach. *Heliyon*, 6(6), e04284. 10.1016/j.heliyon.2020. e0428432613132

Permarupan, P. Y., Xuan, K. Z., & Ling, T. K. (2021). Factors Influencing Consumers' Purchasing Decision on Local Products. In Alareeni, B., Hamdan, A., & Elgedawy, I. (Eds.), *The Importance of New Technologies and Entrepreneurship in Business Development: In the Context of Economic Diversity in Developing Countries. ICBT 2020. Lecture Notes in Networks and Systems* (Vol. 194). Springer. 10.1007/978-3-030-69221-6_32

Pingxuan, R. (2020). AR 3D Magic Book: A Healthy Interactive Reading Device Based on AR and Portable Projection. CIPAE 2020: Proceedings of the 2020 International Conference on Computers, Information Processing and Advanced Education October 2020, pp. 244-250. 10.1145/3419635.3419714

Porter, M. (1985). *Competitive Advantage. Creating and Sustaining Superior Performance*. The Free Press.

Pratas, J., & Oliveira, Z. (2023). QR Codes Research in Marketing: A Bibliometric and Content Analysis. In Reis, J. L., Peter, M. K., Varela González, J. A., & Bogdanović, Z. (Eds.), *Marketing and Smart Technologies. Smart Innovation, Systems and Technologies* (Vol. 337). Springer. 10.1007/978-981-19-9099-1_19

Purnomo, Y. J. (2023). Digital Marketing Strategy to Increase Sales Conversion on E-commerce Platforms. *Journal of Contemporary Administration and Management*, 1(2), 54–62. 10.61100/adman.v1i2.23

Qin, Z. (2022). *E-Commerce. Concepts, Principles, and Application*. Springer. 10.1007/978-981-19-6438-1

Raimbekov, Z., Sładkowski, A., Syzdykbayeva, B., Azatbek, T., & Sharipbekova, K. (2022). Improving the Efficiency of Transportation and Distribution of Goods in Modern Conditions. In Sładkowski, A. (Ed.), *Modern Trends and Research in Intermodal Transportation. Studies in Systems, Decision and Control* (Vol. 400). Springer., 10.1007/978-3-030-87120-8_4

Salina, T. (2023). A Review of Augmented Reality for Informal Science Learning: Supporting Design of Intergenerational Group Learning. *Visitor Studies*, 26(1), 1–23. 10.1080/10645578.2022.2075205

Santos, S., & Martins Gonçalves, H. (2021). The consumer decision journey: A literature review of the foundational models and theories and a future perspective. *Technological Forecasting and Social Change*, 173, 121117. 10.1016/j.techfore.2021.121117

Saw, C. C., & Inthiran, A. (2022). Designing for Trust on E-Commerce Websites Using Two of the Big Five Personality Traits. *Journal of Theoretical and Applied Electronic Commerce Research*, 17(2), 375–393. 10.3390/jtaer17020020

Schwarz, J. A., & Tan, B. (2021). Optimal sales and production rollover strategies under capacity constraints. *European Journal of Operational Research*, 294(2), 507–524. 10.1016/j.ejor.2021.01.040

Shammar, E. A., & Zahary, A. T. (2020). The Internet of Things (IoT): A survey of techniques, operating systems, and trends. *Library Hi Tech*, 38(1), 5–66. 10.1108/LHT-12-2018-0200

Sharma, N. (2024). A digital cohort analysis of consumers' mobile banking app experience. *International Journal of Consumer Studies*, 48(1), e12989. 10.1111/ijcs.12989

Sharma, P., Ueno, A., Dennis, C., & Turan, C. P. (2023). Emerging digital technologies and consumer decision-making in retail sector: Towards an integrative conceptual framework. *Computers in Human Behavior*, 148, 107913. 10.1016/j.chb.2023.107913

Sharma, S., Mahajan, S., & Rana, V. (2019). A semantic framework for e-commerce search engine optimization. *International Journal of Information Technology : an Official Journal of Bharati Vidyapeeth's Institute of Computer Applications and Management*, 11(1), 31–36. 10.1007/s41870-018-0232-y

Sharma, T., & Bashir, M. (2020). Use of apps in the COVID-19 response and the loss of privacy protection. *Nature Medicine*, 26(8), 1165–1175. 10.1038/s41591-020-0928-y32457443

Singh, U. S. (2021). (in press). A study on the revolution of consumer relationships as a combination of human interactions and digital transformations. *Materials Today: Proceedings*. 10.1016/j.matpr.2021.05.578

Soto Setzke, D., Riasanow, T., Böhm, M., & Krcmar, H. (2023). Pathways to Digital Service Innovation: The Role of Digital Transformation Strategies in Established Organizations. *Information Systems Frontiers*, 25(3), 1017–1037. 10.1007/s10796-021-10112-0

Stocchi, L., Pourazad, N., Michaelidou, N., Tanusondjaja, A., & Harrigan, P. (2022). Marketing research on Mobile apps: Past, present and future. *Journal of the Academy of Marketing Science*, 50(2), 195–225. 10.1007/s11747-021-00815-w34776554

Tae-Woo Lee, P., Chhetri, P., Liu, W., & Lin, C. W. (2024). Integrated transport and logistics for sustainable global trade. *International Journal of Logistics*, 27(3), 359–362. 10.1080/13675567.2024.2307198

Toussaert, S. (2021). Upping uptake of COVID contact tracing apps. *Nature Human Behaviour*, 5(2), 183–184. 10.1038/s41562-021-01048-133479504

Türker, C., Altay, B. C., & Okumuş, A. (2022). Understanding user acceptance of QR code mobile payment systems in Turkey: An extended TAM. *Technological Forecasting and Social Change*, 184, 121968. 10.1016/j.techfore.2022.121968

Valamede, L. S., de Oliveira, G. G., Munhoz, I. P., & Akkari, A. C. S. (2022). Digital Technologies Adoption to Face COVID-19 Pandemic: An Exploratory Approach. In: Iano, Y., Saotome, O., Kemper Vásquez, G.L., Cotrim Pezzuto, C., Arthur, R., Gomes de Oliveira, G. (Eds) *Proceedings of the 7th Brazilian Technology Symposium (BTSym'21). BTSym 2021. Smart Innovation, Systems and Technologies*. Springer, Cham. 10.1007/978-3-031-08545-1_17

Valette-Florence, R., & Valette-Florence, P. (2020). Effects of emotions and brand personality on consumer commitment, via the mediating effects of brand trust and attachment. [English Edition]. *Recherche et Applications en Marketing*, 35(1), 84–110. 10.1177/2051570720905703

Verma, S., & Dixit, G. K. (2023). The Future of E-commerce: Trends, Challenges, and Opportunities. *International Journal for Research in Applied Science and Engineering Technology*, 11(VII), 934–937. https://www.ijraset.com/best-journal/the-future-of-ecommerce-trends-challenges-and-opportunities. 10.22214/ijraset.2023.54758

Wajid, R., & Alam, K. (2024). Role of Modern Technology in COVID-19 Care Management. In Alam, K., Daniel, S., Alzahrani, A., & Hassan Almalki, W. (Eds.), *Nursing Practice during COVID-19: Preparation, Education and Support*. Springer. 10.1007/978-3-031-52110-2_5

Wang, L., Chen, H., & Zhang, X. (2023). Make a good impression: Recommend different products for self-presentation. *Australian Journal of Management*, 0(0). 10.1177/03128962231166246

Wang, X. V., & Wang, L. (2021). A literature survey of the robotic technologies during the COVID-19 pandemic. *Journal of Manufacturing Systems*, 60, 823–836. 10.1016/j.jmsy.2021.02.00533612914

Wara, A. A., & Dugga, S. (2019). Enhancing User Experience using Mobile QR-Code Application. *International Journal of Computer and Information Technology*, 3(6), 1310–1315. https://www.ijcit.com/archives/volume3/issue6/Paper030620.pdf

Wihardja, C. E., & Widianto, M. H. (2023). *E-Commerce Website: A Systematic Literature Review.* International Conference on Informatics, Multimedia, Cyber and Informations System (ICIMCIS), Jakarta Selatan, Indonesia. 10.1109/ICIMCIS60089.2023.10349018

Wisnicki, B. (2020). Impact of R&D Cartelization with Endogenous Product Differentiation. In Tsounis, N., & Vlachvei, A. (Eds.), *Advances in Cross-Section Data Methods in Applied Economic Research. ICOAE 2019. Springer Proceedings in Business and Economics*. Springer. 10.1007/978-3-030-38253-7_13

Xia, Y., Xie, J., Zhu, W., & Liang, L. (2021). Pricing strategy in the product and service market. *Journal of Management Science and Engineering*, 6(2), 211–234. 10.1016/j.jmse.2021.02.001

Yamin, M. A. Y., & Abdalatif, O. A. A. (2024). Examining consumer behavior towards adoption of quick response code mobile payment systems: Transforming mobile payment in the fintech industry. *Humanities & Social Sciences Communications*, 11(1), 675. 10.1057/s41599-024-03189-w

Yao, Y., Wang, L., & Shen, J. (2022). Features and Applications of QR Codes. *International Journal for Innovation Education and Research*, 10(5), 166–169. 10.31686/ijier.vol10.iss5.3762

Zha, D., Foroudi, P., Melewar, T. C., & Jin, Z. (2024). Examining the Impact of Sensory Brand Experience on Brand Loyalty. *Corporate Reputation Review*. 10.1057/s41299-023-00175-x

Chapter 9
The Transaction War Between Google Pay and Phonepe

A. B. Mishra
https://orcid.org/0000-0003-4429-4058
International Institute of Management Studies, Pune, India

Vinod Gaikwad
International Institute of Management Studies, Pune, India

ABSTRACT

The transaction war between Google Pay and PhonePe has been a focal point in the digital payment landscape, reflecting the intense competition and evolving dynamics within the market. Key insights reveal the distinctive strengths of Google Pay, such as its brand recognition and integration with the Google ecosystem, alongside PhonePe's advantages, including its affiliation with Flipkart and extensive merchant network. Both platforms contend with regulatory competitive pressures, technological advancements, innovation, and strategic partnerships. PhonePe's revenue of Rs 2,914 crore for the financial year 2023 indicates significant growth for the digital payments platform. Meanwhile, Google Pay's annual revenue of 305.63 billion U.S. dollars 2023 highlights the massive scale and global reach of Google's payment services. Beyond the transaction war itself, this case study sheds light on broader trends and implications for the digital payment industry, offering valuable insights for industry practitioners, policymakers, and researchers navigating the dynamic landscape of digital finance

1. INTRODUCTION

In India, the digital payment landscape has witnessed a fierce competition between Google Pay and PhonePe, two leading players in the market. The battle for dominance in digital transactions has led to an array of strategies, innovations, and countermeasures from both sides. (Mishra, 2023) PhonePe's revenue of Rs 2,914 crore for the financial year 2023 indicates significant growth for the Indian digital payments platform. Meanwhile, Google Pay's annual revenue of 305.63 billion U.S. dollars throughout 2023 highlights the massive scale and global reach of Google's payment services. Both figures reflect the increasing adoption and reliance on digital payment solutions in today's economy. (Ruchin Goyal, 2022) This case study delves into the transaction war between Google Pay and PhonePe, analyzing their

DOI: 10.4018/978-1-6684-7840-0.ch009

competitive strategies, market positioning, and the broader implications for the Indian digital payment ecosystem. (Ranjan et al., 2023) This case study explores the transaction war between Google Pay and PhonePe, offering insights into the competitive rivalry, regulatory environment, technological innovations, and strategic implications for stakeholders. By examining both platforms and analyzing factors influencing the digital payment landscape, this study provides a comprehensive understanding of the transaction war and its implications. this study contributes to the broader discourse on digital payments in India and offers practical implications for digital payment providers, policymakers, and other stakeholders navigating the complexities of the digital economy. Overall, this case study serves as a valuable resource for understanding the transaction war between Google Pay and PhonePe, shedding light on the competitive landscape, regulatory challenges, technological innovations, and strategic considerations shaping the future of digital payments in India.

2. PROBLEM STATEMENT

The transaction war between Google Pay and PhonePe in the Indian digital payment market presents a complex set of challenges and opportunities for both companies. As they vie for dominance, it is essential to identify and address the key issues impacting their market position, user experience, and long-term sustainability. The primary objective is to analyze the competitive dynamics, regulatory hurdles, technological innovations, and consumer preferences that shape the battleground. By identifying and strategically tackling these issues, both Google Pay and PhonePe can optimize their strategies, enhance user experiences, and fortify their market positions amidst the ongoing transaction war.

3. METHODOLOGY

Adopt a qualitative research approach to explore the transaction war between Google Pay and PhonePe comprehensively. Qualitative methods allow for in-depth analysis of the nuances, dynamics, and intricacies of the competition between the two platforms. Gather secondary data from various sources, including financial reports, company announcements, press releases, industry publications, regulatory documents, market research reports, and academic literature. This data will provide context, background information, and supporting evidence for the case study analysis. Structure the case study narrative into coherent sections, including background information on Google Pay and PhonePe, competitive analysis, regulatory challenges, technological innovations, consumer behavior insights, and strategic implications. Present real-world examples, anecdotes, and case studies to illustrate key points and provide concrete evidence supporting the analysis and conclusions. Subject the case study to peer review by experts in the field of digital payments, market research, and strategic management. Validate the findings and recommendations through discussions with industry practitioners, regulators, and other relevant stakeholders to ensure practical relevance and applicability. By this methodology, the case study will provide valuable insights into the transaction war between Google Pay and PhonePe, contributing to a deeper understanding of the competitive dynamics, challenges, and opportunities in the Indian digital payment market.

4. BACKGROUND

PhonePe: PhonePe is a digital payments platform based in India. Founded in December 2015 by Sameer Nigam, Rahul Chari, and Burzin Engineer, PhonePe initially started as a unified payments interface (UPI) app, (Kashyap, 2023) enabling users to make peer-to-peer payments and pay utility bills. It gained prominence as one of the leading digital payment platforms in India, (N.L. Sarda, 2024) offering a range of financial services, including mobile recharges, bill payments, and merchant transactions (Tolety, 2018). In 2016, PhonePe was acquired by Flipkart, one of India's largest e-commerce companies, providing it with significant backing and resources for growth (Mishra & Dodke, 2024). Since then, PhonePe has expanded its offerings, introduced innovative features, and established itself as a key player in India's digital payment ecosystem (Pulse, 2023).

Table 1. Timeline of PhonePe

Year	Activity
December 2015	PhonePe is founded by Sameer Nigam, Rahul Chari, and Burzin Engineer.
August 2016	Flipkart acquires PhonePe, providing it with significant resources and access to Flipkart's extensive user base.
2016-2017	PhonePe focuses on building its user base and enhancing its platform's features, including peer-to-peer payments and bill payments.
April 2017	PhonePe launches its UPI-based app, allowing users to make seamless transactions using their bank accounts.
2018	PhonePe introduces several new features and services, including mobile recharges, in-app games, and merchant transactions.
2019	PhonePe crosses the milestone of one billion transactions on its platform, cementing its position as one of India's leading digital payment platforms.
2020	PhonePe expands its offerings by introducing financial products such as insurance and mutual funds on its platform.
2021	PhonePe introduces innovative features such as PhonePe Switch, enabling users to access a wide range of third-party services within the app.
Present	PhonePe remains a key player in India's digital payment landscape, competing with other major players such as Google Pay and Paytm while continuously innovating and expanding its offerings

Source: Accumulated Data

Google Pay: Google Pay is a digital wallet platform and online payment system developed by Google. It allows users to make payments, send money to friends, pay bills, and purchase goods and services online or in stores (Ugia, 2023). Initially launched in 2015 as Android Pay and later rebranded as Google Pay in 2018, the platform has since expanded its services globally, catering to users across various countries (Mishra & Singh, 2023). Google Pay leverages Google's extensive infrastructure and partnerships to offer a seamless and secure payment experience to its users.

continued on following page

Table 2. Continued
Table 2. Timeline of Google Pay

Year	Activity
September 2015	Google launches Android Pay, a mobile wallet platform that allows users to make payments using their Android devices.
2016	Android Pay expands its services to additional countries, including the United Kingdom, Australia, and Singapore.
January 2018	Google announces the merger of Android Pay and Google Wallet into a single platform called Google Pay, streamlining its payment services.
February 2018	Google Pay is officially launched, integrating features from both Android Pay and Google Wallet into a unified platform.
2018-2019	Google Pay expands its services globally, adding support for more countries and partnering with various banks and financial institutions to offer enhanced features and services.
October 2018	Google Pay introduces its app for iOS devices, allowing iPhone users to make payments and send money using the platform.
2019	Google Pay launches new features such as Google Pay for Business, enabling merchants to accept payments through the platform.
2020	Google Pay introduces several new features and updates, including support for contactless payments, transit passes, and integration with Google Photos for sending money.
2020-2021	Google Pay experiences significant growth in user adoption and transaction volume, driven by increased demand for digital payments amid the COVID-19 pandemic.
2021	Google Pay introduces new features such as Plex, a digital banking platform offering checking and savings accounts in partnership with banks and credit unions.

Source: Accumulated Data

5. LITERATURE REVIEW

The most common form of digital payment is still using a laptop, tablet, or smartphone to browse a website and make purchases or make other payments (Usman, 2023). Over the projected period, it is expected that consumer interest in online transactions would increase due to the rising acceptability of mobile apps, digital currencies, mobile wallets, net banking, point of sale, and debit and credit cards (Mishra, Satarkar, et al., 2023). When compared to traditional payment methods, cashless transactions offer several advantages, such as increased speed, convenience, and security (Usman M et al., 2023). Cashless payments benefit businesses because they improve tracking, revenue, and customer satisfaction. Due to their ease of use and the numerous benefits of online transactions, e-wallets have grown in popularity over time (Mishra, 2023). Financial service providers employ digital technologies to enhance client satisfaction, optimise operational efficiency, and foster innovation. The digital transformation of the financial sector includes technologies such as artificial intelligence (AI), cloud computing, block chain, data, and the Internet of Things (IoT) (Mohseni, 2022). Frequently, what motivates them is their ambition to challenge reputable financial organisations. Given their growing consumer popularity, especially among a younger demographic more accustomed to digital technology, fintech companies are exerting pressure on more traditional financial institutions to change their offers or risk losing market share. Transitioning from a traditional analogue workplace to a modern, digitally connected one may be difficult (Mishra A. B., 2023). The rapid growth of digital payments in India has been extensively documented in the literature. Researchers have highlighted factors such as increasing smartphone penetration, government initiatives promoting digital transactions, and the emergence of Unified Payments Interface (UPI) as key drivers of the digital payment ecosystem (Garg, 2022). The competition between Google Pay and PhonePe has been analyzed in several studies. These studies examine factors such as market share trends, user acquisition strategies, technological innovations, and competitive positioning. For example, an analysis provides insights into the strategies and market performance of both platforms, shedding light on their strengths, weaknesses, opportunities, and threats. Regulatory challenges and policy developments in the digital payment sector have been a subject of research interest. Studies have examined issues such as data privacy laws, interoperability requirements, and regulatory compliance burdens faced by Google Pay, PhonePe, and other digital payment providers (Singh, 2024). Understanding consumer behavior and preferences is crucial for digital payment providers (Varma & Mishra, 2015). Research has explored factors influencing consumer adoption, usage patterns, satisfaction levels, and switching behavior. McKinsey & Company conducted a study on consumer trends in digital payments, offering insights into the drivers and barriers to adoption and usage (Mishra A. B., 2023). Technological innovations play a vital role in shaping the digital payment landscape. Scholars have investigated the impact of emerging technologies such as artificial intelligence, blockchain, and biometrics on digital payment platforms. Google's blog post (Year) provides updates on new features and technological advancements in Google Pay, highlighting the company's commitment to innovation (Usman, 2023). Strategic decisions and initiatives undertaken by Google Pay and PhonePe have been analyzed in academic and industry literature. Case studies and strategic analyses offer insights into partnerships, product development strategies, and competitive positioning strategies adopted by both platforms (Ruchin Goyal, 2022) By synthesizing insights from these studies, this case study aims to provide a comprehensive analysis of the transaction war between Google Pay and PhonePe, offering valuable insights for stakeholders in the digital payment ecosystem (D'Cruze, 2023).

6. DIGITAL PAYMENT LANDSCAPE

Online buying decisions, which are described as buying things and/or paying for services through a website/browser on a computer, mobile device etc (Mishra, 2015) continues to lead the field of online payment categories. In the last year, 73% of participants said they have made a digital payment of such a nature (Mishra, 2023).

Figure 1. Digital Payment Adaptation

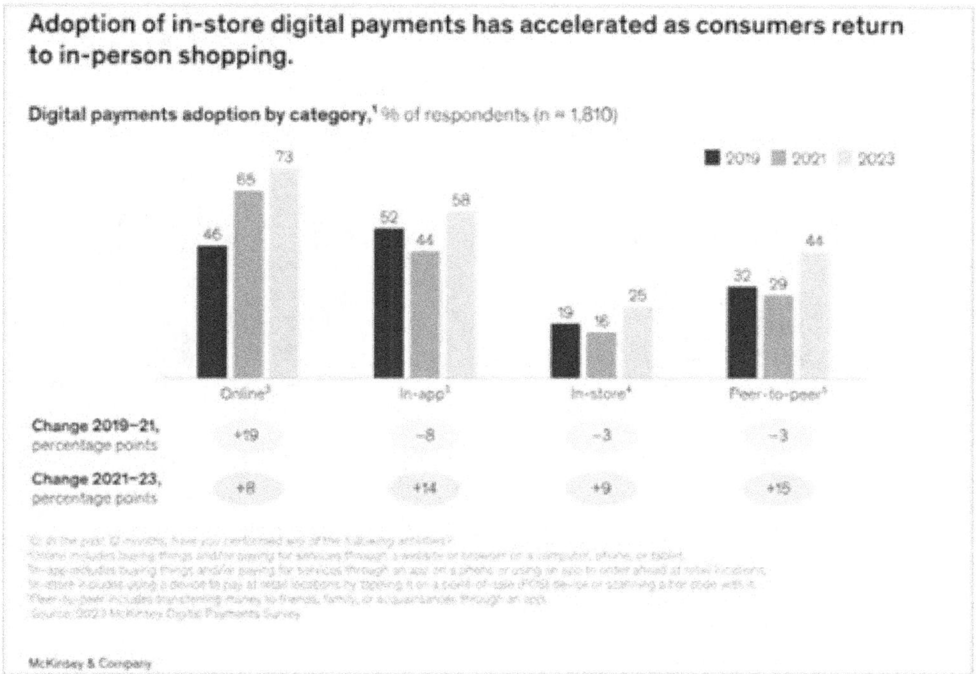

Source: Mckinsey.com

A significant development is the tendency of digital wallet consolidation. 30% of customers predicted that by 2021, they would have three or more digital wallets (like Google Pay and PhonePe) on their phones. This percentage dropped to 20% in 2023. The percentage of respondents who anticipated using a single wallet, on the other hand, increased from 21% to 31% during the same time frame. With 69% of respondents ranking security and provider trust as top considerations, these attributes have cemented their position as essential when choosing a wallet. Easy to use and low cost, which were chosen by 58 and 46 percent of respondents, respectively, were the next most often mentioned qualities, and they separated out from the pack in comparison to previous studies (Mishra, 2023).

6.1 Pestle Analysis Of Digital Payment Landscape

PESTLE analysis highlights the multifaceted factors shaping the digital payment landscape, including political regulations, economic conditions, social trends, technological advancements, legal frameworks, and environmental considerations.

Figure 2. PESTLE Analysis of Digital Payment Landscape

Source: Accumulated Data

By considering these factors, digital payment companies can better understand the external environment in which they operate and make informed decisions regarding strategy, risk management, and innovation.

7. THE TRANSACTION WAR

The "Transaction War" refers to the fierce competition among companies in the digital payment industry to capture a larger share of the market and increase transaction volume. This competition is driven by several factors:

7.1 Market Penetration

Google Pay initially gained traction by leveraging its integration with popular Google services and Android devices, securing a large user base. PhonePe capitalized on its association with Flipkart, integrating its payment option into the e-commerce giant's platform and leveraging its extensive customer base (Kashyap, 2023).

Figure 3. National Payments Corporation of India (NPCI) data (March 2023)

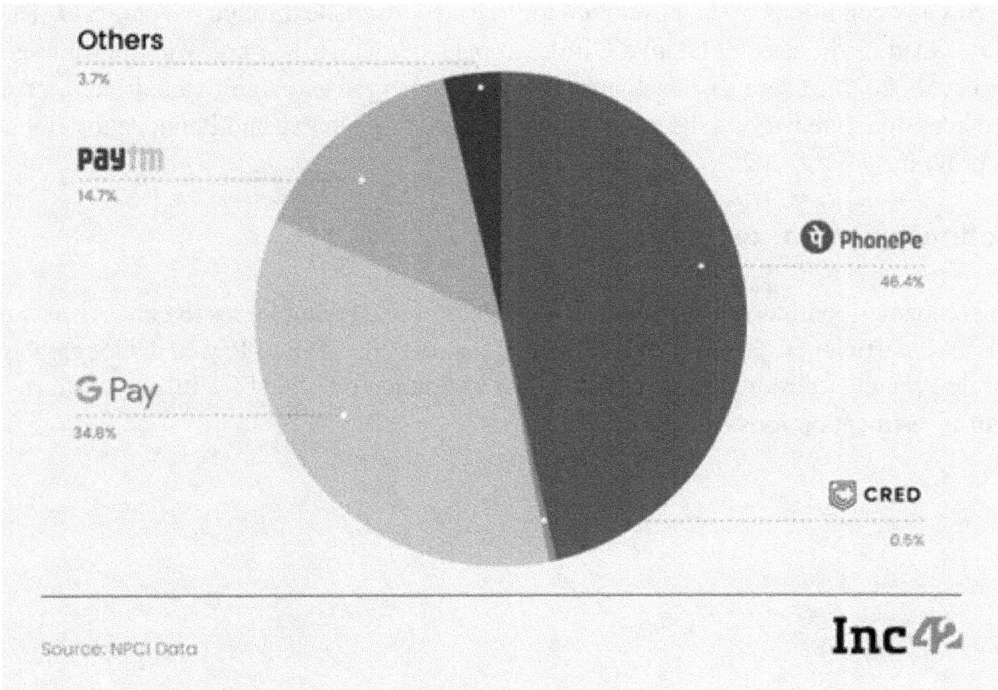

Source: inc42.com

In March 2023, the Unified Payments Interface (UPI) marked a significant milestone by processing a record-breaking 868.5 crore transactions, amounting to INR 14.1 trillion (Singh, 2024). Data provided by the National Payments Corporation of India (NPCI) indicates a notable month-over-month increase, with transactions rising by 15.33% and transaction value by 14.1% throughout 2023 (Mishra, Ranjan, et al., 2023). During this period, PhonePe maintained its position as the leading UPI app, facilitating 407.63 crore transactions valued at INR 7.07 trillion in March 2023 alone. With a market share of 49.45% in transaction value and 46.38% in transaction count, PhonePe demonstrated its enduring popularity and dominance in the digital payments landscape (Garg, 2022). Following closely behind, Google Pay processed 305.44 crore UPI transactions amounting to INR 4.83 trillion, capturing 34.75% of total transactions and 33.75% of transaction value. Despite being the runner-up, Google Pay's substantial transaction volume underscores its significant presence and competitiveness in the UPI ecosystem (Kashyap, 2023).

7.2 Cash back Incentives

Google Pay aggressively implemented cashback rewards programs to incentivize user transactions, referrals, and other interactions, with rewards ranging from 5 to 30 available to both new and existing users. These cashback rewards, visible in the rewards channel, aim to enhance user retention and attract new users to the platform. (Mishra & Karjodkar, 2022). Users must utilize their cashback rewards within seven days of redemption, after which they expire if unused. Cashbacks are directly credited to the user's bank account linked to Google Pay, provided it supports UPI transactions (Tanwar, 2019).

Similarly, PhonePe offers Payback Rewards, where users can earn cashback or scratch cards based on the terms and conditions of the promotion for transactions made through the platform. The cashback amount is added to the user's PhonePe Gift Card balance, which is a non-withdrawable gift voucher (Mohseni et al., 2022). These cashback incentives have emerged as a significant driver for user engagement and adoption, intensifying the competition between Google Pay and PhonePe to offer compelling rewards programs (Garg, 2022).

7.3 Technological Innovations

Both companies continuously introduced new features and technologies to enhance user experience and transaction efficiency. Google Pay introduced features like 'Tap to Pay' and 'Google Pay for Business,' while PhonePe introduced innovations such as 'PhonePe Switch' for in-app services and 'Super Funds' for investment options.

Figure 4. Technological Innovations

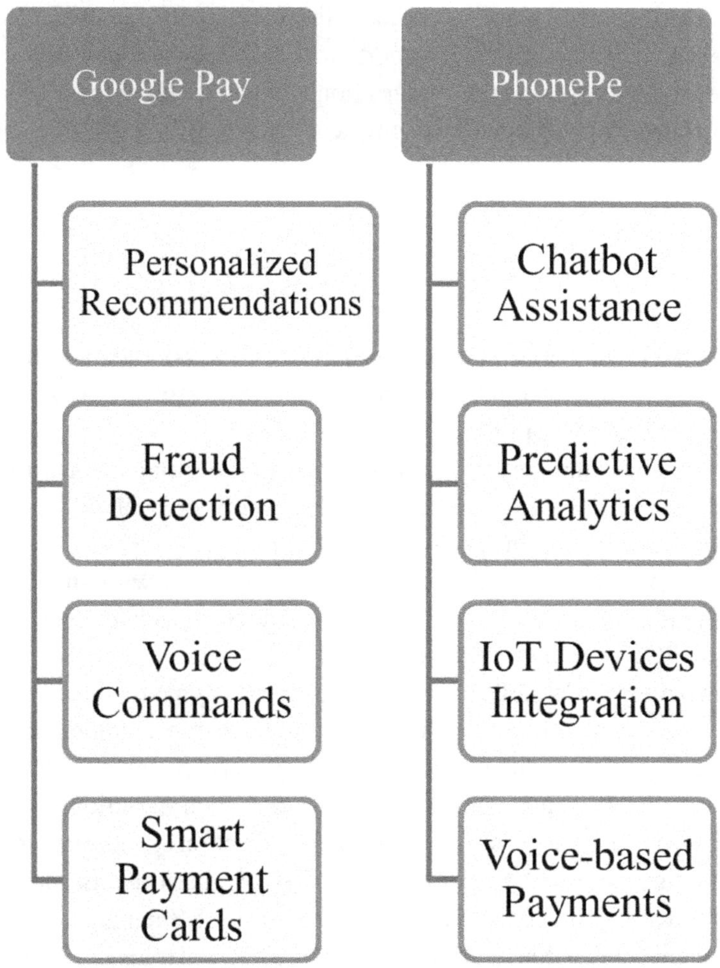

Source: Accumulated Data

Google Pay

- **Personalized Recommendations:** Google Pay leverages AI algorithms to analyze user transaction data and preferences, providing personalized recommendations for offers, discounts, and loyalty programs. This enhances user engagement and encourages repeat usage of the platform (Ugia, 2023).
- **Fraud Detection:** AI-powered fraud detection systems in Google Pay analyze transaction patterns, detect anomalies, and identify potentially fraudulent activities in real-time. This helps to safeguard users' accounts and prevent unauthorized transactions (Nilesh Kate, 2022).

- **Voice Commands:** Google Pay integrates with Google Assistant, allowing users to initiate transactions and check their account balance using voice commands. This IoT integration enables hands-free interactions and enhances accessibility for users (Rana et al., 2022).
- **Smart Payment Cards:** Google Pay supports IoT-enabled smart payment cards, allowing users to make contactless payments using their smartphones or wearable devices. This enhances convenience and security by eliminating the need for physical cards (Mishra, 2020).

PhonePe

- **Chatbot Assistance:** PhonePe employs AI-powered chatbots to provide customer support and assistance to users. These chatbots can answer queries, resolve issues, and guide users through various features and functionalities of the app (Kashyap, 2023).
- **Predictive Analytics:** PhonePe utilizes AI and machine learning algorithms to analyze transaction data and user behavior, enabling predictive analytics for personalized recommendations, targeted promotions, and fraud detection (D'Cruze, 2023).
- **IoT Devices Integration:** PhonePe supports IoT integration with smart devices and wearables, allowing users to make payments using IoT-enabled devices such as smartwatches, fitness trackers, and IoT-enabled POS terminals (Mohseni, 2022).
- **Voice-based Payments:** PhonePe enables voice-based payments through integration with virtual assistants and voice-enabled devices. Users can initiate transactions and perform other banking tasks using voice commands, enhancing accessibility and convenience (Mishra, Allen, et al., 2024). Unlike many merchants content with debit card or UPI transactions, those with high Average Transaction Values (ATV) necessitate credit card transaction capabilities, facilitated either through Electronic Data Capture (EDC) machines or UPI. To safeguard against identity theft, Custom Photo QRs were introduced, followed by the implementation of SmartSpeakers for real-time payment validation. PhonePe's SmartSpeakers validate over 100 crore transactions monthly on average, bolstering merchant capabilities across more than 17,000 postal codes and deploying over 4.4 million devices across India (Mishra A. B., 2023). The deployment of devices even in remote locations underscores the widespread adoption of this technology in rural areas (Mishra, Varma Anil, et al., 2021). Recently, PhonePe introduced a celebrity voice feature for SmartSpeakers, allowing merchants to confirm payments using voices like the renowned Hindi voice of Mr. Amitabh Bachchan. This addition enhances the appeal to both customers and merchants, resonating with millions of Indians.A significant advancement in PhonePe's payment solution suite is the introduction of their new point-of-sale device. Running on the Android operating system, this device revolutionizes checkout processes for businesses, whether at delivery locations, restaurant tables, retail counters, or anywhere with cellphone connectivity (Pulse, 2023).

7.4 Strategic Partnerships

Both Google Pay and PhonePe forged strategic partnerships with banks, financial institutions, and other businesses to expand their ecosystem and offer additional services to users. These partnerships enabled both platforms to offer a wide range of financial services beyond basic peer-to-peer transactions, further enhancing their competitiveness.

Strategic Partnerships With Google Pay

- **Banks and Financial Institutions:** HDFC Bank, ICICI Bank, Axis Bank, State Bank of India (SBI), and other major banks in India have partnered with Google Pay to enable seamless integration with users' bank accounts for fund transfers, bill payments, and other financial transactions (Mishra A. B., 2023).
- **Merchants and Businesses:** Google Pay has partnerships with a wide range of merchants and businesses, including retail chains, restaurants, online marketplaces, and service providers, allowing users to make payments for purchases and services through the platform (Garg, 2022).
- **Mobile Network Operators (MNOs):** Google Pay collaborates with mobile network operators such as Bharti Airtel, Vodafone Idea, and Reliance Jio to enable mobile recharge and bill payments directly through the app (Mishra, Goel, et al., 2022).
- **Third-Party Apps and Services:** Google Pay integrates with third-party apps and services such as Zomato, Swiggy, Uber, BookMyShow, and more, allowing users to make payments seamlessly within these apps (D'Cruze, 2023).

Strategic Partnerships With PhonePe

- **Flipkart:** PhonePe is backed by Flipkart, one of India's largest e-commerce companies. This strategic partnership enables seamless integration of PhonePe's payment services with Flipkart's platform, allowing users to make payments for purchases on the e-commerce platform (Thathoo, 2023).
- **Merchants and Retailers:** PhonePe has partnerships with a diverse range of merchants and retailers, including offline stores, online marketplaces, and service providers, facilitating digital payments for a wide variety of products and services (Mehta, 2021).
- **Utility and Service Providers:** PhonePe collaborates with utility companies, service providers, and government agencies to enable bill payments, recharges, and other utility services directly through the app (Mishra, Chand, et al., 2022).
- **Banks and Financial Institutions:** PhonePe has strategic partnerships with several banks and financial institutions to offer banking services, including savings accounts, loans, insurance, and investment options, through the app (Varma & Mishra, 2013).

These strategic partnerships enhance the offerings, user experience, and market presence of Google Pay and PhonePe, contributing to their growth and success in the competitive digital payment landscape.

7.5 Merchant Acquisition

Google Pay and PhonePe aggressively pursued merchant acquisition strategies, offering incentives and discounts to businesses to accept digital payments through their platforms. This led to widespread adoption of digital payments among merchants, further intensifying the competition between Google Pay and PhonePe for market share (Mehta, 2021).

7.6 SWOT Analysis of Google Pay and PhonePe

SWOT analysis is a strategic planning tool used by organizations to identify and evaluate their internal strengths and weaknesses, as well as external opportunities and threats. The importance of SWOT analysis lies in its ability to provide a structured framework for assessing the current state of an organization or a specific project and informing strategic decision-making.

Figure 5. SWOT analysis of Google Pay

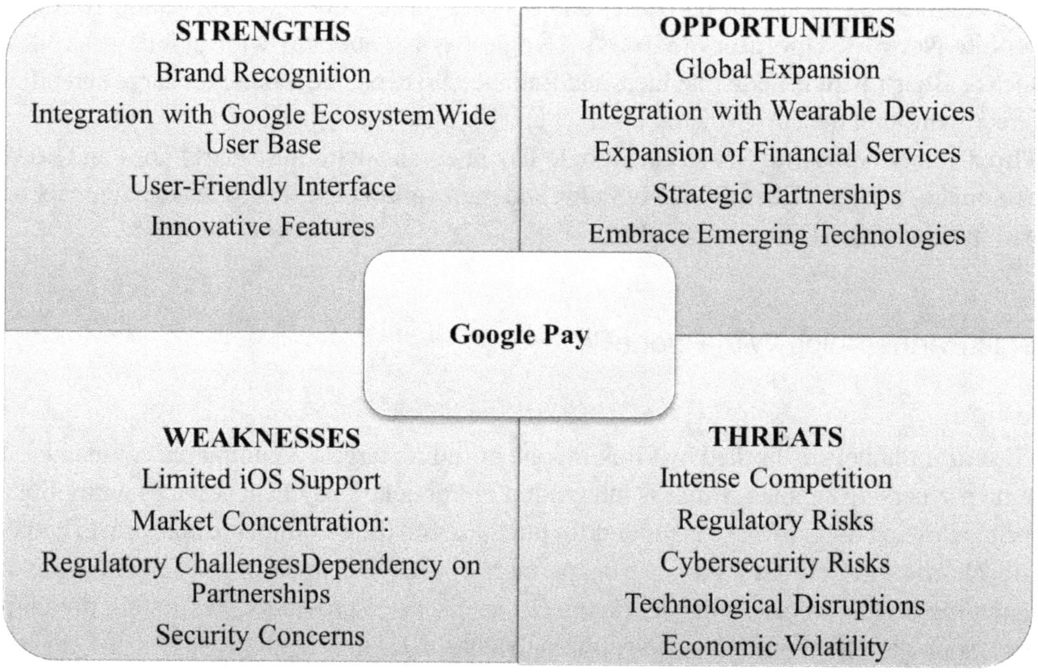

Source: Accumulated Data

Figure 6. SWOT analysis of PhonePe

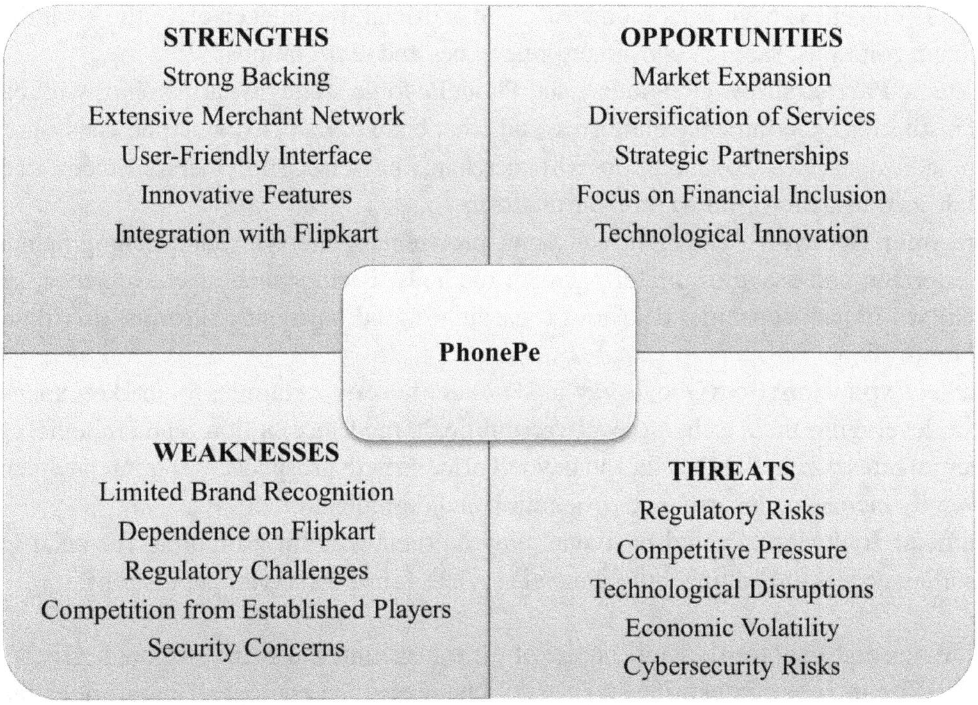

Source: Accumulated Data

By systematically assessing their internal capabilities and external environment, organizations can make informed decisions and enhance their competitiveness and resilience over time both Google Pay and PhonePe have their respective strengths and weaknesses, understanding these factors is crucial for strategic decision-making and maintaining competitive advantage in the dynamic digital payment landscape.

8. FINDINGS

- **Competitive Dynamics:** Google Pay and PhonePe engage in fierce competition, leveraging their respective strengths to gain market share and enhance their positions in the digital payment landscape. Both platforms invest heavily in marketing campaigns, user acquisition strategies, and product innovations to attract and retain users.
- **Regulatory Challenges:** Google Pay and PhonePe face regulatory challenges in India, including compliance with data localization laws, interoperability mandates, and consumer protection regulations. Regulatory uncertainties and changes pose risks to their operations and growth strategies, necessitating proactive compliance measures and engagement with policymakers.

- **Technological Innovations:** Both Google Pay and PhonePe introduce innovative features and functionalities to improve user experience, security, and convenience. Technological advancements such as contactless payments, biometrics, and artificial intelligence drive the evolution of digital payment solutions, shaping consumer preferences and expectations.
- **Strategic Partnerships:** Google Pay and PhonePe forge strategic partnerships with banks, financial institutions, e-commerce platforms, and other businesses to expand their ecosystems and offer value-added services. Collaborations with merchants and service providers enhance user engagement and drive transaction volume on their platforms.
- **Consumer Behavior:** Changing consumer preferences, lifestyles, and demographics influence the adoption and usage of digital payment methods. Factors such as convenience, security, and incentives impact consumer decisions regarding digital payment platforms, driving competition and innovation.
- **Market Expansion:** Both Google Pay and PhonePe have opportunities for market expansion beyond India, leveraging their technological capabilities, brand recognition, and strategic partnerships. Emerging markets in South Asia and beyond offer growth prospects for digital payment providers, driven by increasing smartphone penetration and digitalization efforts.
- **Financial Inclusion:** Digital payments play a crucial role in promoting financial inclusion by providing access to banking and financial services for underserved populations.

The findings highlight the dynamic nature of the transaction war between Google Pay and PhonePe, characterized by intense competition, regulatory challenges, technological innovations, and strategic collaborations. Understanding these findings is essential for digital payment providers, policymakers, and other stakeholders seeking to navigate the complexities of the digital economy and drive sustainable growth in the digital payment ecosystem.

9. CONCLUSION AND RECOMMENDATIONS

The transaction war between Google Pay and PhonePe has been characterized by intense competition, innovative strategies, and relentless pursuit of market dominance. Both platforms have significantly contributed to the growth of digital payments in India, driving financial inclusion and transforming the way transactions are conducted (Mishra & Ranjan, 2022). As the battle continues, the Indian digital payment landscape remains dynamic, with Google Pay and PhonePe vying for supremacy amidst evolving consumer preferences, regulatory challenges, and technological advancements (Garg, 2022). The integration of AI and IoT technologies in Google Pay and PhonePe enhances the efficiency, security, and user experience of digital payments, driving innovation and differentiation in the competitive digital payment landscape (Mishra & Singh, 2024). Google Pay and PhonePe should continue to monitor regulatory developments, engage with policymakers, and proactively address compliance requirements to mitigate regulatory risks and ensure sustained operations and growth (Mishra, Satarkar, et al., 2024). Both platforms should prioritize investments in technological innovation, exploring emerging technologies such as blockchain, artificial intelligence, and biometrics to enhance security, improve user experience, and drive differentiation (Tanwar, 2019). Google Pay and PhonePe should explore opportunities to expand their ecosystems through strategic partnerships with banks, financial institutions, merchants, and service providers, offering value-added services and enhancing user engagement (Mishra, Raikwar, et al., 2024). Google Pay and PhonePe can contribute to financial inclusion by expanding access to banking and financial services for underserved populations, including rural communities, small businesses, and low-income individuals, through tailored products and initiatives (Mishra, 2022). Both platforms should prioritize user experience, offering intuitive interfaces, seamless transactions, and personalized recommendations to enhance user satisfaction, loyalty, and retention (Mehta, 2021). Google Pay and PhonePe can explore opportunities to diversify revenue streams beyond transaction fees, such as offering financial products, advertising services, and premium features, to ensure sustainable monetization and profitability (Mishra, Sahu, et al., 2021). By implementing these recommendations, Google Pay and PhonePe can strengthen their competitive positions, drive innovation, and contribute to the continued growth and development of the digital payment ecosystem in India and beyond.

REFERENCES

D'Cruze, D. (2023). *Google Pay now supports UPI payments via RuPay credit cards; check how to use it.* Business Today. https://www.businesstoday.in/

Desk, T. (2023). Google Pay now supports UPI payments using RuPay credit cards. *Indian Express.* https://indianexpress.com/

Devi, S., & Periyasamy, N. (2023). A Study On Users Perception Towards Google Pay With Special Reference To Puducherry. *Journal of Namibian Studies: History Politics Culture*, 38, 1995–2003.

Garg, A. (2022). *Google Pay, PhonePe and other UPI apps may soon impose transaction limit.* INDIA TODAY.

Kashyap, H. (2023). *PhonePe, Google Pay, Paytm Process 94% Of UPI Transactions In March 2023.* Inc42.

Lohar, A., Gajare, Y. Y., & Kumar, A. (2018). Key growth drivers and barriers to adoption of e-payments: A review. *National Journal of Research in Marketing, Finance and HRM, 3*(1), 01-12.

Manickam, T., Vinayagamoorthi, G., Gopalakrishnan, S., Sudha, M., & Mathiraj, S. P. (2022). Customer inclination on mobile wallets with reference to Google-Pay and PayTM in Bengaluru City. [IJEBR]. *International Journal of E-Business Research*, 18(1), 1–16. 10.4018/IJEBR.293295

Mathiraj, S. P., & Mala, M. (2021). A study on users' opinion about google pay. *IJAR*, 7(12), 161–164.

Mehta, R. (2021). Phonepe Vs Google Pay which is better? *Times of India.*timesofindia.indiatimes.com

Mishra, A. (2020). E-payment system: A rising trend of economy. *New Paradigm in Business & Education*, 1, 1–6.

Mishra, A. B. (2015). *Mobile Commerce in Modern Business Era.* Research Gate. https://www.researchgate.net/publication/351840817_Mobile_Commerce_in_Modern_Business_Era

Mishra, A. B. (2020). E- Payment System: A Rising Trend Of Economy. *New Paradigm in Business and Education.* Research Gate. https://www.researchgate.net/profile/Anitha-K-2/publication/349605501_E-LEARNING_THROUGH_GAMIFICATION-_AN_ITINERARY_TO_GAIN_IN-DEPTH_KNOWLEDGE/links/6037d566299bf1cc26ef9597/E-LEARNING-THROUGH-GAMIFICATION-AN-ITINERARY-TO-GAIN-IN-DEPTH-KNOWLEDGE.pdf#page=10

Mishra, A. B., Varma Anil, & Ranjan Nitin. (2021). PUTSCH BUYER TENDENCY AND CLIMBING SALES OF MOBILE TRADE BUSINESS. Manager –. *British Journal of Administrative Management*, 58(152), 54–60.

Mishra, A. B. (2022). SAHYADRI FARMS: INDIA'S LARGEST FARMER PRODUCER COMPANY. *International Journal of Advance and Applied Research*, 10, 996–998. https://ijaar.co.in/wp-content/uploads/2022/11/1001175.pdf

Mishra, A. B. (2023). Dynamics of Digital Payments Enable the World's Safest Way to Pay. *Journal of Informatics Education and Research*, 3(2).

Mishra, A. B., Allen, M., & Tirkey, P. (2024). *Disruption causes to Micromax by once a Market leader now a Myth*. https://www.iimspune.edu.in/images/pdf/Journal/Vol3I1-Paper11.pdf

Mishra, A. B., Chand, K., & Kaith, K. (2022). Influencer Marketing as Emerging Promotional Tool in Modern Era and Opportunities to Uprising Sales. *International Journal of Emerging Research in Engineering, Science, and Management*, 1(3). 10.58482/ijeresm.v1i3.3

Mishra, A. B., & Dodke, S. D. (2024). ZARA: Technological Influence on Becoming the Fashion Industry's Market Leader. In Global, I. G. I. (Ed.), (pp. 204–215)., 10.4018/979-8-3693-2643-5.ch012

Mishra, A. B., Goel, A., & Jajoo, P. (2022). A Case Study of Amul: Implementation of Extension Strategy to Repositioning Brand During Covid-19 Period. *International Journal of Emerging Research in Engineering, Science, and Management*, 1(4). 10.58482/ijeresm.v1i4.3

Mishra, A. B., & Karjodkar, R. (2022). A Case Study of Air India - Maharajah Back to Home. *International Journal of Emerging Research in Engineering, Science, and Management*, 1(3). 10.58482/ijeresm.v1i3.5

Mishra, A. B., Raikwar, A., & Tiwari, A. (2024). *Britannia: Marketing Initiatives Boost A Fledgling Business's Transformation To One Of The Largest Fmcg Brands*. https://www.iimspune.edu.in/images/pdf/Journal/Vol3I1-Paper12.pdf

Mishra, A. B., & Ranjan, N. (2022). INTERNET OF THINGS BASED EMERGING SMART TOOLS FOR NEW EDGE EDUCATION. *Mukt Shabd Journal*, 11(10), 80–87. 10.0014.MSJ.2022.V11I10.0086781.1135708

Mishra, A. B., Ranjan, N., Sharma, K. M., Padhye, P., & Chand, K. (2023). Advancement of Digital Transformation to Boost Financial Services Industry. *Journal of Informatics Education and Research*, 3(2), 2435–2440.

Mishra, A. B., Sahu, T., Ranjan, N., & Varma, A. (2021). Green Marketing Practices Prevailing In Hotel Industry. *Journal of Contemporary Issues in Business and Government*, 27(02). 10.47750/cibg.2021.27.02.145

Mishra, A. B., Satarkar, M., & Joshi, S. (2023). IKEA - Phygital Transformation in Furniture Manufacturing Industry. *International Journal of Emerging Research in Engineering, Science, and Management*, 2(3), 6–9. 10.58482/ijeresm.v2i3.2

Mishra, A. B., Satarkar, M., & Joshi, S. (2024). *Capitalizing the Retail Industry by Automation and Artificial Intelligence (AI): Case Study of IKEA*. IGI Global. 10.4018/979-8-3693-2643-5.ch014

Mishra, A. B., Satarkar, M., & Joshi, S. (2024). *Capitalizing the Retail Industry by Automation and Artificial Intelligence (AI): Case Study of IKEA*. IGI Global. 10.4018/979-8-3693-2643-5.ch014

Mishra, A. B., & Singh, A. (2023). Brand Positioning in the Indian Smartphone Market: A Case Study of OnePlus. *International Journal of Emerging Research in Engineering, Science, and Management*, 2(3). 10.58482/ijeresm.v2i3.1

Mishra, A. B., & Singh, A. (2023). Brand Positioning in the Indian Smartphone Market: A Case Study of OnePlus. *International Journal of Emerging Research in Engineering, Science, and Management*, 2(3). 10.58482/ijeresm.v2i3.1

Mishra, A. B., & Singh, A. (2024). *The Mumbai Dabbawalas : An Efficient and Sustainable Lunchbox Delivery System.* IGI Global. 10.4018/979-8-3693-1544-6.ch007

Mishra, A. S. A., & Singh, A. (2023). Brand positioning in the Indian smartphone market: A case study of OnePlus. *International Journal of Emerging Research in Engineering Science and Management,* 2(3). 10.58482/ijeresm.v2i3.1

Mohseni, M., Othman, B. A., Raturi, P., Mishra, A. B., Priya, S. J., & Saravanan, V. (2022). The Role of Parallel Computing Towards Implementation of Enhanced and Effective Industrial Internet of Things (IOT) Through Manova Approach. *2022 2nd International Conference on Advance Computing and Innovative Technologies in Engineering (ICACITE),* (pp. 160–164). IEEE. 10.1109/ICACITE53722.2022.9823698

Nilesh Kate, P. P. (2022). Studies on Anti-Virus Software Tools: Strong Weapon to Protect Systems. *International Conference on Innovative Practices in Technology and Management (ICIPTM).*

Nooteboom, B. (1992). Towards a dynamic theory of transactions. *Journal of Evolutionary Economics,* 2(4), 281–299. 10.1007/BF01200127

Pulse, P. (2023). *Innovation leading to accelerated growth: The merchant journey.* PhonePe.

Rana, S., Cavaliere, L. P. L., Mishra, A. B., Padhye, P., Singh, R. R., & Khanna, R. (2022). Internet of Things (IOT) Based Assessment for Effective Monitoring Data Against Malicious Attacks on Financial Collectors. *2022 2nd International Conference on Advance Computing and Innovative Technologies in Engineering (ICACITE),* (pp. 177–181). IEEE. 10.1109/ICACITE53722.2022.9823612

Ranjan, N., Mishra, A. B., & Padhye, P. (2023). Dynamics of Digital Payments Enable the World's Safest Way to Pay. *Journal of Informatics Education and Research,* 3(2). 10.52783/jier.v3i2.406

Ruchin Goyal, P. R. (2022). Digital Payments in India: A US$10 Trillion Opportunity. *BCG.Com.*

N.L. Sarda, G. S. (2024). *An introduction to NPCI and its various products.* National Payments Corporation of India (NPCI).

Sharma, S. P. (2022). *RBI releases guidelines for interoperability-Prepaid Payment Instruments (PPIs).* PHD Chamber of Commerce and Industry.

Singh, M. (2024). Indian parliamentary panel red-flags PhonePe and Google Pay cornering 83% of India's UPI payments. *techcrunch.com.*

Tanwar, S. (2019). The Indian government can thank Google for the popularity of its digital payment system. *Quartz.*

Thathoo, C. (2023). PhonePe Separation: Flipkart Begins $700 Mn ESOP Payouts. *Inc42.* https://inc42.com/

Tolety, R. K. (2018). E-Wallets–Their cause, Rise and Relevance. International. *Journal of Research in IT and Management,* 8(7).

Tolety, R. K. (2018). E-Wallets–Their cause, Rise and Relevance. International. *Journal of Research in IT and Management,* 8(7).

Usman M, Sheoliha N, Prabhakar P V, Mishra, A. B., & Dondapati. (2023). Leading Strategies for Organizational Adaptation and Growth in Digital Transformation in Marketing. *Journal of Informatics Education and Research.*

Usman, M. S. (2023). Leading Strategies for Organizational Adaptation and Growth in Digital Transformation in Marketing. *Journal of Informatics Education and Research.*

Varma, S. R., & Mishra, A. B. (2013). *Distribution Channels of Indian Insurance Business - A Study*. Abhinavan.

Varma, S. R., & Mishra, A. B. (2015). Study of Consumer Buying Behaviour in General Insurance Industry. In *Excellence through creativity, Research, innovation in field of IT and Management*. Research Gate.

Chapter 10
Personalized Healthcare in the Era of E-Business 5.0:
Harnessing the Power of Big Data

S. C. Vetrivel
https://orcid.org/0000-0003-3050-8211
Kongu Engineering College, India

V. P. Arun
JKKN College of Engineering and Technology, India

K. C. Sowmiya
Sri Vasavi College, India

V. Sabareeshwari
Amrita School of Agricultural Sciences, India

ABSTRACT

In the dynamic landscape of modern healthcare, the convergence of E-Business 5.0 and big data is unlocking unprecedented opportunities for personalized medicine. This chapterexplores the transformative potential of E-Business 5.0, characterized by enhanced connectivity, artificial intelligence, and automation, in redefining patient-centered care through the utilization of vast data sets. The chapter examine how big data technologies, including data mining, machine learning, and predictive analytics, are enabling healthcare professionals to offer tailored treatment plans, improve diagnosis accuracy, and enhance patient outcomes. By integrating these technologies within E-Business 5.0 frameworks, healthcare systems can deliver more responsive and efficient services, ultimately leading to a new era of personalized healthcare.

DOI: 10.4018/978-1-6684-7840-0.ch010

1. INTRODUCTION

1.1. Overview of the Current Healthcare Landscape

The global healthcare landscape has been marked by a dynamic interplay of challenges and advancements. The ongoing COVID-19 pandemic has underscored the critical importance of healthcare infrastructure and highlighted existing disparities in access to medical resources. Across the globe, efforts to expand healthcare coverage and enhance resilience against future pandemics have been intensified. Telehealth has experienced a significant surge in adoption, offering remote consultations and monitoring, thereby transforming traditional healthcare delivery models (Hulsen, 2021). Advancements in precision medicine, genomics, and artificial intelligence have opened new frontiers in diagnosis and treatment. However, the rising cost of healthcare remains a persistent concern, and various countries are exploring innovative models to achieve better cost-efficiency without compromising the quality of care (Gubbi et al., 2013). As the healthcare landscape continues to evolve, the integration of technology, emphasis on preventive care, and global collaborative efforts will play crucial roles in shaping the future of healthcare.

1.2. The Need for Personalized Healthcare

Personalized healthcare, also known as precision medicine, is an innovative approach to medical treatment that takes into account individual differences in patients' genes, environments, and lifestyles (Gillum, 2013). The need for personalized healthcare arises from several factors, each contributing to the potential benefits and advancements in medical care:

- Genetic Variability: Individuals differ in their genetic makeup, leading to variations in how they respond to diseases and treatments. Personalized healthcare utilizes genetic information to tailor medical interventions, making them more effective and reducing the risk of adverse reactions.
- Targeted Treatments: Personalized healthcare enables the development of targeted therapies that are designed to address specific genetic or molecular characteristics of a patient's condition. This approach can enhance treatment efficacy while minimizing side effects.
- Disease Prevention: Understanding an individual's genetic predispositions can help identify potential health risks before symptoms manifest (Reiser, 1991). This allows for proactive measures such as lifestyle modifications, early screening, and personalized prevention strategies to reduce the likelihood of developing certain diseases.
- Optimizing Medication Response: Genetic variations can influence how individuals metabolize and respond to medications. Personalized healthcare aims to identify these variations to optimize drug selection, dosage, and treatment plans, improving overall patient outcomes and reducing the risk of adverse reactions.
- Reducing Healthcare Costs: Tailoring treatments based on individual characteristics can lead to more efficient healthcare resource utilization. By avoiding unnecessary and ineffective treatments, healthcare costs can be reduced, and resources can be directed toward interventions that are more likely to be successful.
- Advancements in Technology: Recent advancements in genomic sequencing, data analytics, and other technologies have made it more feasible and cost-effective to gather and analyze individual health data. This has accelerated the integration of personalized healthcare into clinical practice.

- Patient Empowerment: Personalized healthcare empowers patients by involving them in decision-making processes and making them active participants in their healthcare. This shift from a one-size-fits-all approach to a personalized one fosters a more patient-centric model of care.
- Improved Diagnosis Accuracy: Genetic and molecular information can enhance the accuracy of disease diagnosis. Identifying specific markers associated with diseases allows for earlier and more precise diagnosis, facilitating timely and targeted interventions.
- Research and Innovation: The emphasis on personalized healthcare encourages ongoing research and innovation in genomics, bioinformatics, and related fields. This not only benefits individual patient care but also contributes to the broader understanding of diseases and the development of new therapeutic approaches.

1.3. Big Data and its Relevance to Healthcare

Big data has emerged as a transformative force in healthcare, revolutionizing the way information is collected, analyzed, and utilized to enhance patient outcomes and streamline healthcare processes. The vast and complex datasets generated in healthcare, encompassing electronic health records, medical imaging, genomics, and patient-generated data, constitute what is collectively known as big data (Alansari et al., 2018; Belgaum et al., 2018). The relevance of big data in healthcare lies in its ability to uncover valuable insights, patterns, and correlations that traditional methods may overlook. Through advanced analytics and machine learning algorithms, healthcare professionals can identify trends, predict disease outbreaks, personalize treatment plans, and optimize resource allocation. This data-driven approach not only improves clinical decision-making but also enhances patient engagement and empowers individuals to actively manage their health. Additionally, big data facilitates medical research by expediting the discovery of new treatments and interventions. Despite the immense potential, addressing challenges related to data security, privacy, and interoperability is crucial to realizing the full benefits of big data in healthcare.

2. DIGITAL TECHNOLOGIES IN HEALTHCARE

2.1 Electronic Health Records (EHR)

Electronic Health Records (EHR) are digital versions of patients' paper charts in a healthcare setting. These records contain a patient's medical history, diagnoses, medications, treatment plans, immunization dates, allergies, radiology images, and laboratory test results. EHRs aim to provide comprehensive and real-time information about a patient's health to authorized users, facilitating better and more efficient healthcare delivery (Miraz et al., 2015). Implementing EHRs has several benefits, including improved patient care, enhanced communication among healthcare providers, increased efficiency, and better data accuracy. However, challenges such as interoperability issues, data security concerns, and the initial costs of implementation and training have been part of the ongoing discussion in the healthcare industry.

The key components and features of Electronic Health Records are:

- Patient Demographics: EHRs include basic information about patients, such as name, date of birth, gender, contact details, and emergency contacts.
- Medical History: Comprehensive records of a patient's medical history, including previous illnesses, surgeries, hospitalizations, and family medical history.
- Medications: A list of current and past medications, including dosage, frequency, and duration. EHRs often include alerts for potential drug interactions.
- Allergies: Information about any known allergies or adverse reactions to medications, foods, or environmental factors.
- Immunizations: Records of vaccinations and dates to ensure patients are up-to-date with preventive healthcare measures.
- Laboratory Test Results:EHRs store data from various diagnostic tests, such as blood tests, imaging studies, and pathology reports. Trend analysis helps healthcare providers monitor changes over time.
- Radiology Images:Integration of medical imaging files, such as X-rays, MRIs, and CT scans, directly into the electronic record for a comprehensive view of a patient's health.
- Clinical Notes:Healthcare providers can enter notes documenting each patient encounter, including symptoms, diagnoses, treatment plans, and progress.
- Electronic Prescribing: EHR systems often support electronic prescription capabilities, making it easier for healthcare providers to send prescriptions directly to pharmacies.
- Interoperability: EHRs aim to facilitate interoperability, allowing different healthcare systems to exchange and use health information seamlessly. This promotes continuity of care, especially when patients see multiple providers or move between healthcare facilities.
- Security and Privacy: Robust security measures are in place to protect patient information, and access to EHRs is typically restricted to authorized healthcare professionals.
- Patient Portals: Many EHR systems have patient portals that allow individuals to access their own health information, schedule appointments, communicate with healthcare providers, and view test results.

2.1.2 Electronic Medical Records (EMR)

Electronic Medical Records (EMR) are digital versions of the paper charts in clinician offices, clinics, and hospitals. They contain notes and information collected by and for the clinicians in that office, clinic, or hospital and are used by providers for diagnosis and treatment. EMRs are more beneficial than paper records because they enable providers to track data over time, identify patients for preventive visits and screenings, and monitor how patients are doing on certain parameters such as blood pressure readings or vaccinations. Key benefits of EMRs include:

- Improved Efficiency and Accuracy: EMRs streamline the workflow for healthcare providers, reduce the time spent on documentation, and minimize errors related to handwriting or transcription.
- Enhanced Patient Care: With instant access to comprehensive and up-to-date patient information, healthcare providers can make better-informed decisions and provide higher quality care.
- Better Coordination of Care: EMRs facilitate the sharing of patient information among different healthcare providers, ensuring that everyone involved in a patient's care has access to the same information.

- Increased Patient Participation: Some EMR systems allow patients to access their health records, test results, and treatment plans, which can help them be more engaged in their care.
- Data Security: EMRs can be more secure than paper records, with proper encryption and access control measures in place to protect patient information.

Despite these benefits, the implementation of EMRs can be challenging due to high initial costs, the need for training, and concerns about data privacy and security. However, as technology advances, the integration of EMRs continues to grow, playing a crucial role in the modernization and improvement of healthcare systems worldwide.

2.2 Wearable Devices and Internet of Things (IoT)

Wearable devices and the Internet of Things (IoT) represent two interconnected realms that have significantly transformed the landscape of technology and personal connectivity. Wearable devices, encompassing smartwatches, fitness trackers, and augmented reality glasses, have seamlessly integrated into our daily lives, providing users with real-time health monitoring, communication, and enhanced productivity (Moore & Benbasat, 1991; Nasi et al., 2015). These devices serve as extensions of ourselves, collecting and analyzing data to offer personalized insights into our well-being and activities. The synergy between wearables and IoT amplifies their impact, as these devices become nodes in a vast interconnected network. The Internet of Things expands the scope beyond individual wearables by enabling seamless communication and data exchange among various smart devices, creating a web of interconnectedness that enhances efficiency, automation, and the overall user experience. From smart homes with interconnected appliances to healthcare systems that monitor patients remotely, the fusion of wearable devices and IoT is catalyzing a paradigm shift in how we interact with technology, fostering a more connected, data-driven, and personalized future.

2.3 Data Storage and Processing Infrastructure

The Data Storage and Processing Infrastructure in Big Data Technologies for Healthcare is a comprehensive ecosystem that encompasses distributed storage systems, databases, processing frameworks, and security measures. This infrastructure empowers healthcare providers to manage, analyze, and derive valuable insights from the ever-growing volumes of healthcare data. Below are key components of the Data Storage and Processing Infrastructure in the context of Big Data Technologies in Healthcare:

1. Data Storage:

    - Distributed File Systems: Technologies such as Hadoop Distributed File System (HDFS) provide scalable and distributed storage for large datasets. This is crucial for storing diverse healthcare data, including electronic health records (EHRs), medical images, genomic data, and sensor data.
    - Data Warehouses: Healthcare organizations use data warehouses like Amazon Redshift, Google BigQuery, or Snowflake for efficient storage and retrieval of structured data. These platforms are designed to handle large volumes of data and support complex queries.

- NoSQL Databases: Non-relational databases, such as MongoDB or Cassandra, are employed for storing unstructured or semi-structured data, including patient notes, social media data, and other text-based information.
- Object Storage: Technologies like Amazon S3 or Azure Blob Storage are used to store large amounts of unstructured data, such as medical images, videos, and other multimedia files.

2. Data Processing:

- Batch Processing: Technologies like Apache Spark or Apache Flink are employed for processing large datasets in batch mode. Batch processing is useful for tasks such as aggregating historical patient data, running analytics, and generating reports.
- Stream Processing: Real-time data processing is crucial in healthcare for monitoring patients, detecting anomalies, and responding to emergencies. Technologies like Apache Kafka and Apache Flink enable the processing of streaming data in real-time.
- Machine Learning (ML) and Artificial Intelligence (AI): Big Data technologies facilitate the implementation of machine learning algorithms and AI models for predictive analytics, disease detection, and personalized medicine. Frameworks like TensorFlow and PyTorch are commonly used in healthcare ML applications.
- Graph Processing: Graph databases like Neo4j can be employed for analyzing complex relationships within healthcare data, such as understanding disease networks, patient pathways, and social determinants of health.

3. Security and Compliance:

- Data Encryption: Healthcare data is sensitive, and encryption mechanisms (both in transit and at rest) are implemented to ensure the security and privacy of patient information.
- Access Controls: Role-based access controls (RBAC) and other authentication mechanisms are applied to regulate access to healthcare data, ensuring that only authorized personnel can view or modify specific information.
- Compliance Measures: Healthcare organizations must adhere to regulatory standards such as HIPAA (Health Insurance Portability and Accountability Act) to ensure the confidentiality, integrity, and availability of patient data. Big Data technologies are implemented with features that support compliance with these regulations.

2.4 Data Security and Privacy Concerns

Data security and privacy concerns in healthcare are of paramount importance, especially when leveraging big data technologies. The integration of large-scale data analytics tools and platforms in the healthcare sector offers unprecedented opportunities for improving patient outcomes, optimizing treatment plans, and advancing medical research. However, the vast amounts of sensitive and personal health information involved make it imperative to address potential risks. One primary concern is the potential for unauthorized access to patient data. Big data technologies often involve the storage and processing of massive datasets, creating a tempting target for cybercriminals (Shameer et al., 2017). Healthcare organizations must implement robust security measures, including encryption, access controls, and regular audits, to safeguard patient information from unauthorized access or data breaches. Furthermore, the interoperability of various healthcare systems and the sharing of data across platforms raise privacy concerns. As patient data flows between hospitals, clinics, and research institutions, ensuring that proper consent mechanisms are in place becomes crucial. Transparent and well-defined consent processes, coupled with strong data governance policies, are essential to protect patient privacy and maintain trust in the healthcare system.

Anonymizing patient data is another critical aspect of addressing privacy concerns. While aggregated and de-identified data can be valuable for research and analysis, there is always a risk of re-identification (Yin et al., 2016). Healthcare organizations must adopt advanced anonymization techniques to minimize the chances of connecting individual patients to their medical records. Compliance with data protection regulations, such as the Health Insurance Portability and Accountability Act (HIPAA) in the United States or the General Data Protection Regulation (GDPR) in the European Union, is non-negotiable. Adhering to these regulations ensures that healthcare providers and organizations meet stringent standards for data security and privacy, with hefty penalties for non-compliance.

3 APPLICATIONS OF BIG DATA IN PERSONALIZED HEALTHCARE

3.1 Predictive Analytics for Disease Prevention

Predictive analytics, in conjunction with big data, has emerged as a transformative force in the realm of personalized healthcare, particularly in disease prevention. The integration of vast datasets, encompassing individual health records, genetic information, lifestyle choices, and environmental factors, allows for the development of sophisticated predictive models. These models leverage advanced algorithms to analyze patterns and identify potential health risks, enabling a proactive approach to disease prevention. In personalized healthcare, the use of big data in predictive analytics is pivotal for tailoring preventive strategies to an individual's unique characteristics (Mayer-Schönberger & Cukier, 2013). This approach goes beyond a one-size-fits-all methodology, taking into account the intricacies of genetic predispositions, lifestyle habits, and environmental influences. By harnessing the power of big data, healthcare professionals can predict the likelihood of specific diseases in an individual, allowing for early intervention and targeted preventive measures. Furthermore, the continuous monitoring of health metrics through wearable devices and other connected technologies contributes valuable real-time data to the predictive analytics ecosystem. This dynamic feedback loop enables healthcare providers to adapt preventive strategies based on evolving health patterns, ensuring a more responsive and personalized approach (Olla & Shimskey, 2015). One notable application of predictive analytics in personalized healthcare is the identification of risk factors associated with chronic conditions such as diabetes, cardiovascular diseases, and certain types of cancer. By analyzing historical data and incorporating real-time information, predictive models can not only assess current health status but also forecast future health trajectories. This proactive approach empowers individuals to make informed lifestyle choices, receive timely interventions, and ultimately mitigate the risk of developing serious health conditions.

3.2 Genomic Data Analysis for Personalized Medicine

Genomic data analysis has emerged as a cornerstone in the realm of personalized medicine, revolutionizing healthcare by tailoring treatments to individual genetic profiles. The integration of big data technologies has played a pivotal role in advancing the field, allowing for the processing and interpretation of vast amounts of genomic information at an unprecedented scale. The Human Genome Project, completed in 2003, marked a significant milestone by sequencing the entire human genome, paving the way for personalized medicine to harness the power of genomic data. In personalized healthcare, the analysis of genomic data involves scrutinizing an individual's genetic makeup to identify variations that may influence disease susceptibility, treatment response, and overall health (Anne-Lindsay, n.d.). The sheer volume and complexity of genomic data demand sophisticated computational tools and infrastructure, which is where big data technologies come into play. These technologies enable the storage, management, and analysis of massive datasets, including genomic information from diverse populations.

One of the key applications of genomic data analysis in personalized medicine is the identification of genetic markers associated with specific diseases. By analyzing large datasets comprising genetic information and clinical outcomes, researchers can pinpoint variations that may contribute to disease development or progression (Obermeyer & Emanuel, 2016). This knowledge allows for the development of targeted therapies designed to address the unique genetic characteristics of individual patients, thereby maximizing treatment efficacy. The integration of big data analytics facilitates the identification of patterns and correlations within genomic datasets. Machine learning algorithms, for instance, can analyze genomic information alongside clinical data to predict disease risk, optimize treatment plans, and enhance diagnostic accuracy. This data-driven approach empowers healthcare practitioners to make more informed decisions, tailoring interventions to the specific genetic signatures of each patient. In practical terms, the impact of genomic data analysis and big data in personalized medicine is exemplified by initiatives such as the Precision Medicine Initiative in the United States. This ambitious project aims to collect and analyze vast amounts of genomic, clinical, and lifestyle data to develop a comprehensive understanding of individual health profiles. As more individuals contribute their genomic data to research databases, the depth and breadth of available information continue to expand, fueling advancements in personalized healthcare.

3.3 Real-Time Monitoring and Intervention

Real-time monitoring and intervention in personalized healthcare have become increasingly sophisticated with the integration of Big Data analytics. The marriage of advanced technologies and vast datasets allows for a proactive approach to healthcare, tailoring interventions to individual needs. Real-time monitoring involves the continuous collection and analysis of patient data, encompassing vital signs, physiological parameters, and even lifestyle choices. This wealth of information is then processed through Big Data analytics, which can rapidly identify patterns, anomalies, and trends. One of the significant advantages of real-time monitoring and intervention is its potential to detect health issues before they escalate. For instance, wearable devices and sensors can continuously stream data, alerting healthcare professionals to deviations from baseline parameters (Ed Corbett, 2017). According to a study published in the Journal of Medical Internet Research, continuous monitoring significantly reduced the rate of hospital readmissions among chronic disease patients.

The implementation of Big Data in personalized healthcare also enables predictive analytics. By analyzing historical data from diverse sources, algorithms can forecast potential health risks for an individual. This allows for timely interventions, such as lifestyle modifications, medication adjustments, or preventive measures, to be implemented (Bresnick, 2017). A study conducted by Pricewaterhouse-Coopers indicates that predictive analytics, when integrated with personalized healthcare, can lead to a 20% reduction in hospitalizations and emergency room visits. Further, real-time monitoring facilitates patient engagement and empowerment. Patients can access their personalized health data through mobile apps or online platforms, fostering a sense of responsibility for their well-being. According to a report by McKinsey & Company, this increased patient engagement not only enhances adherence to treatment plans but also contributes to better health outcomes.

3.4 Patient Engagement and Empowerment

Patient engagement and empowerment are crucial components of modern healthcare, and the integration of big data has revolutionized personalized healthcare delivery. Patient engagement refers to the active participation of individuals in their own health management, fostering a collaborative relationship between patients and healthcare providers. Empowerment involves providing patients with the knowledge, tools, and resources needed to make informed decisions about their health. Big data, with its vast and diverse datasets, plays a pivotal role in achieving these goals by enabling a more personalized approach to healthcare. In the realm of personalized healthcare, big data allows for the analysis of large volumes of patient information, including genetic data, electronic health records, wearables, and lifestyle data. This comprehensive view facilitates the identification of unique patterns and trends, enabling healthcare providers to tailor treatment plans that are specific to each patient's needs. This personalized approach not only enhances treatment efficacy but also fosters a sense of empowerment as patients become active participants in decisions regarding their health (Moore, 2001). Moreover, big data analytics can predict and prevent health issues by identifying risk factors and suggesting preventive measures. This proactive approach contributes to patient engagement by encouraging individuals to take preventive actions and make lifestyle choices that positively impact their well-being. Patients can access their health data, monitor progress, and receive personalized recommendations, promoting a sense of control over their health.

Communication and shared decision-making between patients and healthcare providers are also enhanced through big data. Real-time data exchange allows for more meaningful and timely discussions about treatment options, potential side effects, and lifestyle modifications. This collaborative environment fosters trust and empowers patients to actively engage in their care by understanding the implications of various choices. However, it's crucial to address privacy and security concerns associated with handling sensitive health data. Striking the right balance between leveraging big data for personalized healthcare and ensuring the protection of patient information is paramount for the success of patient engagement and empowerment initiatives.

4 CHALLENGES AND CONSIDERATIONS

4.1 Data Privacy and Security

The integration of Big Data in personalized healthcare presents numerous opportunities to revolutionize medical treatments and patient outcomes. However, this transformative potential comes with a myriad of challenges and considerations, particularly in the realm of data privacy and security. One significant challenge is the sheer volume and diversity of data generated and utilized in personalized healthcare. Personal health records, genetic information, and real-time monitoring data contribute to vast datasets that are attractive targets for cyber threats. Ensuring the confidentiality and integrity of this sensitive information is crucial to prevent unauthorized access, data breaches, and potential misuse. Moreover, the interoperability of diverse healthcare systems and platforms poses a considerable challenge. Integrating data from various sources while maintaining privacy standards requires robust technical solutions and standardized protocols (Apple, 2017). Achieving a balance between data sharing for research purposes and safeguarding individual privacy becomes a delicate task, as personalized healthcare heavily relies on comprehensive datasets for meaningful insights. Ethical considerations are paramount in the context of data privacy in personalized healthcare. The use of patient data for research and development raises questions about informed consent, transparency, and the potential for unintended consequences. Striking the right balance between individual privacy rights and the collective benefits of data-driven healthcare advancements requires careful ethical deliberation. Regulatory compliance is another major consideration (Yann, 2015). Healthcare data is subject to stringent regulations, such as the Health Insurance Portability and Accountability Act (HIPAA) in the United States and the General Data Protection Regulation (GDPR) in the European Union. Adhering to these regulations while harnessing the potential of Big Data in personalized healthcare necessitates robust governance frameworks and secure infrastructure.

4.2 Integration of Data From Various Sources

The integration of data from various sources in the context of personalized healthcare within the framework of big data necessitates a meticulous approach to data privacy and security. As healthcare systems increasingly leverage vast and diverse datasets, including electronic health records, wearable devices, genetic information, and more, the need for seamless integration becomes paramount for deriving meaningful insights. However, this integration must be conducted with a rigorous commitment to safeguarding the privacy and security of sensitive personal health information (Balandin et al., 2013). Data privacy is a critical concern as it involves handling sensitive patient information, and adherence to regulations such as the Health Insurance Portability and Accountability Act (HIPAA) and the General Data Protection Regulation (GDPR) is imperative. Any integration strategy should prioritize anonymization and encryption techniques to protect patient identities and health records. Furthermore, implementing access controls and monitoring mechanisms ensures that only authorized personnel can access and manipulate the integrated data. In tandem with data privacy, maintaining robust security measures is fundamental. Big data platforms utilized in personalized healthcare must employ state-of-the-art security protocols to prevent unauthorized access, data breaches, and cyber threats. Encryption of data in transit and at rest, regular security audits, and the use of secure communication channels contribute to a fortified security posture. Additionally, adopting advanced authentication mechanisms, such as multi-factor authentication, enhances access control and mitigates the risk of unauthorized data access. To foster trust among patients and healthcare providers, transparency about data usage and adherence to ethical guidelines are paramount (Kahn et al., 2010). Clear communication regarding the purpose of data integration, the measures in place to ensure privacy and security, and the potential benefits for personalized healthcare helps build a foundation of trust and ensures the responsible handling of sensitive information. In conclusion, the integration of data from various sources in personalized healthcare within the realm of big data demands a harmonious balance between deriving valuable insights and upholding the highest standards of data privacy and security.

4.3 Standardization and Interoperability

Standardization and interoperability play pivotal roles in ensuring robust data privacy and security within the realm of personalized healthcare when utilizing big data. Standardization involves establishing uniform guidelines and protocols for data collection, storage, and transmission, creating a cohesive framework that promotes consistency across diverse healthcare systems. This is crucial in the context of big data in personalized healthcare, where a multitude of data sources, such as electronic health records, wearables, and genomic information, contribute to a comprehensive patient profile. Interoperability, on the other hand, refers to the seamless exchange and integration of data across different platforms and systems (Wiesner & Pfeifer, 2014). In the context of personalized healthcare and big data, interoperability ensures that health data can be shared and utilized effectively, allowing for comprehensive analysis and personalized treatment strategies. It facilitates the convergence of various data streams, fostering a holistic understanding of an individual's health status.

Incorporating standardized formats and protocols ensures that sensitive health information is handled uniformly, reducing the risk of data breaches and unauthorized access. Moreover, interoperability ensures that health data can be securely exchanged among different healthcare providers and stakeholders, promoting collaborative and integrated care without compromising data security. Data privacy and security are paramount concerns in personalized healthcare, given the highly sensitive nature of personal health information. Standardization and interoperability not only enhance the efficiency of data utilization but also establish a secure foundation. Compliance with standardized security measures, encryption protocols, and access controls becomes more manageable when interoperability is built into the system, creating a comprehensive and secure ecosystem for big data in personalized healthcare (Hoens et al., 2013). Ultimately, by adhering to standardized practices and ensuring interoperability, the healthcare industry can harness the potential of big data to advance personalized medicine while safeguarding patient privacy and data security. This approach fosters trust among patients, healthcare providers, and other stakeholders, contributing to the responsible and ethical evolution of personalized healthcare in the era of big data.

4.4 Ethical Concerns in Personalized Healthcare

The advent of big data in personalized healthcare has brought about a revolution in medical treatment and patient care. However, this transformation is not without its ethical concerns, particularly in the realm of data privacy and security. Personalized healthcare relies heavily on the collection and analysis of vast amounts of sensitive patient data, ranging from genetic information to medical histories. The ethical dilemma arises from the need to balance the potential benefits of personalized treatments with the protection of individuals' privacy. One primary concern is the potential misuse or unauthorized access to this wealth of personal health information (Varshney, 2014). As big data systems store and process immense volumes of data, the risk of security breaches increases, potentially leading to the compromise of sensitive patient details. Unauthorized access to such information could result in identity theft, financial fraud, or even discrimination based on health conditions. Striking a balance between utilizing this data for medical advancements and safeguarding individuals' privacy is a significant ethical challenge. Another ethical concern is the informed consent process. Patients may not fully understand the implications of sharing their data for personalized healthcare purposes. Issues may arise regarding transparency, as individuals might not be aware of how their information is being used, who has access to it, and for what purposes. Ensuring that patients are well-informed and have the ability to control their data is essential to maintaining trust in personalized healthcare systems. Moreover, there's a risk of bias in the data collected and analyzed for personalized healthcare. If certain demographic groups are underrepresented in the data sets, it could lead to biased outcomes and treatment recommendations (Junglas et al., 2009). This raises ethical questions about fairness and justice in healthcare delivery, as personalized treatments should ideally be accessible and beneficial to all, irrespective of demographic characteristics.

5. CASE STUDY

5.1 BM Watson for Oncology

IBM Watson for Oncology is an example of personalized healthcare implementation that utilizes Big Data and artificial intelligence to assist healthcare professionals in cancer treatment decisions. This system analyzes vast amounts of medical literature, clinical trial data, and patient records to provide evidence-based treatment options.

5.2 Key Components

- Data Integration: The system integrates structured and unstructured data, including medical literature, clinical trial information, and individual patient records.
- Cognitive Computing: IBM Watson, a powerful cognitive computing system, processes and analyzes the integrated data to identify relevant patterns, treatment options, and potential clinical trials.
- Personalized Treatment Recommendations: Based on the analysis of the patient's medical history and the latest medical knowledge, the system generates personalized treatment recommendations.
- Clinical Decision Support: Healthcare professionals can use these recommendations as a valuable resource in their decision-making process, helping them tailor treatment plans to the individual patient.

5.3 Success Factors

- Improved Treatment Accuracy: By leveraging Big Data and AI, IBM Watson for Oncology aims to provide more accurate and personalized treatment recommendations, potentially improving patient outcomes.

- Efficiency in Decision-Making: The system assists oncologists in quickly accessing a vast amount of medical information, reducing the time needed to make informed decisions about treatment options.
- Staying Updated with Research: The platform continuously learns from new medical literature and clinical trial results, ensuring that healthcare professionals have access to the latest information in the field.
- Global Reach: Since the system can analyze data from various sources globally, it facilitates a broader perspective on treatment options, considering regional and international best practices.

5.4 Challenges

- Data Privacy and Security: Handling sensitive patient data requires robust security measures to ensure privacy and compliance with healthcare regulations.
- Integration with Existing Systems: Integrating personalized healthcare solutions into existing healthcare infrastructure can be challenging but is crucial for seamless adoption.

6. FUTURE TRENDS AND OPPORTUNITIES

6.1 Advancements in Artificial Intelligence and Machine Learning

Advancements in artificial intelligence (AI) and machine learning (ML) are ushering in a transformative era in personalized healthcare, with the integration of big data playing a pivotal role. The convergence of these technologies is enabling healthcare professionals to extract valuable insights from massive datasets, leading to more precise diagnostics, personalized treatment plans, and improved patient outcomes (Asri et al., 2015). One significant trend is the utilization of AI and ML algorithms to analyze diverse and complex healthcare datasets, including electronic health records, genomics, and wearable device data. These technologies can identify patterns and correlations that may be imperceptible to human observers, facilitating early disease detection and personalized risk assessments. Machine learning models are becoming increasingly sophisticated in predicting patient outcomes, optimizing treatment strategies, and identifying potential adverse reactions to specific medications.

Moreover, the integration of big data allows healthcare providers to create comprehensive patient profiles by aggregating information from various sources. This holistic approach enables a more nuanced understanding of an individual's health, considering genetic predispositions, lifestyle factors, and environmental influences. As a result, healthcare professionals can tailor interventions and treatment plans to each patient's unique characteristics, optimizing therapeutic efficacy and minimizing side effects. In the realm of diagnostics, AI is making remarkable strides by enhancing medical imaging interpretation. Machine learning algorithms can rapidly analyze radiological images, aiding in the early detection of diseases such as cancer and neurological disorders. This not only expedites diagnosis but also contributes to the development of more targeted and personalized treatment plans (Dorr et al., 2006; Sanaei & Sepehri, 2020). The future holds numerous opportunities for the continued advancement of AI and ML in personalized healthcare. Predictive analytics powered by big data can be leveraged to identify disease trends, allocate resources efficiently, and design preventive healthcare strategies. Additionally, the ongoing evolution of AI-driven virtual assistants and chatbots can enhance patient engagement and provide real-time health monitoring, fostering a proactive approach to healthcare management. While the potential benefits of these advancements are vast, challenges such as data privacy, ethical considerations, and the need for regulatory frameworks must be addressed. Striking a balance between innovation and safeguarding patient rights will be crucial in realizing the full potential of AI, ML, and big data in personalized healthcare. Overall, the synergy between these technologies is poised to revolutionize the healthcare landscape, offering more effective, efficient, and personalized care to individuals around the world.

6.2 Integration of Block chain for Secure Data Sharing

The integration of block chain technology into the realm of personalized healthcare, particularly in the context of secure data sharing facilitated by big data, represents a significant advancement with promising future trends and opportunities. Block chain, known for its decentralized and immutable nature, offers a robust solution to the challenges associated with data security and privacy in healthcare. In personalized healthcare, where patient-specific data is crucial for tailoring treatments and interventions, the incorporation of big data analytics has become increasingly prevalent. However, the sharing of sensitive health information poses inherent risks, such as unauthorized access and data breaches. Blockchain addresses these concerns by providing a decentralized and tamper-resistant ledger that ensures the integrity and confidentiality of health data.

One of the key advantages of integrating blockchain with big data in personalized healthcare is the establishment of a transparent and secure ecosystem. Each transaction or data entry is cryptographically linked, forming a chain of blocks that cannot be altered retroactively. This feature not only enhances the traceability of data but also ensures that patients have control over who accesses their health information. Blockchain technology enables the creation of smart contracts, which are self-executing contracts with predefined rules. These smart contracts can automate the consent management process, allowing patients to grant and revoke access to their data seamlessly (Dhar, 2014). This not only empowers individuals to have greater control over their health information but also streamlines the data-sharing process among healthcare providers, researchers, and other relevant stakeholders. As for future trends and opportunities, the integration of blockchain in personalized healthcare is likely to witness increased adoption and refinement. The interoperability of blockchain with emerging technologies, such as artificial intelligence and the Internet of Things, could further enhance the depth and breadth of health data analysis (Bydon, Schirmer, Oermann, Kitagawa, Pouratian, Davies, Sharan, & Chambless, 2020). Additionally, the development of standardized protocols and frameworks for blockchain implementation in healthcare settings will contribute to a more cohesive and interoperable ecosystem.

6.3 Patient-Centric Healthcare Ecosystems

Patient-centric healthcare ecosystems represent a transformative approach to healthcare delivery that places the individual at the center of their own care. This paradigm shift is increasingly gaining momentum, particularly as it intersects with future trends and opportunities driven by the integration of big data in personalized healthcare. The essence of patient-centric ecosystems lies in fostering a holistic and personalized approach to healthcare, tailoring medical interventions to individual needs, preferences, and circumstances. In this context, big data plays a pivotal role by providing a wealth of information derived from various sources, including electronic health records, wearable devices, genetic data, and lifestyle inputs (Sanaei & Sepehri, 2019). The aggregation and analysis of this massive and diverse dataset empower healthcare providers with insights into each patient's unique health profile, enabling more accurate diagnoses, treatment plans, and preventive strategies. Real-time monitoring through wearable devices and continuous data feedback further enhances the dynamic nature of personalized healthcare, allowing for timely adjustments based on an individual's changing health status. The integration of big data into patient-centric healthcare ecosystems also facilitates proactive and preventive measures. Predictive analytics, fueled by machine learning algorithms, can identify potential health risks before they manifest clinically, enabling early interventions and lifestyle modifications (Bydon, Schirmer, Oermann, Kitagawa, Pouratian, Davies, Sharan, & Chambless, 2020). This not only enhances the quality of care but also contributes to cost-effectiveness by reducing the burden of treating advanced-stage illnesses.

The collaboration between healthcare providers, researchers, and technology developers is critical for the evolution of patient-centric ecosystems. The collective efforts in data sharing and interdisciplinary research pave the way for innovative solutions and the development of cutting-edge technologies, such as telemedicine, remote patient monitoring, and personalized treatment plans (Peek et al., 2014). As patient-centric healthcare ecosystems continue to evolve, ethical considerations around data privacy and security become paramount. Striking a balance between harnessing the potential of big data and safeguarding individual privacy is essential for maintaining trust in these evolving healthcare models.

7 CONCLUSION

The integration of Big Data in personalized healthcare has the potential to revolutionize patient outcomes by providing a tailored and more effective approach to medical treatment. The vast amount of data generated from diverse sources, including electronic health records, genomics, wearable devices, and patient-reported outcomes, enables healthcare professionals to gain deeper insights into individual health profiles. This wealth of information allows for the identification of specific biomarkers, genetic predispositions, and personalized risk factors, paving the way for targeted interventions and treatment strategies. Personalized healthcare powered by Big Data facilitates a shift from a one-size-fits-all model to a more nuanced and patient-centric approach. Treatment plans can be customized based on an individual's unique genetic makeup, lifestyle, and environmental factors, leading to more precise diagnoses and therapeutic interventions. This tailored approach not only enhances the effectiveness of medical treatments but also minimizes potential side effects and adverse reactions, ultimately improving patient safety and satisfaction.

Furthermore, the use of Big Data in personalized healthcare contributes to a more proactive and preventive healthcare model. Predictive analytics and machine learning algorithms can anticipate potential health issues, allowing healthcare providers to intervene early and prevent the progression of diseases. This shift towards preventive care not only improves patient outcomes but also reduces the burden on healthcare systems by minimizing the need for costly and resource-intensive treatments. The incorporation of Big Data in personalized healthcare holds immense promise for transforming patient outcomes. By harnessing the power of data analytics, healthcare professionals can move towards a future where treatments are not only more effective but also tailored to the individual, ushering in a new era of precision medicine that prioritizes personalized and patient-centered care.

REFERENCES

Alansari, Z., Soomro, S., Belgaum, M. R., & Shamshirband, S. (2018). The Rise of Internet of Things (IoT) in Big Healthcare Data: Review and Open Research Issues. In *Progress in Advanced Computing and Intelligent Engineering* (pp. 675-685). Springer.

Anne-Lindsay, B. (n.d.). A case study on Dignity Health: Analytics helps prevent deadly infections. *Insights Editor*.

Apple. (2017). *ResearchKit 1.5.3*. ResearchKit.

Asri, H., Mousannif, H., Al Moatassime, H., & Noel, T. (2015). Big data in healthcare: Challenges and opportunities. *Cloud Technologies and Applications (CloudTech), International Conference*. IEEE.

Balandin, S., Balandina, E., Koucheryavy, Y., Kramar, V., & Medvedev, O. (2013). —Main Trends in mHealth Use Scenarios,||. *J. Sel. Top. Nano Electron. Comput*, 1(1), 64–70. 10.15393/j8.art.2013.3022

Belgaum, M. R., Soomro, S. U., Alansari, Z., & Alam, M. (2018). Treatment of Reactive Routing Protocols Using Second Chance Based on Malicious behavior of Nodes in MANETS. *Pakistan Journal of Engineering, Technology & Science, 6*(2).

Bydon, M., Schirmer, C. M., Oermann, E. K., Kitagawa, R. S., Pouratian, N., Davies, J., Sharan, A., & Chambless, L. B. (2020). Big data defined: A practical review for neurosurgeons. *World Neurosurgery*, 133, e842–e849. 10.1016/j.wneu.2019.09.09231562965

Dhar, V. (2014). Big data and predictive analytics in health care. *Big Data*, 2(3), 113–116. 10.1089/big.2014.152527442491

Dorr, D. A., Jones, S. S., Burns, L., Donnelly, S. M., Brunker, C. P., Wilcox, A., & Clayton, P. D. (2006). Use of health-related, quality-of-life metrics to predict mortality and hospitalizations in community-dwelling seniors. *Journal of the American Geriatrics Society*, 54(4), 667–673. 10.1111/j.1532-5415.2006.00681.x16686880

Ed Corbett, M. D. (2017). *The Real-World Benefits of Machine Learning in Healthcare*. Health Catalysyt.

Gillum, R. F. (2013). From papyrus to the electronic tablet: A brief history of the clinical medical record with lessons for the digital Age. *The American Journal of Medicine*, 126(10), 853–857. 10.1016/j.amjmed.2013.03.02424054954

Gubbi, J., Buyya, R., Marusic, S., & Palaniswami, M. (2013). Internet of Things (IoT): A vision, architectural elements, and future directions. *Future Generation Computer Systems*, 29(7), 1645–1660. 10.1016/j.future.2013.01.010

Hoens, T. R., Blanton, M., Steele, A., & Chawla, N. V. (2013). —Reliable medical recommendation systems with patient privacy,||. *ACM Transactions on Intelligent Systems and Technology*, 4(4), 67. 10.1145/2508037.2508048

Hulsen, T. (2021). Challenges and solutions for big data in personalized healthcare. In *Big Data in Psychiatry# x0026; Neurology* (pp. 69-94). Academic Press. 10.1016/B978-0-12-822884-5.00016-7

Bresnick, J. (2017). *Machine Learning in Healthcare: Defining the Most Common Terms*. Thinkstock.

Junglas, C., Abraham, C., & Ives, B. (2009). Abraham, and B. Ives, —Mobile technology at the frontlines of patient care: Understanding fit and human drives in utilization decisions and performance,||. *Decision Support Systems*, 46(3), 634–647. 10.1016/j.dss.2008.11.012

Kahn, J. G., Yang, J. S., & Kahn, J. S. (2010). 'Mobile' health needs and opportunities in developing countries. *Health Affairs (Project Hope)*, 29(2), 252–258. 10.1377/hlthaff.2009.096520348069

Mayer-Schönberger, V., & Cukier, K. (2013). *Big data: A revolution that will transform how we live, work, and think*. Houghton Mifflin Harcourt.

Miraz, M. H., Ali, M., Excell, P. S., & Picking, R. (2015, September). A review on Internet of Things (IoT), Internet of everything (IoE) and Internet of nano things (IoNT). In *Internet Technologies and Applications (ITA)* (pp. 219-224). IEEE.

Moore, G. C., & Benbasat, I. (1991). Development of an instrument to measure the perceptions of adopting an information technology innovation. *Information Systems Research*, 2(3), 192–222. 10.1287/isre.2.3.192

Moore, S. K. (2001). Unhooking medicine. *IEEE Spectrum*, 38(1), 107–108, 110. 10.1109/6.901156

Nasi, G., Cucciniello, M., & Guerrazzi, C. (2015). The role of mobile technologies in health care processes: The case of cancer supportive care. *Journal of Medical Internet Research*, 17(2), e26. 10.2196/jmir.375725679446

Obermeyer, Z., & Emanuel, E. J. (2016). Predicting the future — Big data, machine learning, and clinical medicine. *The New England Journal of Medicine*, 375(13), 1216–1219. 10.1056/NEJMp160618127682033

Olla, P., & Shimskey, C. (2015). mHealth taxonomy: A literature survey of mobile health applications,||. *Health and Technology*, 4(4), 299–308. 10.1007/s12553-014-0093-8

Peek, N., Holmes, J. H., & Sun, J. (2014). Technical challenges for big data in biomedicine and health: Data sources, infrastructure, and analytics. *Yearbook of Medical Informatics*, 23(01), 42–47. 10.15265/IY-2014-001825123720

Reiser, S. J. (1991). The clinical record in medicine part 1: Learning from cases*. *Annals of Internal Medicine*, 114(10), 902–907. 10.7326/0003-4819-114-10-9022014953

Sanaei, A., & Sepehri, M. M. (2019). *Quality improvement through intensive care registries: the value of big data in clinical decision making*. Arch Anesth Crit Care.

Sanaei, A., & Sepehri, M. M. (2020). Quality Improvement through Intensive Care Registries: The Value of Big Data in Clinical Decision Making. *Archives of Anesthesia and Critical Care.*

Shameer, K., Badgeley, M. A., Miotto, R., Glicksberg, B. S., Morgan, J. W., & Dudley, J. T. (2017). Translational bioinformatics in the era of real-time biomedical, health care and wellness data streams. *Briefings in Bioinformatics*, 18(1), 105–124. 10.1093/bib/bbv11826876889

Varshney, U. (2014). Mobile health: Four emerging themes of research,||. *Decision Support Systems*, 66, 20–35. 10.1016/j.dss.2014.06.001

Wiesner, M., & Pfeifer, D. (2014). Health recommender systems: Concepts, requirements, technical basics and challenges,||. *International Journal of Environmental Research and Public Health*, 11(3), 2580–2607. 10.3390/ijerph11030258024595212

Yann, L. (2015). Deep learning. *Nature, 521*(7553).

Yin, Y., Zeng, Y., Chen, X., & Fan, Y. (2016). The internet of things in healthcare: An overview. *Journal of Industrial Information Integration*, 1, 3–13. 10.1016/j.jii.2016.03.004

Chapter 11
Embracing the Fourth Industrial Revolution in the Petrochemical Industry

Xiaohua Bai
Universiti Brunei Darussalam, Brunei

Mohammad Nabil Almunawar
https://orcid.org/0000-0001-5296-2576
Universiti Brunei Darussalam, Brunei

ABSTRACT

The petrochemical sector is undergoing significant transformations in the era of the Fourth Industrial Revolution (IR 4.0). This chapter delves into the opportunities and challenges posed by IR 4.0 for the petrochemical sector, exploring how advancements in IoT, AI, and big data analytics among others are optimizing its operations, improving its productivity, and reducing its costs. By analyzing industry use cases and literature review, this chapter aims to provide insights into recommendations for the petrochemical sector to navigate the digital transformation effectively.

1. INTRODUCTION

As a basic industry, the petrochemical sector plays a pillar role in the economic development. By producing a wide range of petroleum and chemical products, it serves as the backbone for many end-market industries including automotive, construction, agriculture, aviation, textile, healthcare, and pharmaceuticals among others. As such, it creates countless direct jobs in research & development, engineering, construction and manufacturing areas as well as indirect jobs in related sectors like logistics, trading, finance, IT and so on. In addition, it usually develops into industrial parks, attracting a cluster of related industries and driving infrastructure building to create synergies in waste reduction, energy efficiency and supply chain optimization.

However, the production processes in the petrochemical industry are often characterized by complex operations, substantial energy consumption, and high risks such as flammability, explosiveness, toxicity, and pollution due to the inherent nature of chemical materials and chemical reactions. This requires a

DOI: 10.4018/978-1-6684-7840-0.ch011

strong emphasis to be placed by both the regulators and enterprises on autonomous operation, energy conservation, and robust safety and environmental protection measures. The emergence of the Fourth Industrial Revolution (IR 4.0) provides significant support to the advancement of this important industry.

The emergence of IR 4.0 heralds a fundamental shift in the global industry including the petrochemical industry and society, driven by a number of digital and physical advanced technologies. The confluence of these technologies is now forming a greater physical-to-digital-to-physical connection, bringing unprecedented levels of automation, connectivity, and innovation to a wide range of industries. Artificial Intelligence (AI), the Internet of Things (IoT), Big Data Analytics, robots, 3D printing, Blockchain, Cloud Computing, and virtual reality (VR) are some of the major technologies propelling this revolution.

In the context of the petrochemical industry, IR 4.0 is revolutionizing traditional operational processes and business models by providing advanced technologies like cloud computing and storage, IoT, big data analytics, and artificial intelligence systems. These technologies open up new opportunities for boosting productivity, reducing consumption, increasing safety, improving quality, and enhancing sustainability.

This chapter is aimed to fulfill the following objectives: (1) explore the implications and opportunities brought by IR 4.0 for the petrochemical sector; (2) investigate the challenges faced by the petrochemical sector in adapting to IR 4.0; (3) analyze case studies of petrochemical companies that have successfully implemented IR 4.0 technologies; and (4) provide recommendations to petrochemical companies for their successfully navigating the digital transition.

The rest of the chapter is organized as follows: The next section provides an understanding of IR 4.0 and its use in the petrochemical industry, followed by a discussion on its impact. Section 4 discusses the challenges of the petrochemical sector in adopting IR 4.0. The chapter continues with case studies of industries implementing IR 4.0, followed by recommendations on how the petrochemical industry should adopt IR 4.0. Finally, we conclude the chapter.

2. UNDERSTANDING IR 4.0 IN PETROCHEMICAL SECTOR

2.1 Definition and Characteristics of IR 4.0

IR 4.0 is the next phase in the digitization of the manufacturing sector, driven by disruptive trends such as the rise of data and connectivity, analytics and intelligence, human-machine interaction, and improvements in robotics. It builds upon the digital revolution (IR 3), which was marked by the wide application of computers, the Internet, and other electronic technologies (Boer, 2022).

In the petrochemical sector, IR 4.0 is characterized by the adoption of the Internet of Things (IoT), Big Data Analytics, High-Performance Computing (HPC), Artificial Intelligence (AI), digital twins, and cloud computing solutions to optimize processes, enhance productivity, and facilitate rapid decision-making.

2.2 Key Technologies Driving IR 4.0 in the Petrochemical Sector

IR 4.0 in the petrochemical industry is built upon several pillars such as the Internet of Things (IoT), Blockchain, Cloud Computing, Artificial Intelligence (AI), Virtual Reality (VR), Robotics and Automation, Digital Twins, and Big Data Analytics. These technological advancements have transformed assets and processes into smart, data-driven, and integrated systems, fostering greater efficiency and innovation across the petrochemical sector.

IoT. Normally, IoT sensors are installed throughout petrochemical plants to monitor the performance of all the assets. These sensors record their physical conditions such as machine operations, column and vessel statuses, pipeline conditions, spare parts availability, hazardous chemical levels, and environmental factors. They transmit the real-time data back to the central control room, enabling convenient monitoring and manipulation of critical parameters. The seamless data flow from IoT sensors facilitates fast decision-making, ensuring the normal steady performance, safety, and efficiency of plant operations. By harnessing IoT, petrochemical plants can proactively manage assets, optimize processes, and maintain stringent safety standards in a dynamic operational environment (Precedence Research, 2023)

Blockchain. Blockchain offers transparency, reliability, and privacy, creating an auditable database for all stakeholders in the supply chain. When combined with smart contracts, blockchain enhances efficiency, security, and transparency while reducing paperwork. This integration can also create a global market for assets, further increasing market transparency (Aksahan, 2021). The petrochemical industry can benefit significantly from blockchain technology due to its various properties. Supply chain tracking is crucial in this industry as petroleum products pass through multiple channels like manufacturers, suppliers, contractors, refineries, and retailers. Disruptions in this process can have significant economic and social impacts.

Cloud Computing. Cloud Computing, especially the enterprise one revolutionizes how complex data from plants are manipulated. Through this technology, data is not only gathered but also analyzed and integrated within designated data centers. This approach grants management seamless access to data from any location and at any time, drastically enhancing decision-making efficiency. By leveraging the flexibility and scalability of cloud solutions, organizations can streamline operations, improve collaboration, and stay agile in a rapidly evolving industry landscape.

Big Data Analytics. Big Data Analytics plays a crucial role in the era of digitalization. After capturing vast amounts of real-time production data, dynamic equipment operation data, and other unstructured data from operational processes, petrochemical companies can utilize big data analytics tools to swiftly process and analyze them for the identification of patterns, prediction of trends, optimization of product quality, reduction of transitional materials, and more efficient energy consumption strategies. This data-driven approach empowers organizations to make faster and better decisions, drive innovation, and improve overall operational performance in the petrochemical sector (Eissa, 2020).

Artificial Intelligence (AI). AI finds wide applications in the petrochemical industry. For instance, the Advanced Process Control (APC) software powered by AI is used in production plants for optimizing complex production processes and minimizing energy consumption. Recently, it has been reported that generative AI can also help chemical manufacturers deconstruct complex contracts by summarizing the contract, including the parties involved, the crucial terms, duration and other critical factors and even identifying compliance issues (Katz, 2023).

Robotics and Automation. Robotic systems have revolutionized various industries, including petrochemical plants, by introducing robotic systems to substitute humans in performing repetitive and hazardous tasks. These systems also handle automatic maintenance activities, reducing human factors and enhancing safety, productivity, and precision in plant operations. As a result, human resources can redirect their focus towards more productive and creative aspects of the business, leading to overall efficiency in the industry (Samiha Al Zadjali, 2021). The integration of robotics and automation not only streamlines processes but also ensures consistent and reliable performance, contributing to sustainable growth and competitiveness in the market.

Digital Twins. This technology refers to virtual models of processes, products, or plants. The systems allow for mathematical modeling and simulation of processes by utilizing real-time data. In the petrochemical sector, digital twins are often used to provide simulation training to learners so that they can practice and enhance their operation skills in a safe and controlled environment without any risk to personnel or equipment. Furthermore, digital twins offer a solution to transform the petrochemical industry by improving efficiency and reducing risk. According to researchers, these virtual models of physical assets seamlessly connect with real-time data across assets, columns, reactors, piping, and equipment. Despite changes in crude oil quality, catalyst composition, and process conditions, digital twins continuously analyze industrial data to predict and optimize processes (Bhatt, 2024).

Virtual Reality (VR). Production activities in the petrochemical sector carry a significant risk due to the flammable and explosive nature of their components. One of the primary prevention methods is to provide operators with adequate training covering all potential real-life scenarios they may encounter. Virtual reality technology plays a crucial role in this by allowing operators to gain risk-free experience in various scenarios. For instance, virtual reality can simulate risky situations like hydrocarbon leakage during production, helping operators understand and respond effectively to such hazards through regular desktop or live drills (Kumar et al., 2021).

Office Automation (OA) and Teleconferencing. The two technologies have significantly boosted communication, collaboration, and productivity among the workforce by automating and streamlining routine workflows, accelerating information exchanges, and overcoming physical environment barriers. For example, in a refinery setting, where numerous approvals are required daily, OA streamlines and standardizes the approval process, making it much more efficient.

3. IMPACT AND OPPORTUNITIES BROUGHT BY IR 4.0 TO PETROCHEMICAL SECTOR

The adoption of IR 4.0 technologies has transformed the petrochemical sector into a connected, data-driven smart manufacturing ecosystem. Using real-time and high-value support systems, coordinated and performance-oriented smart manufacturers respond quickly to customer demands and minimize energy and material usage, while radically improving sustainability, productivity, innovation, and economic competitiveness. (Zhihong Yuan, 2017) This transformation covers various stages throughout the value chain of petrochemical companies, such as raw materials procurement, inventory management, production planning & scheduling, operation management, asset monitoring and maintenance, energy utilization optimization, HSSE (health, safety, security, and environment) management, and financial budgeting and management. This paper intends to highlight some of the key implications and opportunities as follows.

3.1 Improved Operational Efficiency

Through big data analytics and AI-driven optimization leveraging detectors, sensors, and software, real-time visibility into plant operations is achieved. This leads to improved communication between board operators and field operators, agile production scheduling adaptable to changing conditions, alignment of production plans with market dynamics, enhanced product quality and yields, reduced labor and energy requirements, and minimized operational upsets and costs, ultimately resulting in increased operational efficiency.

For example, the APC (Advanced Process Control) technology widely used in chemical plants leverages soft sensors that provide real-time data, neural networks, and statistical models to assist operators in achieving plant operation excellence. This not only significantly reduces the variance of process variables, allowing smooth running of plants, but also achieves "constraint pushing", significantly improving plant efficiency by minimizing raw material and energy consumption, optimizing product throughput and quality, and enhancing production flexibility. Implementing APC techniques can significantly increase plant profit margins by 2 to 10%, and in some exceptional cases, such improvements have led to profit increases as high as 15 to 20%, equating to substantial financial gains of up to 2 million Euros per year (Nicolae et al., 2019).

3.2 Enhanced Asset Health and Reliability

IR 4.0 enables the petrochemical industry to implement comprehensive asset performance management (APM) solutions, combining real-time monitoring, predictive analytics, and maintenance optimization. By analyzing real-time data from various sources like sensors, cameras, and drones, it can efficiently detect anomalies and faults in equipment, providing precise recommendations for preventive actions. This proactive approach minimizes downtime, reduces failures, enhances worker and equipment safety, and optimizes operational efficiency, ultimately reducing costs and improving reliability in the petrochemical sector.

3.3 Data-Driven Decision Making

Cloud Computing and storage technology enable seamless integration of advanced database management systems, software and AI algorithms including among others MES (Manufacturing Execution System), ERP (Enterprise Resource Planning), DCS (Distributed Control System), APC (Advanced Process Control), SIS (Safety Instrumented System), GDS (Gas Detection System), CCS (Compressor Control System), this integration equipes decision-makers with objective and reliable information, actionable insights, and even instantly generates customized response plans based on prescriptive scenarios, and allows them to make swift and informed responses under various circumstances including resource allocation, production planning, and emergency management.

3.4 Elevated Safety and Environmental Performance

IR 4.0 technologies empower petrochemical companies to utilize sophisticated instrumentation for early prediction of any abnormal conditions, initial automatic treatment, and timely alarms to prompt operator intervention or safe plant shutdown, thus substantially improving plant safety while reducing material loss and emissions, minimizing environmental impact, and aligning with regulatory requirements and corporate sustainability goals.

3.5 Supply Chain Optimization

IR 4.0 revolutionizes the supply chain in the petrochemical industry through the integration of advanced technologies that elevate efficiency, visibility, and flexibility across the entire supply chain spectrum. Leveraging predictive analytics for demand forecasting, IoT for real-time inventory monitoring, blockchain for transparent transaction security, and robotics for manual task automation, it streamlines operations and optimizes the entire supply chain process.

Some predictions regarding the Potential Results of the Industrial Revolution 4.0 (IR 4.0) for Non-Resource Sector Enterprises. This prediction provides valuable insights into the potential tangible impacts of IR 4.0 on the petrochemical sector, shedding light on how this technological revolution could shape the industry's future trajectory. By analyzing these predictions, we can better understand and anticipate the transformative effects of IR 4.0 on petrochemical enterprises, including advancements in automation, data analytics, and digital technologies that are poised to revolutionize production costs, operational efficiencies, productivity, agility, and competitiveness within the sector.

Table 1. Potential results of the industrial revolution IR 4.0 for non-resource sector enterprises

Application Area	Opportunities	Result
Production quality	Digital quality management Advanced process control (APC) Statistical process control (SPC)	10–20% reduction in quality assurance costs %
Time to introduce the product to the market	Fast modeling and experimentation Concurrent engineering Open innovation/collaboration with customers	Reduction of time of introduction to the market by 20–50%
Equipment operation modes	Smart energy consumption; Informatization of production Optimization of equipment operation in real-time	3–5% increase in productivity
Loading of production equipment	The flexibility of the routing Flexibility in the use of equipment; remote monitoring and control; predictive maintenance An augmented reality to maintain	30-50% reduction of equipment downtime
Efficiency and safety of labor	Human-robot interaction Remote monitoring Digital performance management	45-55% increase in productivity of technical functions due to automation of labor
Logistics	3D printing on site Real-time supply chain optimization Optimization of batch sizes	20-50% cost reduction of storing inventory

Source: "Digital Russia: New Reality", July 2017, McKinsey, forecast to 2025. (Deberdieva E M, 2019)

4. CHALLENGES FACED BY PETROCHEMICAL SECTOR IN ADOPTING IR 4.0

4.1 Technological Disruption and Legacy Systems

The first primary challenge confronting the petrochemical sector in the age of IR 4.0 is the integration of disruptive technologies into existing systems and infrastructure. Numerous petrochemical factories continue to rely on outdated equipment and systems, making the integration of new digital solutions with existing infrastructure a complex task. Achieving interoperability and ensuring seamless collaboration between legacy systems and the latest digital technologies are critical to facilitating a smooth transition.

4.2 Investment Costs and ROI Considerations

The initial capital expenditure required for implementing IR 4.0 technologies can be significant for petrochemical companies. This includes expenses associated with identifying practical needs, engaging qualified technology vendors, procuring technology, upgrading infrastructure, and providing workforce training. Evaluating the return on investment (ROI) and long-term value proposition of IR 4.0 initiatives is crucial for informed decision-making and gaining support from stakeholders. Despite the compelling benefits of IR 4.0 as identified in the previous section, such as increased efficiency, reduced downtime, and enhanced competitiveness, petrochemical businesses frequently struggle to accurately assess the financial implications and risks associated with the adoption.

4.3 Workforce Transition and Skills Gap

Unlike nimble high-tech companies that prioritize technological agility and innovation, petrochemical enterprises have historically focused more on operational continuity and efficiency within established processes. This traditional approach has led to a workforce that may be proficient in conventional methods but may struggle to adapt to and leverage emerging digital tools and systems effectively because of initially lacking essential digital knowledge. Therefore, embracing IR 4.0 requires an ongoing commitment to upskill and reskill the workforce to remain competitive in an environment characterized by rapidly evolving technologies.

4.4 Cybersecurity Risks and Data Privacy Concerns

As petrochemical manufacturers embrace IR 4.0 technologies, enhanced connectivity and data sharing bring many concomitant challenges, particularly in terms of cybersecurity and data privacy. The interconnectedness of IoT devices, reliance on cloud infrastructure, and extensive data networks open up new possibilities for potential cybersecurity threats and data breaches. These vulnerabilities expose petrochemical enterprises to risks such as sabotage, intellectual property theft, and unauthorized access to sensitive information. Hence, petrochemical enterprises must invest in robust cybersecurity measures, employee awareness training, and regulatory compliance to mitigate cyber risks effectively.

4.5 Regulatory Compliance and Environmental Standards

The advent of IR 4.0 technologies has significantly heightened regulators' expectations for petrochemical businesses, especially regarding operational safety and industrial emissions. For instance, in response to mounting pressure from environmental advocates and organizations, government bodies are progressively implementing carbon tax policies. Consequently, adherence to regulatory mandates and environmental benchmarks stands as a pivotal concern for petrochemical companies. Furthermore, fluctuations in regulations, emissions thresholds, and safety standards demand continual monitoring, reporting, and adaptation of operational practices. This inevitably translates into increased costs for operators as they strive to comply with evolving standards while investing in innovative solutions to mitigate environmental impact and ensure sustainable practices within their operations.

4.6 Resistance to Change and Cultural Barriers

The adoption of IR 4.0 technologies in the petrochemical sector may encounter resistance from both the workforce and stakeholders. This resistance can stem from various factors, including concerns about job displacement, fear of disruption to established roles and processes, and reluctance to move beyond comfort zones (Min Xu, 2018).

5. CASE STUDIES ON IMPLEMENTATION OF IR 4.0 IN PETROCHEMICAL SECTOR

5.1 Sinopec Zhenhai Branch

In 2016, the Sinopec Zhenhai Branch completed the construction of a smart petrochemical plant utilizing IR 4.0 technologies, marking a significant leap in operational efficiency. The integration of production plans, dispatcher instructions, and material movement was seamlessly achieved through the establishment of a comprehensive online dispatching and command system leveraging AI, big data analytics and enterprise cloud. This system transformed the original segmented planning, scheduling, and production practice into a fully online closed-loop management system. As a result, production efficiency has seen a notable boost, with labor hours reduced by 20 people/day and work efficiency increasing by 15%.

Moreover, the implementation of IoT, infrared, and industrial robot technology has led to the creation of a fully enclosed, highly automated, and unmanned polypropylene 3D warehouse. This innovative warehouse management system enables automated processes for solid product packaging, warehouse operations, and unmanned loading and delivery, fostering synergies among smart factories and industrial parks.

Furthermore, significant strides have been made in digital equipment management and predictive maintenance, enhancing operational continuity and efficiency. The adoption of an asset health and reliability management system allows for online monitoring and analysis of critical equipment, facilitating fault location and life prediction through advanced data analytics tapping into expert knowledge databases. This has resulted in reduced unplanned shutdowns, further contributing to operational efficiency improvements.

Additionally, the company's implementation of online energy optimization technology has led to online real-time optimization of steam, electricity, fuel gas, and overall plant energy consumption utilizing data mining and modeling for developing dynamic target values. This holistic approach not only balances energy usage but also reduces emissions, curbs costs, and improves overall efficiency, resulting in annual energy cost savings exceeding 7 million yuan.

5.2 Sinopec Maoming Branch

In 2017, the Sinopec Maoming Branch achieved a milestone with the completion of its cutting-edge petrochemical facility, powered by Industry 4.0 technologies. This advanced plant utilizes big data analytics for thorough operational analysis, resulting in a remarkable boost in productivity. By scrutinizing over 1.1 billion production data points and the complex composition of feedstock naphtha, the facility curated an extensive library of operational samples. These samples are invaluable in fine-tuning process parameters, leading to notable achievements such as a 0.14% increase in gasoline yield, a 0.9-point rise in octane number, and an annual profitability surge of 6.78 million yuan.

Moreover, the facility pioneered a groundbreaking mobile Health, Safety, and Environment (HSE) management model for field operations. Leveraging on-site industrial sensors, industrial wireless networks, and smart terminals, this innovative approach overhauled digital work ticket management by consolidating time, location, ticket, and operator data into a unified system. Consequently, safety management standards for on-site operations have been significantly raised, ensuring comprehensive oversight and real-time monitoring.

Additionally, the company implemented a collaborative incident command system based on coordinated response and resource-sharing mechanisms. Utilizing technologies like communication integration and three-dimensional digitization, they substantially slashed response costs while maximizing emergency response efficiency. Through numerical and three-dimensional accident propagation simulations and drills employing VR technologies, the company's emergency response capabilities have been greatly enhanced.

5.3 Hengyi Petrochemicals

In 2022, Hengyi Petrochemicals encountered frequent unplanned downtime due to a compressor malfunctioning over 30 times in a year, resulting in production losses, product quality, extended maintenance time and increased costs. Employing real-time monitoring, the company gathered operating data from compressor sensors and other data from maintenance and training records to develop predictive models for failures, which identified cause-and-effect relationships, generating alerts and recommendations for the compressor's performance. This initiative resulted in a 70% reduction in unplanned downtime and saved approximately $500,000 annually in operational costs. As part of its operational transformation, Hengyi Petrochemicals plans to extend similar asset management systems to other critical assets across the plant.

5.4 BASF

Chemical companies can enhance capacity optimization through demand forecasting and responsive scheduling. For instance, BASF is implementing a predictive analytics approach that integrates the company's historical data with economic data to forecast demand effectively. This forecasting model incorporates various external factors such as seasonal effects, macroeconomic indicators for customer industries on national and regional scales, regulatory alterations, as well as internal factors like BASF's strategic decisions—such as expansions, mergers, acquisitions, divestitures, and other transactions. By utilizing this forecasting model, BASF can strategically plan and adjust its plant operations in response to changing demand dynamics (Blackburn et al., 2015).

6. RECOMMENDATIONS

6.1 Leadership Commitment and Vision

Strong executive leadership is crucial for successful IR 4.0 adoption. Leaders must champion digital transformation, set clear objectives, and allocate resources to support innovation. By fostering a culture of learning and collaboration, leaders can drive alignment, empower employees, and accelerate digital innovation.

6.2 Investment in Digital Infrastructure and Talent Development

Investing in digital infrastructure and talent development is essential. This includes upgrading equipment, deploying IoT sensors, and implementing AI and big data analytics platforms. Concurrently, prioritizing workforce training builds digital capabilities and fosters a culture of innovation and agility, unlocking growth opportunities in the digital age.

6.3 Collaboration With Technology Vendors and Industry Associations

Being part of the digital ecosystem by partnering with technology vendors, universities and industrial organizations is vital for accessing cutting-edge solutions and expertise. Strategic partnerships enable co-creation and accelerate technology adoption, fostering innovation and agility in the industry.

6.4 Regulatory Compliance

The petrochemical sector must prioritize regulatory compliance as part of its IR 4.0 strategy. This includes staying abreast of changing regulations, standards, and guidelines related to safety, environmental protection, and sustainability, and ensuring compliance across all operations and activities.

6.5 Cyber Risk Management

In intensifying their engagement with digital ecosystem partners, petrochemical manufacturers should prioritize the development of robust risk management frameworks, contingency plans, and cybersecurity measures. These efforts are essential for mitigating risks inherent in technology adoption, such as cyber threats, data breaches, and operational disruptions.

7. CONCLUSION

In conclusion, IR 4.0 is poised to reshape the operation strategies of the petrochemical sector, and petrochemical manufacturers need to embrace IR 4.0 and integrate their digital and physical assets across different stages of the value chain. By leveraging IR 4.0 technologies such as AI, IoT, robotics, 3D printing, and big data analytics, petrochemical companies can optimize asset performance, enhance plant productivity, drive cost savings, improve energy efficiency, and reduce risks. However, realizing the full potential of IR 4.0 requires overcoming various challenges, including investment costs, technological barriers, workforce upskilling, resistance to change on the individual level and organizational level, regulatory compliance, and cyber risk. Through strategic leadership, investment in digital capabilities, and collaboration with technology vendors, petrochemical companies can navigate the digital transformation successfully and emerge as leaders in the global economy.

REFERENCES

Aksahan, F. (2021, April). *Industry 4.0 in the Oil and Gas Industry*. ResaerchGate. https://www.researchgate.net/publication/352994741_Industry_40_in_the_Oil_and_Gas_Industry

Bhatt, M. (2024, January 29). *Digital Twins: Upcoming Revolution in Refining sector.* Linkedin. https://www.linkedin.com/pulse/digital-twins-upcoming-revolution-refining-sector-meet-bhatt-0pixf/?trk=article-ssr-frontend-pulse_more-articles_related-content-card

Blackburn, R., Lurz, K., Priese, B., Göb, R., & Darkow, I.-L. (2015). A predictive analytics approach for demand forecasting in the process industry. *International Transactions in Operational Research*, 22(3), 407–428. 10.1111/itor.12122

Boer, E. d. (2022, August 17). *What are Industry 4.0, the Fourth Industrial Revolution, and 4IR?* Mckinsey & Company. https://www.mckinsey.com/featured-insights/mckinsey-explainers/what-are-industry-4-0-the-fourth-industrial-revolution-and-4ir

Deberdieva, E. M., Vechkasova, M. V., Golikava, H. S., Borisova, A. A., & Lysenko, A. F. (2019). Experience in the management of business processes with the use of digital technologies by Russian companies of a petrochemical complex. *IOP Conference Series. Materials Science and Engineering*, 483, 483. 10.1088/1757-899X/483/1/012066

Eissa, H. (2020, January 13). *Unleashing Industry 4.0 Opportunities: Big Data Analytics in the Midstream Oil & Gas Sector.* OnePetro. https://onepetro.org/IPTCONF/proceedings-abstract/20IPTC/3-20IPTC/154550

Katz, J. (2023, August 7). *Generative AI in the Chemical Industry.* Chemical Processing. https://www.chemicalprocessing.com/automation-it/article/33008789/ai-in-the-chemical-industry-from-molecule-discovery-to-contract-compliance

Kumar, V. V., Carberry, D., Beenfeldt, C., Andersson, M. P., Mansouri, S. S., & Gallucci, F. (2021). Virtual reality in chemical and biochemical engineering education and training. *Education for Chemical Engineers*, 36, 143–153. 10.1016/j.ece.2021.05.002

Nicolae, N., Popescu, M., & Pătrăşcioiu, C. (2019). *Implementation of Advanced Process Control in Refineries.*, 10.1109/ICSTCC.2019.8885801

Precedence Research. (March, 2023). *Internet of Things (IoT) in Chemical Market.* Precedence Research. https://www.precedenceresearch.com/internet-of-things-in-chemical-market

Samiha Al Zadjali, A. U. (2021). Impact of Industry 4.0 in Manufacturing Sector. *International Journal of Management Science and Business Administration*, 25-33.

Xu, M. (2018). The Fourth Industrial Revolution: Opportunities and Challenges. *International Journal of Financial Research*, 90-94.

Yuan, Z. W. Q. (2017). *Smart Manufacturing for the Oil Refining and Petrochemical Industry.* Elsevier.

Chapter 12
Omnichannel Supply Chain in India:
A Study Using SAP-LAP Approach

Siva Kumar Pujari
https://orcid.org/0000-0002-9178-4220
Christ University, India

C. S. Sooryendhu
Christ University, India

ABSTRACT

Organizations are increasingly adding new service delivery channels to make their products and services readily available in such an environment. Omnichannel retailing will help organizations to provide better consumer service while making it easy for them to do business when appropriately implemented. By implementing omnichannel retailing, organizations will benefit from high operational efficiency, better financial performance, smoother communication, and a satisfied, loyal customer base. Therefore, this study tries to explore the current situation of the retail industry in India, the major actors or players of the business ecosystem, and processes adopted in organizations to provide products and services to their customers. The study will be qualitative in nature and is approached through an SAP (situation-actor-processes) – LAP (learnings-actions-performance) framework to synthesize learning from the current scenario to propose actions and set the performance measures.

1. INTRODUCTION

The retail sector has witnessed unprecedented changes over the past two decades, with the evolution of the digital world and the advent of the direct-to-consumer online channel (Gallino & Moreno, 2014; Piotrowicz & Cuthbertson, 2014; Verhoef, Kannan, & Inman, 2015). The online channel has become quite prominent in various retail markets, and this might be called a disruptive trend (Christensen & Raynor, 2003). Consumers are increasingly adopting shopping via multiple channels, with companies continually adding new channels to make their products and services available anywhere and anytime (Avery, Steenburgh, Deighton, & Caravella, 2012; Balasubramanian, Peterson, & Jarvenpaa, 2002). As

DOI: 10.4018/978-1-6684-7840-0.ch012

the race to provide better customer service remains the deciding factor in gaining competitive advantage, companies are increasingly adopting omni-channel retailing. Omni-channel retailing is defined as integrating service channels or customer touchpoints to improve customer experience (Avery, Steenburgh, Deighton, & Caravella, 2012; Verhoef, Kannan, & Inman, 2015). The natural borders between channels are blurred in omni-channel retailing; therefore, the new channels will break down geographical barriers and customer ignorance, which were previously employed by traditional businesses to gain a market advantage (Dorman, 2013; Bell, Gallino, & Moreno, 2014).

Lack of integrated fulfilment processes, isolation of information databases, and misaligned corporate goals could all be threats during channel transition due to the fast-changing retail industry (Lewis, Whysall, & Foster, 2014; Hubner, Holzapfel, & Kuhn, 2016; Hubner, Kuhn, & Wollenburg, 2016). Another reason pertaining to why most companies' supply chains hesitate from adopting omnichannel is the inherent difficulty in layering the newly required capabilities on top of the legacy systems. This necessitates larger and deeper reforms within organizations to match increased customer expectations in terms of consumer experience, customisation, and faster response time while keeping delivery costs under control.

As a result of the entry of various new players, the Indian retail business has emerged as one of the world's most dynamic and fast-paced industries. The retail industry in India is expected to increase to $1.5 trillion by 2030, up from $0.793 trillion in 2020, due to socio-demographic and economic reasons such as urbanisation, income growth, and increase in number of nuclear families. This sector accounts for more than ten percent of the country's GDP and roughly eight percent of employment. India has emerged to become the world's fifth-largest global destination in the retail space.

The e-commerce industry in India is expected to cross $350 billion by 2030, growing at a CAGR of 23%. The first half of 2021 saw the e-commerce industry bagging nearly a third of several electronic categories, half of smartphones sold, and about a fifth of all apparel sales in India. More than $8 billion in PE/VC funding was raised by e-commerce and consumer internet companies in 2020, with 400 deals (excluding investments in Jio). With an expected annual gross merchandise value of $350 billion, India will become the third largest online retail industry by 2030.

The Indian retail market is largely unorganized, accounting about 88 percent in 2019. Although, there has been approximately a growth of 50% in the organized retail sector from 2012 to 2020, it still accounts for only 12% of retail. By 2025, the modern Indian retail business is predicted to grow at a 15 percent compound annual growth rate (CAGR) to reach 18 percent. Apparel and accessories (18%), consumer electronics (6%), and home & living (6%), among other major retail categories (by percent organised retail penetration), will drive the growth in organised retail this decade. This increased growth of Indian retail sector calls for better management of resources, technology and advantages that omnichannel supply chain promises so as to improve the customer offerings.

Brick-and-mortar stores in India, such as Lifestyle, Arvind Fashions, and Shoppers' Stop, are known for utilizing technology to attract younger customers to remain competitive. Smart displays, in-store services, smart shelves, home delivery, brand optimization options, supply chain optimization, and logistics automation are just a few instances of how technology has improved the retail ecosystem. Internet of Things (used in customer experience, supply chain, and channel-revenue streams), SMAC (Social, Mobile, Analytics, and Cloud), Big data, and Omni channel retail adoption are some trends that have impacted the Indian retail business over the years.

According to McKinsey's FashionScope, India's apparel market will be valued at $59.3 billion in 2022, making it the world's sixth-largest, equivalent to the United Kingdom's $65 billion and Germany's $63.1 billion. Between now and 2025, the targeted population's total income (individuals earning more than $9,500 per year) is predicted to triple. Indian players are innovating to build momentum around traditional stores: merchants embrace technology to improve the in-store experience with digital marketing displays and improved checkout. Madura Fashion & Lifestyle, for example, established the Van Heusen Style Studio, which uses augmented reality to show clients ensembles.

Customers' improved computer savvy fuelled the apparel sector's expansion. From five million smartphones in the country and 45 million internet users ten years ago, these figures have risen to 355 million and 460 million, respectively, in 2018. This has turned up the scope of selling through varied channels for retailers.

Considering that the retail settings and participating players are all critical to channel operation (Verhoef, Kannan, & Inman, 2015), issues affecting the success of omni-channel retailing could include channel operation, supply chain readiness, and consumer technology acceptance. According to a review of the available research, most omni-channel studies focus on mature and developed retail markets (Rigby, 2011, Verhoef, Kannan, & Inman, 2015; Picot- Coupey, Hure, & Piveteau, 2016), with emerging economies such as India receiving very little attention. Because the Indian retail industry differs from its counterparts in developed countries due to its vast size, rapid expansion, and diverse tastes, the drivers and barriers found in other countries may not apply to the Indian retail market.

In order to inspect and understand the drivers/ enablers and barriers/inhibitors of successful omnichannel implementation in the Indian market, this research investigates the same via the retail industry. An overall study of the market, major players and the underlying regulations within the Indian market, will be done through SAP LAP (situation, actor, process, learning, action, performance) framework to answer the following research questions:

RQ1: What are the omni-channel retailing barriers and enablers in a fast-growing retail market like India?

RQ2: How to improve the performance of omnichannel supply chains in retail market in India?

In order to answer the above research question, the authors conduct extensive literature review. Forther, formulate the following research objective:

→ To propose a conceptual framework to improve performance of omnichannel supply chains in retail market in India

2. LITERATURE REVIEW

Verhoef et al (2017) introduce a framework that delves into the transformation of consumer connectivity within the omnichannel context. The authors highlight the role of mobile-oriented technologies, emphasizing their facilitation of connections between consumers and People, Objects, and Physical Environments. Kannan PK (2017) introduces a framework for digital marketing research that establishes a connection between marketing strategy, the marketing process, and digital technology. Within this framework, the authors pinpoint emerging issues, pose research questions, and delineate a comprehensive agenda for future research in the domain of digital marketing. Kembro et al.,(2018) perform a systematic literature review focusing on warehouse operations and design within the context of omni-channel logistics. Their findings reveal a noticeable imbalance, with less emphasis placed on the specific realm of warehouse operations and design. Instead, the existing discussions predominantly centre around shifts in consumer demand and network design. The authors extract ten key themes from the available literature pertaining to omni-channel warehousing, crafting a thorough and organized agenda for future research. This agenda takes into consideration critical factors such as network design, channel management, and the value proposition. In their investigation of the logistics networks issue within omni-channel grocery retailing. Hilken et al., (2018) investigate the enhancement of customers' omnichannel experiences through the utilization of the emerging technology of augmented reality (AR). The authors observe that AR can contribute to achieving seamless omnichannel experiences, addressing and alleviating current challenges within the omnichannel environment. Wollenburg et al. (2018) observe that channel integration has a more pronounced positive impact on the logistics benefits of non-food products. However, they note that the logistics design for grocery retailing is contingent upon various factors such as the nature of the product, market dynamics, and the retailer's specific characteristics.

Lim and Winkenbach (2018) examine how retailers implement last-mile delivery to fulfil omnichannel demand. In their study, they create a typology of last-mile distribution by integrating considerations of product variety and delivery responsiveness. Lim and Srai (2018) delve into the interaction between last-mile supply networks and the underlying mechanisms to understand their impact on omnichannel performance. The authors note a scarcity of attention to this issue in the operations management literature. The new mechanism proposed for last-mile supply networks in their paper offers valuable design implications for retailers. They recommend that managers take into account factors such as product types and delivery responsiveness when designing a suitable last-mile supply network. Marchet et al (2018) recognize 11 logistics variables within the omni-channel management strategy, categorized across four aspects: distribution, fulfilment, delivery, and returns management. The authors emphasize the absence of a universal or "one-fits-all" business logistics model, underscoring the need for tailored approaches in omni-channel logistics.

Galipoglu et al., (2018) provide an overview of relevant literature in the context of omni-channel retailing, with a specific focus on the research domain of logistics and supply chain management. The authors highlight a limitation in the consideration of logistics and supply chain management literature within the omni-channel retailing context. Furthermore, they advocate for increased emphasis on conceptual and analytical research in this field. Hossain et al (2020) emphasize that despite widespread adoption of omnichannel strategies, there's a gap in understanding factors influencing integration quality (INQ) across channels. This paper, based on interviews, focus groups, and surveys from multichannel banking customers, validates a hierarchical INQ model with four primary dimensions and ten sub-dimensions. The research establishes that INQ influences cross-buying behaviour and acts as a partial mediator between INQ and perceived value in an omnichannel environment.

The study by Sales-Vivó et al (2021) investigates value co-creation and relationship quality in a B2B industrial setting. It dissects social and economic satisfaction within the framework of relationship quality, exploring alternative models that incorporate value co-creation. Analyzing data from 77 firms in the Spanish Furniture Market Observatory, the research demonstrates that the influence of relationship quality on economic satisfaction is strengthened by the inclusion of value co-creation, notably in the manufacturer-supplier relationship. The study by Quach, S., Barari, M., Moudrý, D. V., & Quach, K. (2022), investigates the influence of service integration components, specifically service consistency and service transparency, on customer experience and loyalty. Utilizing flow theory and hyperbolic discounting theory, the research, based on 786 survey responses, the study reveals that service consistency significantly affects flow and perceived risk, while service transparency only impacts flow. Both flow and perceived risk correlate with customer loyalty. Additionally, showrooming behaviour and location-based service usage moderate the relationship between service consistency and privacy risk, offering valuable insights for retailers in omnichannel strategy development.

The article by SZTORC and SAVENKOVS, (2023) aims to examine changes in the adoption of modern technological solutions by large enterprises in response to regulations promoting digital sovereignty, as outlined in the European Digital Decade strategy. Utilizing data from Eurostat related to large enterprises in the European Union from 2014 to 2022, the research employs PCA and VIKOR methods along with the ICT dissemination index. The results reveal substantial disparities in the digitization level and technology adoption intensity among large enterprises. Foroughi et al,. (2023) investigates the factors influencing the intention to reuse augmented reality (AR) apps, utilizing data from 439 IKEA Place app users. The study analysed the data through 'partial least squares' (PLS) and 'fuzzy-set qualitative comparative analysis' (fsQCA), the study reveals that AR attributes significantly impact perceived ease of use, perceived usefulness, and confirmation. The technology continuance theory is largely supported, with recreational consciousness moderating the influence of attitude on reuse intentions. The study contributes to the literature by exploring AR app reuse drivers, extending technology continuance theory, demonstrating the moderating role of recreational consciousness, and utilizing the PLS-fsQCA approach. The findings offer insights for developing strategies and designing AR apps to retain users.

Sharma and Fatima 's (2024) study delves into the impact of omnichannel shopping habits on customers' perceived value and usage, utilizing customer value theory. The analysis of survey data from 512 omnichannel shoppers in Australia reveals that shopping habits play crucial roles as antecedent, mediator, and moderator in the relationship between perceived value and usage. The findings underscore the significance of prioritizing security and privacy, fostering social communications, and providing personalized services to reinforce habitual buying.

As evident from the literature review that many studies on omni-channel retailing were conducted in developed nations, but only a few were done in developing countries such as India. Further, there are limited conceptual studies that offer a way to improve performance in omnichannel supply chains. Given the tremendous growth of e-commerce and omni-channel retailing in India in recent years, academics and practitioners need to investigate and understand the key strategic hurdles to omni-channel retailing adoption in this rapidly developing industry.

3. METHODOLOGY

Secondary sources were used to compile the information for the study. Secondary information was gathered from published sources and websites. Peer-reviewed journals, business newspapers, corporate news, articles, and material available on consulting firms' websites make up the majority of the published material.

In the literature, there are a variety of opinions on how firms have adopted omnichannel supply chains and the modifications they have made. Given that identifying the driver, enabler, barriers, and inhibitors for omnichannel involve numerous participants and underlying situations, a framework for analyzing these issues should be developed to accommodate various perspectives of the omnichannel supply chain. This technique should record the current scenario, field players, and methods employed to conduct a full investigation that may be used to recommend improvements and measure performance. The SAP-LAP framework is one such methodology.

(Sushil, 2019) suggests examining the above-mentioned needs using the SAP-LAP approach. There are two steps to this process. The dynamic parameters of a case are highlighted through the three dynamic interfaces in the first stage, SAP analysis. Situations (S), actors (A), and processes (P) are the interfaces (P). The LAP synthesis is the next stage. LAP is made up of three parts. These include learning problems (L), recommended actions (A), and expected performance (P). The actors consistently assess the situation, follow processes, and take actions to enhance their performance, and based on the outcomes, either the processes are updated or the same processes are repeated in the future.

3.1. SAP- LAP linkage framework

The SAP-LAP linkages framework is a development of the SAP-LAP framework. It is concerned with the interactions between the situation, the actor, the processes, the learning, the action, and the performance. The SAP's cross-interaction provides linkages between current situations, actors, and processes, answering the questions "what," "who," and "how." The influence of situation on actor(s) and process(es) is depicted in linkages 1 and 2, respectively, whereas linkage 3 interprets the roles performed by various players in various processes in the form of an interpretive matrix (Sushil 2005). The insights gathered from the existing situation, actor(s), and process(es) are depicted in linkages 4, 5, and 6 to define causality in terms of 'why' it is happening in that manner, delivering the learning from the analysis of existing context. The foundation for desired theory development in the form of LAP links is learned in terms of 'why' about the present system. The connection 7 describes the learning to action leads, including the 'when' and 'where' the action(s) will be taken, 'who' will do it, and 'how' it will be performed. The influence of action on performance, i.e., the intended 'what' to be attained, is given by linkage 8. Finally, connection 9 provides feedback from performance to help students study more effectively. As a result, the SAP-LAP linkages initially establish relationships between existing 'what,' 'who,' and 'how,' as well as insights into all of the fundamental issues (why, where, when, who, how, and what) that provide the conceptual foundation for the theory to be tested.

Self-interaction matrices exist among separate SAP-LAP components in addition to cross-interaction matrices. Minimum two self-interaction matrices for 'activity' and 'performance' should be established to help theory development. The self-interaction matrix for 'actions' (binary and interpretive) displays the interaction of actions in terms of their driver-dependence relationships, which can be simulated using TISM (Sushil, 2018). Similarly, a self-interaction matrix of performance aspects will give the intended structure for what is to be accomplished.

Figure 1. Framework for theory building using SAP-LAP framework

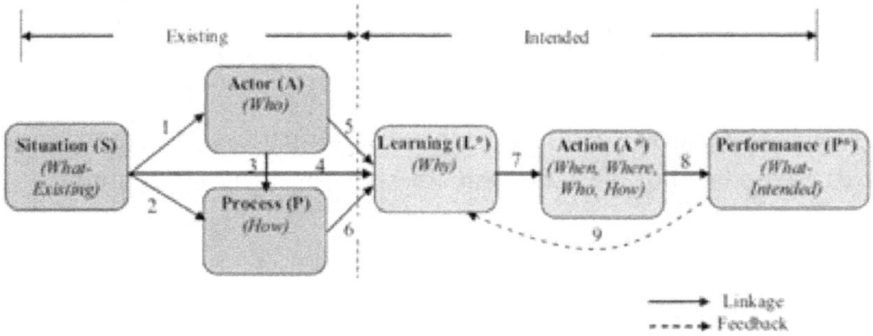

The above-mentioned generic framework for theory development created a theoretical foundation for the omnichannel supply chain. In the context of an omnichannel supply chain, the following broad elements of SAP-LAP components are recognized and explained:

3.1.1. Situation

This component of the SAP-LAP methodology elaborates on the 'what' question of the existing system. The current supply chain has been witnessing unprecedented changes due to changes in customer requirements, technological advancements, e-commerce boom, changes in purchasing power, income growth, urbanization, and changes in governmental policies. The current unorganized retail sector uses archaic methods to source and sell products to customers. The current situation of the retail supply chain can be summarised as follows:

S1: Rising customer expectation
S2: Boom in e-commerce
S3: Socio-demographic and economic factors
S4: Government policies on the retail sector

3.1.2. Actors

The fundamental question of "who" is addressed in terms of relevant actors or stakeholders. The retail supply chain consists of several players who profoundly impact the supply chain. While one might think that the consumers are the only significant player- the online shoppers in India are expected to reach ~500mn in 2030 from +150Mn in 2020 (*Retail Industry in India - Indian Retail Sector, Market Size*, n.d.) there are other players. They are the e-commerce market which is expected to touch $350 Bn in GMV by 2030; the Indian retail market- consisting of organized and unorganized players- which is estimated to reach 1.5bn by 2030 from $0.793 in 2020 (*Retail Industry in India - Indian Retail Sector, Market Size*, n.d.)and lastly the Government who has been making policies to protect the domestic business by altering the FDI policies.

A1: Consumers
A2: Retailers -Organised and Unorganised sector
A3: E-commerce market

A4: Government

3.1.3. Process

The processes that answer the question of "how" to address the circumstance serve as a focal point for identifying the theory that surrounds it and determining the study's scope(Sushil, 2019). The omni-channel supply chain is a way to meet increased customer expectations by allowing customers to shop across several channels – online through phone or laptop, in real brick-and-mortar stores, or at wholesale outlets – while receiving a consistent, holistic experience. Shifting to an omni-channel strategy has numerous advantages. According to a 2017 Harvard Business Review study, omni-channel customers spend 4% more in-store and 10% more online than single-channel customers on every purchasing occasion.. (*Forbes India - Rethinking Supply Chains From The Lens Of Omni-Channel Retailing*, n.d.).

P1: Information integration for supply chain visibility
P2: Omnichannel fulfilment strategies
P3: Centralization of procurement process

3.1.4. Learning

The learning explains 'why' by reflecting on the current condition in terms of both challenges/inhibitors and opportunities/enablers in the existing system using insights gathered through SAP analysis of the existing omnichannel supply chain. These learnings act as barriers to achieve better performance in omnichannel supply chains. Therefore, negative implications of barriers to be tackled with appropriate measures or actions.

L1: Lack of proper redesigning of fulfilment process
L2: Lack of an integrated information platform to monitor supply chain inventory
L3: Lack of systems to centralize the procurement process
L4: Failure to deploy human capital to train staff and provide skill development
L5: Lack of involvement of senior management
L6: Lack of channel performance measures and incentives to motivate change

3.1.5. Actions

The actions that result from the learning insights should be described in terms of 'when' the activities should be carried out (time frame) and 'where' they should be done (location). These actions act as enablers or drivers of performance in omnichannel supply chains. Furthermore, a strong action plan must assign responsibilities for answering the question "who" as well as the modalities (how) in which the actions are to be carried out (Sushil, 2019).

A1: Customer centric supply chain strategy
A2: Network ecosystem of the future
A3: End-to-end planning and information flow
A4: Omnichannel fulfilment through node operations
A5: Omnichannel fulfilment through transportation and LSP management
A6: Operating model and change management

A1: Customer centric supply chain strategy - By keeping a customer-centric approach, the omnichannel supply chain should combine best practices with digital innovation to build an omnichannel supply chain. The customer-centric supply chain strategy involves meeting the customer needs across all channels and making all decisions by having a deep understanding of the consumer. The companies need to be absolutely clear about the customer segments to deliver great service to the segments which matter the most. This comes from the underlying fact that the resources are limited, hence targeting the most important segment will be beneficial.

The customer-centric approach is followed by three strategic supply chain elements namely the network and ecosystem of the future, operating model, and digitization and process automation. The supply chain process which acts as enabler are end-to-end planning and information flow, omnichannel fulfilment through node operations, and omnichannel fulfilment through transportation.

A2: Network and ecosystem of the future - The transition to omnichannel is compelling consumer goods enterprises to reassess their supply chain frameworks. Achieving consumer-service goals across channels necessitates the strategic selection of distribution centres (DCs), incorporation of new node types, and partnerships. A collaborative approach involving all stakeholders, from suppliers to consumers, is vital for an effective supply chain ecosystem. The ability to adapt to evolving consumer demands hinges on the seamless exchange of information throughout the value chain and the optimal utilization of all network assets and capabilities.

A3: End-to-end planning and information flow - Omnichannel operations encompass diverse sales channels, numerous network nodes, and decentralized inventory, contributing to increased operational complexity. Despite this challenge, customers expect prompt access to the right products at the right locations. Overcoming the operational difficulties in omnichannel supply chains involves a focus on three key elements: forecasting, inventory management, and seamless information flow throughout the end-to-end planning process (McKinsey, 2021). Therefore, end-to-end planning and information flow is essential for better performance.

A4: Omnichannel fulfilment through node operations - Consumer-product firms must rethink their fulfilment networks, which are critical to their supply chains, as the volume of in-store purchases shifts to e-commerce. To attain competitive costs and consistent quality while managing the complexities of omnichannel operations, omnichannel players must develop critical capabilities related to product flow (McKinsey, 2021). By adding e-commerce offering to offline business, the companies are often exposed to difficulties regarding fulling orders which come in the inherent differences between online orders and shipping of seasonal stock. While online orders emphasis on the need for short lead times, the seasonal stock replenishment focuses on cost over delivery speed.

A supply chain designed specifically for omnichannel will account for the various channel requirements. Warehouse automation is a viable alternative that can increase speed, quality, and efficiency.

A5: Omnichannel fulfilment through transportation and LSP management - Because each channel has different requirements, transportation and logistics-service provider (LSP) management are much more complicated for organisations with various channels to serve. Orders from brick-and-mortar consumer product stores can usually be scheduled ahead of time and delivered by truck. E-commerce providers, on the other hand, must process a large number of individual orders in a short amount of time via couriers or postal services. Omnichannel players must ensure that all customers receive reliable, timely service while maintaining competitive transportation costs.

A6: Operating model and change management - Companies must completely restructure their operational models to reap the full benefits of omnichannel, which includes rethinking processes, structures, mindsets, capabilities, and performance management. This begins with having a team spearheading the change management for omnichannel. Collaboration with value-chain partners is also essential to implement omnichannel.

Figure 2. SAP LAP framework for setting up omnichannel supply chain

LEARNING

L1: Lack of proper redesigning of fulfilment process

L2: Lack of an integrated information platform to monitor supply chain inventory

L3: Lack of systems to centralize the procurement process

L4: Failure to deploy human capital to train staff and provide skill

FEEDBACK

PERFORMANCE

P1: Customized service delivery

P2: Faster Delivery

P3: Reduced overall cost

P4: Increased supply chain visibility with optimized inventory

ACTION

A1: Customer centric supply chain strategy

A2: Network ecosystem of the future

A3: End-to-end planning and information flow

A4: Omnichannel fulfilment through node operations

A5: Omnichannel fulfilment through transportation and LSP management

A6: Operating model and change

3.1.6. Performance

The purpose of the performance is to express the desired outcome (what) in order to carry out the activities in a focused manner (Sushil, 2019). Omnichannel supply chains have become the cornerstone of contemporary retail, providing customers with a seamless shopping experience across various channels. Enhancing the performance of omnichannel supply chains requires a multifaceted approach, integrating key performance indicators (KPIs) such as:

P1: Customized service delivery

P2: Faster Delivery

P3: Reduced overall cost

P4: Increased supply chain visibility with optimized inventory

P1: Customized service delivery - The initiation of personalized service delivery within omnichannel supply chains involves comprehending and fulfilling individual customer preferences. The adoption of robust customer relationship management (CRM) systems facilitates the gathering and examination of customer data, empowering businesses to customize their services based on unique preferences. KPIs in this domain encompass customer satisfaction scores, repeat purchase rates, and Net Promoter Scores (NPS). Further, improving the personalized service experience necessitates the incorporation of real-time order tracking. Granting customers visibility into the real-time status and location of their orders cultivates trust and enhances satisfaction. KPIs related to order tracking comprise on-time delivery rates, order accuracy, and the frequency of delivery updates.

Improving the performance of omnichannel supply chains is a multifaceted endeavor that requires a holistic approach. Implementing KPIs such as customized service delivery, faster delivery, reduced overall cost, and increased supply chain visibility with optimized inventory enables businesses to navigate the complexities of the modern retail landscape successfully. By focusing on these key performance indicators, organizations can enhance customer satisfaction, achieve operational efficiency, and stay competitive in the dynamic world of omnichannel commerce.

P2: Faster Delivery - Minimizing delivery times necessitates attention to last-mile logistics. Employing advanced routing algorithms and capitalizing on local distribution centers can streamline and enhance last-mile delivery. Essential metrics for this optimization process encompass average delivery time, delivery cost per order, and delivery accuracy.

The increasing demand for swift delivery options has become prominent. Providing same-day or next-day delivery services can distinguish businesses in a competitive landscape. KPIs for these services encompass the percentage of orders delivered within the stipulated timeframe and customer feedback regarding delivery speed.

P3: Reduced overall cost - Effective inventory management is essential for cost reduction in omnichannel supply chains. Utilizing demand forecasting tools and implementing just-in-time inventory practices helps minimize holding costs, with KPIs including inventory turnover ratio, stockout rates, and carrying costs. Streamlining the distribution network through consolidated centres reduces transportation costs, measured by KPIs like transportation cost per unit and warehouse efficiency metrics. Strong collaboration with suppliers, including favourable negotiations and vendor-managed inventory systems, leads to efficient and cost-effective supply chains, with metrics involving supplier lead time, order accuracy, and achieved cost savings.

P4: Increased supply chain visibility with optimized inventory - Achieving enhanced supply chain visibility involves implementing real-time data analytics tools, providing insights into inventory, demand, and potential disruptions. KPIs in this area include data accuracy, time-to-insight, and the percentage of real-time tracked inventory.

For inventory optimization, accurate demand forecasting is essential. Advanced algorithms and machine learning models improve forecast accuracy, with metrics including demand variability and the frequency of forecasting updates.

Crucial to inventory management is collaboration across the supply chain. Sharing inventory data with partners enhances demand planning and reduces excess stock, with KPIs like fill rate, order fulfilment times, and stockout frequency playing a pivotal role.

4. MANAGERIAL IMPLICATIONS

The proposed flexible theoretical model aids SC managers with omnichannel supply chain management concerns related to the SC's "situation, actors, process, learning, actions, and resilient performance. The rising customer expectations are pushing the organizations to adopt digitalization and automation. Managers are required to strategize to meet these expectations through a slew of changes at the management level and the technical level. While all the above proposed Actions are crucial, seamless integration of information and planning tools across channels are also important to meet the customer expectation and facilitate management and decision making.

Digitization and automation techniques must be implemented in a holistic manner. Separately managed initiatives are frequently less than the sum of their parts and fail to produce the essential step shift in consumer service. But it's also important to realize that smart analytics and automation alone won't make significant impact; organizations will need a completely new operational model to see these changes through and provide omnichannel excellence.

Adopting omnichannel supply chain can seem as a daunting task for the managers. Hence, there is no one-size- fits-all approach to prioritizing. Organizations can adopt a "crawl, walk, run" approach to set up omnichannel.

The goal for prospective omnichannel players at the "crawl" portion of the journey should be to master the fundamentals. Above all, defining a competitive service proposition for the omnichannel journey is critical; businesses must be clear on essential questions such as which services to offer and how to differentiate themselves. After mastering the fundamentals, players should focus on implementing omnichannel best practises and, lastly, establishing unique omnichannel solutions. The operating model will function seamlessly to align incentives and key performance indicators (KPIs) at the conclusion of this process to avoid competition for limited resources. This method ensures that the various channels complement one other, which is the omnichannel driving principle. The synthesis of SAP-LAP portions has been presented in the form of tables in Appendix section. The framework present in Figure 2 is result of the LAP synthesis.

5. CONCLUSION

India has been witnessing rapid changes in the retailing industry, which has been compounded by internet proliferation, wide usage of smartphones, and systematic differences in the sociodemographic features of the country. In lieu of this, consumers have upped their expectations of services from organizations within the retail industry. To live up to this demand, organizations have been trying to incorporate new service channels to improve their product availability. Given that managing several channels can be a difficult task, omnichannel retailing offers a better solution that integrates all the channels. Omnichannel retailing calls for organizations to integrate their logistics, information, inventory, fulfillment, and distribution, thereby promising operational efficiency, financial performance, and business efficiency.

This paper studies the current state of the omnichannel supply chain in India and proposes a framework for organizations which are in their course to adopt omnichannel supply chain. The framework has been developed through SAP LAP approach which analyses “situation”, “actor” and “process” to derive “learning” to propose “action” and establish “performance” measures. The basic questions which are addressed by the general framework of theory building are what, who, how, why, when, where. The paper gives a broad theory building framework for omnichannel supply chain, and it has been illustrated in a generic sense with the example of omnichannel adoption in retail sector. As a result, the study's primary weakness is its lack of real-world testing and validation. The framework could be fine-tuned over time as it was put to use in different scenarios. The paper brings up new research avenues in both omnichannel supply chain and theory development.

REFERENCES

Avery, J., Steenburgh, T., Deighton, J., & Caravella, M. (2012). Adding bricks to clicks: Predicting the patterns of cross- channel elasticities over time. *Journal of Marketing*, 76(3), 96–111. 10.1509/jm.09.0081

Balasubramanian, S., Peterson, R., & Jarvenpaa, S. (2002). Exploring the implications of m- commerce for markets and marketing. *Journal of the Academy of Marketing Science*, 30(4), 348–361. 10.1177/009207002236910

Beck, N., & Rygl, D. (2015). Categorization of multiple channel retailing in multi-, cross-, and omni-channel retailing for retailers and retailing. *Journal of Retailing and Consumer Services*, 2015(27), 170–178. 10.1016/j.jretconser.2015.08.001

Bell, D., Gallino, S., & Moreno, A. (2014). How to win in an omni- channel world. *MIT Sloan Management Review*, 56(1), 45–53.

Brynjolfsson, E., Hu, Y., & Rahman, M. (2013). Competing in the age of omni- channel retailing. *MIT Sloan Management Review*, 54(4), 1–7.

Cao, L. (2014). Business model tranformation in moving to a cross- channel retail strategy: A case study. *International Journal of Electronic Commerce*, 18(4), 69–96. 10.2753/JEC1086-4415180403

Cao, L., & Li, L. (2014). The impact of cross- channel integration on retailers' sales growth. *Journal of Retailing*, 91(2), 198–216. 10.1016/j.jretai.2014.12.005

Christensen, C. M., & Raynor, M. E. (2003). *The Innovator's Solution*. Harvard Business Press.

Coelho, F., & Easingwood, C. (2008). A model of the antecedents of multiple channel usage. *Journal of Retailing and Consumer Services*, 15(1), 32–41. 10.1016/j.jretconser.2007.03.002

Daniel, T., & Sebastian, B., A., M. K., & Paul, M. (2019). Omnichannel fulfillment strategies: Defining the concept and building an agenda for future inquiry. *International Journal of Logistics Management*, 30(3), 863–891.

De Leeuw, S., Minguela-Rata, B., Sabet, E., Boter, J., & Sigurðardóttir, R. (2016). Trade - offs in managing commercial consumer returns for online apparel retail. *International Journal of Operations & Production Management*, 36(6), 710–731. 10.1108/IJOPM-01-2015-0010

Dorman, A. (2013). *Omni- channel retail and the new age consumer: an empirical analysis of direct- to - consumer channel interaction in the retail industry*. CMC Senior Theses, Claremont McKenna College.

Foroughi, B., Hongsachart, H., Asadi, S., Iranmanesh, M., Ghobakhloo, M., & Tirkolaee, E. B. (2023). Reuse intention of augmented reality apps: Recreational consciousness as moderator. *Service Industries Journal*, 1–42.

Galipoglu, E., Kotzab, H., Teller, C., Yumurtaci Hüseyinoglu, I. Ö., & Pöppelbuß, J. (2018). Omni-channel retailing research–state of the art and intellectual foundation. *International Journal of Physical Distribution & Logistics Management*, 48(4), 365–390. 10.1108/IJPDLM-10-2016-0292

Gallino, S., & Moreno, A. (2014). Integration of online and offline channels in retail: The impact of sharing reliable inventory availability information. *Management Science*, 60(6), 1434–1451. 10.1287/mnsc.2014.1951

Herhausen, D., Binder, J., Schoegel, M., & Herrmann, A. (2015). Integrating bricks and clicks: Retailer-level and channel- level outcomes of online- offline channel integration. *Journal of Retailing*, 91(2), 309–325. 10.1016/j.jretai.2014.12.009

Hilken, T., Heller, J., Chylinski, M., Keeling, D. I., Mahr, D., & de Ruyter, K. (2018). Making omnichannel an augmented reality: The current and future state of the art. *Journal of Research in Interactive Marketing*, 12(4), 509–523. 10.1108/JRIM-01-2018-0023

Hossain, T. M. T., Akter, S., Kattiyapornpong, U., & Dwivedi, Y. (2020). Reconceptualizing Integration Quality Dynamics for omnichannel marketing. *Industrial Marketing Management*, 87, 225–241. 10.1016/j.indmarman.2019.12.006

Hubner, A., Holzapfel, A., & Kuhn, H. (2016). Distribution systems in omni- channel retailing. *Business Reseach*, 44(33), 228–247.

Hubner, A., Kuhn, H., & Wollenburg, J. (2016). Retail logistics in the transition from multi- channel to omni- channel. *International Journal of Physical Distribution & Logistics Management*, 46(6/7), 562–561. 10.1108/IJPDLM-08-2015-0179

Kannan, P. K., & Li, H. A. (2017). Digital marketing: A framework, review and research agenda. *International Journal of Research in Marketing*, 34(1), 22–45. 10.1016/j.ijresmar.2016.11.006

Kembro, J. H., Norrman, A., & Eriksson, E. (2018). Adapting warehouse operations and design to omni-channel logistics: A literature review and research agenda. *International Journal of Physical Distribution & Logistics Management*, 48(9), 890–912. 10.1108/IJPDLM-01-2017-0052

Lewis, J., Whysall, P., & Foster, C. (2014). Drivers and technology related obstacles in moving to multichannel retailing. *International Journal of Electronic Commerce*, 18(4), 43–68. 10.2753/JEC1086-4415180402

Lim, S. F. W., & Srai, J. S. (2018). Examining the anatomy of last-mile distribution in e-commerce omnichannel retailing: A supply network configuration approach. *International Journal of Operations & Production Management*, 38(9), 1735–1764. 10.1108/IJOPM-12-2016-0733

Lim, S. F. W., & Winkenbach, M. (2019). Configuring the last-mile in business-to-consumer e-retailing. *California Management Review*, 61(2), 132–154. 10.1177/0008125618805094

Lui, S., Ngo, H., & Hon, A. (2006). Coercivestrategy in inter firm cooperation: Mediating roles of interpersonal and inter organizational trust. *Journal of Business Research*, 59(4), 466–474. 10.1016/j.jbusres.2005.09.001

Marchet, G., Melacini, M., Perotti, S., Rasini, M., & Tappia, E. (2018). Business logistics models in omni-channel: A classification framework and empirical analysis. *International Journal of Physical Distribution & Logistics Management*, 48(4), 439–464. 10.1108/IJPDLM-09-2016-0273

McKinsey. (2021). *Omnichannel shopping and retail*. McKinsey. https://www.mckinsey.com/industries/retail/our-insights/into-the-fast-lane-how-to-master-the-omnichannel-supply-chain#The%20Importance%20of%20Omnichannel:%20E-Commerce%20Is%20Booming,%20But%20Physical%20Stores%20Remain%20Important

Neslin, S. A., Dhruv, G., Robert, L., Venkatesh, S., & Marije, L. (2006). Challenges and oppurtunities in multichannel customer management. *Journal of Service Research*, 9(2), 95–112. 10.1177/1094670506293559

Pauwels, K., & Neslin, S. (2015). Building with bricks and mortar: The revenue impact of opening physical stores in multichannel environment. *Journal of Retailing*, 91(2), 182–197. 10.1016/j.jretai.2015.02.001

Picot- Coupey, K., Hure, E., & Piveteau, L. (2016). Channel design to enrich customers' shopping experiences; synchronizing clicks with bricks in an omni- channel perspective- the direct optic case. *International Journal of Retail & Distribution Management*, 44(3), 336–368.

Piotrowiccz, W., & Cuthbertson, R. (2014). Introduction to the special issue information technology in retail: Toward omnichannel retailing. *International Journal of Electronic Commerce*, 18(4), 5–16. 10.2753/JEC1086-4415180400

Quach, S., Barari, M., Moudrý, D. V., & Quach, K. (2022). Service integration in omnichannel retailing and its impact on customer experience. *Journal of Retailing and Consumer Services*, 65, 102267. 10.1016/j.jretconser.2020.102267

Rigby, D. (2011). The future of shopping. *Harvaed Business REview. Vil*, 89(12), 65–76.

Sales-Vivó, V., Gil-Saura, I., & Gallarza, M. G. (2021). Comparing relationship of quality-satisfaction models: Effects of B2B value co-creation. *International Journal of Retail & Distribution Management*, 49(7), 941–957. 10.1108/IJRDM-10-2020-0394

Sharma, N., & Fatima, J. (2024). Influence of perceived value on omnichannel usage: Mediating and moderating roles of the omnichannel shopping habit. *Journal of Retailing and Consumer Services*, 77, 103627. 10.1016/j.jretconser.2023.103627

Sushil. (2018). How to check correctness of total interpretive structural models? *Annals of Operations Research, 270*(1–2), 473–487. 10.1007/s10479-016-2312-3

Sushil. (2019). Theory building using SAP-LAP linkages: an application in the context of disaster management. *Annals of Operations Research, 283*(1–2), 811–836. 10.1007/s10479-017-2425-3

Sztorc, M., & Savenkovs, K. (2023). Shaping The Digital Potential Of The Large Enterprise Sector Following The Implementation Of The European Digital Decade Strategy. *Scientific Papers of Silesian University of Technology. Organization & Management/Zeszyty Naukowe Politechniki Slaskiej. Seria Organizacji i Zarzadzanie*, (178).

Taylor, D., Brockhaus, S., Knemeyer, A. M., & Murphy, P. (2019). Omnichannel fulfillment strategies: Defining the concept and building an agenda for future inquiry. *International Journal of Logistics Management*, 30(3), 863–891. 10.1108/IJLM-09-2018-0223

Verhoef, P., Kannan, P., & Inman, J. (2015). From multi- channel retailing to omni- channel retailing. Introduction to the special issue on multi- channel retailing. *Journal of Retailing*, 91(2), 174–181. 10.1016/j.jretai.2015.02.005

Verhoef, P. C., Stephen, A. T., Kannan, P. K., Luo, X., Abhishek, V., Andrews, M., Bart, Y., Datta, H., Fong, N., Hoffman, D. L., Hu, M. M., Novak, T., Rand, W., & Zhang, Y. (2017). Consumer connectivity in a complex, technology-enabled, and mobile-oriented world with smart products. *Journal of Interactive Marketing*, 40(1), 1–8. 10.1016/j.intmar.2017.06.001

Wollenburg, J., Holzapfel, A., Hübner, A., & Kuhn, H. (2018). Configuring retail fulfillment processes for omni-channel customer steering. *International Journal of Electronic Commerce*, 22(4), 540–575. 10.1080/10864415.2018.1485085

Zhang, D., Dai, H., Dong, L., Wu, Q., Guo, L., & Liu, X. (2019). The value of pop- up stores on retailing platforms: Evidence from a field experiment with Alibaba. *Management Science*, 65(11), 5142–5151. 10.1287/mnsc.2019.3410

Compilation of References

Abdel-Basst, M., Mohamed, R., & Elhoseny, M. (2020). A novel framework to evaluate innovation value proposition for smart product–service systems. *Environmental Technology & Innovation*, 20, 101036. 10.1016/j.eti.2020.101036

Abid, H., & Javaid, M. (2019). Industry 5.0 and its applications in orthopaedics. *Journal of Clinical Orthopaedics and Trauma*, 10(4), 807–808. 10.1016/j.jcot.2018.12.01031316261

Adadi, A., & Berrada, M. (2018). Peeking inside the black-box: A survey on explainable artificial intelligence (XAI). *IEEE Access : Practical Innovations, Open Solutions*, 6, 52138–52160. 10.1109/ACCESS.2018.2870052

Adamopoulou, E., & Moussiades, L. (2020). Chatbots: History, technology, and applications. *Machine Learning with Applications*, 2, 100006. 10.1016/j.mlwa.2020.100006

Agarwal, P., Malhotra, S. K., & Swami, S. (2024). The role of smart technologies in managing supply chain post pandemic: an exploratory scientific procedures and rationales for systematic literature review. *Journal of Science and Technology Policy Management.*

Agmeka, F., Wathoni, R. N., & Santoso, A. S. (2019). The Influence of Discount Framing towards Brand Reputation and Brand Image on Purchase Intention and Actual Behaviour in E-commerce. *Procedia Computer Science*, 161, 851–858. 10.1016/j.procs.2019.11.192

Agost, M. J., Vergara, M., & Bayarri, V. (2021). The Use of New Presentation Technologies in Electronic Sales Environments and Their Influence on Product Perception. In Yamamoto, S., & Mori, H. (Eds.), Lecture Notes in Computer Science: Vol. 12765. *Human Interface and the Management of Information. Information Presentation and Visualization. HCII 2021*. Springer. 10.1007/978-3-030-78321-1_1

Ahmed, E. O. (2023). The Study of Software Engineering for Development and Maintenance of Software Systems. *International Journal of Intelligent Systems and Applications in Engineering*, 12(8s), 128–137. https://ijisae.org/index.php/IJISAE/article/view/4102

AI Business. (n.d.). Case Study: How Alibaba Uses AI Chatbots to Serve a Billion Customers. *AI Business.*https://aibusiness.com/ml/the-alibaba-challenge-how-to-effectively-engage-with-a-billion-customers-

Aksahan, F. (2021, April). *Industry 4.0 in the Oil and Gas Industry*. ResaerchGate. https://www.researchgate.net/publication/352994741_Industry_40_in_the_Oil_and_Gas_Industry

Akter, S., Wamba, S. F., Gunasekaran, A., Dubey, R., & Childe, S. J. (2016). How to improve firm performance using big data analytics capability and business strategy alignment? *International Journal of Production Economics*, 182, 113–131. 10.1016/j.ijpe.2016.08.018

Alansari, Z., Soomro, S., Belgaum, M. R., & Shamshirband, S. (2018). The Rise of Internet of Things (IoT) in Big Healthcare Data: Review and Open Research Issues. In *Progress in Advanced Computing and Intelligent Engineering* (pp. 675-685). Springer.

Al-Gindy, A., Yasin, N., Aerabe, M., & Omar, A. A. C. (2022). *"Integrating Digital Technology in Enterprise and Entrepreneurship Education," in Technology and Entrepreneurship Education: Adopting Creative Digital Approaches to Learning and Teaching*. Springer International Publishing.

Ali, O., Osmanaj, V., Kwiatek, P., Alryalat, M., Chimhundu, R., & Dwivedi, Y. K. (2023). The impact of technological innovation on marketing: individuals, organizations and environment: a systematic review. *Ekonomska Istrazivanja*, 36(3), 2210661. 10.1080/1331677X.2023.2210661

Almusaed, A., Yitmen, I., & Almssad, A. (2023). Reviewing and Integrating AEC Practices into Industry 6.0: Strategies for Smart and Sustainable Future-Built Environments. *Sustainability (Basel)*, 15(18), 13464. 10.3390/su151813464

Al-Omoush, K. S., Al Attar, M. K., Saleh, I. H., & Alsmadi, A. A. (2020). The drivers of E-banking entrepreneurship: An empirical study. *International Journal of Bank Marketing*, 38(2), 485–500. 10.1108/IJBM-03-2019-0113

Ameen, N., Hosany, S., & Tarhini, A. (2021). Consumer interaction with cutting-edge technologies: Implications for future research. *Computers in Human Behavior*, 120, 106761. 10.1016/j.chb.2021.106761

Amini, M., & Jahanbakhsh Javid, N. (2023). A Multi-Perspective Framework Established on Diffusion of Innovation (DOI) Theory and Technology, Organization and Environment (TOE) Framework Toward Supply Chain Management System Based on Cloud Computing Technology for Small and Medium Enterprises. *Organization and Environment (TOE) Framework Toward Supply Chain Management System Based on Cloud Computing Technology for Small and Medium Enterprises (January 2023).International Journal of Information Technology and Innovation Adoption*, 11, 1217–1234.

Andersson, G. (2018). Internet interventions: Past, present, and future. *Internet Interventions : the Application of Information Technology in Mental and Behavioural Health*, 12, 181–188. 10.1016/j.invent.2018.03.00830135782

Angelopoulos, A., Michailidis, E. T., Nomikos, N., Trakadas, P., Hatziefremidis, A., Voliotis, S., & Zahariadis, T. (2020). Tackling faults in the industry 4.0 era—A survey of machine-learning solutions and key aspects. *Sensors (Basel)*, 20(1), 109. 10.3390/s2001010931878065

Anne-Lindsay, B. (n.d.). A case study on Dignity Health: Analytics helps prevent deadly infections. *Insights Editor*.

Apple. (2017). *ResearchKit 1.5.3*. ResearchKit.

Arora, N., Dreze, X., Ghose, A., Hess, J. D., Iyengar, R., Jing, B., Joshi, Y., Kumar, V., Lurie, N., Neslin, S., Sajeesh, S., Su, M., Syam, N., Thomas, J., & Zhang, Z. J. (2008). Putting one-to-one marketing to work: Personalization, customization, and choice. *Marketing Letters*, 19(3), 305–321. 10.1007/s11002-008-9056-z

Artificial Intelligence Coined at Dartmouth. (1956). Dartmouth. https://home.dartmouth.edu/about/artificial-intelligence-ai-coined-dartmouth

Aslam, F., Aimin, W., Li, M., & Ur Rehman, K. (2020). Innovation in the era of IoT and industry 5.0: Absolute innovation management (AIM) framework. *Information (Basel)*, 11(2), 124. 10.3390/info11020124

Asongu, S. A. (2021). The Effects of Mobile Phone Technology, Knowledge Creation and Diffusion on Inclusive Human Development in Sub-Saharan Africa. *Journal of the Knowledge Economy*, 12(3), 1367–1398. 10.1007/s13132-020-00668-8

Asri, H., Mousannif, H., Al Moatassime, H., & Noel, T. (2015). Big data in healthcare: Challenges and opportunities. *Cloud Technologies and Applications (CloudTech), International Conference*. IEEE.

Ataman, K., Myhr, N., & Nistor, C. (2023). Disruptive Innovation as a Network Dilemma: A Conceptual Model. *Journal of Behavioral and Applied Management*, 23(2), 104–113. https://jbam.scholasticahq.com. 10.21818/001c.84555

Augmented Work for an Automated, AI-driven World. (2023). *IBM Institute for Business Value.* https://www.ibm.com/thought-leadership/institute-business-value/en-us/report/augmented-workforce

Avelar, S., Borges-Tiago, T., Almeida, A., & Tiago, F. (2024). Confluence of sustainable entrepreneurship, innovation, and digitalization in SMEs. *Journal of Business Research*, 170, 114346. 10.1016/j.jbusres.2023.114346

Avery, J., Steenburgh, T., Deighton, J., & Caravella, M. (2012). Adding bricks to clicks: Predicting the patterns of cross-channel elasticities over time. *Journal of Marketing*, 76(3), 96–111. 10.1509/jm.09.0081

Babamiri, B., Bahari, D., & Salimi, A. (2019). Highly sensitive bioaffinity electrochemiluminescence sensors: Recent advances and future directions. *Biosensors & Bioelectronics*, 142, 111530. 10.1016/j.bios.2019.11153031398687

Badawi, B. (2019). A smart fuzzy auto-suggestion system for a multilayer QR code generator. *Journal of Theoretical and Applied Information Technology*, 19(13), 3585–3603. https://www.jatit.org/volumes/Vol97No13/5Vol97No13.pdf

Bai, Q., & Tian, S. (2020). Innovate or die: Corporate innovation and bankruptcy forecasts. *Journal of Empirical Finance*, 59, 88–108. 10.1016/j.jempfin.2020.09.002

Balandin, S., Balandina, E., Koucheryavy, Y., Kramar, V., & Medvedev, O. (2013). —Main Trends in mHealth Use Scenarios,||. *J. Sel. Top. Nano Electron. Comput*, 1(1), 64–70. 10.15393/j8.art.2013.3022

Balasubramanian, S., Peterson, R., & Jarvenpaa, S. (2002). Exploring the implications of m- commerce for markets and marketing. *Journal of the Academy of Marketing Science*, 30(4), 348–361. 10.1177/009207002236910

Ballester, D., Malo, S., & Paché, G. (2020). The effects of the industry 4.0 on the operational performance of SMEs. *Journal of Manufacturing Technology Management*, 31(4), 950–972. 10.1108/JMTM-06-2019-0187

Barney, J. B. (1991). Firm resources and sustained competitive advantage. *Journal of Management*, 17(1), 99–120. 10.1177/014920639101700108

Barney, J. B. (1995). Looking inside for competitive advantage. *The Academy of Management Perspectives*, 9(4), 49–61. 10.5465/ame.1995.9512032192

Barney, J. B., & Arikan, A. M. (2001). The resource-based view: Origins and implications. In Hitt, M. A., Freeman, R. E., & Harrison, J. S. (Eds.), *The Blackwell Handbook of Strategic Management* (pp. 124–188). Blackwell Publishers.

Beck, N., & Rygl, D. (2015). Categorization of multiple channel retailing in multi-, cross-, and omni- channel retailing for retailers and retailing. *Journal of Retailing and Consumer Services*, 2015(27), 170–178. 10.1016/j.jretconser.2015.08.001

Behl, A., Dutta, P., Lessmann, S., Dwivedi, Y. K., & Kar, S. (2019). A conceptual framework for the adoption of big data analytics by e-commerce startups: A case-based approach. *Information Systems and e-Business Management*, 17(2-4), 285–318. 10.1007/s10257-019-00452-5

Belgaum, M. R., Soomro, S. U., Alansari, Z., & Alam, M. (2018). Treatment of Reactive Routing Protocols Using Second Chance Based on Malicious behavior of Nodes in MANETS. *Pakistan Journal of Engineering, Technology & Science, 6*(2).

Bell, D., Gallino, S., & Moreno, A. (2014). How to win in an omni- channel world. *MIT Sloan Management Review*, 56(1), 45–53.

Benitez-Amado, J., Llorens-Montes, J., & Perez-Arostegui, M. N. (2019). Organizational learning, innovation, and performance in high-tech firms: The moderating role of the human resource management approach. *Journal of Business Research*, 95, 319–326. 10.1016/j.jbusres.2018.10.036

Berman, S. J. (2012). Digital transformation: Opportunities to create new business models. *Strategy and Leadership*, 40(2), 16–24. 10.1108/10878571211209314

Bhatt, M. (2024, January 29). *Digital Twins: Upcoming Revolution in Refining sector.* Linkedin. https://www.linkedin.com/pulse/digital-twins-upcoming-revolution-refining-sector-meet-bhatt-0pixf/?trk=article-ssr-frontend-pulse_more-articles_related-content-card

Biswas, P. K., & Li, S. (2022). A hybrid recommender system for recommending smartphones to prospective customers. *Expert Systems with Applications*, 208, 118058. 10.1016/j.eswa.2022.118058

Blackburn, R., Lurz, K., Priese, B., Göb, R., & Darkow, I.-L. (2015). A predictive analytics approach for demand forecasting in the process industry. *International Transactions in Operational Research*, 22(3), 407–428. 10.1111/itor.12122

Boer, E. d. (2022, August 17). *What are Industry 4.0, the Fourth Industrial Revolution, and 4IR?* Mckinsey & Company. https://www.mckinsey.com/featured-insights/mckinsey-explainers/what-are-industry-4-0-the-fourth-industrial-revolution-and-4ir

Bohórquez, E., Pérez, M., Alvarez, R., & Villón, S. (2024). Marketing Strategies and Sales: Key Factors for Positioning and Growth in the Market. In Reis, J. L., Del Rio Araujo, M., Reis, L. P., & dos Santos, J. P. M. (Eds.), *Marketing and Smart Technologies. ICMarkTech 2022. Smart Innovation, Systems and Technologies* (Vol. 344). Springer., 10.1007/978-981-99-0333-7_27

Bonfanti, A., De Crescenzo, V., Simeoni, F., & Adaui, C. R. L. (2024). Convergences and divergences in sustainable and social entrepreneurship research: A systematic review and research agenda. *Journal of Business Research*, 170, 114336. 10.1016/j.jbusres.2023.114336

Bresnick, J. (2017). *Machine Learning in Healthcare: Defining the Most Common Terms.* Thinkstock.

Brito, R. D., Correia de Souza, E., & Moita, R. (2024). Separating Vertical from Horizontal Differentiation. *Review of Industrial Organization*, 64(2), 183–218. 10.1007/s11151-023-09924-y

Brown, D. G., & Wobst, H. J. (2021). A decade of FDA-approved drugs (2010–2019): Trends and future directions. *Journal of Medicinal Chemistry*, 64(5), 2312–2338. 10.1021/acs.jmedchem.0c0151633617254

Brynjolfsson, E., Hu, Y., & Rahman, M. (2013). Competing in the age of omni- channel retailing. *MIT Sloan Management Review*, 54(4), 1–7.

Bydon, M., Schirmer, C. M., Oermann, E. K., Kitagawa, R. S., Pouratian, N., Davies, J., Sharan, A., & Chambless, L. B. (2020). Big data defined: A practical review for neurosurgeons. *World Neurosurgery*, 133, e842–e849. 10.1016/j.wneu.2019.09.09231562965

Byrne, D. P., Imai, S., Jain, N., & Sarafidis, V. (2022). Instrument-free identification and estimation of differentiated products models using cost data. *Journal of Econometrics*, 228(2), 278–301. 10.1016/j.jeconom.2021.12.006

Camilleri, M. A., Cricelli, L., Mauriello, R., & Strazzullo, S. (2023). Consumer Perceptions of Sustainable Products: A Systematic Literature Review. *Sustainability (Basel)*, 15(11), 8923. 10.3390/su15118923

Campisi, T., Russo, A., Basbas, S., Bouhouras, E., & Tesoriere, G. (2023). A literature review of the main factors influencing the e-commerce and last-mile delivery projects during COVID-19 pandemic. *Transportation Research Procedia*, 69, 552–559. 10.1016/j.trpro.2023.02.207

Cao, L. (2014). Business model tranformation in moving to a cross- channel retail strategy: A case study. *International Journal of Electronic Commerce*, 18(4), 69–96. 10.2753/JEC1086-4415180403

Cao, L., & Li, L. (2014). The impact of cross- channel integration on retailers' sales growth. *Journal of Retailing*, 91(2), 198–216. 10.1016/j.jretai.2014.12.005

Capacity. (2023). *Evolution of Chatbots*. Capacity. https://capacity.com/chatbots/evolution-of-chatbots/

Carayannis, E. G., Christodoulou, K., Christodoulou, P., Chatzichristofis, S. A., & Zinonos, Z. (2021). Known unknowns in an era of technological and viral disruptions—Implications for theory, policy, and practice. *Journal of the Knowledge Economy*, 1–24.

Casheekar, A., Lahiri, A., Rath, K., Prabhakar, K. S., & Srinivasan, K. (2024). A contemporary review on chatbots, AI-powered virtual conversational agents, ChatGPT: Applications, open challenges and future research directions. *Computer Science Review*, 52, 100632. 10.1016/j.cosrev.2024.100632

Cassani, L., Fiszman, S., Alvarez, M. V., Moreira, M. R., Laguna, L., & Tarrega, A. (2020). Emotional response evoked when looking at and trying a new food product, measured through images and words. A case study with novel fruit and vegetable smoothies. *Food Quality and Preference*, 84, 103955. 10.1016/j.foodqual.2020.103955

Chae, B. K., Koh, S., & Prybutok, V. R. (2014). Information technology capability and firm performance: Contradictory findings and their possible causes. *Management Information Systems Quarterly*, 38(1), 305–326. 10.25300/MISQ/2014/38.1.14

Chandel, A., & Sharma, R. (2023). Artificial Intelligence and Value Creation at the Crossroads of Industry 5.0: A Bibliometric and Content Analysis Discourse. In Dadwal, S. (Eds.), *Opportunities and Challenges of Business 5.0 in Emerging Markets* (pp. 58–78). IGI Global., 10.4018/978-1-6684-6403-8.ch004

Chatzoglou, P., Chatzoudes, D., Savvidou, A., Fotiadis, T., & Delias, P. (2022). Factors affecting repurchase intentions in retail shopping: An empirical study. *Heliyon*, 8(9), e10619. 10.1016/j.heliyon.2022.e1061936158093

Chemnad, K., Alshakhsi, S., Almourad, M. B., Altuwairiqi, M., Phalp, K., & Ali, R. (2022). Smartphone usage before and during COVID-19: A Comparative Study Based on Objective Recording of Usage Data. *Informatics (MDPI)*, 9(4), 98. 10.3390/informatics9040098

Chen, H. (2010). Business and Market Intelligence 2.0. *IEEE Computer Society*. IEEE. https://citeseerx.ist.psu.edu/document?repid=rep1&type=pdf&doi=2a143d9d55854e0852a1401054b2fa12839987b2

Chen, Y. W. O. M. D. C. K. (2024, February 14). Case Study: How Alibaba Uses AI Chatbots to Serve a Billion Customers. *AI Business*. https://aibusiness.com/ml/the-alibaba-challenge-how-to-effectively-engage-with-a-billion-customers-#close-modal

Chen, I. J., & Paulraj, A. (2004). Towards a theory of supply chain management: The constructs and measurements. *Journal of Operations Management*, 22(2), 119–150. 10.1016/j.jom.2003.12.007

Chen, M., & Bashir, R. (2022). Role of e-commerce and resource utilization for sustainable business development: Goal of economic recovery after Covid-19. *Economic Change and Restructuring*, 55(4), 2663–2685. 10.1007/s10644-022-09404-5

Chen, M., Mao, S., & Liu, Y. (2014). Big data: A survey. *Mobile Networks and Applications*, 19(2), 171–209. 10.1007/s11036-013-0489-0

Chinese Academy of Cyberspace Studies. (2023). World Information Technology Development. In *World Internet Development Report 2021*. Springer. 10.1007/978-981-19-9323-7_3

Chodak, G. (2024). Measuring the Impact of E-Commerce on the Economy. In *The Future of E-commerce*. Palgrave Macmillan. 10.1007/978-3-031-55225-0_1

Chodak, G. (2024). *The Future of E-commerce. Innovations and Developments*. Springer. 10.1007/978-3-031-55225-0

Choi, S. W., & Nam, J. H. (2019). The use of AI chatbot as an assistant tool for SW education. *Journal of the Korea Institute of Information and Communication Engineering*, 23(12), 1693–1699.

Chong, T., Yu, T., Keeling, D. I., & de Ruyter, K. (2021). AI-chatbots on the services frontline addressing the challenges and opportunities of agency. *Journal of Retailing and Consumer Services*, 63, 102735. 10.1016/j.jretconser.2021.102735

Chouaib Dakouan, M., & Redouane Benabdelouahed, M. (2019). Digital Inbound Marketing: Particularities of Business-to-Business and Business-to-Customer Strategies. In Kavoura, A., Kefallonitis, E., & Giovanis, A. (Eds.), *Strategic Innovative Marketing and Tourism. Springer Proceedings in Business and Economics*. Springer. 10.1007/978-3-030-12453-3_14

Christensen, C. M., & Raynor, M. E. (2003). *The Innovator's Solution*. Harvard Business Press.

Cioffi, R., Travaglioni, M., Piscitelli, G., Petrillo, A., & Parmentola, A. (2020). Smart manufacturing systems and applied industrial technologies for a sustainable industry: A systematic literature review. *Applied Sciences (Basel, Switzerland)*, 10(8), 2897. 10.3390/app10082897

Clark, T., Azab, C., & Key, T. M. (2024). Marketing's next era: The scope and impact of marketing's future, the reach and legacy of Shelby Hunt. *Journal of Business Research*, 170, 114278. 10.1016/j.jbusres.2023.114278

Cloitre, A., Dos Santos Paulino, V., & Theodoraki, C. (2023). The quadruple/quintuple helix model in entrepreneurial ecosystems: An institutional perspective on the space case study. *R & D Management*, 53(4), 675–694. 10.1111/radm.12547

Ćoćkalo, D., Tadić, D., Bakator, M., Stanisavljev, S., & Makitan, V. (2023). Managing the Transition Process to Society 5.0. *Management: Journal of Sustainable Business and Management Solutions in Emerging Economies*.

Coelho, F., & Easingwood, C. (2008). A model of the antecedents of multiple channel usage. *Journal of Retailing and Consumer Services*, 15(1), 32–41. 10.1016/j.jretconser.2007.03.002

Cornell, J., & Cornell, J. (2024, January 12). 12 Essential Chatbot Features to Consider in 2024. Chat Blog. https://www.proprofschat.com/blog/chatbot-features/

Corner, P. D., Singh, S., & Pavlovich, K. (2017). Entrepreneurial resilience and venture failure. *International Small Business Journal*, 35(6), 687–708. 10.1177/0266242616685604

D'Cruze, D. (2023). *Google Pay now supports UPI payments via RuPay credit cards; check how to use it.* Business Today. https://www.businesstoday.in/

da Silva, B. D. (2001). A Tecnologia é uma Estratégia. In Dias, P. (Ed.), *Freitas, C. V. de (Org.). Actas da II Conferência Internacional Desafios 2001* (pp. 839–859). Centro de Competência da Universidade do Minho do Projecto Nónio.

Daniel, T., & Sebastian, B., A., M. K., & Paul, M. (2019). Omnichannel fulfillment strategies: Defining the concept and building an agenda for future inquiry. *International Journal of Logistics Management*, 30(3), 863–891.

Danneels, E. (2003). Tight-loose coupling with customers: The enactment of customer orientation. *Strategic Management Journal*, 24(6), 559–576. 10.1002/smj.319

Dargan, S., Bansal, S., Kumar, M., Mittal, A., & Kumar, K. (2023). Augmented Reality: A Comprehensive Review. *Archives of Computational Methods in Engineering*, 30(2), 1057–1080. 10.1007/s11831-022-09831-7

Dave, D. M. (2023). Revolutionizing Medical Device Implants: Unleashing the Power of Industry 5.0. *International Journal of Computer Trends and Technology*, 71(10), 1–11. 10.14445/22312803/IJCTT-V71I10P101

Davenport, T. H., & Harris, J. (2007). *Competing on analytics: The new science of winning*. Harvard Business Press.

De Leeuw, S., Minguela-Rata, B., Sabet, E., Boter, J., & Sigurðardóttir, R. (2016). Trade - offs in managing commercial consumer returns for online apparel retail. *International Journal of Operations & Production Management*, 36(6), 710–731. 10.1108/IJOPM-01-2015-0010

Deberdieva, E. M., Vechkasova, M. V., Golikava, H. S., Borisova, A. A., & Lysenko, A. F. (2019). Experience in the management of business processes with the use of digital technologies by Russian companies of a petrochemical complex. *IOP Conference Series. Materials Science and Engineering*, 483, 483. 10.1088/1757-899X/483/1/012066

Deepa, N., Pham, Q. V., Nguyen, D. C., Bhattacharya, S., Prabadevi, B., Gadekallu, T. R., & Pathirana, P. N. (2022). A survey on blockchain for big data: Approaches, opportunities, and future directions. *Future Generation Computer Systems*, 131, 209–226. 10.1016/j.future.2022.01.017

Dehning, B., Stratopoulos, T. C., & Zan, L. (2003). The financial performance of internet versus non-internet firms: A comprehensive study. *Journal of Electronic Commerce Research*, 4(3), 143–157. 10.1108/eb028855

Desk, T. (2023). Google Pay now supports UPI payments using RuPay credit cards. *Indian Express.*https://indianexpress.com/

Devi, S., & Periyasamy, N. (2023). A Study On Users Perception Towards Google Pay With Special Reference To Puducherry. *Journal of Namibian Studies: History Politics Culture*, 38, 1995–2003.

Dhar, V. (2014). Big data and predictive analytics in health care. *Big Data*, 2(3), 113–116. 10.1089/big.2014.152527442491

Díaz-Díaz, R., Muñoz, L., & Pérez-González, D. (2017). The business model evaluation tool for smart cities: Application to SmartSantander use cases. *Energies*, 10(3), 262. 10.3390/en10030262

Diebold, F. X. (2012). On the Origin(s) and Development of the Term 'Big Data'. PIER Working Paper n. 12-037. https://ssrn.com/abstract=2152421

Dolega, L., Rowe, F., & Branagan, E. (2020). Going digital? The impact of social media marketing on retail website traffic, orders and sales. *Journal of Retailing and Consumer Services*, 60, 102501. 10.1016/j.jretconser.2021.102501

Dong, A. (2020). AI chatbot behind Alibaba's $38 billion Single's Day sales miracle. *Digital Innovation and Transformation.* Harvard Press. https://d3.harvard.edu/platform-digit/submission/ai-chatbot-behind-alibabas-38-billion-singles-day-sales-miracle/

Dorman, A. (2013). *Omni- channel retail and the new age consumer: an empirical analysis of direct- to - consumer channel interaction in the retail industry*. CMC Senior Theses, Claremont McKenna College.

Dorr, D. A., Jones, S. S., Burns, L., Donnelly, S. M., Brunker, C. P., Wilcox, A., & Clayton, P. D. (2006). Use of health-related, quality-of-life metrics to predict mortality and hospitalizations in community-dwelling seniors. *Journal of the American Geriatrics Society*, 54(4), 667–673. 10.1111/j.1532-5415.2006.00681.x16686880

du Plessis, C. (2022). A Scoping Review of the Effect of Content Marketing on Online Consumer Behavior. *SAGE Open*, 12(2). 10.1177/21582440221093042

Du, Z., Liu, J., & Wang, T. (2022). Augmented Reality Marketing: A Systematic Literature Review and an Agenda for Future Inquiry. *Frontiers in Psychology*, 13, 925963. 10.3389/fpsyg.2022.92596335783783

Ed Corbett, M. D. (2017). *The Real-World Benefits of Machine Learning in Healthcare*. Health Catalysyt.

Edwards, C. (2022). Evaluating the Tipping Point of a Complex System: The Case of Disruptive Technology. *TechRxiv.* https://www.techrxiv.org/doi/full/10.36227/techrxiv.21126292.v1

Eissa, H. (2020, January 13). *Unleashing Industry 4.0 Opportunities: Big Data Analytics in the Midstream Oil & Gas Sector.* OnePetro. https://onepetro.org/IPTCONF/proceedings-abstract/20IPTC/3-20IPTC/154550

Fan, X., Deng, N., Qian, Y., & Dong, X. (2022). Factors Affecting the Effectiveness of Cause-Related Marketing: A Meta-Analysis. *Journal of Business Ethics*, 175(2), 339–360. 10.1007/s10551-020-04639-6

Farmer, K., & Schelnast, M. (2021). Product Differentiation, Decreasing Costs, and Intra-Sectoral Trade. In *Growth and International Trade. Springer Texts in Business and Economics.* Springer. 10.1007/978-3-662-62943-7_13

Fatimah, Y. A., Kannan, D., Govindan, K., & Hasibuan, Z. A. (2023). Circular economy e-business model portfolio development for e-business applications: Impacts on ESG and sustainability performance. *Journal of Cleaner Production*, 415, 137528. 10.1016/j.jclepro.2023.137528

Fedorko, R., Krail, S., & Bacik, R. (2022). Artificial Intelligence in E-Commerce: A Literature Review. Springer.

Feedstuffs.com. (2019). Kroger, Microsoft partner on digital solutions. Retrieved January 9, 2019 from https://www.feedstuffs.com/news/kroger-microsoft-partner-digital-solutions

Flynn Meyer, E. (2021). *Mastering Inbound Marketing: Your Complete Guide to Building a Results-Driven Inbound Strategy* (1st ed.). BookBaby.

Föckler, P., Zeidler, T., Brombach, B., Bruns, E., & Bimber, O. (2005). PhoneGuide: Museum guidance supported by on-device object recognition on mobile phones. In *Proceedings of the 4th International Conference on Mobile and Ubiquitous Multimedia* (pp. 3–10). ACM. 10.1145/1149488.1149490

Forecast, G. M. D. T. (2019). *Cisco visual Networking index: global mobile data traffic forecast update, 2017-2022.* CISCO. https://www.cisco.com/c/en/us/solutions/service-provider/visualnetworking-index-vni/index.html

Foresti, R., Rossi, S., Magnani, M., Bianco, C. G. L., & Delmonte, N. (2020). Smart society and artificial intelligence: Big data scheduling and the global standard method applied to smart maintenance. *Engineering (Beijing)*, 6(7), 835–846. 10.1016/j.eng.2019.11.014

Foroughi, B., Hongsachart, H., Asadi, S., Iranmanesh, M., Ghobakhloo, M., & Tirkolaee, E. B. (2023). Reuse intention of augmented reality apps: Recreational consciousness as moderator. *Service Industries Journal*, 1–42.

Fraga-Lamas, P., Lopes, S. I., & Fernández-Caramés, T. M. (2021). Green IoT and edge AI as key technological enablers for a sustainable digital transition towards a smart circular economy: An industry 5.0 use case. *Sensors (Basel)*, 21(17), 5745. 10.3390/s2117574534502637

Fridhi, A., & Frihida, A. (2019). GIS 3D and Science of Augmented Reality: Modeling a 3D Geospatial Environment. *Journal of Soft Computing in Civil Engineering*, 3-4, 78–87. 10.22115/SCCE.2020.212254.1148

Galipoglu, E., Kotzab, H., Teller, C., Yumurtaci Hüseyinoglu, I. Ö., & Pöppelbuß, J. (2018). Omni-channel retailing research–state of the art and intellectual foundation. *International Journal of Physical Distribution & Logistics Management*, 48(4), 365–390. 10.1108/IJPDLM-10-2016-0292

Gallino, S., & Moreno, A. (2014). Integration of online and offline channels in retail: The impact of sharing reliable inventory availability information. *Management Science*, 60(6), 1434–1451. 10.1287/mnsc.2014.1951

Gamayanto, I., & Nurhindarto, A. (2020). Developing Smart City 5.0 Framework To Produce Competency. *Journal of Applied Intelligent System*, 5(1), 23–31. 10.33633/jais.v5i1.4228

García-Salirrosas, E. E., Acevedo-Duque, Á., Marin Chaves, V., Mejía Henao, P. A. M., & Olaya Molano, J. C. (2022). Purchase Intention and Satisfaction of Online Shop Users in Developing Countries during the COVID-19 Pandemic. *Sustainability (Basel)*, 14(10), 6302. 10.3390/su14106302

Garg, A. (2022). *Google Pay, PhonePe and other UPI apps may soon impose transaction limit.* INDIA TODAY.

Garratt, M. (2018). *Why Disruption Is Coming for Your Industry -- And How to Embrace It.* Entrepreneur.com. https://www.entrepreneur.com/article/324260

Gartner Predicts 25% of People Will Spend at Least One Hour Per Day in the Metaverse by 2026 (2022). *Gartner Inc. Press Release*. Newsroom. https://www. gartner.com/en/newsroom/press-releases/2022-02-07-gartner-predicts-25-percentof-people-will-spend-at-least-one-hour-per-day-in-the-metaverse-by-2026

Get ahead start into the world of conversational messaging. (2023, July 22). Sinch Engage. https://engage.sinch.com/blog/ai-chatbots-in-e-commerce/#:~:text=AI%20chatbots%20can%20be%20great,leave%20with%20the%20best%20product

Ghasemi, Y., Jeong, H., Choi, S. H., Park, K.-B., & Lee, J. Y. (2022). Deep learning-based object detection in augmented reality: A systematic review. *Computers in Industry*, 139, 103661. 10.1016/j.compind.2022.103661

Ghobakhloo, M., Fathi, M., Iranmanesh, M., Maroufkhani, P., & Morales, M. E. (2021). Industry 4.0 ten years on: A bibliometric and systematic review of concepts, sustainability value drivers, and success determinants. *Journal of Cleaner Production*, 302, 127052. 10.1016/j.jclepro.2021.127052

Ghobakhloo, M., Hong, T. S., Sabouri, M. S., & Zulkifli, N. (2017). Strategies for successful information technology adoption in small and medium-sized enterprises. *Information Systems*, 65, 41–53. 10.1016/j.is.2017.01.006

Ghosh, M. (2024). Meta-analytic review of online purchase intention: Conceptualising the study variables. *Cogent Business & Management*, 11(1), 2296686. 10.1080/23311975.2023.2296686

Gillum, R. F. (2013). From papyrus to the electronic tablet: A brief history of the clinical medical record with lessons for the digital Age. *The American Journal of Medicine*, 126(10), 853–857. 10.1016/j.amjmed.2013.03.02424054954

Görög, M., Zabál, P., & Szűts, Z. (2021). Digital transformation and its role in enhancing the competitiveness of SMEs. *Sustainability*, 13(12), 6999. 10.3390/su13126999

Govindarajan, V., Kopalle, P. K., & Danneels, E. (2011). The effects of mainstream and emerging customer orientation on radical and disruptive innovations. *Journal of Product Innovation Management*, 28(s1), 121–132. 10.1111/j.1540-5885.2011.00865.x

Grabowska, S., & Saniuk, S. (2022). Assessment of the competitiveness and effectiveness of an open business model in the industry 4.0 environment. *Journal of Open Innovation*, 8(1), 57. 10.3390/joitmc8010057

Gross-Gotacka, E. (2023). Integration of Intellectual Capital, Sustainable Development, and Business 5.0. In: Rzepka, A. *Innovation in Digital Economy: New Approaches to Management for Industry 5.0* [Translated by Jakub Prachowski] (pp.135-148). Routledge. https://www.routledge.com/Innovation-in-the-Digital-Economy-New-Approaches-to-Management-for-Industry/Rzepka/p/book/9781032469935

Gross-Gotacka, E. (2023). The Concept of Inclusion and Diversity as an Accelerator for Building Society 5.0 and Creating a Managed Organization in the 5.0 Era. In: Rzepka, A. *Innovation in Digital Economy: New Approaches to Management for Industry 5.0* [Translated by Jakub Prachowski] (pp. 62-72). Routledge. https://www.routledge.com/Innovation-in-the-Digital-Economy-New-Approaches-to-Management-for-Industry/Rzepka/p/book/9781032469935

Grubor, A., & Milovanov, O. (2017). Brand strategies in the era of sustainability. *Interdisciplinary Description of Complex Systems*, 15(1), 78–88. 10.7906/indecs.15.1.6

Gubbi, J., Buyya, R., Marusic, S., & Palaniswami, M. (2013). Internet of Things (IoT): A vision, architectural elements, and future directions. *Future Generation Computer Systems*, 29(7), 1645–1660. 10.1016/j.future.2013.01.010

Guenther, A., Eisenbart, B., & Dong, A. (2020). Creativity and successful product concept selection for innovation. *International Journal of Design Creativity and Innovation*, 9(1), 3–19. 10.1080/21650349.2020.1858970

Guidotti, R., Monreale, A., Ruggieri, S., Turini, F., Giannotti, F., & Pedreschi, D. (2018). A survey of methods for explaining black box models. *ACM Computing Surveys*, 51(5), 1–42. 10.1145/3236009

Gupta, H., Kumar, A., & Kumar, S. (2021). Investigating the antecedents of digital transformation for sustainable development in Indian manufacturing SMEs. *Journal of Manufacturing Technology Management*, 32(7), 1521–1547. 10.1108/JMTM-04-2020-0181

Haddad, E. (2024). Leveraging social media, big data, and smart technologies for intercultural communication and effective leadership: Empirical study at the Ministry of Digital Economy and Entrepreneurship. *International Journal of Data and Network Science*, 8(2), 857–870. 10.5267/j.ijdns.2023.12.019

Hair, J. F., Hult, G. T. M., Ringle, C. M., & Sarstedt, M. (2017). *A primer on partial least squares structural equation modeling (PLS-SEM)*. Sage Publications.

Haleem, A., Javaid, M., & Khan, I. H. (2019). Current status and applications of artificial intelligence (AI) in the medical field: An overview. *Current Medicine Research and Practice*, 9(6), 231–237. 10.1016/j.cmrp.2019.11.005

Hanan, S. A. S., Elhadad, A., & Ghareeb, A. (2021). Rapid and Blind Watermarking Approach of the 3D Objects Using QR Code Images for Securing Copyright. *Computational Intelligence and Neuroscience, vol. 2021. Computational Intelligence and Neuroscience*, 2236866, 1–11. 10.1155/2021/2236866

Haorongbam, L., Nagpal, R., & Sehgal, R. (2022). *Service Oriented Architecture (SOA): A Literature Review on the Maintainability, Approaches and Design Process. 12th International Conference on Cloud Computing, Data Science & Engineering (Confluence)*, Noida, India. 10.1109/Confluence52989.2022.9734153

Hendricks, S., & Mwapwele, S. D. (2024). A systematic literature review on the factors influencing e-commerce adoption in developing countries. *Data and Information Management*, 8(1), 100045. 10.1016/j.dim.2023.100045

Herhausen, D., Binder, J., Schoegel, M., & Herrmann, A. (2015). Integrating bricks and clicks: Retailer-level and channel-level outcomes of online- offline channel integration. *Journal of Retailing*, 91(2), 309–325. 10.1016/j.jretai.2014.12.009

He, W., Zhang, Z. J., & Li, W. (2021). Information technology solutions, challenges, and suggestions for tackling the COVID-19 pandemic. *International Journal of Information Management*, 57, 102287. 10.1016/j.ijinfomgt.2020.10228733318721

Hildebrand, C., & Bergner, A. (2019). AI-Driven Sales Automation: Using Chatbots to Boost Sales. *NIM Marketing Intelligence Review*, 11(2), 36–41. 10.2478/nimmir-2019-0014

Hilken, T., Heller, J., Chylinski, M., Keeling, D. I., Mahr, D., & de Ruyter, K. (2018). Making omnichannel an augmented reality: The current and future state of the art. *Journal of Research in Interactive Marketing*, 12(4), 509–523. 10.1108/JRIM-01-2018-0023

Hill, G. N., & Whitty, M. A. (2021). Embedding metadata in images at time of capture using physical Quick Response (QR) codes. *Information Processing & Management*, 58(3), 102504. 10.1016/j.ipm.2021.102504

Hoens, T. R., Blanton, M., Steele, A., & Chawla, N. V. (2013). —Reliable medical recommendation systems with patient privacy,||. *ACM Transactions on Intelligent Systems and Technology*, 4(4), 67. 10.1145/2508037.2508048

Hoffman, D. L., Moreau, C. P., Stremersch, S., & Wedel, M. (2022). The Rise of New Technologies in Marketing: A Framework and Outlook. *Journal of Marketing*, 86(1), 1–6. 10.1177/00222429211061636

Hootsuite. (2021). *Digital 2021: global digital overview*. Hootsuite. https://datareportal.com/reports/digital-2021-global-overview-report

Hopkins, J. L. (2021). An investigation into emerging industry 4.0 technologies as drivers of supply chain innovation in Australia. *Computers in Industry*, 125, 103323. 10.1016/j.compind.2020.103323

Hossain, M. I., Tabash, M. I., Siow, M. L., Ong, T. S., & Anagreh, S. (2023). Entrepreneurial intentions of Gen Z university students and entrepreneurial constraints in Bangladesh. *Journal of Innovation and Entrepreneurship*, 12(1), 1–34. 10.1186/s13731-023-00279-y36919091

Hossain, T. M. T., Akter, S., Kattiyapornpong, U., & Dwivedi, Y. (2020). Reconceptualizing Integration Quality Dynamics for omnichannel marketing. *Industrial Marketing Management*, 87, 225–241. 10.1016/j.indmarman.2019.12.006

Hoyer, W. D., Kroschke, M., Schmitt, B., Kraume, K., & Shankar, V. (2020). Transforming the Customer Experience Through New Technologies. *Journal of Interactive Marketing*, 51, 57–71. 10.1016/j.intmar.2020.04.001

Hubner, A., Holzapfel, A., & Kuhn, H. (2016). Distribution systems in omni- channel retailing. *Business Reseach*, 44(33), 228–247.

Hubner, A., Kuhn, H., & Wollenburg, J. (2016). Retail logistics in the transition from multi- channel to omni- channel. *International Journal of Physical Distribution & Logistics Management*, 46(6/7), 562–561. 10.1108/IJPDLM-08-2015-0179

Hulsen, T. (2021). Challenges and solutions for big data in personalized healthcare. In *Big Data in Psychiatry# x0026; Neurology* (pp. 69-94). Academic Press. 10.1016/B978-0-12-822884-5.00016-7

Hyams-Ssekasi, D., & Yasin, N. (2022). *Technology and Entrepreneurship Education*. Springer International Publishing. 10.1007/978-3-030-84292-5

Ietto, B., Ancillai, C., Sabatini, A., Carayannis, E. G., & Gregori, G. L. (2022). The role of external actors in SMEs' human-centered industry 4.0 adoption: An empirical perspective on Italian competence centers. *IEEE Transactions on Engineering Management*.

Imoize, A. L., Adedeji, O., Tandiya, N., & Shetty, S. (2021). 6G enabled smart infrastructure for sustainable society: Opportunities, challenges, and research roadmap. *Sensors (Basel)*, 21(5), 1709. 10.3390/s2105170933801302

Irmak, E., & Bozdal, M. (2018) Internet of Things (IoT): The Most Up-To-Date Challenges, Architectures, Emerging Trends and Potential Opportunities. *International Journal of Computer Applications* (0975 – 8887). https://core.ac.uk/download/pdf/286715999.pdf

Irons, B. T. (2020). Current and Future Applications of 3D Printing Using Custom-Made Material. [Thesis, USD]. https://red.library.usd.edu/honors-thesis/89/

Islam, J. U., Ahmed, S., Ali, M., Islam, S., & Moe, T. N. (2022). Investigating the relationships among digital innovation, digital transformation, and organizational performance: The role of digital leadership. *Information Systems Frontiers*, 1–20. 10.1007/s10796-022-10440-0

Janadari, N., & Preena, G. R. (2020). *"The Gig Economy and Workforce", Contemporary Developments in Human Resource Management book, I.* SSN.

Jing, F., Lin, J., Zhang, Q., & Qian, Y. (2022). New technology introduction and product rollover strategies. *European Journal of Operational Research*, 302(1), 324–336. 10.1016/j.ejor.2021.12.025

Junglas, C., Abraham, C., & Ives, B. (2009). Abraham, and B. Ives, —Mobile technology at the frontlines of patient care: Understanding fit and human drives in utilization decisions and performance,||. *Decision Support Systems*, 46(3), 634–647. 10.1016/j.dss.2008.11.012

Jwala, K. (2019). Developing a Chatbot using. *Machine Learning*, 8(1). https://www.ijrte.org/wp-content/uploads/papers/v8i1S3/A10170681S319.pdf

Kahn, J. G., Yang, J. S., & Kahn, J. S. (2010). 'Mobile' health needs and opportunities in developing countries. *Health Affairs (Project Hope)*, 29(2), 252–258. 10.1377/hlthaff.2009.096520348069

Kalgotra, P., Gupta, A., & Sharda, R. (2021). Pandemic information support lifecycle: Evidence from the evolution of mobile apps during COVID-19. *Journal of Business Research*, 134, 540–559. 10.1016/j.jbusres.2021.06.00234565948

Kamble, S. S., Gunasekaran, A., Gawankar, S. A., & Papadopoulos, T. (2019). Industry 4.0 and lean management: A proposed integration model and research agenda. *Production Planning and Control*, 30(8-9), 698–710. 10.1080/09537287.2019.1601963

Kannan, D., Senthil, S., & Tiwari, M. K. (2015). A review of lean manufacturing implementation techniques. *Procedia CIRP*, 26, 12–17. 10.1016/j.procir.2015.07.005

Kannan, P. K., & Li, H. A. (2017). Digital marketing: A framework, review and research agenda. *International Journal of Research in Marketing*, 34(1), 22–45. 10.1016/j.ijresmar.2016.11.006

Kashyap, H. (2023). *PhonePe, Google Pay, Paytm Process 94% Of UPI Transactions In March 2023*. Inc42.

Katsumata, S., Ichikohji, T., Nakano, S., Yamaguchi, S., & Ikuine, F. (2022). Changes in the use of mobile devices during the crisis: Immediate response to the COVID-19 pandemic. *Computers in Human Behavior Reports*, 5, 100168. 10.1016/j.chbr.2022.10016835079660

Katz, J. (2023, August 7). *Generative AI in the Chemical Industry*. Chemical Processing. https://www.chemicalprocessing.com/automation-it/article/33008789/ai-in-the-chemical-industry-from-molecule-discovery-to-contract-compliance

Kaufmann, P. J., & Dant, R. P. (1999). Franchising and the domain of entrepreneurship research. *Journal of Business Venturing*, 14(1), 5–16. 10.1016/S0883-9026(97)00095-5

Kembro, J. H., Norrman, A., & Eriksson, E. (2018). Adapting warehouse operations and design to omni-channel logistics: A literature review and research agenda. *International Journal of Physical Distribution & Logistics Management*, 48(9), 890–912. 10.1108/IJPDLM-01-2017-0052

Kendall, K., & Kendall, J. (2021). *Systems Analysis and Design* (10th ed.). Pearson.

Khang, A., Gupta, S. K., Rani, S., & Karras, D. A. (Eds.). (2023). *Smart Cities: IoT Technologies, big data solutions, cloud platforms, and cybersecurity techniques*. CRC Press. 10.1201/9781003376064

Khan, R., & Arif, Z. U. (2023). *Systematic Review of Disruptive Innovation (DI)*. Research in Agriculture and Future Direction of Research. 10.1016/j.teler.2023.100079

Kim, S. (2020). Empirical investigation of digital marketing activity, digital marketing environment, and organizational performance. *Journal of Organizational and End User Computing*, 32(2), 52–71. 10.4018/JOEUC.2020040104

Kim, S., Baek, T. H., & Yoon, S. (2020). The effect of 360-degree rotatable product images on purchase intention. *Journal of Retailing and Consumer Services*, 55, 102062. 10.1016/j.jretconser.2020.102062

Kjeldsen, K., Nodeland, M., Fagerstrøm, A., & Pawar, S. (2023). The relative impact of QR codes on omnichannel customer experience and purchase intention. *Procedia Computer Science*, 219, 1049–1056. 10.1016/j.procs.2023.01.383

Knox, J. (2022). The Metaverse, or the Serious Business of Tech Frontiers. *Postdigit Sci Educ*, 4(2), 207–215. 10.1007/s42438-022-00300-9

Korkut, E. H., & Surer, E. (2023). Visualization in virtual reality: A systematic review. *Virtual Reality (Waltham Cross)*, 27(2), 1447–1480. 10.1007/s10055-023-00753-8

Kraus, N., Kraus, K., Manzhura, O. L. E. K. S. A. N. D. R., Ishchenko, I. N. N. A., & Radzikhovska, Y. U. L. I. I. A. (2023). Digital Transformation of Business Processes of Enterprises on the Way to Becoming Industry 5.0 in the Gig Economy. *WSEAS Transactions on Business and Economics*, 93(20), 1008–1029. 10.37394/23207.2023.20.93

Kremez, Z., Frazer, L., Weaven, S., & Quach, S. (2021). Ecommerce structures for retail and service franchises: Ecommerce implementation in mature franchise systems. *Asia Pacific Journal of Marketing and Logistics*, 33(6), 1292–1308. 10.1108/APJML-11-2018-0461

Krishen, A. S., Dwivedi, Y. K., Bindu, N., & Kumar, K. S. (2021). A broad overview of interactive digital marketing: A bibliometric network analysis. *Journal of Business Research*, 131, 183–195. 10.1016/j.jbusres.2021.03.061

Kshetri, N. (2018). Blockchain's roles in meeting key supply chain management objectives. *International Journal of Information Management*, 39, 80–89. 10.1016/j.ijinfomgt.2017.12.005

Kumar, V. V., Carberry, D., Beenfeldt, C., Andersson, M. P., Mansouri, S. S., & Gallucci, F. (2021). Virtual reality in chemical and biochemical engineering education and training. *Education for Chemical Engineers*, 36, 143–153. 10.1016/j.ece.2021.05.002

Lambert, D. M., & Cooper, M. C. (2000). Issues in supply chain management. *Industrial Marketing Management*, 29(1), 65–83. 10.1016/S0019-8501(99)00113-3

Lamine, W., Fayolle, A., Jack, S., & Audretsch, D. (2023). Impact of digital technologies on entrepreneurship: Taking stock and looking forward. *Technovation*, 126, 102823. 10.1016/j.technovation.2023.102823

Laudon, K. C., & Laudon, J. P. (2021). *Management Information Systems: Managing the Digital Firm* (Global Edition). Pearson Higher Education.

LaVoila, J. J. (2017). *3D User Interfaces: Theory and Practice*. Addison-Wesley Professional.

Law, R., Buhalis, D., & Cobanoglu, C. (2014). Progress on information and communication technologies in hospitality and tourism. *International Journal of Contemporary Hospitality Management*, 26(5), 727–750. 10.1108/IJCHM-08-2013-0367

Lazić, A., Milić, S., & Vukmirović, D. (2024). The Future of Electronic Commerce in the IoT Environment. *Journal of Theoretical and Applied Electronic Commerce Research*, 19(1), 172–187. 10.3390/jtaer19010010

Lee, C. D., & Daiute, C. (2019). Introduction to Developmental Digital Technologies in Human History, Culture, and Well-Being. *Human Development*, 62(1-2), 5–13. 10.1159/000496072

Lee, J., Kao, H. A., & Yang, S. (2014). Service innovation and smart analytics for Industry 4.0 and big data environment. *Procedia CIRP*, 16, 3–8. 10.1016/j.procir.2014.02.001

Lee, S. (2020). Chatbots and Communication: The Growing Role of Artificial Intelligence in Addressing and Shaping Customer Needs. *Business Communication Research and Practice*, 3(2), 103–111. 10.22682/bcrp.2020.3.2.103

Lee, S. M., & Trimi, S. (2021). Convergence Innovation in the Digital Age and in the COVID-19 Pandemic Crisis. *Journal of Business Research*, 123, 14–22. 10.1016/j.jbusres.2020.09.04133012897

Lewis, J., Whysall, P., & Foster, C. (2014). Drivers and technology related obstacles in moving to multichannel retailing. *International Journal of Electronic Commerce*, 18(4), 43–68. 10.2753/JEC1086-4415180402

Lim, S. F. W., & Srai, J. S. (2018). Examining the anatomy of last-mile distribution in e-commerce omnichannel retailing: A supply network configuration approach. *International Journal of Operations & Production Management*, 38(9), 1735–1764. 10.1108/IJOPM-12-2016-0733

Lim, S. F. W., & Winkenbach, M. (2019). Configuring the last-mile in business-to-consumer e-retailing. *California Management Review*, 61(2), 132–154. 10.1177/0008125618805094

Lin, S. (2023). The Influential Factors on Consumer Purchase Intention: A Case Study on MINISO. In: Li, X., Yuan, C., Kent, J. (Eds.) *Proceedings of the 6th International Conference on Economic Management and Green Development. Applied Economics and Policy Studies*. Springer, Singapore. 10.1007/978-981-19-7826-5_121

Lin, B., Chen, Y., & Zhang, L. (2022). Research on the factors influencing the re-purchase intention on short video platforms: A case of China. *PLoS One*, 17(3), e0265090. 10.1371/journal.pone.026509035290393

Lin, X., Featherman, M., Brooks, S. L., & Hajli, N. (2018). Exploring gender differences in online consumer purchase decision making: An online product presentation perspective. *Information Systems Frontiers*, 21(5), 1187–1201. 10.1007/s10796-018-9831-1

Lohar, A., Gajare, Y. Y., & Kumar, A. (2018). Key growth drivers and barriers to adoption of e-payments: A review. *National Journal of Research in Marketing, Finance and HRM, 3*(1), 01-12.

Longo, F., Padovano, A., & Umbrella, S. (2020). Value-oriented and ethical technology engineering in industry 5.0: A human-centric perspective for the design of the factory of the future. *Applied Sciences (Basel, Switzerland)*, 10(12), 4182. 10.3390/app10124182

Lui, S., Ngo, H., & Hon, A. (2006). Coercivestrategy in inter firm cooperation: Mediating roles of interpersonal and inter organizational trust. *Journal of Business Research*, 59(4), 466–474. 10.1016/j.jbusres.2005.09.001

Lv, Z., Lloret, J., & Song, H. (2021). Real-time image processing for augmented reality on mobile devices. *Journal of Real-Time Image Processing*, 18(2), 245–248. 10.1007/s11554-021-01097-9

Mahmood, N. H., Böcker, S., Munari, A., Clazzer, F., Moerman, I., Mikhaylov, K., & Jäntti, R. (2020). *White paper on critical and massive machine type communication towards 6G*. arXiv preprint arXiv:2004.14146.

Mahr, D., & Huh, J. (2022). Technologies in service communication: Looking forward. *Journal of Service Management*, 33(4/5), 648–656. 10.1108/JOSM-03-2022-0075

Makkonen, H., Olkkonen, R., & Frank, L. (2018). Competitive advantage and SMEs: A configurational study. *Journal of Small Business Management*, 56(2), 289–306. 10.1111/jsbm.12319

Manickam, T., Vinayagamoorthi, G., Gopalakrishnan, S., Sudha, M., & Mathiraj, S. P. (2022). Customer inclination on mobile wallets with reference to Google-Pay and PayTM in Bengaluru City. [IJEBR]. *International Journal of E-Business Research*, 18(1), 1–16. 10.4018/IJEBR.293295

Marchet, G., Melacini, M., Perotti, S., Rasini, M., & Tappia, E. (2018). Business logistics models in omni-channel: A classification framework and empirical analysis. *International Journal of Physical Distribution & Logistics Management*, 48(4), 439–464. 10.1108/IJPDLM-09-2016-0273

MarketsandMarkets. (2024). *Conversational AI Market Size, Statistics, Growth Analysis & Trends*. MarketsandMarkets. https://www.marketsandmarkets.com/Market-Reports/conversational-ai-market-49043506.html

Martins, J., Costa, C., Oliveira, T., Gonçalves, R., & Branco, F. (2019). How smartphone advertising influences consumers' purchase intention. *Journal of Business Research*, 94, 378–387. 10.1016/j.jbusres.2017.12.047

Masood, T., & Sonntag, P. (2020). Industry 4.0: Adoption challenges and benefits for SMEs. *Computers in Industry*, 121, 103261. 10.1016/j.compind.2020.103261

Massa, E., & Ladhari, R. (2023). Augmented reality in marketing: Conceptualization and systematic review. *International Journal of Consumer Studies*, 47(6), 2335–2366. 10.1111/ijcs.12930

Mathiraj, S. P., & Mala, M. (2021). A study on users' opinion about google pay. *IJAR*, 7(12), 161–164.

Mayer-Schönberger, V., & Cukier, K. (2013). *Big data: A revolution that will transform how we live, work, and think.* Houghton Mifflin Harcourt.

McAfee, A., & Brynjolfsson, E. (2012). Big data: The management revolution. *Harvard Business Review*, 90(10), 60–68.23074865

McCarthy, J. (2007). *What is Artificial Intelligence?* Stanford. https://www-formal.stanford.edu/jmc/whatisai.pdf

McKinsey. (2021). *Omnichannel shopping and retail.* McKinsey. https://www.mckinsey.com/industries/retail/our-insights/into-the-fast-lane-how-to-master-the-omnichannel-supply-chain#The%20Importance%20of%20Omnichannel:%20E-Commerce%20Is%20Booming,%20But%20Physical%20Stores%20Remain%20Important

Meepung, T., & and Kannikar, P. (2022). Metaverse; Virtual World Challenges and Opportunities for Digital Business. *Journal of Economics, Business and Management, 10.*

Mefoute Badiang, A., & Nkwei, E. S. (2024). Mobile banking adoption its antecedents and post-adoption effects: The role of consumers status orientation in an African context. *Cogent Business & Management*, 11(1), 2321787. 10.1080/23311975.2024.2321787

Mehta, R. (2021). Phonepe Vs Google Pay which is better? *Times of India.*timesofindia.indiatimes.com

Menezes, B., Yaqot, M., Hassaan, S., Franzoi, R., AlQashouti, N., & Al-Banna, A. (2022, October). Digital Transformation in the Era of Industry 4.0 and Society 5.0: A perspective. In *2022 2nd International Conference on Emerging Smart Technologies and Applications (eSmarTA)* (pp. 1-6). IEEE.

Mengalli, N. M., & Carvalho, A. A. (2024). The Learning Experience and the Behavioural Profile: Artificial Intelligence, Upskilling, and Reskilling for the Professions of the Future. In Hai-Jew, S. (Ed.), *Generative AI in Teaching and Learning* (pp. 66–84). IGI Global. 10.4018/979-8-3693-0074-9.ch004

Mengalli, N. M., de Carvalho, A. A., & Galvão, S. M. (2023). Metaverse Ecosystem and Consumer Society 5.0: Consumer Experience and Influencer Marketing in Phygital Transformation. In Bansal, R., Qalati, S., & Chakir, A. (Eds.), *Influencer Marketing Applications Within the Metaverse* (pp. 33–56). IGI Global. 10.4018/978-1-6684-8898-0.ch003

Michael J. (2001). *Knowledge Management and Data Mining for marketing*. Elsevier.

Mihajlović-Milićević, J., & Mitrović, S. (2021, September). A model for agile management of virtual teams for developing smart environments. In *E-business technologies conference proceedings* (*Vol. 1*, No. 1, pp. 201-205).

Miraz, M. H., Ali, M., Excell, P. S., & Picking, R. (2015, September). A review on Internet of Things (IoT), Internet of everything (IoE) and Internet of nano things (IoNT). In *Internet Technologies and Applications (ITA)* (pp. 219-224). IEEE.

Mishra, A. B. (2015). *Mobile Commerce in Modern Business Era*. Research Gate. https://www.researchgate.net/publication/351840817_Mobile_Commerce_in_Modern_Business_Era

Mishra, A. B. (2020). E- Payment System: A Rising Trend Of Economy. *New Paradigm in Business and Education*. Research Gate. https://www.researchgate.net/profile/Anitha-K-2/publication/349605501_E-LEARNING_THROUGH_GAMIFICATION-_AN_ITINERARY_TO_GAIN_IN-DEPTH_KNOWLEDGE/links/6037d566299bf1cc26ef9597/E-LEARNING-THROUGH-GAMIFICATION-AN-ITINERARY-TO-GAIN-IN-DEPTH-KNOWLEDGE.pdf#page=10

Mishra, A. B., & Singh, A. (2024). *The Mumbai Dabbawalas : An Efficient and Sustainable Lunchbox Delivery System*. IGI Global. 10.4018/979-8-3693-1544-6.ch007

Mishra, A. B., Allen, M., & Tirkey, P. (2024). *Disruption causes to Micromax by once a Market leader now a Myth*. https://www.iimspune.edu.in/images/pdf/Journal/Vol3I1-Paper11.pdf

Mishra, A. B., Raikwar, A., & Tiwari, A. (2024). *Britannia: Marketing Initiatives Boost A Fledgling Business's Transformation To One Of The Largest Fmcg Brands*. https://www.iimspune.edu.in/images/pdf/Journal/Vol3I1-Paper12.pdf

Mishra, A. B., Satarkar, M., & Joshi, S. (2024). *Capitalizing the Retail Industry by Automation and Artificial Intelligence (AI): Case Study of IKEA*. IGI Global. 10.4018/979-8-3693-2643-5.ch014

Mishra, A. (2020). E-payment system: A rising trend of economy. *New Paradigm in Business & Education*, 1, 1–6.

Mishra, A. B. (2022). SAHYADRI FARMS: INDIA'S LARGEST FARMER PRODUCER COMPANY. *International Journal of Advance and Applied Research*, 10, 996–998. https://ijaar.co.in/wp-content/uploads/2022/11/1001175.pdf

Mishra, A. B. (2023). Dynamics of Digital Payments Enable the World's Safest Way to Pay. *Journal of Informatics Education and Research*, 3(2).

Mishra, A. B., Varma Anil, & Ranjan Nitin. (2021). PUTSCH BUYER TENDENCY AND CLIMBING SALES OF MOBILE TRADE BUSINESS. Manager –. *British Journal of Administrative Management*, 58(152), 54–60.

Mishra, A. B., Chand, K., & Kaith, K. (2022). Influencer Marketing as Emerging Promotional Tool in Modern Era and Opportunities to Uprising Sales. *International Journal of Emerging Research in Engineering, Science, and Management*, 1(3). 10.58482/ijeresm.v1i3.3

Mishra, A. B., & Dodke, S. D. (2024). ZARA: Technological Influence on Becoming the Fashion Industry's Market Leader. In Global, I. G. I. (Ed.), (pp. 204–215)., 10.4018/979-8-3693-2643-5.ch012

Mishra, A. B., Goel, A., & Jajoo, P. (2022). A Case Study of Amul: Implementation of Extension Strategy to Repositioning Brand During Covid-19 Period. *International Journal of Emerging Research in Engineering, Science, and Management*, 1(4). 10.58482/ijeresm.v1i4.3

Mishra, A. B., & Karjodkar, R. (2022). A Case Study of Air India - Maharajah Back to Home. *International Journal of Emerging Research in Engineering, Science, and Management*, 1(3). 10.58482/ijeresm.v1i3.5

Mishra, A. B., & Ranjan, N. (2022). INTERNET OF THINGS BASED EMERGING SMART TOOLS FOR NEW EDGE EDUCATION. *Mukt Shabd Journal*, 11(10), 80–87. 10.0014.MSJ.2022.V11I10.0086781.1135708

Mishra, A. B., Ranjan, N., Sharma, K. M., Padhye, P., & Chand, K. (2023). Advancement of Digital Transformation to Boost Financial Services Industry. *Journal of Informatics Education and Research*, 3(2), 2435–2440.

Mishra, A. B., Sahu, T., Ranjan, N., & Varma, A. (2021). Green Marketing Practices Prevailing In Hotel Industry. *Journal of Contemporary Issues in Business and Government*, 27(02). 10.47750/cibg.2021.27.02.145

Mishra, A. B., Satarkar, M., & Joshi, S. (2023). IKEA - Phygital Transformation in Furniture Manufacturing Industry. *International Journal of Emerging Research in Engineering, Science, and Management*, 2(3), 6–9. 10.58482/ijeresm.v2i3.2

Mishra, A. B., & Singh, A. (2023). Brand Positioning in the Indian Smartphone Market: A Case Study of OnePlus. *International Journal of Emerging Research in Engineering, Science, and Management*, 2(3). 10.58482/ijeresm.v2i3.1

Mishra, S. K., & Sarkar, A. (2022). Service-oriented architecture for Internet of Things: A semantic approach. *Journal of King Saud University. Computer and Information Sciences*, 34(10, 10 Part A), 8765–8776. 10.1016/j.jksuci.2021.09.024

Misischia, C. V., Poecze, F., & Strauss, C. (2022). Chatbots in customer service: Their relevance and impact on service quality. *Procedia Computer Science*, 201, 421–428. 10.1016/j.procs.2022.03.055

Moenandar, S.-J., Beerends-Pavlovic, S., van den Berg, B., & Coughlan, G. (2022). A Brave New Internet: Hacking the Narrative of Mark Zuckerberg's 2021 Introduction of the Metaverse. *Narrative Works*, 11, 125–148. 10.7202/1108958ar

Mofokeng, T. E., & Tan, A. W. K. (2021). The impact of online shopping attributes on customer satisfaction and loyalty: Moderating effects of e-commerce experience. *Cogent Business & Management*, 8(1), 1968206. 10.1080/23311975.2021.1968206

Mohdhar, A., & Shaalan, K. (2021). The Future of E-Commerce Systems: 2030 and Beyond. In Al-Emran, M., & Shaalan, K. (Eds.), *Recent Advances in Technology Acceptance Models and Theories. Studies in Systems, Decision and Control* (Vol. 335). Springer. 10.1007/978-3-030-64987-6_18

Mohseni, M., Othman, B. A., Raturi, P., Mishra, A. B., Priya, S. J., & Saravanan, V. (2022). The Role of Parallel Computing Towards Implementation of Enhanced and Effective Industrial Internet of Things (IOT) Through Manova Approach. *2022 2nd International Conference on Advance Computing and Innovative Technologies in Engineering (ICACITE),* (pp. 160–164). IEEE. 10.1109/ICACITE53722.2022.9823698

Moore, G. C., & Benbasat, I. (1991). Development of an instrument to measure the perceptions of adopting an information technology innovation. *Information Systems Research*, 2(3), 192–222. 10.1287/isre.2.3.192

Moore, S. K. (2001). Unhooking medicine. *IEEE Spectrum*, 38(1), 107–108, 110. 10.1109/6.901156

Mukherjee, S., & Chittipaka, V. (2022). Analysing the adoption of intelligent agent technology in food supply chain management: An empirical evidence. *FIIB Business Review*, 11(4), 438–454. 10.1177/23197145211059243

Munoz, F., Holsapple, C. W., & Sasidharan, S. (2023). E-commerce. In Nof, S. Y. (Ed.), *Springer Handbook of Automation. Springer Handbooks*. Springer. 10.1007/978-3-030-96729-1_67

Munro, P., Kapitan, S., & Wooliscroft, B. (2023). The sustainable attitude-behavior gap dynamic when shopping at the supermarket: A systematic literature review and framework for future research. *Journal of Cleaner Production*, 426, 138740. 10.1016/j.jclepro.2023.138740

Mustafa, M. J., Chin, J. W., Nungsari, M., & Morris, K. J. (2023). Do proactive students benefit more from university support for entrepreneurship when choosing entrepreneurship as a career choice? An examination of Ghanaian and Malaysian students. *International Journal of Management Education*, 21(3), 100868. 10.1016/j.ijme.2023.100868

N.L. Sarda, G. S. (2024). *An introduction to NPCI and its various products.* National Payments Corporation of India (NPCI).

Nasi, G., Cucciniello, M., & Guerrazzi, C. (2015). The role of mobile technologies in health care processes: The case of cancer supportive care. *Journal of Medical Internet Research*, 17(2), e26. 10.2196/jmir.375725679446

Neslin, S. A., Dhruv, G., Robert, L., Venkatesh, S., & Marije, L. (2006). Challenges and oppurtunities in multichannel customer management. *Journal of Service Research*, 9(2), 95–112. 10.1177/1094670506293559

Nicolae, N., Popescu, M., & Pătrăşcioiu, C. (2019). *Implementation of Advanced Process Control in Refineries.*, 10.1109/ICSTCC.2019.8885801

Niknejad, N., Ismail, W., Ghani, I., Nazari, B., Bahari, M., & Hussin, A. R. B. C. (2020). Understanding Service-Oriented Architecture (SOA): A systematic literature review and directions for further investigation. *Information Systems*, 91, 101491. 10.1016/j.is.2020.101491

Nilesh Kate, P. P. (2022). Studies on Anti-Virus Software Tools: Strong Weapon to Protect Systems. *International Conference on Innovative Practices in Technology and Management (ICIPTM).*

Nimavat, K., & Champaneria, T. (2017). *Chatbots: An overview. Types, Architecture, Tools and Future Possibilities.* Research Gate. https://www.researchgate.net/publication/320307269_Chatbots_An_overview_Types_Architecture_Tools_and_Future_Possibilities

Nooteboom, B. (1992). Towards a dynamic theory of transactions. *Journal of Evolutionary Economics*, 2(4), 281–299. 10.1007/BF01200127

Nor Asshidin, N. H., Abidin, N., & Borhan, H. B. (2016). Consumer Attitude and Uniqueness towards *International Products.Procedia Economics and Finance*, 35, 632–638. 10.1016/S2212-5671(16)00077-0

Nouri-Harzvili, M., Hosseini-Motlagh, S. M., & Zirakpourdehkordi, R. (2024). Evolutionary Marketing Strategies for New High-Technology Product Sales: Effects of Customers' Innovation Adoption. *IEEE Transactions on Engineering Management*, 71, 3158–3171. 10.1109/TEM.2022.3207685

Nozari, H. (Ed.). (2023). *Building Smart and Sustainable Businesses With Transformative Technologies*. IGI Global. 10.4018/979-8-3693-0210-1

OASIS. (2024). *Advancing open standards for the information society*. OASIS. https://www.oasis-open.org/news

Obermeyer, Z., & Emanuel, E. J. (2016). Predicting the future — Big data, machine learning, and clinical medicine. *The New England Journal of Medicine*, 375(13), 1216–1219. 10.1056/NEJMp1606181276820033

Ogunmola, G. A., & Kumar, V. (2023). E-commerce research models: A systematic review and identification of the determinants to success. *International Journal of Business Information Systems*, 43(1), 87–106. 10.1504/IJBIS.2023.131093

Oleárová, M., Bačík, R., & Fedorko, R. (2021). Overview of current trends in mobile commerce: Global perspectives. *Marketing Science & Inspirations*, 16(4), 2–9. 10.46286/msi.2021.16.4.1

Olla, P., & Shimskey, C. (2015). mHealth taxonomy: A literature survey of mobile health applications,||. *Health and Technology*, 4(4), 299–308. 10.1007/s12553-014-0093-8

Onik, M. M., Miraz, M. H., & Kim, C. S. (2018) A recruitment and human resource management technique using blockchain technology for industry 4.0. In *Smart Cities Symposium 2018*. IET.

Oppong, S. A., Yen, D. C., & Merhout, J. W. (2005). A new strategy for harnessing knowledge management in e-commerce. *Technology in Society*, 27(3), 413–435. 10.1016/j.techsoc.2005.04.009

Palvia, P., Ghosh, J., Jacks, T., & Serenko, A. (2021). Information technology issues and challenges of the globe: The world IT project. *Information & Management*, 58(8), 103545. 10.1016/j.im.2021.103545

Pan, D., Ren, X., Zhang, L., Song, Z., Nie, Y., Zhang, L., Ma, M., & Han, D. (2023). A Disruptive Technology Identification Method for New Power Systems Based on Patent Evolution Analysis. *Electronics (Basel)*, 12(9), 2045. 10.3390/electronics12092045

Pang, T. Y., Lee, T.-K., & Murshed, M. (2023). Towards a New Paradigm for Digital Health Training and Education in Australia: Exploring the Implication of the Fifth Industrial Revolution. *Applied Sciences, 13*(11), 6854. MDPI AG. .10.3390/app13116854

Park, S. (2020). The influence of digital transformation on innovation performance in the context of Industry 4.0. *Journal of Open Innovation*, 6(4), 98. 10.3390/joitmc6040098

Paschek, D. (2020). *Business process management using artificial inteligence-an important requirement, success factor and business need for industry 5.0* [Doctoral dissertation, Universitatea „Politehnica" Timişoara, Şcoala Doctorală de Studii Inginereşti, Domeniul de Doctorat Inginerie i Management].

Pauwels, K., & Neslin, S. (2015). Building with bricks and mortar: The revenue impact of opening physical stores in multichannel environment. *Journal of Retailing*, 91(2), 182–197. 10.1016/j.jretai.2015.02.001

Păvăloaia, V.-D., & Necula, S.-C. (2023). Artificial Intelligence as a Disruptive Technology - A Systematic Literature Review. *Electronics, 12*(5), 1102. MDPI AG. .10.3390/electronics12051102

Peek, N., Holmes, J. H., & Sun, J. (2014). Technical challenges for big data in biomedicine and health: Data sources, infrastructure, and analytics. *Yearbook of Medical Informatics*, 23(01), 42–47. 10.15265/IY-2014-001825123720

Peña-García, N., Gil-Saura, I., Rodríguez-Orejuela, A., & Siqueira-Junior, J. R. (2020). Purchase intention and purchase behavior online: A cross-cultural approach. *Heliyon*, 6(6), e04284. 10.1016/j.heliyon.2020.e0428432613132

Perera, S., Jin, X., Das, P., Gunasekara, K., & Samaratunga, M. (2023). A strategic framework for digital maturity of design and construction through a systematic review and application. *Journal of Industrial Information Integration*, 31, 100413. 10.1016/j.jii.2022.100413

Permarupan, P. Y., Xuan, K. Z., & Ling, T. K. (2021). Factors Influencing Consumers' Purchasing Decision on Local Products. In Alareeni, B., Hamdan, A., & Elgedawy, I. (Eds.), *The Importance of New Technologies and Entrepreneurship in Business Development: In the Context of Economic Diversity in Developing Countries. ICBT 2020. Lecture Notes in Networks and Systems* (Vol. 194). Springer. 10.1007/978-3-030-69221-6_32

Peteraf, M. A. (1993). The cornerstones of competitive advantage: A resource-based view. *Strategic Management Journal*, 14(3), 179–191. 10.1002/smj.4250140303

Picot- Coupey, K., Hure, E., & Piveteau, L. (2016). Channel design to enrich customers' shopping experiences; synchronizing clicks with bricks in an omni- channel perspective- the direct optic case. *International Journal of Retail & Distribution Management*, 44(3), 336–368.

Pingxuan, R. (2020). AR 3D Magic Book: A Healthy Interactive Reading Device Based on AR and Portable Projection. CIPAE 2020: Proceedings of the 2020 International Conference on Computers, Information Processing and Advanced Education October 2020, pp. 244-250. 10.1145/3419635.3419714

Piotrowiccz, W., & Cuthbertson, R. (2014). Introduction to the special issue information technology in retail: Toward omnichannel retailing. *International Journal of Electronic Commerce*, 18(4), 5–16. 10.2753/JEC1086-4415180400

Por, M. J., Hosseinzadeh, M., & Moradi, M. (2023). IoT based entrepreneurial opportunities in smart transportation: a multidimensional framework. *International Journal of Entrepreneur behavior and Research*, 1355-2554

Porter, M. (1985). *Competitive Advantage. Creating and Sustaining Superior Performance.* The Free Press.

Porter, M. E. (1985). *Competitive advantage: Creating and sustaining superior performance.* Free Press.

Porter, M. E., & Heppelmann, J. E. (2014). How smart, connected products are transforming competition. *Harvard Business Review*, 92(11), 64–88.

Prajogo, D., & Olhager, J. (2012). Supply chain integration and performance: The effects of long-term relationships, information technology, and sharing, and logistics integration. *International Journal of Production Economics*, 135(1), 514–522. 10.1016/j.ijpe.2011.09.001

Pratas, J., & Oliveira, Z. (2023). QR Codes Research in Marketing: A Bibliometric and Content Analysis. In Reis, J. L., Peter, M. K., Varela González, J. A., & Bogdanović, Z. (Eds.), *Marketing and Smart Technologies. Smart Innovation, Systems and Technologies* (Vol. 337). Springer. 10.1007/978-981-19-9099-1_19

Precedence Research. (March, 2023). *Internet of Things (IoT) in Chemical Market.* Precedence Research. https://www.precedenceresearch.com/internet-of-things-in-chemical-market

Priadythama, I., Herdiman, L., & Susmartini, S. (2020). Role of rapid manufacturing technology in wearable customized assistive technology for modern industry. *AIP Conference Proceedings*, 2217(1), 030076. 10.1063/5.0000747

Pulse, P. (2023). *Innovation leading to accelerated growth: The merchant journey.* PhonePe.

Purnomo, Y. J. (2023). Digital Marketing Strategy to Increase Sales Conversion on E-commerce Platforms. *Journal of Contemporary Administration and Management*, 1(2), 54–62. 10.61100/adman.v1i2.23

Qin, Z. (2022). *E-Commerce. Concepts, Principles, and Application.* Springer. 10.1007/978-981-19-6438-1

Quach, S., Barari, M., Moudrý, D. V., & Quach, K. (2022). Service integration in omnichannel retailing and its impact on customer experience. *Journal of Retailing and Consumer Services*, 65, 102267. 10.1016/j.jretconser.2020.102267

Raimbekov, Z., Sładkowski, A., Syzdykbayeva, B., Azatbek, T., & Sharipbekova, K. (2022). Improving the Efficiency of Transportation and Distribution of Goods in Modern Conditions. In Sładkowski, A. (Ed.), *Modern Trends and Research in Intermodal Transportation. Studies in Systems, Decision and Control* (Vol. 400). Springer., 10.1007/978-3-030-87120-8_4

Raimi, L., Kah, J. M., & Tariq, M. U. (2022). The Discourse of Blue Economy Definitions, Measurements, and Theories: Implications for Strengthening Academic Research and Industry Practice. In Raimi, L., & Kah, J. (Eds.), *Implications for Entrepreneurship and Enterprise Development in the Blue Economy* (pp. 1–17). IGI Global. 10.4018/978-1-6684-3393-5.ch001

Raimi, L., Tariq, M. U., & Kah, J. M. (2022). Diversity, Equity, and Inclusion as the Future Workplace Ethics: Theoretical Review. In Raimi, L., & Kah, J. (Eds.), *Mainstreaming Diversity, Equity, and Inclusion as Future Workplace Ethics* (pp. 1–27). IGI Global. 10.4018/978-1-6684-3657-8.ch001

Rana, S., Cavaliere, L. P. L., Mishra, A. B., Padhye, P., Singh, R. R., & Khanna, R. (2022). Internet of Things (IOT) Based Assessment for Effective Monitoring Data Against Malicious Attacks on Financial Collectors. *2022 2nd International Conference on Advance Computing and Innovative Technologies in Engineering (ICACITE),* (pp. 177–181). IEEE. 10.1109/ICACITE53722.2022.9823612

Rashid, M. A., Riaz, Z., Turan, E., Haskilic, V., Sunje, A., & Khan, N. (2012, July). Smart factory: E-business perspective of enhanced ERP in aircraft manufacturing industry. In *2012 Proceedings of PICMET'12: Technology Management for Emerging Technologies* (pp. 3262-3275). IEEE.

Razak, M., Gunawan, B. I., Fitriany, F., Ashoer, M., Hidayat, M., & Halim, P. K. P. A. (2019). Moving From Traditional to Society 5.0 Case study by Online Transportation Business. *Journal of Distribution Science*, 17(9), 93–102. 10.15722/jds.17.9.201909.93

Regmi, R., Zhang, Z., & Zhang, H. (2023). Entrepreneurship strategy, natural resources management, and sustainable performance: A study of an emerging market. *Resources Policy*, 86, 104202. 10.1016/j.resourpol.2023.104202

Reiser, S. J. (1991). The clinical record in medicine part 1: Learning from cases*. *Annals of Internal Medicine*, 114(10), 902–907. 10.7326/0003-4819-114-10-9022014953

Riedl, R., Fischer, T., Léger, P. M., & Davis, F. D. (2020). A decade of NeuroIS research: Progress, challenges, and future directions. *ACM SIGMIS Database: Database Adv Inform Syst*, 51(3), 13–54. 10.1145/3410977.3410980

Rigby, D. (2011). The future of shopping. *Harvaed Business REview. Vil*, 89(12), 65–76.

Roblek, V., Meško, M., Bach, M. P., Thorpe, O., & Šprajc, P. (2020). The interaction between internet, sustainable development, and emergence of society 5.0. *Data*, 5(3), 80. 10.3390/data5030080

Ruchin Goyal, P. R. (2022). Digital Payments in India: A US$10 Trillion Opportunity. *BCG.Com*.

Rzepka, A. (Ed.). (2023). *Innovation in Digital Economy: New Approaches to Management for Industry 5.0* [Translated by Jakub Prachowski]. Routledge. https://www.routledge.com/Innovation-in-the-Digital-Economy-New-Approaches-to-Management-for-Industry/Rzepka/p/book/978103246993510.4324/9781003384311

Sakız, B., & Gencer, A. H. (2019). Blockchain Technology and its Impact on the Global Economy. *International Conference on Eurasian Economies*. https://avekon.org/papers/2258.pdf

Salem, A. B. M., & Parusheva, S. (2018). Developing a web-based ontology for e-business. *International Journal of Electronic Commerce Studies*, 9(2), 119–132. 10.7903/ijecs.1654

Sales-Vivó, V., Gil-Saura, I., & Gallarza, M. G. (2021). Comparing relationship of quality-satisfaction models: Effects of B2B value co-creation. *International Journal of Retail & Distribution Management*, 49(7), 941–957. 10.1108/IJRDM-10-2020-0394

Salina, T. (2023). A Review of Augmented Reality for Informal Science Learning: Supporting Design of Intergenerational Group Learning. *Visitor Studies*, 26(1), 1–23. 10.1080/10645578.2022.2075205

Sallam, R. L. (2011). *Magic Quadrant for Business Intelligence*. Gartner, Inc.https://in2015.in1.com.br/sites/default/files/magic_quadrant_for_business__210036.pdf

Samiha Al Zadjali, A. U. (2021). Impact of Industry 4.0 in Manufacturing Sector. *International Journal of Management Science and Business Administration*, 25-33.

Sanaei, A., & Sepehri, M. M. (2020). Quality Improvement through Intensive Care Registries: The Value of Big Data in Clinical Decision Making. *Archives of Anesthesia and Critical Care*.

Sanaei, A., & Sepehri, M. M. (2019). *Quality improvement through intensive care registries: the value of big data in clinical decision making*. Arch Anesth Crit Care.

Santos, S., & Martins Gonçalves, H. (2021). The consumer decision journey: A literature review of the foundational models and theories and a future perspective. *Technological Forecasting and Social Change*, 173, 121117. 10.1016/j.techfore.2021.121117

Saw, C. C., & Inthiran, A. (2022). Designing for Trust on E-Commerce Websites Using Two of the Big Five Personality Traits. *Journal of Theoretical and Applied Electronic Commerce Research*, 17(2), 375–393. 10.3390/jtaer17020020

Schwalbe, K. (2015). *Information technology project management*. Cengage Learning.

Schwarz, J. A., & Tan, B. (2021). Optimal sales and production rollover strategies under capacity constraints. *European Journal of Operational Research*, 294(2), 507–524. 10.1016/j.ejor.2021.01.040

Sciendo. (2020). *Chatbot Technologies in Customer Service*. Sciendo. https://www.sciencedirect.com/science/article/pii/S2666827020300062

Sephora Bot. (n.d.). ChatbotGuide.org. https://www.chatbotguide.org/sephora-bot

Shaikh, Z. A., Hajjej, F., Uslu, Y. D., Yüksel, S., Dınçer, H., Alroobaea, R., Baqasah, A. M., & Chinta, U. (2024). A New Trend in Cryptographic Information Security for Industry 5.0: A Systematic Review. *IEEE Access : Practical Innovations, Open Solutions*, 12, 7156–7169. https://ieeexplore.ieee.org/abstract/document/10384336. 10.1109/ACCESS.2024.3351485

Shameer, K., Badgeley, M. A., Miotto, R., Glicksberg, B. S., Morgan, J. W., & Dudley, J. T. (2017). Translational bioinformatics in the era of real-time biomedical, health care and wellness data streams. *Briefings in Bioinformatics*, 18(1), 105–124. 10.1093/bib/bbv11826876889

Shammar, E. A., & Zahary, A. T. (2020). The Internet of Things (IoT): A survey of techniques, operating systems, and trends. *Library Hi Tech*, 38(1), 5–66. 10.1108/LHT-12-2018-0200

Sharma, N. (2024). A digital cohort analysis of consumers' mobile banking app experience. *International Journal of Consumer Studies*, 48(1), e12989. 10.1111/ijcs.12989

Sharma, N., & Fatima, J. (2024). Influence of perceived value on omnichannel usage: Mediating and moderating roles of the omnichannel shopping habit. *Journal of Retailing and Consumer Services*, 77, 103627. 10.1016/j.jretconser.2023.103627

Sharma, P., Ueno, A., Dennis, C., & Turan, C. P. (2023). Emerging digital technologies and consumer decision-making in retail sector: Towards an integrative conceptual framework. *Computers in Human Behavior*, 148, 107913. 10.1016/j.chb.2023.107913

Sharma, S. P. (2022). *RBI releases guidelines for interoperability-Prepaid Payment Instruments (PPIs)*. PHD Chamber of Commerce and Industry.

Sharma, S., Mahajan, S., & Rana, V. (2019). A semantic framework for e-commerce search engine optimization. *International Journal of Information Technology : an Official Journal of Bharati Vidyapeeth's Institute of Computer Applications and Management*, 11(1), 31–36. 10.1007/s41870-018-0232-y

Sharma, T., & Bashir, M. (2020). Use of apps in the COVID-19 response and the loss of privacy protection. *Nature Medicine*, 26(8), 1165–1175. 10.1038/s41591-020-0928-y32457443

Shi, W., Cao, J., Zhang, Q., Li, Y., & Xu, L. (2016). Edge computing: Vision and challenges. *IEEE Internet of Things Journal*, 3(5), 637–646. 10.1109/JIOT.2016.2579198

Siddiqui, W. A. (2023). Design and Fabrication of FPV Racing Drone. *Journal of Mechanical and Construction Engineering*. .10.54060/a2zjournals.jmce.38

Sikder, M. R. (2023). Integrating Circular Economy and Industry 5.0 for Sustainable Supply Chain Management in the Food Industry. *Supply Chain Insider, 9*(1). https://supplychaininsider.org/ojs/index.php/home/article/view/73

Sims, P. (1987). *Basic Robotics Curriculum: An Introductionary Unit for Junior High School Students*. [Thesis, UNF]. https://digitalcommons.unf.edu/etd/52

Singh, M. (2024). Indian parliamentary panel red-flags PhonePe and Google Pay cornering 83% of India's UPI payments. *techcrunch.com.*

Singh, P., & P. (2023, September 1). *10 Must-have Chatbot Features That Make Your Bot a Success*. REVE Chat. https://www.revechat.com/blog/chatbot-features/

Singh, U. S. (2021). (in press). A study on the revolution of consumer relationships as a combination of human interactions and digital transformations. *Materials Today: Proceedings*. 10.1016/j.matpr.2021.05.578

Siqueira, E. H., Fischer, B. B., Bin, A., & Kickul, J. (2023). Entrepreneurial ecosystems' readiness towards knowledge-intensive sustainable entrepreneurship: Evidence from Brazil. *Technovation*, 126, 102820. 10.1016/j.technovation.2023.102820

Siriwardhana, Y., Porambage, P., Liyanage, M., & Ylianttila, M. (2021). A survey on mobile augmented reality with 5G mobile edge computing: Architectures, applications, and technical aspects. *IEEE Communications Surveys and Tutorials*, 23(2), 1160–1192. 10.1109/COMST.2021.3061981

Si, S., Hall, J., Suddaby, R., Ahlstrom, D., & Wei, J. (2023). Technology, entrepreneurship, innovation and social change in digital economics. *Technovation*, 119, 102484. 10.1016/j.technovation.2022.102484

Skuridin, A., & Wynn, M. (2024). Chatbot Design and Implementation: Towards an Operational Model for Chatbots. *Information (Basel)*, 15(4), 226. 10.3390/info15040226

Soto Setzke, D., Riasanow, T., Böhm, M., & Krcmar, H. (2023). Pathways to Digital Service Innovation: The Role of Digital Transformation Strategies in Established Organizations. *Information Systems Frontiers*, 25(3), 1017–1037. 10.1007/s10796-021-10112-0

Stocchi, L., Pourazad, N., Michaelidou, N., Tanusondjaja, A., & Harrigan, P. (2022). Marketing research on Mobile apps: Past, present and future. *Journal of the Academy of Marketing Science*, 50(2), 195–225. 10.1007/s11747-021-00815-w34776554

Subramaniam, M., Iyer, B., & Venkatraman, V. (2019). Competing in digital ecosystems. *Business Horizons*, 62(1), 83–94. 10.1016/j.bushor.2018.08.013

Sushil. (2018). How to check correctness of total interpretive structural models? *Annals of Operations Research, 270*(1–2), 473–487. 10.1007/s10479-016-2312-3

Sushil. (2019). Theory building using SAP-LAP linkages: an application in the context of disaster management. *Annals of Operations Research, 283*(1–2), 811–836. 10.1007/s10479-017-2425-3

Swati, K., & Brijesh, K. (2023) Application of Industry 5.0 in Financial Sector. *Journal of Business and Social Sciences*, (13), 1-7. http://eprints.intimal.edu.my/1822/

Sztorc, M., & Savenkovs, K. (2023). Shaping The Digital Potential Of The Large Enterprise Sector Following The Implementation Of The European Digital Decade Strategy. *Scientific Papers of Silesian University of Technology. Organization & Management/Zeszyty Naukowe Politechniki Slaskiej. Seria Organizacji i Zarzadzanie*, (178).

Tae-Woo Lee, P., Chhetri, P., Liu, W., & Lin, C. W. (2024). Integrated transport and logistics for sustainable global trade. *International Journal of Logistics*, 27(3), 359–362. 10.1080/13675567.2024.2307198

Tang, J., Zheng, Q. H., Wang, W. Z., Deveci, M., Bacanin, N., & Aws, A. A. Z. (2023). Analyzing Information Security Factors in Adoption of Intelligent Technologies for Medical Waste Management Systems. *IEEE Transactions on Consumer Electronics*.

Tanwar, S. (2019). The Indian government can thank Google for the popularity of its digital payment system. *Quartz*.

Tariq, M. U. (2024). Multidisciplinary Service Learning in Higher Education: Concepts, Implementation, and Impact. In S. Watson (Ed.), Applications of Service Learning in Higher Education (pp. 1-19). IGI Global. 10.4018/979-8-3693-2133-1.ch001

Tariq, M. U. (2024). Emerging Trends and Innovations in Blockchain-Digital Twin Integration for Green Investments: A Case Study Perspective. In Jafar, S., Rodriguez, R., Kannan, H., Akhtar, S., & Plugmann, P. (Eds.), *Harnessing Blockchain-Digital Twin Fusion for Sustainable Investments* (pp. 148–175). IGI Global. 10.4018/979-8-3693-1878-2.ch007

Tariq, M. U. (2024). Emotional Intelligence in Understanding and Influencing Consumer Behavior. In Musiolik, T., Rodriguez, R., & Kannan, H. (Eds.), *AI Impacts in Digital Consumer Behavior* (pp. 56–81). IGI Global. 10.4018/979-8-3693-1918-5.ch003

Tariq, M. U. (2024). Enhancing Cybersecurity Protocols in Modern Healthcare Systems: Strategies and Best Practices. In Garcia, M., & de Almeida, R. (Eds.), *Transformative Approaches to Patient Literacy and Healthcare Innovation* (pp. 223–241). IGI Global. 10.4018/979-8-3693-3661-8.ch011

Tariq, M. U. (2024). Equity and Inclusion in Learning Ecosystems. In Al Husseiny, F., & Munna, A. (Eds.), *Preparing Students for the Future Educational Paradigm* (pp. 155–176). IGI Global. 10.4018/979-8-3693-1536-1.ch007

Tariq, M. U. (2024). Fintech Startups and Cryptocurrency in Business: Revolutionizing Entrepreneurship. In Kankaew, K., Nakpathom, P., Chnitphattana, A., Pitchayadejanant, K., & Kunnapapdeelert, S. (Eds.), *Applying Business Intelligence and Innovation to Entrepreneurship* (pp. 106–124). IGI Global. 10.4018/979-8-3693-1846-1.ch006

Tariq, M. U. (2024). Leveraging Artificial Intelligence for a Sustainable and Climate-Neutral Economy in Asia. In Ordóñez de Pablos, P., Almunawar, M., & Anshari, M. (Eds.), *Strengthening Sustainable Digitalization of Asian Economy and Society* (pp. 1–21). IGI Global. 10.4018/979-8-3693-1942-0.ch001

Tariq, M. U. (2024). Metaverse in Business and Commerce. In Kumar, J., Arora, M., & Erkol Bayram, G. (Eds.), *Exploring the Use of Metaverse in Business and Education* (pp. 47–72). IGI Global. 10.4018/979-8-3693-5868-9.ch004

Tariq, M. U. (2024). Revolutionizing Health Data Management With Blockchain Technology: Enhancing Security and Efficiency in a Digital Era. In Garcia, M., & de Almeida, R. (Eds.), *Emerging Technologies for Health Literacy and Medical Practice* (pp. 153–175). IGI Global. 10.4018/979-8-3693-1214-8.ch008

Teo, T. S. H., Lin, S., & Lai, K. H. (2009). Adopters and non-adopters of e-procurement in Singapore: An empirical study. *Omega*, 37(5), 972–987. 10.1016/j.omega.2008.11.001

Thakur, V. K., Gularte, M. S., Raj, R. G., & Kessler, M. R. (2015). *Green composites: Polymer composites and the environment.* Springer.

Thathoo, C. (2023). PhonePe Separation: Flipkart Begins $700 Mn ESOP Payouts. *Inc42.* https://inc42.com/

The CEO's Guide to Generative AI What You Need to Know and Do to Win with Transformative Technology. (2024). *IBM Institute for Business Value.* IBM. https://www.ibm.com/downloads/cas/BN9Y6QPN

The Economic Potential of Generative AI: The Next Productivity Frontier. (2023). McKinsey & Company. https://www.mckinsey.com/~/media/mckinsey/business%20functions/mckinsey%20digital/our%20insights/the%20economic%20potential%20of%20generative%20ai%20the%20next%20productivity%20frontier/the-economic-potential-of-generative-ai-the-next-productivity-frontier-vf.pdf?shouldIndex=false

Tidio. (2024). *Chatbot Statistics: Trends and Predictions for 2024.* Tidio. https://www.tidio.com/blog/chatbot-statistics/

Tolety, R. K. (2018). E-Wallets–Their cause, Rise and Relevance. International. *Journal of Research in IT and Management*, 8(7).

Tornjanski, V., Knežević, S., & Mirčetić, V. (2023, June). The role of healthy e-business in Society 5.0: The empowerment of the human-centric era. In *E-business technologies conference proceedings* (*Vol. 3,* No. 1, pp. 22-27).

Tornjanski, V., Knežević, S., Ljubanić, D., Glišić, V., Žižić, D., & Travica, J. (2021, September). Towards secured digital business ecosystems: From threats to opportunities. In *E-business technologies conference proceedings* (*Vol. 1,* No. 1, pp. 1-14).

Toussaert, S. (2021). Upping uptake of COVID contact tracing apps. *Nature Human Behaviour*, 5(2), 183–184. 10.1038/s41562-021-01048-133479504

Treiblmaier, H., Rejeb, A., & Strebinger, A. (2020). Blockchain as a driver for smart city development: Application fields and a comprehensive research agenda. *Smart Cities*, 3(3), 853–872. 10.3390/smartcities3030044

Turban, E., Sharda, R., Aronson, J. E., & King, D. (2015). *Business intelligence: A managerial approach*. Pearson Education.

Türker, C., Altay, B. C., & Okumuş, A. (2022). Understanding user acceptance of QR code mobile payment systems in Turkey: An extended TAM. *Technological Forecasting and Social Change*, 184, 121968. 10.1016/j.techfore.2022.121968

Turker, D., & Altuntas, S. (2014). Sustainable supply chain management in the fast fashion industry: An analysis of corporate reports. *European Management Journal*, 32(5), 837–849. 10.1016/j.emj.2014.02.001

Tyrväinen, O., Karjaluoto, H., & Saarijärvi, H. (2020). Personalization and hedonic motivation in creating customer experiences and loyalty in omnichannel retail. *Journal of Retailing and Consumer Services*, 57, 102233. 10.1016/j.jretconser.2020.102233

Usman M, Sheoliha N, Prabhakar P V, Mishra, A. B., & Dondapati. (2023). Leading Strategies for Organizational Adaptation and Growth in Digital Transformation in Marketing. *Journal of Informatics Education and Research.*

Usman, M. S. (2023). Leading Strategies for Organizational Adaptation and Growth in Digital Transformation in Marketing. *Journal of Informatics Education and Research.*

Valamede, L. S., de Oliveira, G. G., Munhoz, I. P., & Akkari, A. C. S. (2022). Digital Technologies Adoption to Face COVID-19 Pandemic: An Exploratory Approach. In: Iano, Y., Saotome, O., Kemper Vásquez, G.L., Cotrim Pezzuto, C., Arthur, R., Gomes de Oliveira, G. (Eds) *Proceedings of the 7th Brazilian Technology Symposium (BTSym'21). BTSym 2021. Smart Innovation, Systems and Technologies*. Springer, Cham. 10.1007/978-3-031-08545-1_17

Valenzuela, F., Guenole, N., & Ferrar, J. (2021). The future of work: A literature review. *International Journal of Management Reviews*, 23(3), 453–471. 10.1111/ijmr.12233

Valette-Florence, R., & Valette-Florence, P. (2020). Effects of emotions and brand personality on consumer commitment, via the mediating effects of brand trust and attachment. [English Edition]. *Recherche et Applications en Marketing*, 35(1), 84–110. 10.1177/2051570720905703

Van Alstyne, , MParker, , GChoudhary, , S. P. (2016, April). Pipelines, Platforms and the New Rules of Strategy. *Harvard Business Review*, 94(3), 54–60.

Varma, S. R., & Mishra, A. B. (2015). Study of Consumer Buying Behaviour in General Insurance Industry. In *Excellence through creativity, Research, innovation in field of IT and Management*. Research Gate.

Varma, S. R., & Mishra, A. B. (2013). *Distribution Channels of Indian Insurance Business - A Study*. Abhinavan.

Varshney, U. (2014). Mobile health: Four emerging themes of research,||. *Decision Support Systems*, 66, 20–35. 10.1016/j.dss.2014.06.001

Vergaray, A. D., Peralta Robles, W. F., & Salazar Jiménez, J. A. (2023). The Impact of Chatbots on Customer Satisfaction: A Systematic Literature Review. TEM Journal, 1407–1417. https://doi.org/10.18421/TEM123-21

Verhoef, P. C., Stephen, A. T., Kannan, P. K., Luo, X., Abhishek, V., Andrews, M., Bart, Y., Datta, H., Fong, N., Hoffman, D. L., Hu, M. M., Novak, T., Rand, W., & Zhang, Y. (2017). Consumer connectivity in a complex, technology-enabled, and mobile-oriented world with smart products. *Journal of Interactive Marketing*, 40(1), 1–8. 10.1016/j.intmar.2017.06.001

Verhoef, P., Kannan, P., & Inman, J. (2015). From multi- channel retailing to omni- channel retailing. Introduction to the special issue on multi- channel retailing. *Journal of Retailing*, 91(2), 174–181. 10.1016/j.jretai.2015.02.005

Verma, K., Bhardwaj, S., & Arya, R. (2019). Latest Tools for Data Mining and Machine Learning. *International Journal of Innovative Technology and Exploring Engineering (IJITEE).*

Verma, S., & Dixit, G. K. (2023). The Future of E-commerce: Trends, Challenges, and Opportunities. *International Journal for Research in Applied Science and Engineering Technology*, 11(VII), 934–937. https://www.ijraset.com/best-journal/the-future-of-ecommerce-trends-challenges-and-opportunities. 10.22214/ijraset.2023.54758

Voigt, K. I., Buliga, O., & Michl, K. (2017). Industry 4.0–Empirical evidence on productivity gains and employment challenges. *Journal of International Business Studies*, 48(5), 601–606.

Wagg, D.J. (2020). Digital twins: state-of-the-art and future directions for modeling and simulation in engineering dynamics applications. *ASCE-ASME J Risk Uncert Engrg Sys Part B Mech Engrg, 6*(3).

Wajid, R., & Alam, K. (2024). Role of Modern Technology in COVID-19 Care Management. In Alam, K., Daniel, S., Alzahrani, A., & Hassan Almalki, W. (Eds.), *Nursing Practice during COVID-19: Preparation, Education and Support.* Springer. 10.1007/978-3-031-52110-2_5

Wang, Y., Mintz, O., Chen, D., & Chen, K. (2023). How to Effectively Engage with a Billion Customers. *MBR Journal.* https://mbrjournal.com/wp-content/uploads/2023/07/019_Paper-26_AI-3-by-Mintz-Wang-Typeready.pdf

Wang, L., Chen, H., & Zhang, X. (2023). Make a good impression: Recommend different products for self-presentation. *Australian Journal of Management*, 0(0). 10.1177/03128962231166246

Wang, S., Wan, J., Li, D., & Zhang, C. (2016). Implementing smart factory of Industrie 4.0: An outlook. *International Journal of Distributed Sensor Networks*, 12(1), 3159805. 10.1155/2016/3159805

Wang, X. V., & Wang, L. (2021). A literature survey of the robotic technologies during the COVID-19 pandemic. *Journal of Manufacturing Systems*, 60, 823–836. 10.1016/j.jmsy.2021.02.00533612914

Wang, Y. S., & Tang, T. I. (2003). Assessing international Internet marketing performance: The application of the balanced scorecard. *Industrial Management & Data Systems*, 103(4), 253–266. 10.1108/02635570310464625

Wara, A. A., & Dugga, S. (2019). Enhancing User Experience using Mobile QR-Code Application. *International Journal of Computer and Information Technology*, 3(6), 1310–1315. https://www.ijcit.com/archives/volume3/issue6/Paper030620.pdf

Wardana, L. W., Narmaditya, B. S., Wibowo, A., Mahendra, A. M., Wibowo, N. A., Harwida, G., & Rohman, A. N. (2020). The impact of entrepreneurship education and students' entrepreneurial mindset: The mediating role of attitude and self-efficacy. *Heliyon*, 6(9), e04922. 10.1016/j.heliyon.2020.e0492232995616

Wei, L., Zhu, H., Cui, Y., Ren, Y., Li, B., & Liu, J. (2017). Scalable and efficient blockchain-based data sharing scheme for cloud storage. *IEEE Transactions on Cloud Computing*, 6(2), 384–392.

Wernerfelt, B. (1984). A resource-based view of the firm. *Strategic Management Journal*, 5(2), 171–180. 10.1002/smj.4250050207

West, D. M. (2018). *Blockchain for government: Benefits and implications of distributed ledger technology for information sharing.* Brookings Institution.

What Is a Chatbot? (n.d.). IBM. https://www.ibm.com/topics/chatbots

Wibowo, B., Clarissa, H., & Suhartono, D. (2020). The Application of Chatbot for Customer Service in E-Commerce. Engineering, MAthematics and Computer Science (EMACS). *Journal*, 2(3), 91–95. 10.21512/emacsjournal.v2i3.6531

Wiesner, M., & Pfeifer, D. (2014). Health recommender systems: Concepts, requirements, technical basics and challenges,||. *International Journal of Environmental Research and Public Health*, 11(3), 2580–2607. 10.3390/ijerph11030258024595212

Wihardja, C. E., & Widianto, M. H. (2023). *E-Commerce Website: A Systematic Literature Review.* International Conference on Informatics, Multimedia, Cyber and Informations System (ICIMCIS), Jakarta Selatan, Indonesia. 10.1109/ICIMCIS60089.2023.10349018

Williamson, P. J., & De Meyer, A. (2012). Ecosystem advantage: How to successfully harness the power of partners. *California Management Review*, 55(1), 24–46. 10.1525/cmr.2012.55.1.24

Wisnicki, B. (2020). Impact of R&D Cartelization with Endogenous Product Differentiation. In Tsounis, N., & Vlachvei, A. (Eds.), *Advances in Cross-Section Data Methods in Applied Economic Research. ICOAE 2019. Springer Proceedings in Business and Economics*. Springer. 10.1007/978-3-030-38253-7_13

Wollenburg, J., Holzapfel, A., Hübner, A., & Kuhn, H. (2018). Configuring retail fulfillment processes for omni-channel customer steering. *International Journal of Electronic Commerce*, 22(4), 540–575. 10.1080/10864415.2018.1485085

Wu, H., Nguyen, G. T., Chorppath, A. K., & Fitzek, F. (2017). Network slicing for conditional monitoring in the industrial internet of things. *Transport*, 2018.

Xia, Y., Liu, X., Wang, X., Deng, H., Han, C., Liu, Z., & Tsai, S. B. (2023). The power of role models in a team: The impact of lead entrepreneur's digital leadership on digital entrepreneurial success. *Information Processing & Management, 60*(6).

Xia, Y., Xie, J., Zhu, W., & Liang, L. (2021). Pricing strategy in the product and service market. *Journal of Management Science and Engineering*, 6(2), 211–234. 10.1016/j.jmse.2021.02.001

Xu, M. (2018). The Fourth Industrial Revolution: Opportunities and Challenges. *International Journal of Financial Research*, 90-94.

Xu, L. D., He, W., & Li, S. (2014). Internet of Things in industries: A survey. *IEEE Transactions on Industrial Informatics*, 10(4), 2233–2243. 10.1109/TII.2014.2300753

Yamin, M. A. Y., & Abdalatif, O. A. A. (2024). Examining consumer behavior towards adoption of quick response code mobile payment systems: Transforming mobile payment in the fintech industry. *Humanities & Social Sciences Communications*, 11(1), 675. 10.1057/s41599-024-03189-w

Yang, K., Chen, M., Zhang, Y., & Wang, S. (2017). Big data and cloud computing: Innovation opportunities and challenges. *International Journal of Digital Earth*, 10(1), 13–53. 10.1080/17538947.2016.1239771

Yann, L. (2015). Deep learning. *Nature, 521*(7553).

Yao, Y., Wang, L., & Shen, J. (2022). Features and Applications of QR Codes. *International Journal for Innovation Education and Research*, 10(5), 166–169. 10.31686/ijier.vol10.iss5.3762

Yazici, A. M., Özkan, A., & Özkan, H. (2024). Meta: XR-AR-MR and Mirror World Technologies Business Impact of Metaverse. *Journal of Metaverse*, 4(1), 21–32. 10.57019/jmv.1344489

Yin, Y., Zeng, Y., Chen, X., & Fan, Y. (2016). The internet of things in healthcare: An overview. *Journal of Industrial Information Integration*, 1, 3–13. 10.1016/j.jii.2016.03.004

Yuan, Z. W. Q. (2017). *Smart Manufacturing for the Oil Refining and Petrochemical Industry*. Elsevier.

Zemčík, T. (2019). *A Brief History of Chatbots. DEStech Transactions on Computer Science and Engineering*.

Zha, D., Foroudi, P., Melewar, T. C., & Jin, Z. (2024). Examining the Impact of Sensory Brand Experience on Brand Loyalty. *Corporate Reputation Review*. 10.1057/s41299-023-00175-x

Zhang, S., & Wen, J. (2018). Research on construction of smart tourism service system based on big data and cloud computing. In *2018 IEEE International Conference on Big Data (Big Data)* (pp. 5155-5162). IEEE.

Zhang, D., Dai, H., Dong, L., Wu, Q., Guo, L., & Liu, X. (2019). The value of pop- up stores on retailing platforms: Evidence from a field experiment with Alibaba. *Management Science*, 65(11), 5142–5151. 10.1287/mnsc.2019.3410

Zhu, Q., Huang, L., & Wang, W. (2016). The adoption of blockchain technology in financial services: A comparative study. In *2016 13th International Conference on Service Systems and Service Management (ICSSSM)* (pp. 1-6). IEEE.

Zhu, Q., Sarkis, J., Lai, K. H., & Geng, Y. (2012). Green supply chain management in China: Pressures, practices, and performance. *International Journal of Operations & Production Management*, 32(5), 519–543. 10.1108/01443571211228747

About the Contributors

Elena G. Popkova – Doctor of Science (Economics), the founder and president of the Institute of Scientific Communications (Russia) and Professor of Peoples' Friendship University of Russia. Her scientific interests include the theory of economic growth, sustainable development, globalization, humanization of economic growth, emerging markets, social entrepreneurship, and the digital economy and Industry 4.0. Elena G. Popkova organizes Russian and international scientific and practical conferences and is the editor and author of collective monographs, and serves as a guest editor of international scientific journals. She has published more than 300 works in Russian and foreign peer-reviewed scientific journals and books.

***

Poorva Agrawal completed her Ph. D degree in Computer Science & Engineering from Symbiosis International (Deemed University), Pune, India. She is currently working as Assistant Professor in Department of Computer Science at Symbiosis Institute of Technology, Nagpur. She has more than 11 years of experience in teaching. Her area of interests includes NLP, AI/ML, soft computing Data Science, and Image processing.

Haji Mohammad Nabil Almunawar is currently an associate professor at the School of Business and Economics, Universiti of Brunei Darussalam (UBDSBE), Brunei Darussalam. He was the former dean of UBDSBE. He received his bachelor's degree in 1983 from Bogor Agricultural University, Indonesia, master's degree (MSc) from the Department of Computer Science, University of Western Ontario, London, Canada in 1991, and Ph.D in Computer Science/Information Systems from the University of New South Wales in 1998. Dr. Almunawar has published more than 150 papers in refereed journals, books, book chapters, encyclopedias, and international conference proceedings. He has more than 30 years of teaching experience in the area of information systems. His overall research interests include applications of IT in management, e-business/commerce, digital marketplace/platform, digital business ecosystem, health informatics, information security, and cloud computing. Currently, he focuses his research on digital transformation, digital marketplace, digital platform, and digital business ecosystem.

Xiaohua Bai is an MBA student at the School of Business and Economics, Universiti Brunei Darussalam. He earned his bachelor's degree in Business English from Northeast Petroleum University. Currently, Xiaohua Bai works at Hengyi Industries SDN BHD, where he excels in project contracts management and serves as a project liaison officer. His professional interest centers on foreign direct investment (FDI) projects liaison and management within the petrochemical industry. Xiaohua Bai is deeply passionate about exploring the intricacies of FDI projects and their profound influence on the global stage.

Sooryendhu C.S. is a MBA Student in Lean Operations & Systems Division at School of Business and Management, Christ University, India. Her area of interest includes Omni-channel Supply Chain, E-Commerce and Lean Operations.

Antonio Carvalho is a PhD in Business Administration from the Municipal University of São Caetano do Sul USCS (2020); Master in Education, Administration and Communication from Universidade São Marcos (2007); Postgraduate MBA Management and Innovation in Distance Learning USP (2015); Postgraduate MBA in Marketing from USP ESALQ (2017); Post graduation in Financial Administration from the Methodist University of São Paulo (1997); Bachelor in Business Administration from the Municipal University of São Caetano do Sul (1980); Bachelor in Economic Sciences from the Municipal University of São Caetano do Sul (1982). He is currently coordinator and professor of the undergraduate course in Business Administration at Faculdade São Bernardo do Campo - FASB.

Anita Chaudhary pursuing a Ph.D. in Electronics Engineering from Shri Guru Granth Sahib World University, Fatehgarh, Punjab, India. She earned her B.Tech-M.Tech. in ECE from Lovely Professional University, Phagwara, India in 2012. She is an Assistant Professor (Senior Scale) at the Eternal University Baru Sahib, H.P. India. She has 10 years of teaching and research experience at various reputed Universities in India.

About the Contributors

Suhashini Awadhesh Chaurasia has twenty-six years of teaching experience. Her area of research is Machine Learning. She has published seven Indian patents; She is also chief editor for a special issue on Interdisciplinary Perspectives On Artificial Intelligence Systems: From Theory To Application; Two books are authored namely Linux Operating System and Software Engineering. Eight edited international book chapters published. Taken two copyrights on literary work. Four papers published in reputed IEEE Scopus indexed journals and one Springer book chapter. Two books chapters published in International edited book AI Tools and Applications for Women's Safety. Three book chapters published in Impact of AI on Advancing Women's Safety. One book chapter is published in Wearable Devices, Surveillance Systems, and AI for Women's Wellbeing. Two book chapters published in Enhancing Security in Public Spaces Through Generative Adversarial Networks (GANs). Three papers are published in UGC peer reviewed journals. Two papers are published in peer reviewed journals. Two international conference papers presented and published. Two national conference papers presented and published. Two research articles published in the newspaper. Speaker at international conferences and colleges. She is a reviewer in 3rd International Conference on Advanced Communication and Intelligent Systems. She is also a reviewer in IGI-Global International Publisher Journal for AI Tools and Applications for Women's Safety and other for edited books. Member of board of studies at Rashtrasant Tukadoji Nagpur University, Nagpur. Working as head of the department in the college and CHB at VMV college. Attended and organized many FDPs, Orientation, Refresher programs, workshops and symposium. She can be contacted at ssuhashinc@gmail.com

Gagandeep Kaur completed her Ph. D degree in Computer Science & Engineering from LPU, Punjab, India. She is currently working as Assistant Professor in Department of Computer Science at Symbiosis Institute of Technology, Nagpur. She has more than 11 years of experience in teaching. Her area of interests includes NLP, AI/ML, Data Science, and Image processing.

Sowmiya KC, an accomplished Ph.D. scholar at Sri Vasavi College in Erode, emerges as a dynamic and vibrant researcher with a rich educational background. Having laid the foundation with a B.Ed. degree and furthered her academic pursuits with post-graduation at PSGR Krishnammal College for Women, she has adeptly positioned herself at the forefront of scholarly exploration.Her commitment to advancing knowledge is exemplified through her proactive involvement in two conferences in 2023, where she not only showcased her research prowess but also actively engaged with peers and experts, fostering meaningful discussions. Notably, the recognition garnered from presenting her research findings at these conferences has resulted in the acceptance of her journal article for publication later this year.This noteworthy achievement not only underscores Sowmiya's dedication to the academic realm but also highlights her impactful contributions to the scholarly discourse. As a Ph.D. scholar, she stands as a vibrant and influential contributor to the ever-evolving landscape of research and academic exploration, leaving an indelible mark on her field.

V.P. Arun is a driven and accomplished professional with a diverse educational background and extensive hands-on experience across various industries. Graduating with honors, Arun earned his Master of Business Administration (M.B.A) with a specialization in Human Resources and Marketing from the renowned Sona School of Management in Salem in 2018, where he excelled academically with an impressive 8.3 Cumulative Grade Point Average (CGPA). Before pursuing his MBA, Arun laid a solid foundation by obtaining a Bachelor of Engineering degree from Kongu Engineering College in 2014. Throughout his academic journey, Arun displayed an unwavering commitment to learning and personal growth, actively seeking opportunities to expand his knowledge and skills beyond the confines of traditional education. He sought practical experiences to complement his theoretical understanding, such as a 45-day summer internship focused on conducting a feasibility study for R-Doc Sustainability in the market. Additionally, Arun broadened his horizons through a 7-day industrial visit to Malaysia and Singapore, immersing himself in diverse cultural and professional environments. Arun's academic pursuits were further enriched by his involvement in hands-on projects, including a comprehensive study on Employee Job Satisfaction at Roots Cast Private Limited.

Shruti Maheshwari has submitted her PhD thesis in mechanical engineering from IIT BHU, India. She is currently working as assistant professor in Symbiosis Institute of Technology, Pune. She has more than 7 years of experience in teaching. Her area of interest includes industrial engineering, optimization, operation management, machine learning.

Neli Mengalli is a senior professional who has been working for over twenty years in the educational area, interfacing with the areas of knowledge management, monitoring and measuring social media, society 5.0, phygital transformation, and disruptive technologies. She has worked both in the private sector and in public management. Her postgraduate [master's and doctorate] was carried out at the Pontifical Catholic University of São Paulo with an emphasis on new technologies. A highlight of the works produced is in communities of practice, in the management of online contexts, in disruptive technologies and in transform(active) methodologies. She participated in research groups with the theme of technology at the Pontifical Catholic University of São Paulo and in workshops that associated the language, education, and technology at FASB - Faculdade São Bernardo do Campo. In the professional trajectory are basic education, higher education, course evaluation, advisory in public policies, and mentoring for startups. She was an interlocutor in the implementation of public policies in the educational area.

Nitish Kumar Minz is an exceptional Bachelor of Commerce student specializing in Business Administration and Management at K.R. Mangalam University. With an unwavering commitment to excellence and a remarkable work ethic, Mr. Minz has consistently demonstrated his dedication to academic and professional pursuits. His academic achievements extend beyond the classroom, as he has made significant contributions to several research papers and book chapters that are currently in the final stages of publication. His insightful contributions and research expertise have earned him recognition within his field of study. Nitish Kumar Minz, as the President of the Student Council at K.R. Mangalam University, holds a prestigious position. In this leadership role, he has demonstrated exceptional skills in managing various projects and strategic initiatives. His internship at KEIC (KRMU Entrepreneurship & Incubation Center) has allowed him to further refine his project management and strategic planning abilities, providing valuable hands-on experience in the field. Furthermore, he has been selected as NEP SAARTHI- Student Ambassador for Academic Reforms in Transforming Higher Education at K.R. Mangalam University. This esteemed role demonstrates his passion for educational reforms and his commitment to improving the quality of higher education. As a Student Ambassador, Mr. Minz actively engages with fellow students, faculty, and staff, promoting a culture of academic excellence and facilitating positive changes within the university. Recognizing his outstanding accomplishments and exceptional contributions, he has recently been honored with the prestigious CHANCELLOR'S EXCELLENCE AWARD. This esteemed award serves as a testament to his dedication, hard work, and exemplary performance throughout his academic journey. Mr. Nitish Kumar Minz's academic prowess, research contributions, leadership roles, and recognition through awards highlight his exceptional abilities and potential for future success. He continues to inspire and make a significant impact within the academic community, demonstrating his commitment to excellence in all his endeavors.

A. B. Mishra, Presently serving as an Associate Professor in International Institute of Management Studies, Pune. India. Dr. Mishra earned his PhD in Business Management and brings a wealth of corporate experience from renowned Multinational Companies in Sales & Marketing. With extensive tenure in both academia and industry, he blends practical insights with scholarly rigor. Dr. Mishra is an alumnus of the Faculty Development Program at IIM Kozhikode and has actively engaged in numerous seminars, conferences, and workshops across prestigious educational and corporate platforms. Dr. Mishra has actively participated in a myriad of seminars, conferences, and workshops hosted by eminent educational and corporate platforms. His research endeavors have left an indelible mark, with publications gracing the pages of reputable journals like SCOPUS, ABDC, and Web of Science and other leading journals. Not stopping there, he is also credited as an author of books and holds patents, showcasing his multifaceted contributions to the field. Not content with merely domestic endeavors, Dr. Mishra has broadened his horizons through participation in an International Immersion Program. His research interests are as diverse as they are cutting-edge, encompassing areas such as Phygital, Banking & Insurance, E-business, M-commerce, Artificial Intelligence (AI), Internet of Things (IoT), Consumer Perception of sustainable practices, and more. Beyond research, Dr. Mishra is deeply committed to nurturing the next generation of leaders, imparting invaluable knowledge in core subjects such as Marketing Management, Sales Management, Consumer Behavior, Advertisement & Sales Promotion, and beyond. Through his holistic approach to education, Dr. Mishra inspires students to excel and innovate in the ever-evolving landscape of business and academia.

Latika Pinjarkar has obtained a BE degree in Computer Technology from Nagpur University, MH in 1999 and M. Tech degree in Computer Technology and Application from CSVTU, CG, India in 2008. She obtained her PhD in Computer Science and Engineering from CSVTU CG, India in 2019.She has been engaged in research and teaching for more than 22 years. At present she is Associate Professor and Academic Head in CSE Department at Symbiosis Institute of Technology Nagpur, Symbiosis International (Deemed University) Pune, MH, India. She has presented more than 40 papers in International/National Journals/ Conferences and having 05 Patents to her credit. She has completed one research project sponsored by TEQIP-III. Her research interests include Image Processing, Computer Vision, Content Based Image Retrieval(CBIR) and Machine Learning.

Siva Kumar Pujari received his Doctoral Degree in Supply Chain Resilience from Department of Management Studies, Indian Institute of Technology Roorkee, India. He obtained his Bachelor of Technology in mechanical engineering from Acharya Nagarjuna University, Guntur, Andhra Pradesh, and Master of Technology in Industrial Engineering from National Institute of Technology Tiruchirappalli, Trichy, Tamil Nadu, India. He Presented his work in reputed International Conferences and has published several research papers in journals of international repute. His areas of interest include Supply Chain Resilience, Supply Chain Disruption Management, Risk Management, Resilience of Small and Medium Enterprises (SMEs), Omni-Channel Supply Chain, etc.

Gerardo Reyes Ruiz is an Actuary by training from the Faculty of Sciences-UNAM; he studied a Specialty in Econometrics in the Postgraduate Studies Division of the Faculty of Economics-UNAM; He obtained a Master's and Doctorate in Business Studies (actuarial profile) from the Faculty of Economics and Business of the University of Barcelona, Spain. Later he did a postdoctoral stay at the Center for Economic, Administrative, and Social Studies (CIECAS) of the National Polytechnic Institute (IPN). His work experience has been in public education institutions (UNAM, UAEM, IPN, Centro de Estudios Superiores Navales-CESNAV) where he has taught classes in Bachelor's, Specialty, Master's, and Doctorate degrees. All this accumulated experience allowed him to enter the National System of Researchers (SNI), Social Area, of Mexico (he has the appointment of Level I National Researcher). He is currently attached to the Center for Superior Naval Studies (CESNAV), in Mexico.

About the Contributors

SC Vetrivel is a faculty member in the Department of Management Studies, Kongu Engineering College (Autonomous), Perundurai, Erode Dt. Having experience in Industry 20 years and Teaching 16 years. Awarded with Doctoral Degree in Management Sciences in Anna University, Chennai. He has organized various workshops and Faculty Development Programmes. He is actively involved in research and consultancy works. He acted as a resource person to FDPs & MDPs to various industries like, SPB ltd, Tamilnadu Police, DIET, Rotary school and many. His areas of interest include Entrepreneurship, Business Law, Marketing and Case writing. Articles published more than 100 International and National Journals. Presented papers in more than 30 National and International conferences including IIM Bangalore, IIM Kozhikode, IIM Kashipur and IIM Indore. He was a Chief Co-ordinator of Entrepreneurship and Management Development Centre (EMDC) of Kongu Engineering College, he was instrumental in organizing various Awareness Camps, FDP, and TEDPs to aspiring entrepreneurs which was funded by NSTEDB – DST/GoI

Purushottam D. Shobhane obtained his Ph.D. degree in Mathematics from Gondwana University, Gadchiroli, India in 2018. He obtained his M. Sc. degree in Mathematics from Nagpur University, Nagpur, India in 1990. He is having 32 years' experience of teaching and authored 4 books of Mathematics. At present he is working as Assistant Professor in CSE Department at Symbiosis Institute of Technology, Nagpur, Symbiosis International (Deemed University) Pune, MH, India. He has presented more than 15 papers in International/National Journals/ Conferences. His research interests include General Theory of Relativity & Cosmology, Mathematical Modeling and Inter-disciplinary research.

Muhammad Usman Tariq has more than 16+ year's experience in industry and academia. He has been working as a consultant and trainer for industries representing six sigma, quality, health and safety, environmental systems, project management, and information security standards. His work has encompassed sectors in aviation, manufacturing, food, hospitality, education, finance, research, software and transportation. He has diverse and significant experience working with accreditation agencies of ABET, ACBSP, AACSB, WASC, CAA, EFQM and NCEAC. Additionally, Dr. Tariq has operational experience in incubators, research labs, government research projects, private sector startups, program creation and management at various industrial and academic levels. He is Certified Higher Education Teacher from Harvard University, USA, Certified Online Educator from HMBSU, Certified Six Sigma Master Black Belt, Lead Auditor ISO 9001 Certified, ISO 14001, IOSH MS, OSHA 30, and OSHA 48. He is member of Harvard Business Review Advisory Council.

V. Sabareeshwari currently serves as Assistant Professor in Department of Soil Science, Amrita School of Agricultural Sciences, Coimbatore. Having more than 5 years of research experience and more than 2 years of teaching experience. She got 7 awards in the field of agriculture. Her field of expertise are soil genesis, soil pedological studies as well as soil fertility mapping using advanced software like Arc GIS. She had published 22 research papers and more than 10 book chapters and books in high- impact reputed journals. She has actively participated and presented her papers in more than 20 conferences and seminars. She not only restrict her contribution only in the academic and research part, she had extension experience at farm level (lab to land) with varied crop research.

Sowmiya KC, an accomplished Ph.D. scholar at Sri Vasavi College in Erode, emerges as a dynamic and vibrant researcher with a rich educational background. Having laid the foundation with a B.Ed. degree and furthered her academic pursuits with post-graduation at PSGR Krishnammal College for Women, she has adeptly positioned herself at the forefront of scholarly exploration.Her commitment to advancing knowledge is exemplified through her proactive involvement in two conferences in 2023, where she not only showcased her research prowess but also actively engaged with peers and experts, fostering meaningful discussions. Notably, the recognition garnered from presenting her research findings at these conferences has resulted in the acceptance of her journal article for publication later this year. This noteworthy achievement not only underscores Sowmiya's dedication to the academic realm but also highlights her impactful contributions to the scholarly discourse. As a Ph.D. scholar, she stands as a vibrant and influential contributor to the ever-evolving landscape of research and academic exploration, leaving an indelible mark on her field.

V.P. Arun is a driven and accomplished professional with a diverse educational background and extensive hands-on experience across various industries. Graduating with honors, Arun earned his Master of Business Administration (M.B.A) with a specialization in Human Resources and Marketing from the renowned Sona School of Management in Salem in 2018, where he excelled academically with an impressive 8.3 Cumulative Grade Point Average (CGPA). Before pursuing his MBA, Arun laid a solid foundation by obtaining a Bachelor of Engineering degree from Kongu Engineering College in 2014. Throughout his academic journey, Arun displayed an unwavering commitment to learning and personal growth, actively seeking opportunities to expand his knowledge and skills beyond the confines of traditional education. He sought practical experiences to complement his theoretical understanding, such as a 45-day summer internship focused on conducting a feasibility study for R-Doc Sustainability in the market. Additionally, Arun broadened his horizons through a 7-day industrial visit to Malaysia and Singapore, immersing himself in diverse cultural and professional environments. Arun's academic pursuits were further enriched by his involvement in hands-on projects, including a comprehensive study on Employee Job Satisfaction at Roots Cast Private Limited. These practical experiences not only honed his analytical and problem-solving skills but also showcased his proactive approach to learning and professional development. Transitioning seamlessly from academia to the professional realm, Arun embarked on a remarkable journey, holding pivotal roles in esteemed organizations across various sectors. His professional trajectory includes serving as a Growth Officer at Parle Agro Private Limited, where he played a crucial role in driving sales growth and market expansion.

Index

A

B

C

D

E

F

G

H

I

L

M

N

O

P

Q

S

T

U

ntent.com/pod-product-compliance
e LLC

0926
010B/2674